coalition of the dominant elites yield unprecedented insight into the real nature and inner logic of the 1980 campaign. *The Hidden Election* goes a long way toward laying bare the mainsprings of American politics and clarifying our future political course.

Thomas Ferguson and Joel Rogers are members of the political science departments at the Massachusetts Institute of Technology and Rutgers University (University College/Newark), respectively. Their column, "The Political Economy," appears regularly in *The Nation*.

THE
HIDDEN
ELECTION

THE HIDDEN ELECTION

POLITICS AND ECONOMICS IN THE 1980 PRESIDENTIAL CAMPAIGN

EDITED BY THOMAS FERGUSON AND JOEL ROGERS

87-684

PANTHEON BOOKS   NEW YORK   A *NATION* BOOK

Library of Congress Cataloging in Publication Data
Main entry under title:

The hidden election.

1. Presidents—United States—Election—1980.
I. Ferguson, Thomas, 1949– . II. Rogers, Joel, 1952– .
JK526 1980.H52   324.973'0926   81–47212
ISBN 0–394–51582–X AACR2
ISBN 0–394–74958–8 (pbk.)

Text design by Dana Kasarsky Design

Manufactured in the United States of America

First Edition

Grateful acknowledgment is made to the following for permission to reprint previously
published material:

M. E. Sharpe, Inc.: Review of *Reflections of an Economic Policy Maker: Speeches and Congressional
Statements, 1969–1978* by Leonard A. Rapping, *Challenge,* November/December 1979. Copyright © 1979 by M. E. Sharpe, Inc. Also, excerpt from "The Recycling Problem Revisited"
by Paul L. Volcker, *Challenge,* July/August 1980. Copyright © 1980 by M. E. Sharpe, Inc.

Foreign Affairs: Excerpt from "The New Economic Policy and U. S. Foreign Policy," by C. Fred
Bergsten. *Foreign Affairs,* January 1972. Excerpted by permission. Copyright by Council on
Foreign Relations, Inc.

The Gallup Poll: Material cited from Gallup Opinion Index, Report no. 130, *Religion in America
1976.* Reprinted by permission of The Gallup Poll, Princeton, N.J.

The Nation: Excerpt from "Gene Rostow's Propaganda Club" by Robert Sherrill, *The Nation,*
August 11–18, 1979. Copyright © 1979 by The Nation Associates. Reprinted by permission.

The New York Times: Chart on "How They Voted: Two-Candidate Preferences in 1980 and
1976, by Category of Voters, November 9, 1980." Copyright © 1980 by The New York
Times Company. Reprinted by permission.

The Public Interest: Excerpt from "Toward the New Economics" by Peter Drucker, *The Public
Interest,* Special Edition, 1980. Copyright © 1980 by National Affairs Inc. Also, excerpt from
" 'Rational Expectations' as a Counterrevolution" by Mark Willes, *The Public Interest,* Special
Edition, 1980. Copyright © 1980 by National Affairs Inc.

Politics is business, that's what's the matter with it.
That's what's the matter with everything.
Lincoln Steffens

CONTENTS

CONTENTS

PREFACE

American presidential elections generate enormous amounts of commentary. Months before the opening primaries, the major media are filled with speculation about the upcoming race and gossip about the candidates. As the formal public campaigns get underway, the volume of news and analysis grows exponentially. By election day, media coverage of the major party candidates approaches saturation levels. And no sooner has the election been decided than a flood of hastily written campaign analyses surges into bookstores and newsstands with the final word on how the successful candidate actually won the White House.

In face of this tidal wave of coverage, why yet another election book?

The answer is as simple as it is depressing. While instant election books have become as integral to the beginning of a new presidential term as the Inaugural Ball, they are rarely satisfying. Tending uniformly to explain the campaign outcome in terms of candidate personalities and facile references to the national mood, these "inside accounts" fail to relate campaign dynamics to the broader structure of power in America. They ignore or gloss over the candidates' links to the business community, sources of money, prominent (if unpublicized) supporters, and affiliations with the traditional network of national policymaking. In short, little or nothing is said about the election's significance for the vast array of political coalitions and economic interests that define American public life.

The Hidden Election attempts a sharp break with this "morning after" tradition of political analysis. It not only scrutinizes the public record of the 1980 campaign, from the early primaries to the final vote, but also zeroes in on the "hidden" campaign—that complex process through which the basic structures of economic and social life are transformed into political platforms and electoral coalitions. In so doing, it seeks to identify the underlying sources of political conflict, while mapping out the broad constraints that shape the electoral system as a whole.

Although in no way pretending to be exhaustive, the following essays attempt to cover all the major issues of the campaign. Our own piece explores the political economy of the Reagan victory in detail, with reference to the changing world economy, the current disorders of American mass politics, and the campaign itself. Alexander Cockburn and James Ridgeway follow with an account of the public campaign, candidate organizations, and the press. Walter Dean Burnham analyzes the vote, with a special section on religion and the 1980 race. Gerald Epstein focuses on the Federal Reserve in his discussion of the major economic issues—inflation, unemployment, OPEC, and the fate of the dollar. Bruce Cumings treats foreign policy and defense issues, and the domestic sources of international conflict. Alan Stone considers the struggles over economic regulation and deregulation, and their impact on select industries. David Dickson and David Noble analyze "social" regulation issues and the transformation of science policy. In the final essay, Ira Katznelson investigates the fate of the social welfare constituency—that group which seems most obviously to have lost out in the 1980 campaign—and explores the future of the welfare state.

Together the essays provide signposts not only to the campaign just past, but to the shape of things to come. We hope that their reach is as firm as it is extensive, and that thereby the major political conflicts of the 1980s will be better understood.

In addition to the contributors themselves, who were forced to work to deadlines unfamiliar to many in the academic world, we would like to thank Philip Pochoda, our editor at Pantheon, whose criticism and advice helped shape this collection into a book. We also thank Doug Stumpf and Don Guttenplan of Pantheon Books, and copy editor Jeannine Ciliotta, for their assistance. Finally, we are grateful to Victor Navasky and Kai Bird, editor and associate editor, respectively, at *The Nation,* who gave early and continuing encouragement to the project.

Thomas Ferguson
Joel Rogers

THE
HIDDEN
ELECTION

THE REAGAN VICTORY: CORPORATE COALITIONS IN THE 1980 CAMPAIGN

Thomas Ferguson and Joel Rogers

INTRODUCTION

Among the many stops he made during his long journey to the American presidency, Ronald Reagan's visit to Dallas, Texas, in late August 1980 was surely one of the most memorable. There, in the space of a single day, virtually all the bizarre themes of the 1980 campaign converged.

Reagan had come to the Southwest's commercial capital to shore up his already strong support among "born-again" Christian fundamentalists, who promised to figure as a newly important force in the November election. His visit began with a private meeting with more than two hundred "business and religious leaders" in the ballroom of the Dallas Hyatt Regency.[1] A scene straight out of *Elmer Gantry* or Robert Altman's *Nashville,* the gathering attracted many of the best known and most influential of America's Far Right super-rich. Among those present were billionaire independent oilman Nelson Bunker Hunt, whose errant attempt to become world silver king for a day had only recently failed, triggering the intervention of a specially organized syndicate of banks; Texas Rangers owner and right-wing publicist "Mad" Eddy Chiles; Jesse Helms, the senator from North Carolina, textiles, and tobacco, whom opponents have dubbed the "Six Million Dollar Man" because of his huge campaign war chests; and Fort Worth industrialist T. Cullen Davis, "born again" following his acquittal in his third trial on charges of murdering his wife.

Reagan was preaching to the converted in more senses than one. Typical in his enthusiasm for the candidate was Cullen Davis, who emerged from the meeting to announce: "I'm for him. I hope he gets elected. Ronald Reagan represents the viewpoints of the majority of the people in this country. Everything I have seen or heard about him has been great!"

Afterward, Reagan held a brief press conference, where he astonished the campaign press corps with an abrupt challenge to the theory of evolution. Asked the inevitable question in a city whose public schools must by law afford Charles Darwin and the Book of Genesis equal time in science classes, Reagan replied that "I have a great many questions about evolution. And I think the recent discoveries over the years have pointed out great flaws in it." The candidate then headed off for his main appearance

3

of the day, a speech at a "National Affairs Briefing" staged in Dallas's Reunion Arena by the Religious Roundtable, a born-again group based in Washington, D.C., with which many New Right fundamentalist leaders are affiliated.

According to the *Dallas Times Herald,* prior to Reagan's arrival the audience had been "whipped to a frenzy" by a series of warmup speakers. In an early address, Paul Weyrich, the director of the Committee for the Survival of a Free Congress, warned the audience not to fall prey to the "goo goo syndrome, the good government syndrome," which sees the exercise of the franchise as a good in itself. "I don't want everyone to vote," declared Weyrich. "Our leverage in the election quite candidly goes up as the voting populace goes down. We have no responsibility, moral or otherwise, to turn out our opposition. It's important to turn out those who are with us." Weyrich derided fundamentalist ministers who mobilize their congregations to vote without "telling them who the good guys are and who the bad guys are."

News of good guys and bad guys mounted through the early evening, as a succession of speakers called for a new march of "Christian soldiers" and the lowering of barriers between church and state in American life. A particularly enthusiastic response greeted the Reverend Bailey Smith, president of the 13-million-member Southern Baptist Convention (whose remark at the Roundtable meeting that "God Almighty does not hear the prayer of a Jew" created an uproar later in the campaign). At a counterdemonstration to the Reagan visit held the previous evening, local gay political leader Don Baker had described evangelist James Robison, one of Reagan's hosts during his stay, as a "right wing fanatic." In Reunion Arena, Smith blasted back, charging that "we are in deep trouble in America when they interview a pervert about a preacher. You might as well interview Idi Amin about white supremacy or Hugh Hefner about the value of virginity." The crowd roared.

This faintly surreal atmosphere was only heightened by Reagan's arrival at the hall. Introduced by Robison, who brought the crowd to its feet in anticipation, Reagan delayed his speech while the Briefing's organizers passed the hat for what they claimed was a $100,000 deficit in financing the $350,000 event. When he finally began, Reagan told a cheering crowd (which included Hunt and Davis) that "the First Amendment was written not to protect the people and their laws from religious values, but to protect those values from government tyranny," warned the audience that "Judeo-Christian values based on the moral teachings of religion are undergoing their most serious challenge in our nation's history," and pledged an end to what he described as the federal government's "unconstitutional regulatory vendetta" against independent religious schools. According to a *Herald* story, "cries of 'Amen' and 'God bless you, Ronnie,' echoed from the arena." Sitting in the back of the hall, T. Cullen Davis told reporters how pleased he was with the evening. Responding to questions about the impact of such political mobilization of Christian fundamentalist forces, Davis declared that the only "problem comes with people who don't want church people to exert influence when electing good, moral public officials."[2]

In the flush of first reports, at least one highly placed source in the Carter campaign predicted to press intimates that Reagan's Dallas skylarking would severely damage his image with the rest of the country. But he was wrong. Although most major papers mentioned Reagan's remarks about the theory of evolution, virtually all the media removed them from the context of the earlier meeting with the businessmen, preachers, and Hunt, Davis, and Helms. Even more important, as the campaign went on the media repressed the memory of the event. In sharp contrast to the two Georges—McGovern and Romney—Reagan did not find himself faced at every stop with a battery of reporters asking him if he really rejected the theory of evolution, or with a flurry of newspaper editorials connecting his religious primitivism with his stance on nuclear weapons, or with repeated TV clips of his speech and press conference.

In this moment of vulnerability, the press was kind to Ronald Reagan. Why?

Was it just another instance of the generally favorable media coverage Reagan received throughout the postconvention campaign? After all, the press that picked apart the arithmetic of George McGovern's negative income tax proposals largely failed to challenge the principles of supply-side economics, or even add up the numbers when Reagan pledged simultaneously to cut taxes, balance the budget, preserve essential social spending, and increase military outlays.

Or was it linked more specifically to the circumstances of the Dallas episode? Perhaps a combination of stifling heat, campaign tunnel vision, and shock at Reagan's dismissal of his old friend Bonzo the Chimp's hopes for phylogenic advance?

Perhaps, but we doubt it. Rather, we incline to the view that the press did not cover the Dallas episode adequately for the same reasons it could not cope with the rest of the campaign—because Ronald Reagan's ascent to the presidency announces a sea change in the structure of American politics that defies conventional understanding.

Here was an event that assembled many of the characteristic features of the 1980 race—the mingling of protectionist elites and big-time bankers, the reemergence of the South and Christian fundamentalism as decisive forces in national politics, the hallucinatory rewriting of the Constitution amid single-issue politics and the decay of organized party structures, and the vast mobilization of God and cash in the successful candidacy of a figure once marginal to the "vital center" of American political life. But if Dallas compressed all the mysteries of the 1980 campaign into a single day, it also underscored the difficulties of analyzing what has happened to American politics in recent years. And little wonder.

With 1984 but a single presidential term away, the language and frames of reference that have defined American public life for more than a generation are suddenly irrelevant. Taking their meaning from the political formula of New Deal liberalism, they are useless to describe the collapse of the New Deal system itself—a system whose economic, social, and political foundations are everywhere crumbling, battered beyond repair by double-digit stagflation, protectionist pressures, technological obsolescence, and (save for the periods of punishingly high interest rates) a chronically negative balance of payments.

As in any period of social disintegration, in the interregnum between the death of the old order and the rise of the new, a variety of morbid symptoms have appeared. Among the affluent: a fixation on the therapeutic functions of power and the rewards of competition, manic real estate speculation, mass narcissism, and the ideology of self-improvement. Among the poor and the vulnerable at all levels of society: pentecostalism, fortune telling, satanism, astrology, disaster movies, and the retro craze. Among the press: the inability to explain the sources and meaning of current political conflict.

But not everyone has been incapacitated by the crisis. Parallel to the cultural experimentation of the rank and file has come a drastic restructuring of internal relations among American elites. With obsolete alliances breaking apart, they are scrambling after high ground, on the lookout for new institutions, candidates, and political coalitions to service their needs and withstand the pressures of the 1980s.

For students of American politics, such elite mobilization and regrouping is always of more than passing interest, because it crucially affects the patterns of partisan cleavage and competition evident in a presidential campaign. The enduring structures of power in America must bend to the democratic dispensation, but they rarely break. Instead, they systematically inform the democratic process, providing it with shape and content, setting the agenda of national politics, closing off some courses of state action while endowing others with the cachet of necessity. Indeed, any presidential race can be usefully thought of as consisting of two campaigns. One is public, and unfolds through the primaries and party conventions, speeches, and debates, and final polls and voting results. The other is more obscure, and features the complex process by which pivotal interest groups like oil companies, international banks, weapons producers, labor unions, and even foreign countries coalesce behind particular candidates to advance their own ends. Both campaigns culminate in elections. One election is open; the other is hidden. The task for political analysis is to find the connection between the two, and thus grasp the process by which basic forms of economic conflict and interdependence are translated into electoral movement.[3] Sometimes this connection is self-evident. More often it is not. But never is it unimportant, and in the 1980 case, other factors suggest that its importance is towering.

Many great questions are posed by the Reagan victory, but as a problem of political analysis, the stunning outcome of the 1980 election can be conveniently broken down into a series of smaller puzzles. One major group of these concerns the virtual collapse of the Democratic party leadership.

How did Jimmy Carter go so quickly from healer to heel? Why, like Grover Cleveland and Herbert Hoover, did he persist in the suicidal alienation of his own party base? What explains the peculiar ambivalence he showed toward increased military spending and arms buildup? Sometimes, as in his initial reactions to the Iran and Afghanistan crises, Carter seemed to trumpet increased militarization. On other occasions, and ever more noticeably toward the end of his campaign, he held back. What sense can be made of the strange course of the Kennedy candidacy: its gradual buildup, dramatic collapse, and sudden resurgence stopping just short of success?

Another group of questions cluster around the Republican campaign. One great mystery is the Connally candidacy. Early in his campaign, showing enormous support in the business community, Connally appeared well on his way to installing the *Führerprinzip* as a first principle of American public life. But he quickly faded, leaving only an entry in the *Guinness Book of World Records* for history's most expensive convention delegate. What were the origins of the Bush and Anderson campaigns, and why did Reagan rise so spectacularly after the New Hampshire primary? What was the importance of the deal Reagan almost struck with Gerald Ford at the Republican party convention, and how did he reconcile the bitter disputes within the preconvention campaign to secure almost wall-to-wall support from the American business community before the general election? Finally, what is the enduring significance, if any, of the Reagan presidency?

The historic importance of the 1980 election, the special juncture it occupies in the ongoing process of elite realignment, suggests that none of these questions can be answered without reference to those more powerful springs that drive the American political system as a whole. Here, as in all advanced industrial democratic states, the major dynamics of domestic politics and party competition are determined by two factors: the aggregate balance of power between business and labor within the domestic system, and the competition of industrial sectors within the world economy. But the operative significance of the first factor is limited in the American case by the "exceptionalism" of American politics, which features a weak and politically disorganized labor movement. As a consequence, business provides the driving force behind much of domestic politics, and political conflict is often best analyzed as derivative of conflict between different corporate sectors.

Such business-centered analysis cannot pretend to capture all that is important in the turbulence of domestic politics. But it can provide a key to understanding the sources of power and conflict that shape the public realm. In the aggregate, the varieties of business conflict generate complex patterns of corporate alliance and political coalition. Although these patterns are in constant flux, and wildly unstable at their margins, they tend historically to feature a more durably powerful coalition at their center. Whole political systems can be defined with reference to such core coalitions, which are the system's chief beneficiaries and most important sources of stability.[4] The core of American politics during the Golden Age after World War II may be understood as founded on the alliance of high-technology firms (of which giant integrated petroleum companies were the most numerous and important) and international finance that first emerged in the 1930s.[5]

In these terms, what marks the present period of American politics is the breakup of the core coalition. Nothing is more striking during the present period than the irrevocable disintegration of "politics as usual." This disintegration is a deep and continuing process. It defined the 1980 campaign, making possible the emergence of Ronald Reagan while denying his electoral coalition an enduring victory. What happened in 1980 was not a classical power shift—where one clearly articulated political and economic coalition gained at the expense of another—but a shift in the very structures of interest and power that first constitute such coalitions. In this sense, we will argue, the hidden election had no winner. Its central political actor was neither a candidate nor an interest group but the process of dissolution itself.

In analyzing the 1980 election, two aspects of this process appear crucial. The first derives from the changing structure of the world economy. Its analysis requires reference to the accelerated pace of international economic integration and competition, the relative decline of American industrial power, the tensions among industrialized nations and between the developed and developing worlds, and the vast militarization of thought and action that all these changes in the shape of the international economic system have wrought. The second derives from the spectacular decline of mass politics at home. Its analysis requires reference to the transformation of American political party structures, the atrophy of trade union power, the diminution of extra-party and extra-union forms of mobilization and popular resistance, and the onslaught of business organization and dominance all these have engendered.

Before the dynamics of the 1980 campaign can be appreciated and recognized for what they were, this backdrop must be sketched. The structures of the world economy and domestic mass politics determine the shape of the electoral arena. They furnish the terrain over which the campaign and the complex process of political coalition-building make their laborious course. In the second section of this essay we sketch these broad constraints; in the third, we relate them to the campaign itself.

THE CHANGING WORLD ECONOMY AND THE DECLINE OF MASS POLITICS

Not only America, but the world too, is realigning. The structures of the world economy have been swept up by a deep and accelerating current of rapid economic integration, sharp increases in the mobility of capital, heightened competition among the major industrial powers, and the disintegration of traditional labor markets. This process is complex, but its consequences for the United States may be easily stated. The relative position of the United States in the global economic order has declined drastically. American hegemony has ended. And though the United States still maintains a formidable presence abroad, it does so at ever mounting costs to important sectors of the domestic economy. Those costs are now approaching their breaking point, threatening further collapse of the liberal international economic regime established at the close of World War II.

The United States emerged in 1945 as the world's supreme economic and military power. Though the devastation that total war had wrought on its leading rivals accounted for part of the American advantage at the time, the real secret of America's phenomenal postwar power was the rise to international dominance of a host of key industries: international oil, computers, electronics, aircraft, automobiles, many agricultural commodities, and both investment and commercial finance. As a result, controlling portions of the American business community endorsed a classic "imperialism of free trade," the swift expansion of American multinational industry and finance throughout a world largely powerless to resist them.

Free trade, the integration of once restrictive economic blocs, and global American military authority became the Holy Trinity of the postwar system. America's overwhelming economic power assured its gain from a liberally structured international regime featuring the free flow of goods and capital, as did American dominance of the international monetary institutions and arrangements (including the World Bank, the International Monetary Fund, and the Bretton Woods system of currency exchange) which eased the growth and flow of trade.

The achievements of the liberal system were considerable. There can be little question, for example, that the postwar wave of multinational expansion contributed to the remarkable American prosperity during the 1945–1971 period, or that it successfully integrated other regions—first Europe and Japan, later parts of the Third World—into the process of international economic development. The freedom of movement vouchsafed capital and goods permitted the expansion and relocation of production facilities, lowered input costs, and accelerated the transfer of technological development. It also internationalized the systems of management control and labor organization characteristic of bureaucratic capitalism. The flow of capital generated complex networks of international interdependence, as the inflation-corrected value of direct American foreign investment doubled in the 1950s and doubled again in the 1960s.[6] It fostered trade flows, heightened communication across national boundaries, led to the development of regional planning on a world scale, and massively increased cultural exchange.

But along with these much-advertised "benefits" of the liberal regime came a number of costs. Some of these, notably the perils of unbalanced industrial growth and, more equivocally, the heightened vulnerability of developing regions dependent upon the behavior of advanced industrial states, have been widely discussed. The costs most directly relevant to explaining American politics, however, have on the whole received little attention.

For these to become visible, it is necessary to discriminate among political actors on the basis of their locations in particular industrial sectors (and often in particular firms). The need for such discrimination is perhaps nowhere more evident than in analyzing the sharp disputes within the American business community over United States participation in the global economy. Corporations that produce and sell extensively abroad (as opposed to incidentally procuring foreign raw materials for domestic production) benefit from the liberal regime and continue to promote free trade and direct foreign investment, as do the big commercial and investment banks that finance them. By contrast, declining sectors that cannot make it multinationally, such as shoes, steel, textiles, independent oil (and increasingly rubber, automobiles, and parts of the chemical industry), most small enterprises, and local banks and regional finance seek with increasing desperation to insulate themselves from the pressures of the world economy through tariffs, quotas, investment limitations, and other restrictions on the free flow of goods and capital.[7]

To these declining or nationally centered enterprises, the liberal regime offers nothing but persistent and mounting challenge from expanding foreign industrial centers. This challenge is expressed most obviously in competition for shares of the global export market and the accumulation of national trade surpluses, and is evident in the progressive deterioration of the United States trade position during the postwar years. United Nations data from 1949, for example, indicate positive U.S. trade balances for all major (single-digit) Standard International Trade Classification number commodities,[8] but these across-the-board positive trade balances soon changed under pressure from the rebuilding economies of Western Europe and Japan (and eventually the emergent economies of the Third World). Felt first among older, low-technology industries such as shoe manufacturing and textiles, which showed negative trade balances as early as the middle and late 1950s, the foreign pressure spread gradually to industries employing higher-level technologies, such as iron and steel production, which had a rough parity of exports and imports in 1960 but negative balances a few years later, and road motor vehicles, which turned negative in 1965. By 1970, American trade weakness was evident in heavily negative balances in the basic and miscellaneous manufacturing categories, and in 1971 the first absolute trade deficit in recent United States history appeared.

In addition to such direct import pressure, domestic industry also suffered from the huge capital outflows going to fuel direct foreign investment, whose value had risen to $75.5 billion by 1970. Paralleling the overseas industrial expansion was a gradual internationalization of American banking operations, which rapidly accelerated during the 1960s. Overseas assets of American banks surged from $3.5 billion in 1960 to $52.6 billion by decade's end, and such giants of the international banking community as Bank of America, Chase, J. P. Morgan and Company, and Citibank derived an ever-increasing share of their total profits from foreign operations.[9]

Domestic industry was thus denied those sources of capital it most needed to revamp industrial plants and restore international competitiveness. Lured by more promising opportunities abroad, large-scale investors deserted the United States in record numbers. Although the decline cannot be wholly attributed to capital export, by the late 1960s the average annual rate of increase in real nonresidential fixed capital formation in the United States had dropped to 2.6 percent, off from an early 1960s boom years average of 9.6 percent, and roughly half of the 1949–1966 average of 5 percent.[10] Decline in basic capital formation was reflected in a relative decline in the United States share of world production, which fell steadily during the Golden Years from a late 1940s figure of 60 percent of world manufactures and 40 percent of the world's goods and services to half that share by the late 1970s.[11]

Rising imports and capital outflows were both encouraged and made more complicated by the Bretton Woods system of monetary exchange adopted at the close of World War II. Bretton Woods specified fixed exchange rates between national currencies and designated the U.S. dollar as the principal medium of international exchange while guaranteeing its convertibility into gold. It was the linchpin of stability upon which the liberal system turned. The dollar's role as a reserve currency for the international system, itself dependent upon the supremacy of American industrial power, greatly facilitated the expansion of American industry and investment abroad by limiting the costs of the chronic capital account deficits the United States ran during the period. Foreign governments were willing to buy up the excess dollars flowing all over the world for use as currency reserves, thus insulating the dollar from downward international pressures on its value. The fixed exchange system was ably exploited by the United States, which could buy up additional international power in the form of factories and weapons simply by printing more money, thus exercising what French critics came to call the "exorbitant privilege" of world economic leadership. But while it encouraged direct American foreign investment, the Bretton Woods system worked against the interests of domestic producers. Because of the dollar's role as reserve currency, devaluing it against other currencies would incur costs so enormous that devaluation was effectively foreclosed as a policy option. As imports surged, however, this inflexibility insured that prices of American goods remained artificially high against the prices of foreign competitors, who often deliberately held down their own exchange rates. This discouraged American exports, which remained costly in international markets, and further encouraged imports and additional foreign investment by American firms, which could be purchased with a dollar still strong against other currencies. Domestic producers lost out on both ends.

At no point in the postwar era was the emerging multinational free trade regime without powerful, well-organized opposition. But during the early 1950s, the overwhelming ascendancy of the United States in the world economy limited protests to a few specific parts of the industrial structure—textiles, for example, independent (that is, national) oil companies, a few agricultural commodities, and parts of the chemical industry. As the rest of the world revived, however, the costs mounted on American domestic producers. With more and more sectors meeting stiff competition, a deep chasm began to open within the American business community. Free traders from high-technology, internationally competitive firms and protectionists from domestically centered declining industrial enterprises were pitted against each other in bitter struggle. The Republican party of the Eisenhower years, in which essentially protectionist figures like National Steel's George Humphrey had lived in peaceful (albeit tense) coexistence with multinationalists like Nelson Rockefeller, began to splinter.

The eventual outcome of party infighting was prefigured at its 1960 convention. Nelson Rockefeller, the multinational word made flesh, lost the presidential nomination to Richard Nixon, who was not then and would never become the first choice of most multinationalists, although some had supported his bid for power. Barry Goldwater's victory at the party convention in 1964 marked the consolidation of power by the protectionist wing, represented by such prominent Goldwater supporters as Humphrey, Roger Milliken of Deering Milliken, the giant textile firm, independent oilmen like John Pew and Henry Salvatori, and a host of small and medium-sized enterprises.[12] A call for import restraint was written into the Republican platform, while party elites attacked the Rockefellers, the "eastern liberal establishment," foreign aid, and the United Nations.

Having lost control of the Republican party, multinational free traders found a new home among the Democrats of the 1960s. John Kennedy redeemed early promises of a bipartisan administration by appointing multinational businessmen like Robert McNamara and Douglas Dillon to cabinet posts. He co-sponsored a tax reduction bill with the Committee for Economic Development, and affirmed a strong free trade position with the Trade Expansion Act of 1962 and the ensuing Kennedy Round of massive (35 percent on the average) tariff reductions. Lyndon Johnson followed Kennedy's lead on the decisive free trade issue, ignoring the increasingly protectionist demands of his labor constituency.

While Vietnam and the abortive McGovern movement briefly complicated American politics, by the mid-1960s the present shape of American party politics was already clear. Republican presidential campaigns featured fratricidal battles between conservatives and a diminishing number of liberal "Rockefeller" Republicans. Multinational elites tightened their hold on the Democratic party, while the influence of organized labor markedly declined. Meanwhile, the costs of free trade imperialism soared.

In the mid-1960s the international economy emerged as a pivotal actor in domestic politics. The massive military intervention in Vietnam drained the home economy. Corporate pretax profit rates peaked in 1965 and then went into sharp decline.[13] Inflation made an irresistible entrance on the national stage. Lyndon Johnson, the consensus candidate of Democratic multinationalism, who had promised guns and butter, social welfare and imperial ambition, was forced to drop his reelection bid during the foreign exchange crisis of 1967–1968. The end of the 1960s and the beginning of the new decade saw the first important challenges to the dollar in international monetary markets, the historic 1971 trade deficit, sharpened rivalry between the United States and other economic powers, discord within the International Monetary Fund, protracted defeat in Vietnam, mounting dissent at home, and bitter disputes within NATO over the United States' military future in Europe.

Of particular note were the mounting tensions among the three great centers of industrial might: the United States, Western Europe, and Japan. Discord among domestic elites paralleled and reflected conflict among these "trilateral" states—their inability to agree upon fixed terms of monetary exchange, military strategy and cost sharing, or the ordering of leadership roles within the changing international economic regimes. Western Europe and Japan increasingly declined to play minor roles in the world economy, or subordinate their export-oriented growth strategies to the maintenance of an international order that they believed systematically benefited the United States at the expense of other powers.[14] Although West Germany was eventually squeezed into a modest 10 percent revaluation of the mark, both it and Japan turned aside American entreaties for more substantial currency revaluations, which would have raised the cost of exports to the United States and thus eased the strain on harassed domestic producers. In their bid for new international power and the foreign exchange currencies it required, both countries also ran up substantial trade surpluses that directly threatened American export dominance. In 1952, among members of the IMF, the United States share of exports had been 20.8 percent, while Japan's share was 1.7 percent. Twenty years later, the United States share had dropped to 13.2 percent, while Japan's had more than quadrupled to 7.6 percent. In 1971, when the U.S. trade balance finally turned sharply negative, Japan and West Germany commanded an aggregate trade surplus of $12 billion.[15]

President Richard Nixon responded to the 1971 deficit with his controversial New Economic Policy (NEP). In August of that year, Nixon unilaterally devalued the dollar and suspended its convertibility into gold. He heated up the trade wars by imposing a 10 percent surcharge on virtually all imports. He made blunt requests to Japan, South Korea, Hong Kong, and Taiwan that they slow the tide of textiles surging into the United States and pressured Japan and Western Europe to relax accumulated trade barriers, thus permitting greater American access to their domestic markets.

For domestic producers, the "Nixon shocks" of the NEP were welcome relief and prudent policy. But for multinationalists who had continued to profit from the liberal system, it represented the crudest sort of nativist regress. Such prominent free traders as C. Fred Bergsten, Philip Trezise, and J. Robert Schaetzel deserted the administration for posts at the liberal Brookings Institution and the Council on Foreign Relations (CFR), and Nixon was denounced by virtually all of the "responsible" press. Writing in the CFR journal *Foreign Affairs* a few months after the inauguration of the NEP, Bergsten made clear the depth of multinational reaction:

> In the summer of 1971, President Nixon and Secretary Connally revolutionized U.S. foreign economic policy. In so doing, they promoted a protectionist trend which raises questions about the future of the U.S. economy at least as fundamental as those raised by the abrupt adoption of wage-price controls. In so doing, they have also encouraged a disastrous trend which raises questions about the future of U.S. foreign policy. ... Both the U.S. economy and U.S. foreign policy for the relevant future hang in the balance.
>
> [Nixon] violated the spirit of the reigning international law in both monetary and trade fields. ... The new economic policy went much too far. It set impossible objectives, both quantitatively and qualitatively. ... It is wrong for the American economy. ... It courts disaster for U.S. global interests.[16]

On the heels of Nixon's NEP and the collapse (in several stages) of fixed exchange rates came the soaring oil price hikes engineered by OPEC. Meriting far more attention than we can afford them here, these inaugurated a momentous new chapter in the history of the Third World, by suddenly enriching some countries and immiserating others. They also, however, redefined relations among advanced industrial states. Arab investors now played increasingly important roles in world financial markets and, like other *nouveau riche* before them, became increasingly influential forces within various countries. No less significantly, rivalry among the leaders of the developed world greatly sharpened—rivalry for favorable positions in the rapidly developing Arab markets; rivalry for assured long-term sources of energy; rivalry for export surpluses to pay the oil prices.

Not surprisingly, even before the devastating worldwide recession of 1973–1974 hit, intensifying all these pressures, those parts of each advanced country's business community that expected to profit from an open world economy had begun organizing in self-defense.

Building on the network of transnational foundations, policy organizations, research institutes, and administrative bodies that had been slowly building up since the beginning of the Cold War, major international business groups took the initiative. Several existing organizations, such as the Organization for Economic Cooperation and Development, the International Monetary Fund, and the (U.S.) Council on Foreign Relations, reorganized in varying degrees, took on some new personnel, and expanded their activities. Simultaneously, a flock of new organizations sprang up, of which the Trilateral Commission, organized by Chase Manhattan Bank's David Rockefeller in 1972–1973 (and which quickly enrolled a wide range of multinational banks, industrial corporations, foundations, and media representatives) is by far the best known.[17]

Though important differences exist between these various organizations (the IMF's weighted voting system, for example, affords the United States far more power there than in the OECD), and agreement among their members sometimes embraces little more than bedrock opposition to protectionism, they help to define a network of shared personnel and pooled resources among multinational elites. Together they constitute a new and powerful countervailing force to the centrifugal pressures of the world economy.

But the power of multinational organizations to manage global conflict should not be overestimated. In addition to the domestic resistance their liberal economic programs traditionally inspire, such organizations suffer from the contradictory impulses of the international economic order they were organized to preserve. Nowhere is this more evident than in the multinationals' shifting response to the formulation of East-West diplomatic relations and the role of military force in foreign policy, which in the American case has moved from an early 1970s celebration of American-Soviet détente to the American business community's currently ecumenical militarism. Both because of its enormous consequences for everyday life around the world and because it signally affected the outcome of the 1980 campaign, this final disintegrative pressure of the world economy— the military revival—deserves careful attention.

The origins of détente can be traced directly to the international economic pressures of the 1960s. With the relative decline of the United States as a major profit center, American banks and industry were quickening their search for investment opportunities abroad. One of the most promising candidates for investment was the Soviet Union. The USSR's size and political stability seemed to offer a large long-term market for American capital, technology, and consumer goods, while normalization of relations promised to limit the enormous costs of strategic weapons system, thus easing growing international pressures on the dollar. Major American papers like *The New York Times* and the *Washington Post,* leading academics, and network television all joined in portraying the Soviet Union as a reasonable and responsible nation, thirsty for Pepsi-Cola, hungry for wheat, alive to the beauties of advanced computer technology and, above all, worthy of credit from the major American banks. Pepsi-Cola's bubbling enthusiasm for the project was shared by Chase Manhattan, Caterpillar Tractor, and a host of other multinationals and commercial banks. Richard Nixon, Henry Kissinger, and David Rockefeller all headed off to Moscow. Memories of Hungary, East Berlin, and the (then very recent) brutal Soviet invasion of Czechoslovakia faded. The age of détente began.[18]

Domestic enthusiasm for such an accommodation was never universal, however. The abrupt reversal of foreign policy that détente symbolized was fiercely contested by a broad range of American interests with a stake in the arms race, protection from the pressures of international trade, and preservation of American commitments to such critical client states as those in the Middle East. These included the defense industry and its infrastructure of supply firms and consultants, the Pentagon and its extensive university clientele, declining industrial sectors that would be best served if the United States traded with nobody, government-supported defense contractors, and the myriad supporters of Israel. Highly mobilized from the start, the vast anti-Soviet lobby undermined détente diplomacy by blocking congressional approval of most favored nation (MFN) trade status for the USSR and enlivened the early 1970s with right-wing attacks on the "liberal" policies of Henry Kissinger.

Formidable as it was, domestic opposition to détente would not have reversed the policy had some of its economic assumptions not been proved false. But within only a few years, the Soviet market for bank loans approached saturation, and it became apparent that the financial peculiarities of the Soviet economy favored barter deals and reciprocal production agreements which (especially without MFN status) were most easily exploited by the nearby Western European powers. Especially after the 1973–1974 recession irrefutably demonstrated that the major industrial economies were leveling off, American investors looked increasingly to the less developed countries (LDCs) of the Third World and Southern Europe as offering the greatest potential for growth and the expansion of markets.

Economic growth in these countries had been impressive during the late 1960s and early 1970s. While the American share of world industrial production fell between 1963 and 1977 from 40 to 36 percent, for example, the LDC share during the same period had nearly doubled from 5 to just under 10 percent. Nearly all this growth came after 1970, implying a fantastic expansion of national economies, with extensive capitalization requirements.[19]

The message to hard-pressed American industrialists and international bankers was clear. Particularly after the drastic OPEC oil price rises of 1973, bank lending to the Third World soared. OPEC petrodollars were recycled through commercial banks back to the Third World as public debt. Private bank lending to non-OPEC LDCs increased some threefold, from $34 billion in 1974 to an estimated $120 billion in 1979.[20]

Coupled with the progressive normalization of relations with China (which competes with the Soviet Union to be the big socialist market of the future, and where Europeans have little of the comparative advantage they displayed in trading with the USSR), this shift in investment focus crucially altered foreign policy debate at home. The existence of alternative investment and credit outlets lowered the cost of disrupting American-Soviet relations. Increased economic exposure in Southern Europe and the Third World (along with growing pressures in some countries for political autonomy, and the notorious perils of rapid development) produced simultaneous demands for a "liberalization" of foreign policy, and an enhanced capacity for military intervention abroad. At the same time, continued stagflation in the advanced industrial states exacerbated international economic rivalry among the great powers, highlighting the potential leverage military power provides in international relations, particularly in such critical areas as the Middle East. Virtually every trend in American business interaction with the world economy now swelled the demand for greater military preparedness, leading to extensive elite reorganization.

A major shift began *inside* the American multinational community, as well as among weapons producers and the more obvious champions of increased military spending. For many years, a number of organizations such as the American Security Council and the National Strategy Information Center (NSIC) had religiously promoted anticommunism, arms spending, and military preparedness. Their unchanging message had been sponsored by different parts of the American business community at different points in time. NSIC, for example, had been formed in the early 1960s, during the high noon of the Cold War, with some assistance from the American Bar Association and the support of many major American business figures (including former general Lucius Clay of Continental Can, Sanford Cousins of AT&T, Frank Folsom of RCA, Jack Howard of the Scripps-Howard Newspapers, Don Mitchell of General Telephone & Electronics, and Frank Stanton of CBS). Incorporated by William J. Casey (of whom more later), the group soon launched a massive campaign of advertising, seminars, conferences, and lectures (including one to the American Society of Corporate Secretaries provocatively entitled "New Dimensions in Competition: Clausewitz, Pavlov and Genghis Khan").[21]

But like other such military- and defense-oriented groups, the strength and level of activity of the NSIC varied widely with the changing demands of its corporate supporters. This is graphically reflected in the "gross contributions, gifts, grants and similar amount received category" on their required IRS reporting forms. At the height of détente in 1971, for example, NSIC claimed roughly $620,000 in that category. But as détente collapsed and the demand for militarization heightened in the mid-1970s, NSIC's budget, unlike those of nondefense-related nonprofit groups of the period, surged ahead of inflation. In both 1976 and 1977, for example, the organization collected well over $1.1 million in contributions and gift support.[22] Sensing its deepening support, in the mid-1970s NSIC moved to consolidate and extend its political power. In a May 1976 letter to Yale Law School professor and superhawk Eugene Rostow, NSIC president Frank R. Barnett announced plans to open:

a full-scale Washington office to:

(a) interact with policy echelons in the White House and Pentagon (where we still have many friends);
(b) "tutor" Congressional Staffs, and brief members;
(c) work with Trade Associations—with an interest in "defense"—which have Washington offices;
(d) generate more public information through friends in the Washington press corps who write about military and foreign affairs.[23]

Other defense-related groups, like the American Security Council, show a similar pattern of widening support and ambition during the period.[24] By the late 1970s there were many (usually, though far from invariably, multinationally oriented) organizations promoting increased military spending and pessimistic appraisals of the Soviet Union's defense plans. Important among these were the revamped Georgetown Center for Strategic and International Studies, the (U.S.) Atlantic Council, the Paris-based Atlantic Institute, the London-based International Institute for Strategic Studies and, perhaps most important for U.S. domestic politics, the Committee on the Present Danger (CPD). The last was launched immediately after Carter's victory in November 1976 by a large number of prominent business and (former) military figures, and received a huge startup grant from Hewlett-Packard's David Packard.[25]

But while all important segments of Big Business now championed more defense spending, no consensus had emerged on how large the increment should be or where the funds would be best spent. Nor was there anything approaching a unified view of the proper relationship between the United States and the Soviet Union. Programs like those of the Committee on the Present Danger, which implied annual defense budget increases of 6 percent or more for many years to come, major new strategic weapons systems, and a full-scale renewal of the Cold War, appealed to the suppliers of the weapons, domestic businesses concerned about international competition, the Pentagon, and those multinationals that felt especially vulnerable, (such as many large oil companies). But although these constituted a powerful and effective lobby, they represented only one bloc of American business.

Sentiment inside the financial community, by contrast, was more equivocal. Although commercial bankers and investment houses with stakes in particular regions derive important benefits from some increases in military spending, their enthusiasm for the arms buildup was tempered by fears of the potential inflationary effect of increased military outlays. They feared that higher defense spending spelled further increases in the size of the federal deficit and thus, in the usual Wall Street syllogism, higher inflation. Investment bankers, whose bond business could be severely hurt by double-digit inflation, were especially prominent in their warnings about excessive military expenditures. (During the 1980 presidential campaign, even some of CPD co-chairman Henry Fowler's partners at Goldman Sachs urged defense spending restraint.)[26] Fears about inflation, along with their outstanding loans to Eastern bloc countries, also limited commercial bank enthusiasm for the military buildup. Although their extensive Middle Eastern interests impel them strongly in the opposite direction, the position of American international banks today has some striking similarities to the City of London bankers of the mid-1930s, whose reluctance to rearm in face of the Nazi military buildup is constantly cited by American hawks. In driving up inflation, rising defense expenditures also accelerate international flight from the dollar, thus threatening the huge dollar deposits of the major international banks. Though he endorsed Jimmy Carter's embargo on grain and other exports to the Soviet Union and defended the military buildup in the Middle East, Chase's David Rockefeller argued that "it would be a mistake to go back to the Cold War."[27]

Such a belief was not limited to the financial community. Regardless of the difficulties of domestic implementation of détente, any number of multinationals found the logic of integrating the USSR into the world capitalist economy as compelling as ever. (After Secretary of State Cyrus Vance resigned from the administration in protest over Carter's Iranian rescue venture and the tilt toward militarism at the National Security Council, he was almost immediately welcomed back onto *The New York Times* and IBM corporate boards, which he had left four years before.) And of course the farm belt was still anxious to sell the Russians grain.

Like all the other central conflicts over foreign economic policy, business community disputes over defense spending, the future of American-Soviet relations, and the shape of the United States military presence abroad continued throughout the 1980 campaign, setting the terms of popular debate on the issue of war and peace.

The extensive elite regrouping triggered by changes in the world economy and American industry's strategic position within the international economic (dis)order has taken place largely in the absence of democratic challenge from below. In part this derives from long-term structural changes in the operation of American government and political parties, in part to the continued decline of organized labor and the rollback of community organizations, the civil rights and antiwar movements, and other sources and subjects of democratic mobilization and popular protest of the 1970s. Together these tendencies announce the near-collapse of American mass politics.

As Walter Dean Burnham observes in his essay in this volume, the American electoral arena and its pattern of citizen participation can be sharply distinguished from those that obtain in virtually all other formally democratic advanced industrial states. The present American party system features staggeringly low levels of participation and organizationally weak political parties of the "nonideological" variety. American voter turnout is not only extremely low by comparison to comparably advanced industrial systems, but decisively class skewed, exhibiting sharp variations across levels of income and wealth.[28] Relatively few Americans vote, and the poor vote much less than the rich. Those who need democracy most have it least.

Though the shrinking voter turnout and the withering away of partisan structures constitute the two most commonly discussed aspects of the decline of mass party politics in America, they are far from its most central features. Behind these formal democratic indicators stands a more fundamental process: the decay of independent (that is, nonbusiness dominated, controlled, or oriented) social organizations in general. The most important, though not the only, example of this diminishing pluralism is the decay of organized labor as a force in American politics. Because the strength of organized labor is critical to any independent mass politics, the trade union movement's spectacular decline cries out for sustained attention.

Any number of statistics testify to the gravity of labor's present situation. At the close of World War II, roughly 30 percent of the total American work force was organized into trade unions. Today that figure stands at less than 20 percent. The relative decline of union membership is paralleled by a shift in the emphasis of most existing unions from organizing to bureaucratic maintenance. This shift is reflected roughly in the balance between representation cases (involving union claims to represent workers) and unfair labor practice cases (involving outright violations of the law regulating the protection of concerted activity) coming before the National Labor Relations Board (NLRB). In 1945, 75 percent of the NLRB caseload was composed of representation cases; by 1978, that figure had dropped to a mere 25 percent. In addition, the organizing drives unions do mount are increasingly unsuccessful. As late as the mid-1960s unions were winning roughly 60 percent of their "RC" elections (in which the union seeks to be certified as collective bargaining representative), but by the late 1970s they were winning only slightly more than 40 percent. Along with the decline in organizational success has been a general weakening of the unions' hold on their membership. Deauthorization polls (challenging union security clauses) and decertification elections (challenging the union's status as bargaining representative) are on the rise. In 1950 there were approximately 100 decertification elections involving 9,500 workers. In 1978 there were more than 800 decertification elections involving close to 40,000 workers. Although decertification procedures are often initiated in the murderous jurisdictional disputes that plague the American labor movement, the big winner in most of the current such elections is "no union," as was the case in more than 75 percent of the 1978 decertification elections.[29]

These various percentage declines in union bargaining power and organizational strength are striking enough, but they translate into absolute declines in membership in many of the unions centered in basic manufacturing and transportation. The impact on individual unions has often been staggering. During the 1969–1979 period, for example, the International Association of Machinists and Aerospace Workers lost more than 150,000 workers (nearly a quarter of their membership), the Amalgamated Clothing and Textile Workers lost 149,000 workers (a third of membership), and the Railway, Airline and Steamship Clerks lost some 80,000 workers (40 percent of membership). While such absolute declines in the manufacturing and transportation sectors were offset by gains in government and service sector organizations, even by the generous estimates of the Bureau of Labor Statistics, which includes employee associations such as the National Educational Association and the American Nurses Association in union membership, the growth in absolute union membership during the 1968–1978 period was only 2 million workers, as compared to an increase of some 20 million persons in the total work force.[30]

Unions have also suffered from the rise in aggressive anti-union business organization in the 1970s. To take only one striking example, the Business Roundtable, which first emerged in response to the increasing demands and wage success of the construction building trades during the late 1960s, has almost single-handedly shattered this once impregnable bastion of union power. The dollar volume and industry percentage of nonunionized construction has grown all through the 1970s. Many once exclusively union contractors are now open shop (nonunion), or operate both union and nonunion companies in so-called double-breasted operations. The Associated Builders and Contractors (the major open shop construction trade association) estimates that open shop contractors now account for 60 percent of new annual construction, as compared with the roughly 30 percent of the market they commanded in the early 1970s, when the Roundtable was formed. Elsewhere the Roundtable, in conjunction with the National Association of Manufacturers' Council for a Union Free Environment, the long-standing National Right to Work Committee (and its National Right to Work Legal Defense Foundation), the small-business-dominated National Federation of Independent Business, the revamped United States Chamber of Commerce, and a host of assorted trade associations have been active in the courts and Congress with continuous anti-union legal action and lobbying.[31]

No less unfavorable for unions has been the trend of public opinion. Various polls conducted while Congress considered the recent Labor Law Reform bill showed labor lagging far behind business in both public confidence and faith in its representative character. A majority of those polled also felt that leaders of the larger unions wielded excessive power. In a recent Louis Harris survey published by the U.S. Senate, respondents were asked to indicate their "confidence" in the leadership of a number of leading American institutions. The results showed a general decline in public confidence in institutional leadership, but indicated as well that confidence in labor leadership is notably less than that in the military, major corporations, the Congress, and the federal executive.[32]

More subtle than all these measures of declining labor strength is the progressive deterioration of its position within the Democratic party. Although the unions' power within the Roosevelt New Deal coalition was probably less than most contemporary observers recognized, shared as it was with large numbers of investment and commercial banks, representatives of a variety of high-technology industries, and too many oilmen to count conveniently,[33] from 1935 onward they did exercise significant power within Democratic circles. In addition to co-sponsoring much of the social legislation of the period, unions exercised considerable leverage over Democratic leadership elites. They were, for example, able to compel Harry Truman's 1947 veto of the Taft-Hartley bill.

But by the late 1950s labor's position within Democratic ranks had already begun to deteriorate. A year before the pivotal presidential election of 1960, a Congress top-heavy with Democrats in the wake of the recession-induced landslide of 1958 passed the sharply antilabor Landrum-Griffin Act. In 1965 the most heavily Democratic Congress since Roosevelt's second term declined to amend the 14(b) "right to work" provision of Taft-Hartley, and other Democratic Congresses of the period, despite routine election year promises to labor, contrived to avoid the issue altogether. Thus labor was unable to staunch the flow of shops from the Northeast and Midwest to right to work states in the South. Nor, as noted above, was it able to move an increasingly multinationally oriented succession of Democratic administrations toward import restrictions to stop the loss of jobs in declining industrial sectors like textiles, steel, and shoes, which suffered from the revamped global economy. Throughout the 1960s, the percentage of American workers organized into trade unions continued its disastrous slide, and union members, if not their leaders, looked increasingly to third party candidates to express their dissatisfaction. Despite growing political budgets during the period, the AFL-CIO had ever more serious difficulties in coordinating the voting behavior of its members with the priorities of the national leadership.[34]

Labor's decline within the Democratic party was again vividly illustrated in the late 1970s, when the return of a Democratic administration in 1977 prompted labor leaders to attempt once more to improve their organizing position through legislation. The AFL-CIO proposed a series of amendments to existing labor law whose general thrust was to speed up representation elections, increase penalties for the skyrocketing number of unfair labor practices committed by employers, afford unions access to "captive audience" employer union-busting tactics, and grant the NLRB additional power in "refusal to bargain" cases, while increasing the size of the NLRB and streamlining the review process for administrative law judge findings.

The Labor Law Reform bill was important to unions because of a slowly building crisis within the NLRB administration that directly affected their organization capacity.[35] While too complex to command our full attention here, some aspects of this crisis may be noted. Despite massive productivity gains in the processing of its ever-expanding caseload (up from 13,000 cases in 1955 to more than 50,000 cases in 1978), the NLRB is unable, for example, to maintain previous standards of timeliness in the conduct of representation elections to determine whether a given union will be certified as bargaining representative for a given unit of workers. The gradual lengthening of the period between filing for an election and its actual conduct during the 1960s and 1970s has had disastrous consequences for the unions' ability to maintain the momentum of organizing drives. In 1962 almost 60 percent of representation elections were completed within the calendar month following the month of filing. By 1977 that figure had dropped to 40 percent, and an increasing number of elections took several months to complete. Postelection delays in certifying the results have also drastically increased, a problem largely attributable to a shift in the format of most representation elections from "consent" elections (where the parties waive rights to appeal to the national Board office for resolution of election-related questions) to "stipulated" elections (where those appeal rights are not waived).

During the 1962–1977 period, consent elections accounted for a dwindling share of all NLRB elections, dropping from 46.1 to 8.6 percent, while the share of stipulated elections rose from just under 27 percent to just over 73 percent. The increased number of stipulated elections translates into further postelection delays in "closing" election results and initiating the bargaining process. These delays have the effect of undermining union support and credibility within the bargaining unit. As the delays are further multiplied through the appeal process and widespread employer refusals to bargain, the bargaining strength of the union, measured by its ability to pull employees out on strike, progressively declines. Recent data indicate that even after closing a successful election, unions stand a 20 percent chance of never even securing a contract, while the increase in decertification elections and other challenges to union power within organized shops translates into an additional 13 percent chance that the contracts that are secured will be of only limited duration.[36]

Delays in processing representation elections are further compounded by the NLRB's inability to limit the ever more popular employer strategy of committing massive unfair labor practices against union drives or established unions. Because Board remedies are neither punitive, nor self-enforcing (meaning that to enforce compliance the Board must seek court enforcement), it is commonly cheaper for employers to continue to violate the law in the interest of destroying or preventing unionization. The widely noted instance of the J. P. Stevens textile firm's recidivist violation of the national labor law is only the most glaring example of what has become a common industry tactic. Finally, the use of union-busting consulting firms, used for publicity during organizing drives or for the screening of "prolabor" employees before hiring, has become a major new growth industry in labor-management relations. So confident are these new firms in their ability to stop organizing drives dead in their tracks that many flourish on a contingency fee system. They are paid only if the union is stopped or thrown out. Here again the unions have been unable to gain relief, either through Board procedures or through the reporting and disclosure requirements of the Landrum-Griffin Act.

Despite extensive AFL-CIO mobilization, and the announced support of Jimmy Carter, the Labor Law Reform Bill went down to stunning defeat at the hands of an unprecedentedly broad coalition of anti-union big and small business groups. A catastrophe for organized labor, the loss again underscored labor's inability to extract concessions or support from the putatively friendly ranks of the Democratic party.[37]

Yet another aspect of the decay of the trade union movement has been the progressive absorption of many of its top leaders into a variety of elite business and defense-oriented organizations. For them, the mantle of "responsible labor statesman" hangs irresistibly close at hand, along with the money, public accolades, and outside career options that follow. The Council on Foreign Relations finds willing candidates to provide the 1 percent representation of trade unionists among its membership. Rather more improbably, so does the Trilateral Commission.[38] Trilateralists among recent union leaders have included Leonard Woodcock of the United Auto Workers, who provided Jimmy Carter with a critical, and almost unique, early union endorsement in his campaign for the 1976 presidential nomination and who upon his retirement from the UAW was appointed head of the United States Liaison Office and then ambassador to Peking; I. W. Abel, who steered the United Steelworkers of America through a period of strong rank and file protest, culminating in the victory of his designated successor, Lloyd McBride, over a powerful challenge from insurgent Ed Sadlowski; Glenn Watts, president of the Communications Workers of America, who publicly blasted George Meany for criticizing Jimmy Carter after the reform bill defeat; Sol "Chick" Chaiken of the International Ladies' Garment Workers Union, another strong supporter of Carter (whose early 1980 endorsement of Carter's reelection bid came over substantial internal resistance in his union); and current AFL-CIO president Lane Kirkland. Kirkland and Woodcock have also served time on the Council on Foreign Relations, as has Jerry Wurf, whose American Federation of State, County and Municipal Employees failed notably to mount an effort in support of the reform bill commensurate with its relative size and strength.

Among the 141 founding board members of the Committee on the Present Danger, labor was represented by Chaiken, ILGWU's legislative director Evelyn DuBrow, ACTWU's executive vice-president William DuChessi, Kirkland, Ironworkers president John H. Lyons, American Federation of Teachers president Albert Shanker,[39] Operating Engineers president J. C. Turner, Plumbers and Pipefitters president Martin Ward, and long-time Cold War labor bureaucrat Jay Lovestone, whose role in systematically disorganizing postwar European trade unions has been extensively documented,[40] and who still describes himself as "international affairs" consultant to the AFL-CIO and ILGWU.

The most remarkable example of the integration of industry and union leadership is current AFL-CIO president Lane Kirkland. In addition to service on the CFR, CPD, and Trilateral Commission, Kirkland is a member of the board of the Atlantic Council, the Carnegie Endowment for International Peace, and the Rockefeller Foundation. (Kirkland's assistant in the AFL-CIO secretary-treasurer slot, Thomas Donahue, is a trustee of the Carnegie Corporation of New York, as well as a former official of Radio Free Europe.) Also worth noting is the reliance of progressive unions on the think tanks and policy institutions of predominantly Democratic multinational elites. Thus the Progressive Alliance, the UAW-backed loose federation of unions formed in response to the "class warfare" of the Carter years, relied on Social Science Research Council and Brookings Institution personnel for the articulation of its own program.

The steep decline in labor's ability to influence the direction of national politics had major consequences for the climate of American public life. Because many of these are explored in detail elsewhere in this volume, we discuss them only briefly here.

Perhaps reacting to the turbulent mass politics of the late 1960s, but probably stimulated more by the need to stay abreast of the changing world economy and its attendant social dislocations, a host of foundations (such as the Olin Foundation and the pharmaceutical-based and strongly defense-oriented Smith Richardson Foundation), research institutes (such as the American Enterprise Institute, the National Conservative Research and Education Foundation, and the Coors-sponsored Heritage Foundation), "public interest" legal foundations (such as the Pacific Legal Foundation, Mountain States Legal Foundation, Washington Legal Foundation, and National Right to Work Legal Defense Foundation), and publishers and publications (including the Green Hill Publications, *Conservative Digest*, and *New Right Report*) committed enormous resources to the promotion of public policies that met the needs of what they now viewed as the Brave New World of the 1970s and 1980s.[41] Their political program was varied and their organizational coherence should not be overestimated, but together these many groups mounted a political offensive whose central prongs included demands for a reduction of social welfare expenditures, an attack on antitrust and other economic regulation, an attack on environmental and other "social" regulation, a regressive revision of the tax code, the promotion of religious family life at the expense of women's rights and the secularization of culture, an end to affirmative action for blacks and other minorities, and a rollback of state and national legislation protecting the position of trade unions.

While the new network of subsidized journals, sponsored research institutes, and underwritten publications titillated observers with the prospect that, somehow, "ideas matter again," parts (though not all) of the business community began calling for yet another purge (by our count, the fourth in twentieth-century American history) of the universities. This was a purge they were perfectly positioned to implement, for as David

Dickson and David Noble relate in their essay in this volume, hard-pressed universities had in recent years increasingly turned to business to make up losses imposed by falling enrollments, inflation, and a slowdown in government support.[42]

The rollback of student, "youth," and other university-based popular movements was coupled with a more concrete dismantling and balkanization of many of the civil rights and community organizations that had risen to prominence in the late 1960s and early 1970s. As Ira Katznelson details in his essay, the social welfare constituency in the major cities was the first victim of urban fiscal crisis. Being particularly dependent on state structures and support for the articulation of their political demands, social welfare groups were all the more vulnerable to the contraction of the "claimant state."

Throughout all this, labor sat on the sidelines. It could not afford to compete with the outpouring of conservative Political Action Committees (PACs), and proved largely unable or unwilling to emulate the huge direct mail operations that New Right publicist Richard Viguerie had transformed into a fine art.[43]

Nor surprisingly, the coincidence of sweeping changes in the world economy and drastically enfeebled structures of democratic participation disoriented and threatened many ordinary Americans. With the virtual disappearance of organized alternatives to "business as usual," they embarked on an increasingly desperate search for individualized, nonpolitical means of cognizing personal experience. Along with the skyrocketing numbers of handgun purchases and karate club enrollments, the notable side effects of their many odysseys included a widespread religious revival and the more subtle valorization of the virtues of "civic privatism."

But while the role of the voting half of the population was easily reduced, as so often in recent American politics, to providing data for pollsters intent upon the steady restructuring and adjustment of candidate images, the influence of an infinitely smaller fraction of the population proportionately increased. On the other side of the world of appearance in the 1980 campaign, the elite struggles that constitute the hidden election continued and sharpened.

THE CAMPAIGN

Already certain parts of the puzzle of the 1980 election are beginning to fit together. To the first of the questions posed earlier, an unambiguous answer is emerging: Jimmy Carter's presidency collapsed during and after mid-1978 because the deteriorating world economy undercut all basis for the accommodation of the coalition Carter had originally succeeded in putting together.

As several excellent accounts have related in painstaking detail, multinationally oriented, free trade conscious business groups comprised the hegemonic element in Jimmy Carter's 1976 campaign. Only one major union, the United Auto Workers, supported him in the primaries, but Carter's list of big business supporters was enormous. Eventually it included a dazzling array of the greatest names in American (multinational) business, including Douglas Dillon, Henry Ford II (who, as the Rising Sun rises higher, probably regrets that decision), Felix Rohatyn, Henry Luce III, Roger Altman and several other Lehman Bros. partners, and far too many members of the Trilateral Commission to mention here, including Coca-Cola's J. Paul Austin (who spent several months introducing Carter to other big businessmen), Cyrus Vance, and Zbigniew Brzezinski.[44]

From virtually its first week in office, however, it was apparent that the foundations of this administration were far shakier than the mid-1960s Democratic coalition it superficially resembled. The administration's first choice to head the CIA, corporate attorney Theodore Sorensen (a partner in the Manhattan firm of Paul Weiss Rifkind Wharton & Garrison, a former special assistant to President John Kennedy, and an activist in the 1976 Carter campaign),* withdrew in the face of an all-out attack by the increasingly important anti-détente lobbies. Strongly criticized by the nationalist and protectionist Right, led at that time by Ronald Reagan and Jesse Helms, the top priority of Carter's multinational constituency, the Panama Canal treaty, faced immediate opposition. Originally negotiated by Sol Linowitz (a member of the Trilateral Commission and a nationally prominent Democratic lawyer who held a major interest in Xerox and served as a director of *Time*, Pan Am, and other corporations) and Ellsworth Bunker (who has held many important business and government posts, and was still serving on the board of Atlantic Mutual Insurance and the Asia Foundation), the treaty had to be rescued by a phalanx of multinationals led by Du Pont's Irving Shapiro.

Along with these milestones, there were in addition any number of other battles over the minimum wage, common-situs picketing, health insurance, tax policy, energy policy, defense expenditures, and arms control. But while each of these both registered and added to the pressure building on the administration, none disrupted Carter's basic coalition. The Panama Canal Treaty, after all, finally passed. The administration yielded ground only grudgingly to growing protectionist pressures, and while the defeat of labor law reform embittered relations between the White House and labor, the status quo the measure's failure preserved was not sufficiently threatening in the short run to drive most of labor out of the party, or even to another candidate.

---

*Throughout this essay, we attempt to indicate the most important institutional affiliations of major actors in the 1980 campaign. We consider knowledge of such affiliations as vital to the analysis of contemporary American politics as an awareness of latitude and longitude is to basic navigation. We realize well, however, that this is a view not universally shared, and that regardless of debates within the social sciences, some readers may initially find the inclusion of these data a distraction. The information is therefore presented in parentheses. For those who find them cumbersome, these parenthetic excursions may be hummed.

In the second half of 1978, however, the screws began to tighten.

For all the economic problems bedeviling the United States during Carter's term, the real rate of economic growth continued to remain high (averaging 4 percent a year during the 1977–1978 period), while unemployment slowly declined. As long as these happy circumstances persisted, both increasingly nervous elites and the mass public could postpone major action on their problems, in the hope that something would turn up to make them go away. In 1978, however, this breathing space began to disappear. Though the economy continued to grow, the rate of real growth began dropping. And as it kept sinking throughout 1978, 1979, and 1980, Americans at all income levels began to feel the squeeze—and elites began mobilizing for what were initially described as "hard choices."

Heralding the arrival of the new order was a slowly building dollar crisis. Concerned about the competitiveness of American manufacturing, the volume of OPEC payments, and other issues described by Gerald Epstein in his essay in this volume, Carter, the Treasury, and the Federal Reserve Board had for some time allowed the dollar to drift gradually down. With fears of chronic double-digit inflation mounting, however, foreign exchange markets continued selling off the dollar. Hoping to arrest the drop in the dollar's value, Carter introduced voluntary wage-price controls in October. At nearly the same moment the Fed lifted interest rates, and both the administration and the bankers affirmed their commitment to sustain the value of the dollar.

The new measures, however, accomplished little. While the restraints they imposed on the domestic economy bankrupted a few more small businesses and put additional workers out of jobs, they scarcely affected the underlying inflation rate. As the dollar continued to drop on international markets, the OPEC energy cartel drastically hiked its prices once again, and yet another round of institutional adjustments began.

Just then came the first of several hammer blows that provided the *coup de grâce* to both Carter's coalition and the deeper structures of American politics since the New Deal. In Iran, the best-laid plans of two decades of American diplomats, businessmen, espionage agents, and government officials (and, it was later revealed, handsomely rewarded journalists from major American news media) came disastrously apart. The Shah of Iran, who had been promoted by the United States as a regional leader, was forced to flee the country in the face of a revolutionary religious upsurge. The causes and ramifications of the Iranian debacle will take years to sort out, and the process will no doubt be difficult and contentious. For the 1980 election, however, one consequence of the Iranian revolution overshadows all others: it was a disaster for many of America's largest industrial and service firms. American banks, oil companies, construction firms, weapons suppliers, and any number of other exporters and service enterprises had been deeply involved with the Shah's regime. Many had been active in Iran for years. In addition, the Shah's ambitious, American-encouraged development plans promised many more years of lucrative business. Now, all at once, these projects were consigned to a commercial limbo, and a huge backlog of debts and contracts were placed in question.

The effect of the Shah's collapse on the American big business community was as sweeping as it was predictable. Staggered by their real and prospective losses, American businessmen (and women) suffered something like a collective nervous breakdown. Spurred by the increasingly apparent inability of the United States to influence the unpredictable Khomeni regime, American business woke up to the threat posed by instability in the Third World generally. Many of the biggest firms involved in Iran—notably the big commercial banks and the oil and construction companies—were driven almost to distraction by the awful thought that something similar could happen in Saudi Arabia. As Bruce Cumings describes in detail in his essay in this volume, the chorus of voices demanding rearmament swelled to an insistent roar.

Almost immediately compounding these pressures was another shock from the global economy: the worldwide energy shortage of 1979. Early that year, Jimmy Carter reversed a campaign pledge and announced support for the phased decontrol of oil prices up to the much higher prevailing world market price. At the time, Carter also proposed a modest tax on the huge profits phased decontrol would assure oil firms. While the first of these measures was soon implemented, the "windfall profits" tax part of Carter's proposal was strongly resisted by oil interests and soon mired in interminable congressional debate. As that debate proceeded, the long-building energy crisis exploded in the early summer of 1979. In many parts of the country gasoline briefly became difficult to obtain. Prices soared while anxious motorists were forced to wait in line at overcrowded pumps. Angry and frightened, many Americans suspected that the oil companies had deliberately engineered the shortage to raise prices. While the media worked overtime to quash that rumor (*Time* magazine featured an essay which declared that criticism of oil companies was divisive and should therefore simply cease, while *The New York Times* assembled a panel of social scientists who diagnosed public skepticism of the crisis as "neurotic avoidance")[45] and a parade of oil-company explanations of the shortages marched by (weather, OPEC, the Ayatollah, platform fires in the Gulf of Mexico, Department of Energy rules, and complex gas allocation formulas), various parts of the business community debated what should be done.

No consensus emerged. With a board drawn from mostly second-tier officials of a few national oil companies, major energy consumers (aluminum companies), some defense-related concerns, and some strong supporters of American aid to Israel, Americans for Energy Independence and similar groups strongly supported government-sponsored efforts to find and develop alternative energy sources, such as coal, synthetic fuels, or, for some in their camp, nuclear power. Major figures in the American financial community, greatly concerned about the long-term effect on the dollar of continuing oil-induced deficits and the inability of the big commercial banks to recycle the growing sums of petrodollars, meanwhile began pressing for some combination of conservation, higher prices (which restrain oil imports by forcing a readjustment of demand), and programs to produce limited amounts of new energy, or at least more oil, for hard-pressed Third World countries whose oil payment difficulties were increasingly threatening world financial markets and the stability of the private international banks that loaned to them.[46]

Though some big oil companies were certainly open to the prospect of government support for their developing new lines of business, most major firms thought the best solution to the energy crisis was for the government to allow yet more oil price increases to the cartel-determined world price level (the "free market" solution). Strongly opposed to oil explorations they could not control, the major oil companies also successfully pressured the World Bank to scale back and redesign a program aimed at making loans to non-OPEC Third World potential oil producers.

In these circumstances, Carter was forced to make a decision which, whatever its content, could not avoid harming one or another powerful, well-financed interest in American politics. Not surprisingly, the normal presidential process of staff review and speech preparation broke down completely. The search for more time and the desperate need to build some sort of reliable corporate support inspired Carter to cancel a previously scheduled national energy address and retreat instead to Camp David. There, while the media emphasized his elaborately staged consultations with religious leaders, machine politicians, community activists, and a few labor leaders, a glittering array of high business figures, including prominent members of the oil industry, converged.[47]

The first results of the Camp David deliberations were something of an anticlimax. Though the nationally televised speech Carter gave was generally judged a moderate success, its concrete proposals—a promise that American oil imports had peaked, a request for standby authority to ration gasoline, the establishment of Energy Mobilization and Energy Security Boards to advance the synthetic fuels program and a host of related projects—scarcely added up to high drama. A few weeks later, however, signs multiplied that rather more had been afoot in the Maryland woods. Alluding to decisions reached while he was ensconced at Camp David, Carter dramatically restructured his cabinet. Along with the long-planned resignation of Attorney General Griffin Bell (who quickly materialized on the board of Martin Marietta, a major defense contractor), Carter also accepted the resignations of Energy Secretary James Schlesinger and Transportation Secretary Brock Adams, while he dismissed Health, Education, and Welfare Secretary Joseph Califano and Treasury Secretary Michael Blumenthal. The news hit Washington and the rest of the world like a bombshell. Immediately an outpouring of speculation, gossip, and comment began. Why had Carter done it? What did it mean? How would it affect his political future?

In our view, while much of the discussion may have been misdirected, the summer restructuring of the cabinet and Carter's new appointments merit the closest attention from political analysts. For when they are recognized as the beginning of a series of critical choices Carter made between the middle of 1979 and the spring of 1980, answers emerge to many of the other questions posed about the Carter and Kennedy campaigns at the outset of this essay.

Camp David made obvious what had become increasingly apparent— that the world, and therefore American politics, had become too incoherent to be governed by applications (however creative) of principles derived from the New Deal. Evolved in a time when energy was cheap and the United States was rising both as a military and an economic power, New Deal politics was now obsolete. The conditions under which high-technology industry, international finance, labor unions, and the poor and welfare classes could all happily inhabit the same political party had disappeared. If he wanted to remain in office, Carter now had to experiment with a new political formula.

Carter responded to this imperative in obvious, if ultimately fatal, ways. Elected in 1976 after campaigning in favor of social welfare, ordinary virtues of trust, faith, and integrity, and (very quietly expressed) commitments to free trade, internationalism, and cautious détente, Carter now strengthened his commitments to some of these policies and their constituencies while largely abandoning others. His commitment to free trade and internationalism, for example, never wavered. All through 1979, when almost everything else sometimes seemed to be disintegrating, Special Trade Representative Robert Strauss (a Dallas attorney long active in Democratic politics, owner of small broadcasting and banking firms, and a director, as he entered the administration, of Xerox, Columbia Pictures, and Braniff) continued to push for congressional acceptance of the major trade liberalization package of the Multilateral Trade Negotiation Agreements. He eventually succeeded.

Nor did the cabinet reshuffling mark a change in what one major study of Carter's federal appointments has described as "a select recruitment base which may well be unrivalled in American history."[48] Having filled the administration with free trading elite figures drawn from the Trilateral Commission, the Brookings Institution, and other institutions championing an open world economy, Carter, when he axed Blumenthal, immediately reconfirmed his ties to that part of the American business community. An amusing game of musical chairs began. G. William Miller (the former head of Textron), who was then serving as chairman of the Federal Reserve, replaced Blumenthal. Carter then offered Miller's old job to David Rockefeller, Brown Brothers Harriman partner Robert Roosa, and the Bank of America's A. W. Clausen.[49] When all three declined, the position was awarded to Paul Volcker (a former Chase employee, who was then serving as president of the Federal Reserve Bank of New York, a director of the Council on Foreign Relations, and a member of the Trilateral Commission). After Volcker resigned his outside commitment, Blumenthal replaced him on the CFR board (and was quickly appointed chairman and chief executive officer of Burroughs, as well as a director of Pillsbury, Equitable Life Assurance, and Chemical Bank). Shortly thereafter, Hedley Donovan (the long-time editor of *Time* magazine, a member of the Trilateral Commission, a director of the Council on Foreign Relations, and a trustee of the Ford Foundation and the Carnegie Endowment for International Peace) was appointed a special adviser to Carter. Almost simultaneously, Washington superlawyer Lloyd Cutler (also a member of the Trilateral Commission, a trustee of the Brookings Institution, and a director of the Council on Foreign Relations, American Cyanamid, and the Southeast Banking Corporation) replaced Atlanta attorney Robert Lipshutz as Carter's own general counsel. Alonzo McDonald (a trustee of the CED and formerly of McKinsey & Company, a major international consulting firm) moved over from his post as deputy special trade negotiator to reorganize the White House staff.

Carter's reliance on the multinationally oriented wing of the American business community to fill high government positions continued right through the election campaign. When Commerce Secretary Juanita Kreps left the administration (for personal reasons) later in the year, Carter at once replaced her with Philip Klutznick (formerly a Chicago builder who had since become a limited partner in Salomon Brothers, the big investment bank, and a trustee of the Committee for Economic Development, while serving on the board of Americans for Energy Independence). Other key jobs went to several individuals with similar ties, including Victor Palmieri (a trustee of the Rockefeller Foundation) and Shirley Hufstedler (an Aspen Institute trustee and member of the board of the Colonial Williamsburg Foundation, the Rockefeller family philanthropy).[50]

Other major positions Carter took as he defined his new course were more carefully hedged. On the whole, Carter's energy policy tilted slightly in the direction of major energy consumers (who wanted to keep prices down) and international finance (at least on the issue of World Bank loans to non-OPEC LDCs for oil exploration). It also made concessions to groups (which included some energy companies) favoring synthetic fuels. All these features limited its appeal to most major oil companies (and the nuclear industry, an issue we can only mention here). In addition, virtually all the oil concerns opposed Carter's windfall profits tax proposal, which by opening up a major source of new revenue, mitigated the rapidly developing budget squeeze.

With scarcely a year to go before the election, however, it did not require a crystal ball to see that in a close election Texas would probably emerge as a pivotal state, and that as matters stood then, Carter could well (as he eventually did) lose it. Accordingly, Carter's selection of Deputy Secretary of Defense Charles W. Duncan, Jr., as Schlesinger's successor at the Department of Energy merits more attention than it received at the time. Though virtually all news reports highlighted Duncan's old connection to Coca-Cola (a corporation whose close ties to the Carter administration, like those of the Trilateral Commission, were now a stale joke), Duncan's ties to oil and Texas were numerous and overlapping. After leaving the Coca-Cola presidency in 1974, Duncan had moved to Texas. Still sitting on the board of Coke, he became the head of Rotan Mosle, a Texas-based investment house that had close ties with several institutions dominated by the Moodys, one of the richest families in Texas. He also served as a director of the Great Southern Corporation, the Southern Railway, and a subsidiary of Gulf and Western. Probably even more important than Duncan's own affiliations, however, were those of his brother, John H. Duncan. A long-time member of the Gulf and Western board, the other Duncan had slowly become a major figure in the Texas energy establishment. In the late 1970s, he served on the board of Houston Natural Gas, the Houston Chamber of Commerce, Paktank, a subsidiary of the Dutch multinational Pakhoed Holding, and several banks, including at least one, Texas Bank Shares, which heavily represented the affiliates of many big oil concerns, including Exxon, El Paso Natural Gas, and Getty Oil.[51]

Several other new recruits into Carter's cabinet suggested a similar political shrewdness. At a time of widespread challenge to his policies coming from both the black and feminist communities, he moved Secretary of Housing and Urban Development Patricia Harris, a black woman (who had previously held directorships at the Chase Manhattan Bank, IBM, and Scott Paper) into the HEW slot vacated by Califano. And facing a possible primary fight that would test his control of the party, Carter took the unprecedented step of appointing two big-city mayors to the cabinet. Portland Mayor Neil Goldschmidt became secretary of transportation, and former New Orleans mayor Moon Landrieu (a trustee of the German Marshall Fund who was part of a New Orleans real estate concern that had been in partnership with the Shah of Iran) took over for Harris at HUD.

But while Carter's cabinet shuffle probably strengthened his position with important constituencies, he could not possibly improve his position with them all. It became increasingly apparent over the next few months that Carter was slowly being trapped by the rapidly increasing tension between the requirements of his domestic mass (party) base and American foreign (especially foreign economic) policy. With inflation rising along with business demands for vast increases in defense spending, a squeeze built up on the government budget. After another foreign exchange crisis in October of 1979, the Fed kicked interest rates higher and higher. From this point on, Jimmy Carter was afforded almost no relief.

With an election only months away, the Fed action was exactly what Carter did not need. While the Fed succeeded in propping up the dollar with high interest rates, which attracted funds from abroad and also slowed inflation by throttling back the economy, it sharply raised unemployment levels. In addition, with the economy sluggish, demands on the Treasury rose as unemployment compensation and other federal programs automatically expanded. With the economy flat, however, so were tax collections. Along with the prospective drain on the government budget from additional military spending in the wake of the Soviet invasion of

Afghanistan, these mounting fiscal pressures were too much. Something had to give.

In the business community, the most frequently expressed proposals for controlling inflation stressed the importance of reducing the size of the federal deficit, which implied either a rise in taxes or cuts in spending. With the economy already in trouble, raising taxes was impossible. Accordingly, in the late winter of 1979–1980, all sectors of the business community mobilized in support of more budget cuts. Week after week, a round robin of businessmen and business organizations besieged all levels of government with requests that the recently proposed federal budget be cut back. Their demands were echoed by influential columnists and virtually all the major media, drowning out the protests of groups representing workers, blacks, and the poor who clamored for additional aid during the recession.

In early March, the business efforts reached a climax. The American Assembly, whose trustees represent a cross section of multinational America (and whose most recent additions to the board included Caspar Weinberger, formerly an official in the Nixon administration, and then vice-president and general counsel of giant privately held Bechtel, a member of the Trilateral Commission, and a director of Quaker Oats and Pepsi-Cola), brought together representatives of business and government with a select handful of labor leaders to support Carter's increasingly firm commitment to budgetary restraint.

A few days later, amid widely voiced fears that the market for long-term bonds would disappear if galloping inflation were not immediately slowed to a walk, four investment bankers—Robert Roosa of Brown Brothers Harriman (a long-time Democrat, chairman of the Brookings Institution, vice-chairman of the Rockefeller Foundation, trustee of TIAA/CREF, which arranges pensions for America's college teachers, and a director of the Council on Foreign Relations, American Express, Texaco, the National Bureau of Economic Research, and Owens-Corning Fiberglas); Felix Rohatyn (another important Democrat from the investment banking house of Lazard Freres who, along with his role as Lord Protector of New York City, serves as a director of ITT, South African industrialist Harry Oppenheimer's Minerals & Resources, Ltd., Pfizer, MCA, Eastern Airlines, Howmet Turbine Components, Owens-Illinois, and the giant French holding company Pechiney Ugine Kuhlman); Peter Peterson of Lehman Brothers Kuhn Loeb (a director of the Council on Foreign Relations, American Express, General Foods, 3M, RCA, Illinois Bell, the First National Bank of Chicago, and several other corporations); and Henry Kaufman of Salomon Brothers (a leading economic forecaster)—along with Harvard economist Otto Eckstein (who doubles as the president of Data Resources, a McGraw-Hill subsidiary), gathered with a group of Congressmen organized by Senator Henry Jackson for a "sobering" discussion that began over dinner and stretched late into the night.[52] A few days later, in an atmosphere approaching hysteria, Carter announced sweeping budget cutbacks, and the Federal Reserve announced a series of Draconian credit controls and other measures aimed at direct regulation of the money supply. Carter, Fed chairman Volcker, and the big banks also seized on the crisis to pressure a congressional conference committee into a drastic rewriting of already approved banking legislation. As Alan Stone observes in his essay in this volume, the result was the most sweeping financial regulatory revision since the New Deal.

The budget decisions were among the most fateful and important campaign choices Carter made. Together they confirmed the policy course on which Carter had been heading and cut much of the ground out from under him. For now he was caught in a dilemma. On one hand, his own reaction to Iran, Afghanistan, and other factors previously discussed was fanning the flames of the arms buildup, with its demands for federal spending. On the other, the domestic constituency of the Democratic party —notably labor and the urban poor—was clamoring for more help. But at the same time, international pressures on the dollar, and therefore the government budget, were unyielding.

Thus by early 1980, Jimmy Carter was the first choice of hardly anyone for president of the United States. While defense hardliners could take heart from the increasingly important role assumed by the CIA's "B Team" of superhawk analysts who challenged existing agency estimates of Russian strength and intentions; warm to the replacement of Paul Warnke (a director of the Council on Foreign Relations, member of the Trilateral Commission, and Washington law partner of superlawyer Clark Clifford), who had been strongly criticized by the Right, by former general George Seignious (at that time head of the Citadel, a military college, and a director of the Southern Bancorporation) as the president's chief disarmament negotiator; welcome Zbigniew Brzezinski's efforts to dramatize himself as King of the Khyber Rifles; and hail the Carter administration's moves to restore the position of the CIA, there was simply not enough money in the Carter budget to satisfy them. At the same time, the pressures to accommodate the military also closed off the funds that sustained the party's increasingly disenchanted mass base. It was an awkward corner Carter had been backed into, and one from which he never escaped.

The same analysis that explains why Jimmy Carter persisted in his apparently suicidal election-year efforts to deflate his own constituency also accounts for the peculiar course of the campaign to reject him as the party's nominee.

It is perfectly apparent, for example, that as Carter grew increasingly vulnerable, prominent Democrats like New York Governor Hugh Carey (who promptly opened discussions about a run with Seagram's chairman Edgar M. Bronfman, Warner Communications chairman Steven J. Ross, Norton Simon chairman David Mahoney, American International Group chairman Maurice Greenberg, and a battery of corporate lawyers) would begin dreaming about toppling him.[53] For most of these challengers, however, a head-on attack against a sitting president hardly constituted their best strategy. For them to win, someone else would have to snarl up the nomination by defeating the president in some primaries. Not surprisingly, pressure built on Senator Edward Kennedy, the most likely entrant, to declare his candidacy. But when Kennedy finally did enter the race, of all the many prominent politicians who had been loudly urging him to run, only Chicago mayor Jane Byrne rushed to support him.

Probably even more important as a factor in the abrupt decline of Kennedy's campaign, however, was the derivative character of his early political appeals. The original political formula he tried out on wary elites was essentially the same as that patented by his older brothers in the 1960s. As instanced by John F. Kennedy's administration (in which a cabinet completely dominated by multinational free traders supervised domestic social reform and increased welfare spending), and Robert Kennedy's brief and tragic insurgent candidacy in 1968 (which drew major support from multinational financiers Douglas Dillon and Andre Meyer, among others), that formula called for the simultaneous championing of an open world economy and domestic liberalism. A rather obvious albeit spirited variation on the New Deal, it was a package that enthralled many both in and outside the business community.

But the Kennedys had risen to political prominence during the boom years of the early 1960s. The broad support their domestic liberalism and economic internationalism achieved depended critically on an expanding economy. In the tightening economy of the late 1970s, support for such programs was much thinner. A few leading figures in international finance with long-time ties to the Kennedy family, like World Bank president Robert McNamara, quietly supported Kennedy. So did a handful of mostly second-tier investment bankers, like Robert Towbin of L. F. Rothschild. And early on the Kennedy campaign was joined by Mobil public affairs vice-president and long-time Democrat Herbert Schmertz. (Mobil had strongly criticized Carter's energy proposals. Having proportionately fewer crude oil reserves than most major international oil companies, it stood to gain less from Carter's removal of controls on existing oil supplies than it would have from a tax program weighted more heavily in favor of new oil exploration).[54] But on the whole, when Kennedy trotted out the old bromides about encouraging world trade and innovation (as in his speech to the Investment Association of New York)[55] or the "free market," he was difficult to tell apart from Carter. And, in the budget-cutting year of 1980, when he did differentiate himself from Carter by criticizing the proposed budget cuts, he only succeeded in setting off alarm bells in the business community.

Harassed by savage media attacks, Kennedy's candidacy sank lower and lower. After the loss of the Iowa primary, it seemed about to expire. But it did not fade away. Though he ultimately lost the nomination, Kennedy rebounded vigorously. Picking himself up off the floor, he went on to defeat Carter in a string of important primaries in New York, Pennsylvania, and California, among other states. In the final days before the Democratic nomination, he appeared on the verge of defeating the president. What explains this remarkable turnabout?

An assessment of the nature of the Kennedy campaign more discriminating than either its own self-image or its publicly advertised stereotypes is indispensable to any serious analysis of this question. One must begin by acknowledging that the Kennedy candidacy was neither of two things. First, Kennedy was not Lech Walesa, the union leader who was catapulted almost overnight to the head of the Polish movement for independent trade unions. While he tried to tap popular hostility to Carter's budget-cutting proposals, Kennedy and the key members of his organization had been working together for years. Their views on public policy were well formed, and their network of contacts was largely in place. Second, and even more important, Kennedy's candidacy was only slightly more a vehicle of the organized labor movement than it was a platform for mass protest. Though many unions decided eventually to support him, and most certainly favored the more expansive budgets he championed, as well as his national health insurance proposals, Kennedy's core coalition remained tied to his old (and now rapidly shrinking base) among internationally oriented, high-technology business.

His famous speech at Georgetown University in January 1980, which is usually credited as marking the upturn of his fortunes, had been carefully crafted after emergency discussions with a stellar group of high business figures, including Felix Rohatyn, Otto Eckstein, Arthur Okun (an economist with strong ties to the Brookings Institution, who was a director of Intercapital Funds and for almost a decade an economic consultant to Donaldsen, Lukfin & Jenrette, a major investment banking firm), and Walter Heller (a leading economic policy analyst and member of the Trilateral Commission, who also serves as a director of Northwestern National Life Insurance, the National City Bank of Minneapolis, International Multifoods, and the Commercial Credit Corporation, a subsidiary of giant Minneapolis-based Control Data Computer, a firm with many long-standing ties to high levels of the Democratic party and a leader in developing trade with the Soviet Union).[56]

The speech's proposals were clearly aimed at reestablishing the link welding together the angry mass base of the Democratic party and those portions of the multinational business community who remained interested in and able to afford a coalition with organized labor. Kennedy's pledges, both stated and implied, to cut the budget less savagely than Carter seemed increasingly likely to do were calculated to appeal to the former constituency. By contrast, corporations which, like Control Data, remained interested in trade with the Soviets, and financiers worried about the effect of military spending on the stability of the dollar, were offered the promise of less bellicose foreign policies. The most celebrated of Kennedy's proposals, his call for wage-price controls, was also a device calculated to attract financiers. With the bond market threatening to come completely apart, and fears of another dollar crisis widely voiced, wage-price controls offered a quick fix to the chief anxiety of the business community—double-digit inflation—as Rohatyn pointed out in a speech of his own to the Conference Board only a few weeks later.[57]

For a while, this nostalgic attempt to put the evil genie of the 1970s back into the bottle of the 1960s attracted interest and support. Alan Greenspan, originally a rather right-wing economic forecaster for the Nixon administration, but who had since moved to the center of American corporate life (becoming a director of Morgan Guaranty Trust, General Foods, Mobil, and Alcoa, as well as perhaps the most centrist member of the restructured Hoover Institution board), had already, in December 1979, set up meetings for Kennedy with major investment bankers, including Peter Peterson, Sanford Weill of Shearson Loeb Rhodes, and John Whitehead of Goldman Sachs.[58] Now Max Palevsky, former chairman of Xerox's executive committee and a major fundraiser for McGovern in 1972 and Carter in 1976 (currently a director of Intel), and other liberal Democrats took another look at the senator.

In the end, however, Kennedy garnered only modest support. Though Palevsky and some other businessmen appear to have afforded the campaign some aid, most American elites paused only to notice, and occasionally to praise, Kennedy's "courage." Then they hurried on—in Greenspan's case to the Republicans, in others' to Carter, and in a few unimportant cases to California Governor Jerry Brown. Most, it is clear, were persuaded that the time had passed for the coalition Kennedy now championed. With their overwhelming desires to cut the budget and their deepening commitments to military spending (although, as noted earlier, the range of increases proposed varied widely), continued social spending impressed most businessmen as a luxury that had to be abandoned. To them, accordingly, the preferred way out of the budgetary impasse was the *de facto* elimination of the Democratic party's mass constituency.

As a consequence, in the later stages of his campaign Kennedy experimented with an array of proposals that moved further and further away from his original multinational affiliation. Desperate for leverage against Carter (who, for all his increasingly intractable problems, could count on the support of many businessmen in his fight for the nomination, even if they would not support him in the general election), Kennedy embraced curbs on imported steel in time for the primaries in Pennsylvania, New Jersey, and other heavy industry states. Nowhere did he succeed in articulating a coherent program for international economic policy, however, as reflected in the simultaneous proposals offered during this period for the "reindustrialization" of America, which in contrast to the endorsement of import curbs, resembled proposals Rohatyn was beginning to advance.[59]

Had the choices in the Democratic party been limited to Carter and Kennedy, the Democratic convention would probably have been a much more cut and dried affair than it was. But they were not. As the convention approached, pressure to dump Carter grew from another less obviously active part of the party and country—the Right.

In sharp contrast to all the ink spilled about the programmatic lobbying of groups like the Committee on the Present Danger, or their activities in the Reagan camp, virtually nothing has been written about the activities and weapons and "defense" elites within the Democratic campaign. Their attempts to influence the outcome there, however, were important, and provide grim portents of what American party politics could well become within a few years.

As a powerful group increasingly alienated from Carter, the affluent supporters of arms spending in excess of Carter's already rising levels were of course an inviting target for anyone trying to build a coalition to throw the president out of office. In seeking to attract them, however, Kennedy confronted the same problem Carter did. If he committed himself to more arms spending, he would have to write off the domestic inflation rate (and thus the role of the dollar internationally) or the social welfare constituency of the Democratic party. As a long-time leader of the multinational wing of the Democratic party, and an observant student of the senatorial politicking of Messrs Roosa, Rohatyn & Co. in cutting the budget, Kennedy was well aware that the financial constraint was, in 1980, as much a "given" of the universe of American politics as the principle of gravity.

Accordingly, when after Kennedy's shattering defeat in the Iowa primary superhawk Senator Henry Jackson and five members of the Committee on the Present Danger—Henry Fowler (a former secretary of the Treasury under Lyndon Johnson, and currently a partner at Goldman, Sachs, chairman of the Atlantic Council, trustee of the Alfred P. Sloan Foundation and Japan Society, and director of many corporations, including Corning Glass, Trans World Airlines, the Norfolk and Western Railroad, and the Dillon-family-controlled U.S. and Foreign Securities Corporation), Paul Nitze (one of the original late 1940s cold warriors, currently a director of Schroeder's, Inc., the American subsidiary of the famous British investment bank, the Atlantic Council, the American Security and Trust Company, and Potomac Associates), Eugene Rostow (another former government official now at Yale Law School, who serves on the boards of both the U.S.-based Atlantic Council and the Paris-based Atlantic Institute, a major center of agitation about the Soviet threat), Richard Pipes (the associate director of the Russian Research Center at Harvard, noted for his hawkish analyses of Soviet behavior), and Max Kampelman (a Washington attorney long active in Democratic party politics)—paid a special visit to Kennedy's office to press him to come out for more defense spending, Kennedy declined. Instead he moved quickly toward his Georgetown formula of less defense and more social welfare spending.[60] Nor was there much interaction between the Kennedy campaign and the defense lobby thereafter, although Pipes, Rostow, and other hawks endorsed a minor Kennedy proposal on the organization of the national security policymaking apparatus.[61] The need to free up some resources for the Democratic party's mass constituency continued to hold the groups apart. In the final days before the convention, however, their joint short-run interests in evicting Jimmy Carter from the White House led to sudden cooperation.

Hurt badly by the continuing crisis in Iran (which, immediately after the seizure of the hostages, Carter notoriously exploited in his reelection bid), the controversial resignations of Andrew Young and Cyrus Vance, revelations about brother Billy's dealing with Libya, and the fallout from his deflationary policy choices of earlier in the year, Carter continued sinking in the polls. With his vulnerability increasing daily, a movement developed for an "open" convention—that is, one in which primary delegates would be released from their preconvention commitments. Many of those calling for an open convention were declared Kennedy supporters, or tied closely to obvious Kennedy constituencies, such as Washington D.C. mayor Marion Barry.[62] Almost immediately, however, it became obvious that the movement claimed powerful support from quarters that had no special ties to Kennedy. When forty members of Congress organized a Committee for an Open Convention, Arnold Picker (a businessman with close ties to Washington Senator Henry Jackson) and two members of the Washington congressional delegation stepped in to raise $200,000 for the movement.[63] Almost simultaneously, Henry Jackson announced his support of an open convention, and several Jackson for President Committees formed, including one launched by S. Harrison Dogole, whom the *Washington Post* described blandly as a "Philadelphia Democrat," but who had as well been one of the founding board members of the Committee on the Present Danger (where he identified himself as chairman of Global Security Systems, Inc.).[64] In the final days before the convention, Washington attorney Edward Bennett Williams, a relatively recent addition to the executive committee of the Committee on the Present Danger, attempted to organize all the anti-Carter forces.

These efforts, however, fell just short. Although Kennedy made a memorable speech to an enthusiastic convention audience (the economic proposals of which Carter almost immediately rejected, and was quickly seconded in his condemnation by Robert Roosa),[65] the old coalition seemed able to announce itself only in defeat. As Eugene Rostow and other figures of the party's right wing prepared to move into the Reagan camp, Carter slipped through. Without much enthusiasm, the Democrats prepared for the general election campaign.

By contrast to the Democratic primaries, where the precipitous decline first of Carter and then of his leading rivals required explanation, in the Republican primaries it is the continuing rise of Ronald Reagan, the original front runner, that poses the biggest puzzle. Inheritor of most of the coalition that marched loyally to disaster in 1964 under Barry Goldwater, Reagan stood as recently as 1976 almost wholly outside the mainstream of American public life. As much sharply negative press coverage suggested early in the 1980 campaign, Reagan's predominant public image was that of a shallow, ultraconservative ex-movie actor outrageously mortgaged to the Far Right.

Yet over the course of the campaign Reagan moved gradually to the center of American politics. At length he won support from many individuals whom his original core supporters excoriated, notably David Rockefeller and Henry Kissinger, traditional *bête noires* of the Far Right. As the opening of this essay suggested, an adequate account of this well-nigh miraculous transformation must illuminate as well the collapse of what appeared to be a formidable campaign for John Connally, offer an explanation for the rise and subsequent collapse of the Bush campaign, and account for the rise and subsequent decline of John B. Anderson's independent candidacy.

It is convenient to begin with Reagan himself. As observed earlier, the core of the Goldwater movement consisted of labor-intensive, strongly protectionist manufacturers who disliked both labor unions and foreign competition, independent oil companies (many of whom had long campaigned for tariffs on oil imported by the multinationals), some raw materials producers (who had many reasons to be attracted to Goldwater's strong nationalism), and huge numbers of small and medium-sized businesses for whom an open world economy often meant either little or nothing except threats to economic viability.

The growing flood of foreign, especially Japanese, imports in the late 1960s and early 1970s of course swelled the ranks of these groups. So, clearly, did rising demand for rearmament and opposition to détente although, as noted previously, much of the demand came from multinationals often harshly opposed to protectionism. Representatives of all these groups (especially those promoting increased military spending, who were represented by James Schlesinger, among others) played prominent roles in Reagan's unsuccessful bid to oust Gerald Ford in the 1976 primaries. But little in that campaign, or the subsequent controversies over the Panama Canal and labor law reform in which Reagan took part, was calculated to endear Reagan to the multinationalist interests that dominated the Democratic party and the so-called Eastern Liberal Establishment of the GOP. Only the rising claims for new defense spending suggested that a way might be found to bridge the chasm.

As the campaign opened, the Reagan of 1979 looked very much like the Reagan of 1976, or, more ominously, the Goldwater of 1964. At the center of the campaign was a group of wealthy western businessmen, many of whom had been supporting Reagan for more than a decade: millionaire automobile dealer Holmes Tuttle; former supermarket entrepreneur Theodore Cummings; William Wilson, a rancher and investor; Jack Wrather, the Hollywood producer of *Lassie, The Lone Ranger,* and other All-American favorites, an independent oilman, and director of several corporations, including Capitol Records, Continental Airlines and, appropriately for the sponsor of a candidate offering reassurance to a troubled nation, Muzak, Inc.; nursing-home chain operator Charles Wick; Joseph Coors, the arch-reactionary head of Coors Brewery, a major donor to many conservative policy institutions of the New Right, and a trustee of the Hoover Institution; Nevada Senator Paul Laxalt, previously a close political ally of billionaire Howard Hughes (and as of 1978, although in the Senate, president of Ormby House Hotel and Casino in Carson City, Nevada);[66] William French Smith, Reagan's personal attorney (and a director of Pullman, Pacific Lighting, Pacific Mutual Life, Crocker National Bank, and Pacific Telephone and Telegraph); Alfred Bloomingdale, formerly chairman of the board of the Diners Club and now (along with Mrs. William French Smith) a director of Beneficial Standard, and very active in real estate; plus a handful of others. Among this group, only a few, notably Justin Dart (the head of Dart Industries, a member of the Business Roundtable and leader of the so-called Dart Group which promotes right-wing candidates in California) and Earle Jorgenson (a director of Northrup, Kerr-McGee Oil, and the American Iron & Steel Institute and a trustee of Cal Tech), whose Jorgenson Steel Company claimed Wilson and French Smith as directors, enjoyed links to the upper tiers of the American business community.

Joining this generally close-knit group were a handful of other businessmen, including one superstar, William Simon. Formerly Nixon's secretary of the Treasury, where he made a reputation as an aggressive ideologue, Simon's increasing acceptance on more and more high corporate boards during the middle and late 1970s symbolized the vast changes sweeping through the American industrial structure. By 1979, along with his directorship at Dart Industries, Simon served on the board of Citibank, Xerox, INA, and the Hoover Institution. He also served as president of the Olin Foundation, one of the most aggressive of the foundations financing the resurgence of corporate ideology in America. (A few months after Reagan announced for the presidency, Simon took a new job. He became an investment counselor for Suliman S. Olayan, a leading Saudi businessman who, *The New York Times* recorded a day before the election, has since been elected a director of Mobil Oil.)[67]

Reinforcing this rather thin layer of support were a number of advisers from a variety of Old and New Right think tanks, including Martin Anderson, an economist (and director of the Federal Home Loan Bank of San Francisco) associated with the Hoover Institution (which had slightly widened its network from its circle of regionally based and traditional right-wing supporters), and several figures associated with the Heritage Foundation. The most important of Reagan's foreign policy advisers was Richard Allen. Allen had previously served in the Nixon administration, which he eventually left after several bitter fights with Henry Kissinger. He subsequently became a business consultant, and was president of Potomac International Corporation. A strong nationalist with close ties to groups sympathetic to Israel, Allen was also a member of the Committee on the Present Danger's executive committee.

Along with the assistance he received from right-wing research and policy groups, Reagan profited from his long-standing ties to the various conservative political action groups and regionally centered Republican state officials. In the Republican primaries, in which perhaps 25 percent of the 25 percent of the population that admits to being Republican turns out to vote, this intense local support network gave Reagan real advantages. Very soon, however, a candidate appeared who looked for all the world like someone who could wrest most of the Right from Reagan: John B. Connally. Big business executives who hung back from Reagan flocked to Connally, who projected an image that here, at last, was a man who could make even Amtrak run on time, and whose initial fundraising efforts were so successful that he decided to forego federal matching funds.

As formidable as Connally appeared, however, he was defeated within a few months and pushed out of the race. His rapid collapse poses one of the major mysteries of the campaign. Analyzed carefully, however, most of the mystery evaporates. At the outset, it is well to be clear about one important point. Despite the extensive media identification of Connally as the candidate of big business, neither his past nor his organizational affiliations as he prepared for the race suggested that he was anything of the sort.

Connally's career in Texas politics took off during the 1950s, after he became independent oilman Sid Richardson's attorney. Richardson, like his long-time friend and political ally Clint Murchison, another independent oilman, was fabulously wealthy and played a major role in American politics (having been deeply involved at various times with both Franklin D. Roosevelt and Dwight Eisenhower)[68] and social life (Richardson patronized Billy Graham for years).[69] But the two men were usually at odds with many powerful Eastern interests. Their famous takeover of the New York Central Railroad (on the board of which Connally sat for several years), for example, came after a bitter fight with its previous controlling interests. During his terms as secretary of the navy under Kennedy and as governor of Texas, Connally continued his close relations with the Richardson interests. One source suggests that Governor Connally collected at least $225,000 from the Richardson estate. After he left the governor's post, Connally became a partner in Vinson, Elkins & Searls, one of the most famous law firms in Texas—but still a Texas-based firm. Later he several times advised or represented Nelson Bunker Hunt, whose antagonism toward the GOP liberal establishment is famous. (Indeed, the Hunts's notorious silver play began in the wake of a Connally-arranged meeting between Bunker Hunt and potential Arab investors.)[70] With the possible exception of Texas Instruments, none of the corporation boards on which he served as director before becoming Secretary of the Treasury (including Halliburton, a huge construction company, the First City National Bank of Houston, or the U.S. Trust Company) represented the commanding heights of American business.

In addition, Connally's role at the Treasury during the Nixon shocks made him very controversial. Indeed, many angry multinationalists commonly identify him as the prime villain behind the disruptive NEP. When he returned to private life (after heading up Democrats for Nixon), the limited status Connally enjoyed in the American business community was apparent. As he prepared to run for the presidency, the directorates Connally resigned from were important but scarcely distinguished, featuring Greyhound (a concern greatly interested in deregulation), Dr. Pepper (whose board, like those of its rival soft drink companies, featured several individuals with prominent political ties, in this case mostly to the right wing of the GOP), Continental Airlines, Justin Industries, the First City Bancorporation of Texas, and Falconbridge Nickel Mines, Ltd., a Canadian-based firm. And while Connally's trusteeship at the A. W. Mellon Foundation was of interest in pointing to possible ties to the Mellon family, it did not have the national significance of a Rockefeller or Ford Foundation affiliation.

Nor was Connally's support quite as firm as it was made out to be. Immediately after the Iran debacle, industrialists (including many multinationalists) anxious to spur American rearmament flocked to Connally. So did many protectionist businessmen, attracted by Connally's famous advice on how to handle the American trade deficit with Japan (which the Iran debacle worsened greatly, because the threat it posed to a major source of Japan's oil supplies drove down the value of the yen, leading to lower prices and thus a surge of Japanese exports abroad):

> I would tell them unless you let in . . . American agricultural commodities, you better tell your Japanese people to be prepared to sit on the docks of Yokohama in their Toyotas and watch their own television sets, because they aren't coming to the United States.[71]

They were also intrigued by his references to a North American common market, which would have held back the development of trade with Europe and Japan, and a Reconstruction Finance Corporation to bail out failing businesses, as well as his promise of a massive government-assisted export drive.

Taken together, these proposals briefly provided Connally with an impressive array of backers: Southern Pacific's Ben Biaggini, Robert Stuart of Quaker Oats, Marriott's J. Willard Marriot, James W. Durant of Paine Webber, Robert Malott of FMC, Borg Warner's James F. Beré, AT&T's John deButts, Texas Instruments' J. Erik Jonsson, L. L. Colbert, the former president of Chrysler, Henry Ford (who had been an early supporter of Bush, but moved to Connally as Japanese car import pressures mounted steadily during the campaign), Fred Hartley of Union Oil, Roy Ash of Addressograph Multigraph, Monsanto's John Hanley, Leonard Firestone, James Ferguson of General Foods, E. H. Boullioun of Boeing Commercial Airplane, Robert H. Baldwin of Morgan Stanley (the American investment bank that probably does the most business with Middle East clients), Fluor Corporation's J. Robert Fluor, Citibank's Walter Wriston, Textron's Joseph Collinson, and officials of Exxon, Prudential, and many other firms.

But while this coalition appeared to be a mile wide, it was more crucially only a inch deep. Connally was attempting simultaneously to make high-visibility appeals to multinationals that wanted free trade and an open global economy and to protectionist concerns that sought shelter from international competition. That some right-wing Republicans were suspicious of his candidacy was evident. Jesse Helms, whose textile and tobacco constituencies, had Connally landed them, would have helped him tremendously in the southern primaries against Reagan, held back from a ringing endorsement of either leading Republican candidate. At the same time, Connally allowed himself to be mousetrapped by Henry Kissinger, David Rockefeller, and the rest of the multinational constituency on the delicate question of Israel.

Ever since the formation of the OPEC energy cartel, which converted the Arab states overnight into the leading financial investors, biggest developing market, and greatest sellers of oil in the world, pressure had been building for a tilt in American foreign policy away from Israel in their favor. One of the more urgent desires of many big multinationals, the adjustment of American policy toward the Israeli state, was also one of the most controversial of foreign policy proposals.

Not only by temperament, but by interest as well, Connally was a man who was willing to rush in where others feared to tread. Connally's son, John B. III, served on the board of the Main Bank of Texas, in which, according to the *Atlanta Constitution,* Connally himself had invested.[73] Though the bank was not particularly large, its major (70 percent) owner was important: Sheik Khaled Bin Mahfouz, whose family controlled the largest native-owned bank in Saudi Arabia. Connally had other Arab ties as well.

In the fall of 1979, Connally began mapping out a major speech on the Middle East. While he and his advisers analyzed the problem, he struck up a relationship with the ultimate multinationalists: Henry Kissinger and David Rockefeller. As Rockefeller contributed to his campaign, Kissinger began making unpublicized appearances at cocktail parties on his behalf. In late September, Kissinger attended a fundraising party for Connally sponsored by Henry Seggerman of Boston Fidelity Management. Seggerman later told the *Boston Globe* that Kissinger gave a "tacit endorsement of Connally."[74] The remark almost irresistibly brings to mind Carter Glass's famous one-liner delivered when he was asked if he would support Al Smith's candidacy for president. "I am a Democrat still," said Glass, "very still." Kissinger and Rockefeller supported Connally tacitly, very tacitly. Published sources of great reliability report that Kissinger approved a draft of the famous Connally speech on the Middle East, which proposed a settlement of the Arab-Israeli conflict along the lines proposed in an old Brookings Institution study, and of which most public supporters of Israel strongly disapproved.[75] But neither Kissinger nor Rockefeller (who had some kind words for Connally a few weeks later, delivered while he affirmed his support of Trilateral Commission member George Bush's candidacy) came up to defend the speech during the firestorm of criticism it provoked. Instead, while New York attorney (and Committee on the Present Danger executive committee member) Rita Hauser, financier I. W. Burnham of Drexel Burnham Lambert, and other high Connally officials abandoned his campaign, Rockefeller joined Alton G. Marshall (the head of Rockefeller Center, who had been working on the Bush campaign for months) in official support of George Bush. When Connally next appeared in New York, "there was a flurry of interest when it turned out that no members of the Rockefeller family would attend the New York dinner."[76]

Hurt badly by the refusal of three of the biggest multinationals—ABC, CBS, and NBC—to sell him the TV time his campaign had counted on, Connally's effort staggered on for a few weeks, then collapsed.[77] With his effective withdrawal, the campaign increasingly polarized between Bush and Reagan. For a while a classic confrontation appeared likely to develop between the Republican Right and the liberal Establishment, reminiscent of the Goldwater-Rockefeller battles of the early 1960s. Especially after Bush won the primary in Iowa, a major grain-exporting state, his support among financiers and multinational free traders became obtrusively visible. Along with Rockefeller and Alton Marshall came Steven Fenster (managing director of Lehman Brothers Kuhn Loeb), William Edgerly (chairman of Boston's State Street Bank and Trust Company), Thomas Philips of Raytheon, Albert Gordon of Kidder Peabody, A. G. Monks of the Boston Company, Bristol Myers's Bruce Gelb, Leon Jaworski of Watergate fame, and many Republican members of the Trilateral Commission.[78]

In sharp contrast, many of the most active Connally boosters stampeded to Reagan, at last bringing him support from major business figures. In the Pennsylvania primary, for example, David M. Roderick, the chairman of U.S. Steel, one of the most ardently protectionist corporations in America, helped, along with a bloc of other steel industry figures, raise money for Reagan against Bush.[79] Many advocates of increased armament manufacture, initially attracted to Connally's strong pledges to increase defense spending, also went over to Reagan. No longer hesitant, Jesse Helms began campaigning vigorously for him too.

Before the campaign had a chance to polarize completely, however, the Reagan camp embarked on a series of dramatic moves. Almost unnoticed by the media,[80] Reagan initiated a striking shift in his policies and core constituency. For a few weeks after his defeat in the Iowa primaries, Reagan's campaign was in turmoil. But when he won the New Hampshire primary, his campaign appeared to have regained the "momentum" so beloved by popular political analysts. Only a few hours after his triumph there, however, Reagan astonished seasoned campaign observers by firing John Sears, his campaign manager, and reshuffling his staff.

With Sears out, Edwin Meece (an attorney who had helped prosecute protesting University of California students in the 1960s, a trustee of the Institute for Contemporary Studies, and a one-time vice-president of Rohr Industries, an aircraft parts manufacturer) assumed a major role in the campaign. Also promoted (after he had recently been invited into the campaign by Sears) to a major role was William J. Casey. At the time, the switches triggered extensive debate. In the early weeks of the campaign their net effect appeared to draw the lines more sharply between Bush and Reagan. For within weeks Bush's (and John B. Anderson's) association with the Trilateral Commission and the Rockefellers was being used against him by the Reagan people. Their open criticism of the multinational wing of the GOP created something of a sensation. Though major media (which in many cases, like that of *The New York Times* and *Time* magazine) downplayed the story, the commission attracted a flurry of attention. Rather cautiously deployed by the Reagan campaign staff, the charges received a full airing only in the South. There they clearly made some impact on the electorate. Reagan's Florida co-chairman, Carlos Salmon, insisted to reporters that "the thing that is really beginning to haunt Bush is the Trilateral Commission."[81]

But while the Reagan camp was energizing the *Volk* with its allusions to the shadow world of international finance, another more important process was advancing by slow stages. A close look at Ronald Reagan's career shows a recurring pattern. In the late 1940s, Reagan achieved prominence as a Democratic union official. In slow stages, he traded up from this position by cooperating with major figures in the movie industry on the blacklisting of his fellow actors and several other issues. Coming under the patronage of several of them, notably MCA's Lew Wasserman (a prominent Democrat), Reagan then advanced to his famous slot on *Death Valley Days* (under General Electric sponsorship). Having long since left the world of the average worker far behind, Reagan proceeded to hook up with the arch-enemy of the big multinationals—the Goldwater Republicans—who finally boosted him into public life.

Now Ronald Reagan had the opportunity of a lifetime. As he had left the Screen Actors Guild and GE behind, so now could he exit from the important but limited circle of businessmen who had launched his political career. He had a chance to form positive ties with some of the most powerful men in the world, and also to prevent what had happened to Goldwater from happening to him. From this perspective, one of Casey's several institutional affiliations (in addition to the link with the National Strategy Information Center noted earlier, Casey served as a director of Capital Cities Communications and the Atlantic Council, and had many longstanding ties to the American intelligence community) assumed weighty significance. After leaving public service in the mid-1970s, Casey joined Frank Zarb (former head of the Federal Energy Administration) and Charles W. Robinson in founding the Energy Transition Corporation, a firm that brokered deals between firms seeking energy-related contracts and the federal government.[82]

In 1979, as the campaign heated up, both Casey and Robinson were still with the ETC. Robinson had meanwhile become one of the handful of Americans who sat on the executive committee of the Trilateral Commission, along with David Rockefeller and Henry Kissinger. Making a unique contribution to the Republican-sponsored revival of family values, Robinson had also recently joined the board of the Allen Group, a sizable corporation run by Henry Kissinger's brother Walter.

While Reagan's original core of right-wing supporters watched with mounting apprehension, a slow series of overtures and discreet signals flashed between Reagan and the internationalists. In early spring, George Shultz (president and director of Bechtel, a director of Morgan Guaranty and Sears, a trustee of the Alfred P. Sloan Foundation, and most important, a recently named director of one of the Far Right's favorite targets, the Council on Foreign Relations) joined Trilateralist Caspar Weinberger (Bechtel's general counsel) and endorsed Reagan.

Reagan responded almost immediately. Quickly integrating Shultz and Weinberger into the campaign, Reagan on April 17 announced the formation of a special policy council, headed by William Simon, which included Shultz, Weinberger, Casey, and several other prominent figures from parts of the business community that had not previously enjoyed strong ties to his campaign. Included were Alan Greenspan, Charls Walker (who had originally backed Connally, but who was also the chairman of the American Council on Capital Formation, the treasurer of the Committee on the Present Danger, and an important lawyer and lobbyist for several large corporations, and an enthusiastic promoter of the National Tax Limitation Committee's proposed constitutional amendment to limit government spending), William P. Rogers (former secretary of state under Nixon, a subsequent representative of the Shah of Iran, law partner of William J. Casey, and currently a director of Sohio [owned by giant British Petroleum], Merrill Lynch, and the Gannett newspaper chain), "free market" economist Murray Weidenbaum, neoconservative "Godfather" Irving Kristol (who, along with his role as intellectual in residence at the American Enterprise Institute, was a director of several major corporations, including Warner Lambert), and Donald Rumsfeld (a RAND trustee and director of Bendix, the Atlantic Council, and other organizations). Along with them was a more predictable figure, New York Congressman and New Right hero Jack Kemp, and one whose appearance was truly momentous: John McKetta. Modestly listed by the Reagan campaign as a professor of chemical engineering at the University of Texas, McKetta was in fact a major figure in the oil industry—big oil, not the independents. A director of many Texas-based oil-related concerns, including two subsidiaries of Gulf, McKetta served also as chairman of the editorial committee of *Petroleum Refiner.* Along with Shultz and Weinberger, his presence in the Reagan camp ensured that whatever happened in the general election, Reagan would not become another Goldwater.[83]

With speculation rising and *Business Week* proclaiming that "the battle for the heart and mind of Ronald Reagan has begun,"[84] the campaign now began showing clear signs of internal struggle. A few days after the formation of the policy committee, Reagan announced a list of foreign policy and defense advisers that pointedly excluded Kissinger, and that was tilted heavily in the direction of the far, far Right. It included such notables as Joseph Churba (president of the Institute for International Security), General Louis Walt (a former commander of the Marine Corps), and retired Admiral Thomas Moorer (a walking incarnation of the military-industrial complex, who served as adviser to the Admiral Nimitz Foundation, a consultant to the Georgetown Center for Strategic and International Studies, a director of Fairchild, Texaco, Alabama Drydock and Shipbuilding, and United Services Life Insurance, and president of the Association of Naval Aviation).[85]

As the Bush campaign folded, the tug of war between Reagan's various supporters and the confusion in multinational ranks became more visible.

In the late spring, defeated Republican presidential hopeful John B. Anderson, who had parlayed extraordinarily favorable press coverage and resolutely internationalist policy positions (he was a member of both the Trilateral Commission and the Japan-U.S. Friendship Commission) into a respectable showing in several Republican primaries, seized upon the confused situation to launch an independent third-party campaign for the presidency. For a few months, the uncertainty attending the early stages of Reagan's metamorphosis won Anderson wide support from internationalists of both parties who wanted an alternative to Carter but remained suspicious of Reagan. Chase Manhattan director and Rockefeller family adviser J. Richardson Dilworth, *Time* magazine chariman Andrew Heiskell, Oppenheimer Fund(s) president Leon Levy, Lehman Brothers Kuhn Loeb advisory director Benjamin Buttenwieser, Salomon Brothers partner Daniel Sargent, and Dyson Kittner Moran chairman Charles Dyson (who had played an important role in the 1976 Carter campaign) raised funds for him. Trilateralist investment banker George Ball endorsed him in public. Felix Rohatyn and Henry Kaufman quietly advised him. High officials of the foreign policy establishment, including long-time Council on Foreign Relations official Alton Frye, joined the campaign organization, and money poured in from a number of important multinationalist businessmen, including J. Irwin Miller of Cummins Engine, Robert O. Anderson of ARCO, Irving B. Harris of Standard Shares, Michael Blumenthal, Laurence Rockefeller, and several other members of the Rockefeller family.

In the Eastern press, a lively debate raged over whether Reagan was truly a moderate, or in fact a captive of his right-wing business supporters. Hints were repeatedly dropped that if he would only name his nominee for secretary of state he might well be acceptable, while a campaign led by Congressman Barber Conable, a member of the Trilateral Commission, gathered steam to force the choice of Bush as Reagan's running mate.[87]

While this discussion boiled along, an increasingly alarmed Republican Right mobilized to defend its position. Jesse Helms, New Right publicist Richard Viguerie, and other conservatives campaigned for the selection of a conservative running mate, and John Connally and others helped beat down a brief boomlet that developed for former President Gerald Ford.[88]

In early June, as the convention approached, the tension in the Republican camp rose to fever pitch. Senator Barry Goldwater inserted a discussion of the Trilateral Commission in the *Congressional Record,* along with a complete membership list. And a major fight developed over whether Reagan should dismiss Republican National Chairman William Brock, another member of the commission. Built up in the media as a major test of Reagan's independence from the Right, this last fight unmistakably signaled Reagan's intentions.

An army of moderate Republicans, including Senators John Heinz and John Danforth, Delaware Governor Pierre DuPont IV, and Gerald Ford himself urged Reagan to keep Brock. Paul Laxalt, Lynn Nofziger, and many Republican conservatives wanted him replaced. Casey and Meece, prodded by William Timmons, a Republican strategist who had strong ties to Ford and Brock, pressed Reagan to retain Brock. Reagan kept Brock on. Reagan also moved to compromise some of his previously controversial economic positions. Shunting aside more and more of his "radical" supply-side economic advisers, Reagan accepted the advice of Greenspan, Shultz, and Simon and qualified his endorsement of major tax cuts unaccompanied by measures designed to limit government spending. Following earlier concessions along similar lines by Congressman Jack Kemp to Senator William Roth (yet another member of the Trilateral Commission),[89] Reagan also accepted an emphasis on spending reductions to match the tax cuts.

By mid-June the transformation of the Reagan coalition was well along. Though occasional signs went the other way, by then not only big businesses, but major figures from the multinational community were climbing aboard. On June 17 Reagan unveiled a forty-member business advisory panel, which included R. H. Baldwin of Morgan Stanley, William Agee of Bendix, John Whitehead of Goldman Sachs, J. Robert Fluor of the Fluor Corporation, Richard Schubert of Bethlehem Steel, Alfred Brittain of Bankers Trust, Theodore Brophy of General Telephone and Electronics, Fletcher Byrom of Koppers (a Mellon-controlled concern), and the presidents, chairmen, or chief executive officers of many other large corporations, including Monsanto, Procter & Gamble, Deere, Goodyear, Pfizer, Merrill Lynch, Metropolitan Life, and Weyerhauser.[90]

On July 3 Reagan resorted again to the familiar device of the task force to organize his new supporters. Listed as "domestic and economic advisers" were a host of social scientists, including Edward Banfield, Herman Kahn, Milton Friedman, Irving Kristol, and George Stigler.[91] Many important military and business figures also appeared, including Crocker Bank vice-president Laurence Silberman, Procter & Gamble's Bryce Harlow, Emerson Electric's Edwin Harper, and Clarence Palmby of Continental Oil.

As the convention opened, suspense was still growing over the selection of a vice-president. On the floor of the convention hall Jesse Helms, anti-abortion leaders, and right-wing evangelists jubilated at a string of platform victories. Paying far too much attention to the hijinks in front of the television cameras, many media commentators immediately proclaimed the convention a victory for the right wing. Especially blunt was Mary McGrory's assessment of the situation. Having watched Helms strutting about the floor attacking Henry Kissinger, she wrote from Detroit that "in this city of jobless people, no individual case is more arresting than that of Henry Kissinger, an unemployed Metternich. Apparently when he got to the window of the Ronald Reagan personnel office, he was told what many a laid-off auto worker has heard—'Don't call us, we'll call you.' "[92] Seldom has press judgment proved to be so spectacularly in error.

Only a few hours later, millions of Americans watched in stunned disbelief as the world's most famous multinational foreign policy analyst, the chairman of the international advisory committee of the Chase Manhattan Bank, consultant to Goldman Sachs, director of the Council on Foreign Relations and Atlantic Council, member of the Bilderberg steering committee, senior fellow of the Aspen Institute, consultant to the National Broadcasting Company, and Trilateral Commission executive committee member materialized again at the center of the Republican party. Working with Bryce Harlow, Alan Greenspan, and other key multinationalists, Kissinger persuaded Gerry Ford to consider the number-two slot on the Reagan ticket.

A fantastic series of negotiations now began (for which, however, some precedents existed from Nelson Rockefeller's own tenure as Ford's vice-president).[93] Kissinger, Ford, and company pressed for sweeping concessions as the price for Ford's acceptance of the number-two job, including the delegation to the former president of day-to-day responsibilities for the running of the National Security Council, the Council of Economic Advisors, and the Office of Management and Budget. Opposed by some Reagan advisers as amounting to a subversion of the Constitution, the terms were nevertheless discussed seriously by Reagan, Casey, Meece, and other top aides. Perhaps the most vivid reminder in recent American history of what electorally focused accounts of American politics invariably miss, the negotiations eventually broke down.

Almost immediately Reagan turned aside protests from Jesse Helms, Howard Phillips, Paul Weyrich, Paul Laxalt, and other leaders of the Right and accepted Edwin Meece and Gerry Ford's advice to tap Geroge Bush for the second spot on the ticket. In the general election, Reagan continued his dramatic tilt toward the multinational wing of the party, drawing many former Carter and Anderson supporters into his campaign. Repeatedly employing the "special task force" format for institutionalizing support, Reagan continued to broaden his links in the business community. In August, Shell Oil president John F. Bookout, John McKetta, Robert Quenon of Peabody Coal, and Socal board chairman Harold J. Haynes (a director of Citibank and Boeing) joined other major figures in the energy industry to constitute an energy advisory group for Reagan.[94] On September 19, more stellar advisers appeared, whose affiliations confirmed the direction of the Republican campaign. Exxon vice-president Jack Bennett, Morgan Guaranty's Rimmer de Vries, and Arthur Burns joined an international monetary policy task force.[95] Signaling the defeat of unreconstructed supply-side economics, University of Michigan professor Paul McCracken (a member of the Trilateral Commission and a director of numerous corporations, including Texas Instruments and Dow Chemical) became chairman of the inflation policy task force.[96] In addition, a new economic policy coordinating committee appeared, which included McCracken, Burns, Shultz, Weidenbaum, Charls Walker, Weinberger, and Walter Wriston (the head of Citibank) among its members.[97] A few days later, while Reagan campaigned for the vote of fundamentalist Christians sympathetic to "creationism," an innovation and entrepreneurship task force was announced, with a membership that included the president of the Cetus Corporation (which has heavily invested in microbiology and genetic engineering), the vice-chairman of Intel, and W. J. Sanders III, president of Advanced Micro Research (and a director of Donaldson Lufkin & Jenrette, as well as co-founder of the Semiconductor Industry Association).[98]

Reagan also treaded cautiously around several volatile issues. Though he issued a plan for protection of the steel industry that Carter was forced to trump or face the certain loss of Pennsylvania, Reagan held back from a strong commitment to restrict Japanese imports, persuading Citibank economist Leif Olsen (we suspect too hastily) that he would preserve free trade. He also made noises about aiding New York City, and further modified his original economic program.[99]

In the final days of the campaign, with most polls predicting a very close popular election, Kissinger, Elliot Richardson, and other internationalists announced themselves strongly for Reagan. While the John Birch Society told its members to "forget the Presidency,"[100] Reagan availed himself of the Kissinger and Rockefeller foreign policy network to track Carter's moves to gain the release of the hostages in Iran.

Aside from Warner Communications, Natomas, Seagram, Du Pont, and Phillip Morris, the heads of most major American manufacturing corporations had come out for Reagan by election time, though to the very end incidents like the flap over George Bush's trip to Taiwan fanned doubts. By contrast, among investment bankers, whose bond business was still threatened by double-digit inflation and who (if they did not have particular offsetting interests, such as in the Middle East) were fearful of Reagan's projected military buildup, Carter remained strong. Among the financiers endorsing him were Rohatyn and George Ball (who, like most elite American businessmen, both abandoned the Anderson candidacy as the campaign drew to a close), Salomon Brothers managing partner John Gutfreund, Paine Webber president John Marion, Bear Stearns's Paul Hallingby, Donaldson Lufkin & Jenrette's Richard Jenrette, Harry Jacobs of Bache Halsey Stuart & Shields, and Walter D. Scott of Investors Diversified Services (a major financial company).[101]

CONCLUSION

Though one or two of the final polls hinted at a decisive shift in favor of Ronald Reagan, the size of his margin of victory surprised most observers. Even more astonishing to many was the Republican triumph in the Senate, where the GOP, after vastly outspending their opponents, captured enough seats from liberal Democrats to ensure their control for the first time since the Eisenhower era. On the morning after, many journalists, academics, and even a few politicians rushed to proclaim a new era of American politics.

Unless they are located in the context of the American political system's recent development, such proclamations court serious misunderstanding, and are both premature and inexact.

Ronald Reagan's victory is certainly fraught with major consequences. The domestic economy and all but the most affluent of Americans are certain to be increasingly squeezed over the next several years. Sharpening class divisions, turmoil in the cities, and a general coarsening of American life are sure to come. Still more ominously, Reagan's victory implies an acceleration of the arms buildup initiated under Carter and raises the likelihood of military confrontations in "trouble spots" around the world. In addition, as Reagan's swift abandonment of Carter's human rights policies suggests, the deliberalization of American foreign policy will, especially in the developing world, have immediate and disastrous consequences for the victims of those authoritarian client state regimes shrewd enough to ally with the "free world."

We doubt, however, that Reagan's victory adds up to anything approaching "critical realignment"—the durable recasting of the major constituencies, coalition structures, and partisan cleavages that have periodically renewed organized American politics' capacity to articulate and manage the sources of political conflict. We have argued that what the Reagan victory represents most, in fact, is not critical realignment, but an almost equally fateful *dealignment,* the continued disintegration of those political coalitions and economic structures that have given American party politics some stability and definition during the past generation.

Perhaps the most momentous developments in the campaign came well before the conventions, in the critical interval between the Camp David deliberations and the dramatic night visit of the investment bankers to the congressmen. It was then that the building pressures on the Democratic party came to a head. Facing a difficult reelection fight, an incumbent Democratic president found he could no longer satisfy the competing demands of his party's elite business leadership and mass social base.

No matter how Carter tried to optimize the mix of guns and butter or balance the claims of fiscal austerity and social welfare, decisive parts of both constituencies were bound to be alienated. Under those constraints, he did the best he could. While acceding to demands for fiscal prudence and sharpened military spending (contradictory as they were), Carter strove to preserve something of the heritage of the New Deal, if not the Great Society. But like the low-cost energy and American domination of the world economy that had so long sustained it, the social space of the New Deal had finally vanished. Soon Carter too would disappear, and Reagan's victory would decisively announce that the New Deal system of power no longer defined the shape of American politics.

A world is lost. What will take its place?

For obvious reasons, it is difficult to tell. Any future Democratic presidential aspirant will face even more urgently contradictory demands than Carter. As world economic competition sharpens, so will the demands for increased military spending. But because a stagflating economy dictates that increased military outlays will inevitably come at the expense of the social welfare budget, satisfaction of the military demand will generate serious strains elsewhere in the system. By 1984, it is a fair guess that many Northeastern cities will resemble scenes from *The Clockwork Orange*—barren stretches of decaying buildings broken by oases of fortified high rises (or well-policed "gentrified" brownstone villages), from which the dwindling middle and upper classes peer anxiously at the chaos outside. The regional wars between the Northeast and the booming Sunbelt are sure to worsen. Capital flight will increase. Tensions between business and labor and the poor will surely rise.

To regain electoral viability, we suspect that in the long run the Democratic party must evolve in the direction of some sort of social democracy, American style, featuring the integration of organized labor (and the generally disorganized working population) into a modified system of bureaucratic maintenance and control of domestic production, some investment and wage-price controls, and direct state intervention in a "reindustrialization" program of the sort advanced by Rohatyn, Kennedy, and eventually Carter himself during the campaign. Whether such party development challenges or relies upon steadily declining voter turnouts, the demobilization of ever larger portions of the American electorate and the progressive deterioration of independent mechanisms of popular control is, perhaps, a question. Here the clientism and bureaucratic deformations already endemic in the organized labor movement would assume great importance. But whatever controls are worked out on the national level, their effectiveness will be limited by the increasingly international character of industrial production.

Ronald Reagan's own coalition, it is safe to say, will not hold together either. With more and more corporations coming under the pressure of an integrated global economy, the tensions in the campaign between the late arriving multinationalists and the Republican right wing are sure to worsen. Nor will any foreseeable cuts in domestic spending compensate for arms expenditures on the scale proposed by groups like the Committee on the Present Danger. The riddle of how to increase military spending while reducing inflation will remain unsolved, and the mere presence of a Republican in the White House can hardly be expected to silence the conflicting demands of Reagan's business constituency. His administration is certain to be wracked as well by continuous debates over the proper posture of the United States toward the Soviet Union and the conduct of foreign policy generally—whether some new form of arms limitation agreement should be negotiated; whether the State Department should yield to the National Security Council or the Pentagon; what the pace, extent, and direction of new weapons acquisition and other military expenditures should be. The Middle East poses yet another source of conflict. With Saudi Arabia and other Persian Gulf states rapidly deepening their ties to Western Europe and Japan, pressure increases daily for a dramatic change in American policy toward the region. Such a policy change and its consequences for Israel probably cannot be implemented without some turnover among high administration figures.

And of course there remain always Japan and the other international competitors of the United States. In the 1980s, as Japanese export surpluses continue to mount, the strains on the Republican party's traditional base among protectionist domestic industries will be enormous, as will the effect on any number of multinational firms now feeling the heat of the Rising Sun. Almost certainly, formal and informal barriers to imports will rise in response to ever-broader business community pressure, and explicit protectionist appeals, like those that punctuated the failed Connally campaign, will again be heard.

At some point all this discord is likely to find expression in one or two sharp reversals in the course of Reagan's presidency, along the lines of Nixon's NEP departure. As in the Nixon and Ford administrations before it, intense conflicts within the Reagan administration will yield assorted noisy resignations of top officials, or perhaps a wholesale cabinet reshuffle of the sort embarked upon by Carter. Barring a major war, Ronald Reagan is likely to become the sixth consecutive American president to fail to complete two terms. If so, this will not be because of his advancing age, but because the electoral coalition that brought him to power does not have sufficient strength or durability to recast the structure of the American political system and once more drive it forward.

In the absence of some massive new political initiative, that system will continue its unmistakable disintegration. And as it does, the fabric of American life will be torn, again and again, along the creases so visible in the 1980 campaign.

NOTES

1. For an account of Reagan's visit to Dallas, including this and all other quotations not otherwise attributed, see *Dallas Times Herald,* August 23, 1980, pp. 1A, 22A, and supporting stories in the same issue. We note the reporting of staff writers Mary Barrineau and Richard S. Dunham.

2. The Reverend Bailey Smith's comment on whose prayer God hears is taken from *The New York Times,* September 18, 1980, p. A18. Smith was later criticized for another remark, made a few weeks after the Dallas meeting and broadcast in a sermon from his church in Oklahoma, that Jews have "funny noses." He subsequently apologized for the "funny noses" comment, but refused to "compromise" his "distinctive" belief that God does not hear Jewish prayer. After a meeting between Smith and leaders of the Anti-Defamation League of B'nai B'rith held in December 1980, the League's national director, Nathan Perlmutter, told the press he was satisfied that there was "no anti-Semitic intent" in Smith's remarks. For the "funny noses" comment and the December meeting with B'nai B'rith leaders, see the *Washington Post,* December 27, 1980, p. B12. Cullen Davis's Dallas remark on "the problem" is taken from *Philadelphia Inquirer,* August 24, 1980, p. 9A, which also reports Hunt's presence in Reunion Arena. All other quotes during the Dallas visit are from the *Dallas Times Herald.*

3. It is no secret that most American election analysis (at least since World War II) has concentrated on the first of these processes. But while the point cannot be developed here, there is now a large body of work that explicitly recognizes the limitations of traditional voting analysis. See, for example, R. W. Cobb and C. D. Elder, *Participation in American Politics: The Dynamics of Agenda Building* (Boston: Allyn and Bacon, 1972); Erwin Hargrove's discussion of the impact of public opinion on foreign policy in his *The Power of the Modern Presidency* (New York: Knopf, 1974), pp. 98–122; Adam Przeworski's sharp criticisms of "autonomous actors" interpretations of individual voting behavior in "Institutionalization of Voting Patters, Or Is Mobilization the Source of Decay?" *American Political Science Review, 69* (1975), 65ff; and John O. Field and Ronald E. Anderson's study of the 1964 election and the importance of political parties in shaping public responses to opinion questionnaires (a point which, if pursued, would suggest a quite different relation among elites, parties, and mass politics than that commonly understood) in "Ideology and the Public's Conception of the 1964 Election," *Public Opinion Quarterly, 33* (fall 1969), 380–398.

4. The analysis of political coalitions by reference to industrial sectors is a growing literature. See the seminal works of Eckhart Kehr, *Battleship Building and Party Politics* (Chicago: University of Chicago Press, 1975); and Alexander Gerschenkron, *Bread and Democracy in Germany* (Berkeley: University of California Press, 1943). For more recent attempts to make use of this general analytic framework, see David Abraham, *The Collapse of the Weimar Republic: Political Economy and Crisis* (Princeton: Princeton University Press, 1981). Peter Gourevitch, "International Trade, Domestic Coalitions and Liberty: Comparative Responses to the Crisis of 1873–96," *Journal of Interdisciplinary History, 8,* 2 (autumn 1977), 281–313; and James Kurth, "The Political Consequences of the Product Cycle: Industrial History and Political Outcomes," *International Organization, 33* (winter 1979), 1–34. In his *Critical Realignment: The Fall of the House of Morgan and the Origins of the New Deal* (New York: Oxford University Press, forthcoming), Thomas Ferguson presents a detailed analysis of American political party systems by reference to industrial structures and the balance of power between labor and business.

5. See Ferguson, *Critical Realignment.*

6. See U.S. Department of Commerce, Bureau of the Census, *Historical Statistics of the United States* (Washington, D.C.: Government Printing Office, 1975), Parts I, II, cited in Samuel Bowles and Herbert Gintis, "The Crisis of Liberal Democratic Capitalism," mimeo, August 1980, p. 57.

7. Which industrial sectors are competitive in global markets is a function of technological development, production process design, investment decisions,

the structure of labor markets, and a variety of other factors lying outside the scope of this essay. Suffice it to say that the competitiveness of any given industry can and usually does change over time, and that this change is by no means necessarily unilinear. In addition, aggregating to the level of whole industrial sectors naturally misses some exceptions at the level of individual firms. Both considerations are important in considering the contemporary American textile industry, for example, portions of which are fully competitive in world markets. Where, as here, we generalize in the text for entire industrial sectors, such generalizations should be understood as limited by the historical period under view and the obvious exceptions of some individual firms within the sector.

8. See the extremely useful discussion in Stephen D. Krasner, "United States Commercial and Monetary Policy: Unravelling the Paradox of External Strength and Internal Weakness," in Peter J. Katzenstein (ed.), *Between Power and Plenty: Foreign Economic Policies of Advanced Industrial States* (Madison: University of Wisconsin Press, 1978), pp. 51–87, upon whose data we rely for the discussion of United States sectoral trade balances and bank foreign assets during the period.

9. See Krasner, op. cit., and U.S. Senate Foreign Relations Committee, Subcommittee on Foreign Economic Policy Staff Report, *International Debt, the Banks and U.S. Foreign Policy* (Washington, D.C.: Government Printing Office, 1977). We note that the 1960s trend toward increasing profit shares for American banks from foreign operations has begun to reverse. See the discussion in Gerald Epstein, this volume.

10. Bowles and Gintis, op. cit., p. 51.

11. For details on this decline, see Gerald Epstein, this volume.

12. For a brief but highly informative listing of important Goldwater supporters, see Philip H. Burch, Jr., "The NAM as an Interest Group," *Politics and Society*, 4 (fall 1973), 120–121, note 51.

13. Bowles and Gintis, op. cit., p. 51. For a more extensive (and sometimes divergent) discussion of United States capital formation during the period, see Edward F. Denison, *Accounting for Slower Economic Growth: The United States in the 1970s* (Washington, D.C.: The Brookings Institution, 1979).

14. For an excellent general account of the international monetary instability of the late 1960s and early 1970s, see Fred L. Block, *The Origins of International Monetary Disorder* (Berkeley: University of California Press, 1977).

15. International Monetary Fund, *International Financial Statistics*, 30, 5 (Washington, D.C.: IMF, May 1977), cited in David Gisselquist, *Oil Prices and Trade Deficits: U.S. Conflicts with Japan and West Germany* (New York: Praeger, 1979), pp. 31, 35.

16. Fred Bergsten, "The New Economic Policy and U.S. Foreign Policy," *Foreign Affairs*, 50 (January 1972), pp. 199–200.

17. The Trilateral Commission's activities have stimulated an immense amount of commentary. For accounts of the origins and development of the group that place it in the context of the changing world economy, see Thomas Ferguson and Joel Rogers, "Another Trilateral Election?" *The Nation*, June 28, 1980, pp. 769, 783–787; and the essays gathered in Holly Sklar (ed.), *Trilateralism: The Trilateral Commission and Elite Planning for World Management* (Boston: South End Press, 1980), pp. 61–75.

18. The breathtaking speed with which the United States altered its policy toward the USSR during this period, and then reversed itself again during the late 1970s, offers a warning to those who seek to explain the recent militarization of American foreign policy as a rational response to the character or the behavior of the Soviet regime. As many of the very people who promoted détente in the early 1970s ceaselessly reminded us five years

before and five years after détente began, the Soviet Union flagrantly violates elemental "human rights" and often intervenes militarily abroad, either directly or by proxy. But this was as true in 1972 as it was in 1962 or 1980, and therefore can hardly account for the sweeping fluctuations in American policy. The most influential recent discussions of the Soviet Union's strategic position and commitment to massive military budgets are no less curious, being unpersuasive both in what they say about Soviet military power and what they leave unsaid about American domestic politics. Popular reports on Soviet expansion in the Third World tend to ignore the USSR's growing international isolation, its reversals in formerly friendly countries like Egypt, Guinea, Indonesia, Somalia, and the Sudan, and the critical deterioration of relations between the USSR and its Japanese and Chinese neighbors. Nor is much attention paid to the serious regional conflicts within the Soviet Union, the obvious difficulties it has controlling the domestic policies of Warsaw Pact nations, or the growing political independence of the Third World. The Russians have their own "arc of crisis" stretching from Gdansk to the Khyber Pass, although one might never glean this from reading the national press.

Popular focus on the sheer size of the Soviet military budget is equally misleading. Based on the almost certainly inflated estimates of the CIA, the aggregate figures give no indication of the direction of expenditures (fully one-quarter of which are absorbed by Soviet expenditures against China) or the relative qualitative strengths of superpower weaponry. Even on the basis of the CIA estimates, NATO currently outspends the Warsaw Pact nations. But even if it did not, it is difficult to see why such aggregate budget figures should or could be used to shape American policy. The rate of American defense spending has never been keyed to the Soviet Union's military budget in the past and cannot be in any meaningful way, because behind the money figures stand different production processes with incomparable technologies and capital-labor ratios. Like the "missile gap" of 1960, the "spending gap" of the 1980 campaign was neither accurate nor dispositive.

Even if one accepts the reality of a growing Soviet threat, however, one is no closer to understanding the dynamics of foreign policy formation in the United States. Despite ecumenical militarism, there are continuing debates over the future of SALT II, the wisdom of the MX missile, the proper size of the defense budget, the direction of armed services personnel reform, and the future of American military policy in Western Europe and the Third World. These disputes are not merely tactical; they go to the heart of foreign policy design. And they are surely not explained by hypothesizing a commonly recognized threat from the USSR. Indeed, by assuming that the United States has a discernible "national interest" whose defense should determine our relations with other states, such explanations only serve to obscure the sources of current policy debate and the persistent failure to achieve consensus on international objectives. Rejecting that assumption brings a new world into view, one in which foreign policy formation follows from the interaction between domestic political coalitions and the international economic order, and "consensus-building" merely describes the mobilization of different coalitions for dominance. Such an analysis underlies our discussion of the rise and fall of détente in the text. See as well Thomas Ferguson and Joel Rogers, "The Empire Strikes Back," *The Nation,* November 1, 1980, pp. 436–440.

19. For comparative data on the industrial expansion of the United States, Southern Europe, and the Third World, see William Branson, "Trends in

United States International Trade and Investment since World War II," National Bureau of Economic Research Conference Paper No. 21 (Cambridge, Mass.: National Bureau of Economic Research, 1980), pp. 14–16.

20. *Business Week,* July 2, 1979, p. 79.
21. For the early supporters of the National Strategy Information Center and the details of its early organization, see Internal Revenue Service Forms 1024 (exemption application for organizations claiming tax exemption under section 501(a) of the Internal Revenue Code) and 990 (Return of Organization Exempt from Income Tax, which must be filed annually), various years. Along with the forms are a variety of supporting materials, including a copy of the certificate of incorporation, dated October 4, 1962, signed by Casey, Barnett, and others. For the speech to the corporate secretaries, see the supporting material accompanying the exemption application (Form 1024) dated December 16, 1963. It is perhaps worth noting that Richard Allen was an early lecturer for the organization.
22. National Strategy Information Center IRS Form 990 (Return of Organization Exempt from Income Tax), various years.
23. See the May 24, 1976, letter of Frank R. Barnett to Eugene V. Rostow, reprinted in Robert Sherrill, "Gene Rostow's Propaganda Club," *The Nation,* August 11–18, 1979, pp. 106–110.
24. IRS Form 990 (Return of Organization Exempt from Income Tax) filed by the American Security Council for 1972 indicated $913,480 in "gross contributions, gifts, grants and similar amounts received." For 1977 the comparable figure is $1,654,709. To this should be added $306,576 derived from "sales and receipts from all sources."
25. See the May 17, 1976, letter of Eugene V. Rostow to James Schlesinger, reprinted in Sherrill, op. cit., including comment: "I shall ask Dave to make his contribution for the non-tax-exempt part of our budget, which should be either one-half or one-third of the whole, tentatively, subject to the advice we shall obtain from several key tax lawyers."
26. See, for example, Gary Wenglowski, "After the Recession, More Inflation?" *Washington Post,* July 29, 1980, p. A11.
27. Quoted in the *Los Angeles Times,* March 25, 1980, sec. IV, p. 17.
28. For discussion of the shifting patterns of electoral mobilization and partisan structures in American political history, see Walter Dean Burnham, "The Appearance and Disappearance of the American Voter," in Richard Rose (ed.), *Electoral Participation: A Comparative Analysis* (Beverly Hills: SAGE Publications, 1980), pp. 35–73; "The Changing Shape of the American Political Universe," *American Political Science Review,* 59 (1965), 7–28; and *Critical Elections and the Mainsprings of American Politics* (New York: Norton, 1970).
29. National Labor Relations Board, *Annual Reports* (Washington, D.C.: Government Printing Office), various issues.
30. For a useful statistical survey of union membership over the past two decades, see AFL-CIO Department of Research, *Union Membership and Employment 1959–1979* (Washington, D.C.: AFL-CIO, February 1980).
31. For a discussion of the Business Roundtable's organization and impact on the construction industry and national domestic politics generally, whose significance is far greater than the treatment here can suggest, see Thomas Ferguson and Joel Rogers, "The Knights of the Roundtable," *The Nation,* December 15, 1979, pp. 620–625.
32. Opinion polls during the Labor Law Reform bill reported in Thomas Ferguson and Joel Rogers, "Labor Law Reform and Its Enemies," in Mark Green and Robert Massie, Jr. (eds.), *The Big Business Reader: Essays on Corporate America*

(New York: The Pilgrim Press, 1980), pp. 267–275. Harris survey reported in Daniel Yankelovitch and Bernard Lefkowitz, "The Public Debate on Growth: Preparing for Resolution," mimeo, May 1979, cited in Bowles and Gintis, op. cit., p. 1.

33. See Ferguson, op. cit.

34. For a useful survey of union electoral behavior and organization, see Jong Oh Ra, *Labor at the Polls: Union Voting in Presidential Elections, 1952–1976* (Amherst: University of Massachusetts Press, 1978).

35. For a detailed discussion of administrative maintenance of the post-New Deal system of business unionism, see Joel Rogers, "Regulating Labor: Post New Deal U.S. Labor Policy," unpublished doctoral dissertation (in progress).

36. See the discussion in Richard Prosten, "The Longest Season: Union Organizing in the Last Decade," remarks to the Industrial Relations Research Association, mimeo, August 30, 1978.

37. For a detailed discussion of the fight over labor law reform, see Ferguson and Rogers, "Labor Law Reform and Its Enemies," op. cit.

38. In light of the extreme minority representation of labor in such organizations, labor leadership claims that such organizational affiliations benefit the labor movement as a whole are dubious. Where serious representational issues are at stake in such joint union-industry committees and organizations, union leaders invariably demand parity of representation with business, as in the pay advisory and economic revitalization boards established during the Carter administration. This is strikingly not the case with the organizations under view.

39. We note as well Albert Shanker's involvement with the National Strategy Information Center, notes 21 and 22 above, where he serves on their affiliated American Committee for European Democracy and Security (along with Lane Kirkland). In the spring of 1979, Shanker became the first labor leader ever to address the NSIC. In noting Shanker's affiliation, an NSIC spokesperson introducing his speech reportedly declared: "Sincerely, I think that in Ben Wattenburg's phrase . . . only in America would you have a committee in which Bill Simon and Admiral Gunwald and Bill Casey could serve as lay persons with Lane Kirkland and Albert Shanker; social democrats, liberals, conservatives, democrats and republicans all on the same committee try and support security on both sides of the Atlantic." Shanker reportedly then launched into a speech decrying the "tremendous softening toward the left within the AFL-CIO." In a reported question and answer session afterward, Shanker spoke worlds about the dynamics of contemporary trade union practice in answer to a question about the difficulties labor leaders face in garnering support for defense spending among their union memberships:

> In order to get people to cough up $10 I've got to put down on one side of a sheet of paper 1 or 2 or 3 wonderful things that we just did for them, if we did, and/or 5 or 6 or 7 things that have got to happen to them which will absolutely gobble them up unless we put that money into a fund to defend them. Now I can do that with respect to public schools, tuition tax credits; I can do it for federal aid to education; I can do it in terms of the Supreme Court decision on whether parochial school teachers fall under the National Labor Relations Act—there's no shortage of issues that immediately bother people. But the minute I put out there, "And we're going to support national defense," well, then I've got a terrific debate. Now, I don't mind engaging that debate. As a matter of fact, in every national convention that we hold—and every year we get between 2,000 and 3,000 delegates—there are always at least a dozen resolutions (because any local can send in a resolution) saying that we ought to reduce defense expenditures greatly and use

that money for education. The debate continues, and at some point in that debate I will say, "Well, I just want to say one sentence," and generally people want to know what's going to be said. "You're not going to have a very good school system if you don't have a country." And at that point the resolution is voted down, and that's it.

See "Has Albert Shanker Joined the 'Far Right'?" unsigned, mimeo, 1979 (which includes a transcript of his NSIC session, and from which all quotes are taken). See additional reporting on the speech in *John Herling's Labor Letter,* April 7, 1979; and *NYEA Advocate,* May 15, 1979.

40. For an extensive discussion of "Lovestone Diplomacy—1945–1950," see Ronald Radosh, *American Labor and United States Foreign Policy* (New York: Random House, 1969), pp. 304–347.
41. See the extensive discussion of the "New Right" from a traditional conservative's perspective in Alan Crawford, *Thunder on the Right: The "New Right" and the Politics of Resentment* (New York: Pantheon, 1980). For an overview of the neoconservative movement, see Peter Steinfels, *The Neoconservatives: The Men Who Are Changing America's Politics* (New York: Simon and Schuster, 1979).
42. See as well David F. Noble and Nancy F. Pfund, "Business Goes Back to College," *The Nation,* September 20, 1980, pp. 233, 246–252; and *The New York Times,* November 16, 1980, sec. 3, pp. 1, 25. For a recent example of corporate suppression of critical writing, in this case Gerard Colby Zilg's *DuPont: Behind the Nylon Curtain* (Englewood Cliffs, N.J.: Prentice-Hall, 1974), see Robert Sherrill, "The Nylon Curtain Affair: The Book That DuPont Hated," *The Nation,* February 14, 1981, pp. 172–176.
43. See the discussion of New Right financing in Crawford, op. cit., pp. 42–77, a discussion that does not, in our view, adequately trace the sources of funding, the decisive importance of foreign economic policy in structuring Republican organization and infighting, or the variation within the New Right on basic issues of economic policy. Though space limitations make it impossible to pursue the point at length, the importance of attending to the foreign economic policies recommended by these various groups and institutions can hardly be overemphasized. For reasons discussed in this essay, many prominent American businessmen now favor scaling back domestic social programs while increasing arms spending. Because these twin proposals have traditionally been a central plank in the platform of the right wing of the Republican party, the proliferation of think tanks and research institutes now hard at work inventing rationales for the adoption of such policies often creates the misleading impression that a massive consensus has formed within the business community in favor of the rest of the old Goldwater program. As became evident during the campaign, the decimation of social programs is now a cause popular in those multinational circles that are not, at least at present, hostile to the United Nations, the Rockefeller wing of the Republican party, foreign imports, or even labor unions. If someone wishes to include the policy institutes of these latter interests as part of a broad "New Right," we will not quarrel, but it then becomes vital to distinguish among the New Right's components. While they both celebrate the abstraction of "free enterprise," for example, little else unites figures like William Simon and Jesse Helms.

The case of so-called supply-side economics, which in its pure form acquired some notoriety early in the campaign, is interesting to examine from this standpoint. While supply-side economics quickly developed into a code phrase for the reduction of social expenditures, which has wide support, the original versions of the doctrine also included a flimsy argument for a return to the gold standard. No important American businessman actually favors this, though of course the absolute limit this proposal would place on the money supply makes it attractive as an inflation-fighting fantasy. As such the "theory" received a certain amount of friendly, though openly dubious, encouragement from financial interests deeply concerned about inflation, which had long before become enthusiastic about a managed currency system. The major investment banking firm of Morgan Stanley, for example, gave Lewis Lehrman's gold standard proposals early publicity, although the firm was careful to dissociate itself from Lehrman's views and noted that the proposals were impracticable as they stood. (See John A. Davenport, "The New Allure of the Gold Standard," *Fortune,* April 7, 1980, pp. 86–94.) We note as well that while some influential advocates of a real gold standard support free trade, neither in most theory nor in past practice do gold standards exclude protectionism. Indeed, United States history has often witnessed the two together.

44. For an extensive discussion of Jimmy Carter's early links to the Trilateral Commission and the role commission members played in his 1976 campaign, see Laurence H. Shoup, *The Carter Presidency and Beyond: Power and Politics in the 1980s* (Palo Alto: Ramparts Press, 1980). See as well the discussion in Philip Burch's excellent *Elites in American History: The New Deal to the Carter Administration* (Volume 3 of a three-volume work), pp. 312–315 and notes 13–25 at pp. 345–346, which include the observation that Cyrus Vance originally supported Sargent Shriver for the 1976 Democratic nomination.

45. See "Capping Third World Gushers," *The Nation,* July 28–August 4, 1979, pp. 68–69.

46. See Federal Reserve Bank of New York president Anthony Solomon, "U.S. and the World Economy," remarks before Reuters Annual Dinner, mimeo, May 14, 1980.

47. For a detailed listing of prominent business leaders present at the Camp David event, including the representatives of major oil interests, see "Capping Third World Gushers"; for background on the conflict between the international oil companies and the World Bank, see the correspondence between Exxon chairman Clifton Garvin and Treasury Secretary Michael Blumenthal reprinted therein. The struggle over the design and control of non-OPEC Third World oil exploration continues, of course, and looms large as an issue of the 1980s. See *The New York Times,* August 22, 1979, pp. D1, D5; September 21, 1980, sec. 3, pp. 1, 15; and September 22, 1980, pp. D1, D5.

48. Burch, op. cit., p. 319. For a more detailed account of the Camp David meeting, see "Capping Third World Gushers."

49. Burch, op. cit., p. 356, n. 142.

50. Hufstedler became secretary of education; Palmieri became refugee coordinator. The new secretary of commerce, Philip Klutznick, also had strong ties to groups very sympathetic to Israel. See the discussion in *MERIP Reports,* no. 96, May 1981, pp. 28–30.

51. See Burch, op. cit., p. 341. For Rotan Mosle's ties to the Moody interests and a general discussion of Duncan's oil connections, see Thomas Ferguson and Joel Rogers, "Un President Nationaliste Pour L'Amerique En Crise?" *Le Monde diplomatique,* August 1980, pp. 1, 8–9.

52. For the actions on budgetary restraint by the American Assembly, see *The New York Times,* March 10, 1980, p. D2. For the night meeting of congressmen and bankers, see *The New York Times,* March 13, 1980, p. D4. For Rohatyn and Minerals And Resources, Ltd., see *Financial Times,* December 21, 1979, p. 18. As the *Financial Times* observes, MAR owns shares in Engelhard Resources, on whose board Rohatyn formerly served as director.

53. *The New York Times,* August 15, 1980, p. B1.

54. Towbin's support of Kennedy is noted in Lynn Brenner, "Wall Street Chooses Its Candidates," *Institutional Investor,* March 1980, pp. 55–61. Schmertz's own description of his motives for entering the Kennedy campaign are featured in the *Washington Post,* November 28, 1979, pp. B1, B3. Kennedy's oil holdings in Mokeen Oil and Kenoil are noted in a profile of Kennedy family investment and tax adviser Thomas Walsh in *Forbes,* July 23, 1979, p. 59.

55. For coverage of Kennedy's speech to the Investment Association, see Alexander Cockburn and James Ridgeway, "Kennedy Runs Right," *Village Voice,* October 15, 1979, pp. 1, 11.

56. *Boston Globe,* January 29, 1980, p. 20.

57. *The New York Times,* February 29, 1980, sec. 4, p. 2.

58. See Brenner, op. cit., and *The New York Times,* November 18, 1979, sec. 3, p. 15.

59. *The New York Times,* May 21, 1980, p. A26.

60. For this extremely important meeting, see Rowland Evans and Robert Novak, "Kennedy Arms Dilemma," *Boston Globe,* January 29, 1980, p. 23.

61. *Boston Globe,* May 6, 1980, p. 2.

62. *Washington Post,* July 30, 1980, p. 1.

63. *Boston Globe,* July 29, 1980, p. 6.

64. *Washington Post,* July 29, 1980, p. 1.

65. *Journal of Commerce,* August 15, 1980, pp. 1, 17.

66. See Jack Anderson, "Reagan Chairman a Lackey of Hughes," *Albany Times Union,* September 29, 1980, p. 15.

67. For the business community's appraisal of Olayan's appointment, see *The New York Times,* November 4, 1980, p. D2. Justin Dart's Dart Industries, where Simon served as a director, recently merged with Kraft.

68. See the discussion of Richardson's political activities during the Eisenhower years in Burch, op. cit., pp. 156, 166, 178, 193; and for the Roosevelt years, see Ferguson, op. cit.

69. For a discussion of Richardson's important support of Graham, see Marshall Frady, *Billy Graham* (Boston: Little, Brown, 1979).

70. For Connally's relations with the Richardson estate, see *The New York Times,* February 1, 1977, cited in Burch, op. cit., pp. 287–288, n. 36; for his work with the Hunts, see Harry Hurt III, *Texas Rich: The Hunt Dynasty from the Early Oil Days to the Silver Crash* (New York: Norton, 1981), pp. 319–320, and especially pp. 394–395.

71. *The Wall Street Journal,* August 6, 1979, p. 20. The Yokohama docks advice was reworked and refined throughout Connally's campaign.

72. For coverage of Connally's early business support, see *The New York Times,* July 12, 1979, p. D18; October 1, 1979, p. B1; October 15, 1979, p. D2; *Washington Post,* October 13, 1979, pp. A1, A5; *Time,* July 16, 1979, p. 58.

73. *Atlanta Constitution,* February 11, 1980, cited in *Facts on File* (New York: Facts on File, 1980), p. 129. In the *Facts on File* story, Connally is described, along with the sheik, as one of the bank's "controlling partners." Hurt, op. cit., p. 395, confirms Connally's stake in the Main Bank and adds that Mahfouz bought his shares from their previous owner, Ghaith Pharoan, to spare Connally's presidential campaign any embarrassment resulting from Pharoan's highly publicized association with Bert Lance.

74. *Boston Globe,* October 3, 1979, p. 17.

75. William Safire, "John Connally and Israel," *The New York Times,* October 15, 1979, p. A19.

76. *The New York Times,* November 7, 1979, p. A17.

77. The Carter, Connally, and Reagan campaign organizations all complained about network limitations on half-hour advertising spots, but the network

decision had the most disastrous consequences for Connally. For Connally commications director Julian Read's assessment of the impact of the network decision on the campaign, as well as general coverage of the early advertising wars between the candidates, see *Broadcasting,* November 5, 1979, in particular pp. 36–40.

78. For Bush's early business support, see Brenner, op. cit.; *Boston Globe,* October 3, 1979, p. 17; *The New York Times,* July 12, 1979, p. D18, and August 19, 1979, p. 30.

79. *Boston Globe,* April 16, 1980, p. 5.

80. We noticed it, however. See Ferguson and Rogers, "Another Trilateral Election?"

81. *The New York Times,* March 8, 1970, p. 9.

82. See the coverage in *Business Week,* November 24, 1980. A subsequent phone conversation between the authors and the office of the Energy Transition Corporation confirmed Robinson's role as one of the founders of ETC.

83. *Reagan for President NEWS,* mimeo, April 17, 1980.

84. *Business Week,* April 7, 1980, p. 123.

85. *Reagan for President,* mimeo, April 20, 1980.

86. See the coverage of Anderson's business supporters in *Business Week,* July 7, 1980, p. 24.

87. *Boston Globe,* June 11, 1980, p. 12.

88. *The New York Times,* March 14, 1980, p. A17.

89. *The New York Times,* June 8, 1980, p. C15.

90. *Reagan for President NEWS,* mimeo, June 17, 1980.

91. *Reagan for President NEWS,* mimeo, July 3, 1980.

92. Mary McGrory, "Sad Days for Henry: Alone by the Phone," *Boston Globe,* July 17, 1980, p. 13.

93. Compare the proposed Ford-Reagan convention deal with Ford staffer Robert Hartmann's account in his *Palace Politics* (New York: McGraw-Hill, 1980), of Vice-President Nelson Rockefeller's earlier attempt to persuade Gerald Ford to give him operating responsibility for the Domestic Council. Frankly intended to complement Henry Kissinger's admitted dominance in foreign affairs (Hartmann, p. 304), the proposal, if adopted, would have had much the same effect as the Kissinger-Ford convention proposals to Reagan. Not surprisingly, the Rockefeller move was strongly opposed by the right wing of the Ford administration, led by superhawk Donald Rumsfeld and Howard H. "Bo" Callaway, whose family had long been associated with major textile interests in the South. Like the proposed convention deal, the earlier proposal was blocked before implementation. See Hartmann, chap. 13.

94. Reagan Bush Committee, *NEWS RELEASE,* mimeo, August 21, 1980.

95. Reagan Bush Committee, *NEWS RELEASE,* mimeo, September 19, 1980.

96. Ibid.

97. Ibid.

98. Reagan Bush Committee, *NEWS RELEASE,* mimeo, September 25, 1980.

99. See Olson's later comment in *The New York Times,* November 6, 1980. For Reagan's late campaign reversals on urban, labor, and some social welfare issues, see *The New York Times,* October 9, 1980, pp. A1, B8.

100. Birch Society quoted in *The New York Times,* October 28, 1980, p. A24.

101. For listings of Carter supporters loyal to the end, see *The New York Times,* August 15, 1980, pp. D1, D14; and Carter/Mondale Presidential Committee (Massachusetts), *Carter/Mondale Steering Committee,* mimeo, 1980; and *New York Labor/Business Committee for Carter/Mondale,* mimeo, 1980, among other releases from the Carter-Mondale campaign.

THE WORLD OF APPEARANCE: THE PUBLIC CAMPAIGN

Alexander Cockburn and James Ridgeway

The election of 1980 revolved around uncomplicated emotions: fear for the future, nostalgia for the past, uncertainty about the present. The debate which reached a climax on November 4, 1980, was largely fought across political and intellectual terrain defined by the Right and conceded, in many crucial areas, by liberals almost without a struggle over the preceding years.

Most of the campaign rhetoric, most notably that of Governor Ronald Reagan, was bogus, designed to produce the willing suspension of disbelief. "Supply-side economics" was the mechanism employed in this task. Reality, in the form of a transfer of money from labor to capital, only began to intrude with the Reagan budget of 1981.

In November of 1979 the debate over strategy on the Republican side had by no means been resolved, as the candidacies of John Connally and George Bush as well as Ronald Reagan clearly revealed. Similarly, the challenges to President Carter by Governor Jerry Brown and Senator Edward Kennedy proposed sharply varying political agendas.

Let us then go back to the start of this debate at the end of 1979, review the struggle as it unfolded and listen, across the months, to the words of the principal actors.

AN OMEN

Early in 1979 we went to interview William Winpisinger, president of the International Association of Machinists. Winpisinger, a beefy and combative man, sat quietly behind his desk as we asked:

"Is there any way in which Carter could redeem himself in terms of your political ideas?" Winpisinger paused.

"Yes, there is one way he could do it."

"What?"

"Die."

There was another pause, and then Winpisinger added, "I don't wish that on him, but that's the only goddam way I know that he can."

"So you think he is totally unacceptable for the presidency?"

"I have said so countless times. I don't intend to relent. He's unfit to run this country. He was elected on the crest of the wave of truthsayers, and that son of a bitch has lied through his teeth every day that he's been there. . . . It's quite clear he marches to the drumbeat of the corporate state. . . . Every time he's got a chance to come down on one side or the other of an issue, corporations versus the consumers, he comes down on the corporation side every time."

Winpisinger's boisterous way with words and opinions used to leave some of his fellow labor leaders aghast. "Ah, Winpy . . ." they would sigh. But if Winpisinger was on the far left of the labor spectrum, his hatred of Carter was merely a particularly potent symbol of general resentment and disillusion on the part of labor for Carter. Ahead lay the lunge toward Kennedy as the preferred alternative, and beyond that the possibility that a Republican candidate might make serious inroads on the blue-collar vote.

ANOTHER OMEN

At the end of October 1979, when all eyes were on John Connally as the man most favored by experts to dislodge Ronald Reagan as the Republican candidate, we took a trip to Portland, Maine, for the earliest of the "beauty contests" in which aspirants would parade in front of party members and give them a précis version of their standard stump speeches.

The day-long session in Portland was to be the occasion on which Senate Minority leader Howard Baker would launch his bid and present himself as the "moderate" alternative to Reagan, Connally, Phil Crane, and George Bush. Anderson was already being dismissed as too moderate for serious consideration.

Baker had always been the darling of the Washington press corps. His aides had hired a capacious jet, filled it with reporters, TV teams, and the candidate, and flown it to Portland for the momentous hour. When the day was over, so was the campaign of Howard Baker and his "moderate" challenge. Instead the prize, in this particular contest, had gone to Bush, whose frisky, upbeat paroxysms of preppie polemic disclosed—when you listened carefully—a conservatism quite as robust as that of Reagan.

"Now some of you," Bush cried, "know that I and Barbara lived in a communist country. The first few months we lived in China were fantastic —remember Boswell's Johnson, you're not a man till you've seen the Great Wall of China—then we woke up and we recognized that the freedoms we've taken for granted all our lives simply don't exist, the freedom to hug those children close, to say Can I help you be an engineer or a teacher or whatever, the freedom to worship your God, the freedom to criticize your government, and the freedom to leave your government . . . and I came back to this country blessed with experience that no other candidate has, blessed with a family and sons with a sense of service to their country . . . I have a deep conviction that the United States is honorable and decent . . . I simply believe we have to be strong and I need your help. . . ."

This rhetorical foray into patriotic evangelism had the delegates pounding the floor with their feet. Baker, who came next, utterly misunderstood the spirit of the age. He had dreamed up the dreariest of political campaign pledges, that he was "a politician dedicated to a revival of the 'honorable' profession of politics." As he discoursed in this fashion his delegates sank lower in their chairs and contemplated betrayal. Two hours later Baker was betrayed.

Republicans, it was clear, did not want to hear the gospel of responsibility preached at them. They wanted uplift. This year, you could feel, they sensed that the long nightmare of Watergate was over, and that they were going to win.

* * *

A couple of weeks later, a few miles from Disney World, the Republicans of Florida gathered at the Hyatt House in a clamorous and congenial jamboree which added to the impression that the party was juiced up for victory against the Democrats in 1980 rather than another disastrous bout of the internecine struggles of 1976. This time Reagan, absent from Maine, was on hand for a beauty contest originally contrived by Phil Crane's strategists but now assumed to be a make or break occasion for John Connally.

Reagan's long-planned renaissance had come the previous week when he was unveiled at a $500 a plate dinner at the New York Hilton. They played Cole Porter and screened the blessings of Jimmy Stewart upon his fellow movie star. The lights went up and there was Ronnie, carrying 68 years, a touch of gray at the temples, and The Speech:

"I cannot and will not see this great country destroy itself. Our leaders attempt to blame their failures on circumstances beyond their control, on false estimates by unknown, unidentifiable experts who try to convince us our high standard of living, the result of thrift and hard work, is somehow selfish extravagance which we must renounce as we join in sharing scarcity. . . ."

Just a touch of the old sureness in delivery and timing was missing. Connoisseurs of his style had long observed that Reagan took time to warm up in campaigns. The old warhorse looked better in an informal pose, talking simply to the people about the simple verities of life. And as it was now being unfurled, the political strategy of his campaign adviser John Sears—later fired on the day of the New Hampshire primary—had thrust the candidate onto terrain where he still appeared a trifle unsure of foot.

After months of negotiation, Reagan's issues czar was Representative Jack Kemp of Buffalo, devotee of supply-side economics, the Leonardo of the Laffer curve and of lowered taxes. Poor Reagan stumbled a bit as he labored through the carefully bargained Kemp section of his address: "Business is not a taxpayer. It is a tax collector. Business has to pass its tax burden on to the customer as part of the cost of doing business. You and I pay the taxes imposed on business every time we go to the store. Only people pay taxes and it is political demagoguery or economic illiteracy to try to tell us otherwise. . . . Proposals such as the Kemp-Roth bill would bring about the kind of realistic reductions in tax rates we need. . . ."

There was a wooden quality in the mellifluous voice of the old actor as he recited these novel nostrums, far from the certainties of declamations against red tape. Then suddenly the voice came alive. Some old familiar sentences had heaved into view and Reagan fell upon them: "I have lived through one Depression. I carry with me the memory of a Christmas eve where my brother and I and our parents exchanged our modest gifts. There was no lighted tree as there had been in Christmases past. I remember my father opening an envelope. We all watched, and yes, we were hoping it was a bonus check. It was a notice he no longer had a job. I'll carry with me always the picture of my father sitting there holding that envelope, unable to look at us. I cannot, I will not, stand by while inflation and joblessness destroy the dignity of our people."

The water slipped smoothly over such polished stones of memory, and Reagan smiled his boyish smile during the applause that followed the silence. But there were times—amid all the speculation about his age—when Reagan's face in repose looked drawn, with the resigned dolor of senescence, his mouth like a contracted sphincter muscle. And in his uncertain responses to some questions there was the sense of watching an overly venerable Wallenda of the political high wire, teetering in the wind. Three times—in dealing with the Chrysler bailout, with aid to New York, and with the troubling matter of excess oil profits, he lost his balance and plummeted into the politician's safety net of "inadequate information at this time" and "we must wait till all the facts are in."

But as the week wore on the sureness began to return. *Question:* "Do you see the Soviet Union as an expansionist power that must be confronted?" *Answer:* "Yes, the Soviet Union is an expansionist power and it has never retreated one inch from its determination to one day have the Marxian dream of a one-world Communist state and we had better recognize that." Some things had not changed. On the Friday night the Hyatt, once planned as a condo, almost stillborn in the real estate depression of the early 1970s, now thriving in the Florida real estate boom, pulsed with the roar of the candidates' hospitality suites.

Connally's candidacy had the mark of death upon it, as he hurried forth to seize the ideological initiative and announce that "the Social Security system should be completely revamped" and turned "into a private retirement system." A week earlier in Philadelphia, Connally had come out against affirmative action in a bid to appease a Jewish community deeply affronted by some too-frank remarks on what the United States should do in the Middle East.

He spoke in a monotonic avalanche of bluster, in which the stump slogans and clichés of the previous months ran together in a rhetorical spasm so urgent in its hectoring that more than once he tripped over himself. His was the gospel of rape, burn, and pillage: "We need to open up public lands and strip more coal. Yes, we need to decontrol all government regulations on oil and gas in this country, and lastly we need to build those 92 nuclear plants." Applause. Cries of "Nuke 'em! Nuke those Iranians!" "Of course," Connally added without much conviction, "We need the finest scientific minds to make safe what can be made safe . . . but having done that we need to purge our minds of fear and stop taking advice from Jane Fonda and Ralph Nader. The next Republican president must say, This is a great country, the greatest country on earth. This is the greatest and most compassionate people that ever lived on the face of the earth."

John Connally talking of compassion sounded like a frog trying to whistle Mozart. His type of bluster, minatory and arrogant, was out of key with the tone of the campaign, and signaled his political demise. Connally, talking of trade embargoes and of the Japanese sitting in their own cars on the docks of Yokohama watching their own television sets, offered a contrived ugliness of the soul to his audience which made them ashamed to offer him back the same ugliness from their own hearts. Reagan, through all the long months, never made the word "compassion" sound so shopworn, never—amid all the fearsome threats to bureaucrats, the Russians, and other objects of his wrath—really frightened people.

Amid the speeches and the carousing, delegates unburdened themselves and some problems for George Bush became apparent. Ralph Yoacum: "I'm 67. I've been retired for eight years. I've lost 45 percent of the purchasing power of my fixed income over the past four or five years. I don't mind that. Don't misunderstand me. I'm not blaming anybody. Inflation is the problem. What has it come from? Government spending. I would like to see government cut down to one-tenth of what it is right now in the next three years. You don't build a responsible citizenry by taking responsibility away from them. I support Phil Crane because he's more down to earth than Reagan. George Bush? I don't think we need another military man. I think there are too many regulations in the government favoring military personnel as it is. Bush was in the service. I don't think Reagan was and I don't think Phil was. . . . Iran should not have happened. But we've got it now and there's nothing right now that we can do. But I'll tell you this. I don't think those hostages over there are going to live. If they don't we should just go over and clean that place out. And I mean clean it."

Sunning himself by the pool, a bulky Florida businessman and delegate delivered himself thus:

"George Bush was a member of the Trilateral Commission. The Trilateral controls and orchestrates what is going to happen in the world. George Bush represents nothing but the elitists, the people who are going to

69

control the entire world. The president of my university, the University of Notre Dame, Father Hesburgh, is a member of the Council on Foreign Relations. I wouldn't give the son of a bitch, or the university, a dime till he either resigned or stopped as president of Notre Dame or whatever. He's deluded. The Warburgs, the Loebs, the Rothschilds, Prince Bernard of the Netherlands, these are all people who control the world. . . .

"George Bush's son called me the other day. He said, 'Can you support my father?' and I said, 'Marvin, your father is a fine man, and I'm sure he is a loyal American. He's obviously made a lot of money, and he's been a good businessman and a good husband and father,' but I said, 'Marvin, I cannot support your father. You wanted the truth. Is he a member of the Trilateral Commission?' He said, 'Er . . . er . . .' and I said 'Is he a member, or has he ever been?' And his answer was, 'Yes, he has been and he just resigned three weeks ago,' and I said 'Marvin, you have my answer. Your father cannot in the strictest sense of the word represent this country in any other context but in how it will affect his or the United States' place in the total divine plan orchestrated by the people who control this world.' I said, 'The Bolshevik Revolution was literally underwritten by the Chase Manhattan Bank.' I said, 'It's provable. Go look it up.' I saw him last night and he said, 'You're right.'

"You don't know me from Adam, Sir, and I'm not a stupid person. I went to a fine school and I got a master's from Harvard. I'm telling you George Bush will probably be the nominee. If he is, you can write us off. I'm going to cast my ballot here for Reagan first and for Crane second. These are the only two men here today who truly, corny as it sounds, care about this country. Why Bush? Because they've got a lot of money, a lot of contacts, let's face it, they control the world. David Rockefeller's the head of the whole thing.

"At the rate we're going, my kids are going to live in some form of dictatorship. It's going to be an economic dictatorship. When a couple making 40 or 50 grand can do nothing but pay their bills, that isn't freedom."

Later that evening, in the wake of Reagan's triumph over Connally, at a fund-raising banquet a Florida state representative sighed happily as, along with 800 other Florida Republicans, she ogled Elizabeth Taylor at the head table. This representative had remained uncommitted. Her daughter, also a delegate, had voted for Bush, because he seemed the most reasonable about nuclear power. Her neighbor had voted for Crane. But harmony, not rancor, prevailed. "Look at this," she said with surprise and gratification. "It's a love feast." And so it was, with even journalists from such poison trees of perversion as the *Village Voice* vouchsafed cordial greetings instead of the old glare of the Nixon-Agnew years, when such press persons were regarded as maggots from the underside of a log.

* * *

In Maine, in Florida and elsewhere in those early months you could listen to the Republican candidates and perceive that the main energy being generated by the political process came from the Right. This was not some sudden shift which occurred in the fall of 1979, but further testimony to the direction of the political tides over the last decade.

One could listen to George Bush, Ronald Reagan, John Connally, and even Phil Crane and conclude that despite the palpable errors and illusions of their prescriptions, they felt they had something to say, whereas the Democrats did not.

The Republicans stood ecstatically for growth in the domestic economy, with unshuttered enthusiasm for "unleashing" the private sector. They addressed a central concern of the electorate—inflation—directly with clarion calls for curbs on public spending, clear cutting of federal red tape and regulation. They all called, with varying degrees of bloodthirstiness, for a strong America abroad.

The Democrats found themselves in the peculiar position of echoing, with fainthearted lack of conviction, those same sentiments. Time was when they believed something rather different: bold federal programs to invigorate the economy and cure social ailments, with economic policies designed to that end. Yet when Paul Volcker charged into the chairmanship of the Federal Reserve that fall and adopted traditional Republican, monetarist nostrums, even Ted Kennedy sat on his hands in Congress.

Over the previous four years the Democratic party, which in 1976 was still caroling the ideas of the New Deal, had slid behind the mask of its leader, Jimmy Carter, a spiritless conservative without even the passions of a true Republican creed.

Ronald Reagan rediscovered passion just in time to win the New Hampshire primary, after a shilly-shallying performance in the Iowa caucuses. It was true that Bush blew himself up with a petulant performance in the famous debate, but Reagan finally roared with all the fine old fury in what his aides billed as a "major foreign policy speech" at a Lincoln's Day dinner in Worcester, Massachusetts.

Reagan began quietly by quoting Carter's 1977 speech at Notre Dame. Here, according to Reagan, Carter said that the United States was at last "free of the inordinate fear of communism that once led us to embrace any dictator who shared that fear" and that we were free of "the fear that led from the moral poverty of Vietnam."

His voice began to pick up speed and strength. "When 50,000 Americans made the ultimate sacrifice to defend the people of a small, defenseless country from Communist, godless tyranny that, my friends, is an act of moral courage, not an example of moral poverty." The commander-in-chief, Reagan said, owes an apology to the almost 3 million Americans who served in Southeast Asia and to the memory of the 50,000 who never came home.

Cheers welled up. "Isn't it time," Reagan cried, "that we recognized that those veterans of that war were men who fought as bravely and effectively as any American fighting man ever fought in any war and that they did so with one arm tied behind their backs by their own government? Isn't it time that we told them that never again will we allow the immorality of asking young men to fight and die in a war our government is afraid to let them win."

He coasted for a while, like a runner readying himself for the final sprint. Carter had "systematically" set about to "dismantle a great arsenal of democracy": He had junked the B-1 bomber. "Bowing to Kremlin propaganda," he had abandoned the neutron bomb. He had delayed or postponed the Cruise missile, the MX missile, and the Trident submarine. He had closed down the assembly lines of the Minuteman III missile. And after all these "unilateral concessions" to the Soviets, Paul Warnke (Carter's disarmament negotiator) had brought home the SALT Treaty. Reagan had a clear view here. We should "abandon" not just SALT II but SALT I, until the Soviet Union gets out of Afghanistan. U.S. foreign policy "is bordering on appeasement." The unborn must be protected, the Republican party must come to the rescue of the United States, must liberate the slave states of Eastern Europe. The solution to the energy crisis lies in "the genius of industry." Congress should adopt the Kemp-Roth bill, eliminate the tax on interest on savings deposits, and (rising cheers here) get rid of the federal inheritance tax.

The end was in sight: "For years now, we have witnessed the agony of the refugees of Southeast Asia . . . free Vietnamese struggling ashore in Malaysia from some leaky boat that has made a horrid trip across the South China Sea. Some of those boats make it; many of them don't. But all of those boats carry on them the same inscription: 'This is what happens to friends of the United States.' If there's one message that needs to be sent to all the nations of the world by the next president of the United States it is that there will be no more Taiwans. There will be no more Vietnams. Regardless of price or promise, there will be no more abandonment of our friends by the United States of America." Pause for finale. Then Reagan concluded with quiet passion:

"I want more than anything I have ever done in my life to send that message."

Reagan could say this kind of stuff in his sleep. But by the time of New Hampshire there were signs that "supply-side" Reaganomics, courtesy of the Laffer curve, were having an effect.

The new style Republicanism, espoused by Ronald Reagan, and sometimes referred to as Reaganomics, marked a radical departure from the traditional strategies advocated by GOP politicians. Its adoption marked a new departure for Reagan himself, one which caused deep alarm in an important section of his strategists and advisers.

In the tumultuous weeks before the New Hampshire primary, when it was widely assumed that the Bush campaign was poised for the knockout blow, Ronald Reagan began to fight back. The dirtiest blows were launched on his behalf by William Loeb, publisher of the *Manchester Union-*

Leader. An off-balance Bush, battered by savage polemic, was further undone by the shrill mishandling of the Nashua television debate. But there was strong evidence that the shrewdest blows of all on Reagan's behalf were a series of simple spot ads put together by the former journalist and business consultant Jude Wanniski, former Reagan aide and senatorial candidate Jeffrey Bell, and media consultant Elliott Curson of Philadelphia.

Announcer: "In the past few years, our income has been eroded by the worst peacetime inflation and the largest tax increases in history. Our leaders tell us that in order to help energy consumers, we have to tax energy producers. And to have lower prices, we have to keep federal tax rates high. Ronald Reagan doesn't believe that."

Reagan: "If there's one thing we've seen enough of, it's this idea that for one American to gain, another American has to suffer. When the economy is weak . . . as it has been in recent years . . . everybody suffers . . . especially those who have the least. If we reduce paperwork and unnecessary regulations . . . if we cut tax rates deeply and permanently, we'll be removing many of the barriers that hold everyone back. Those who have the least will gain the most. If we put incentives back into society, everyone will gain. We have to move ahead. But we can't leave anyone behind."

But we can't leave anyone behind. It was this phrase, in what its creators called "The Good Shepherd" ad, that caused hard-jawed traditionalists in the Reagan camp to complain that the former California governor was sounding like a liberal. A couple of weeks later in Florida, an unabashed Reagan was denouncing Carter's anti-inflation plan as likely to cause "unemployment." The unemployment strategy, he told an amazed collection of Republicans in Fort Lauderdale, was "old style" Republicanism.

The battle for Reagan's mind was now on. On the one side were the forces of Jude Wanniski; Congressman Jack Kemp, Reagan's policy coordinator; and Professor Arthur Laffer, the theorist behind the 30 percent tax cut which Reagan was presenting as a campaign plank and which was the most seductive element in his appeal to the working-class and middle-class Democrats who were necessary to propel the governor to victory in November. A less well known adherent at that time was Representative David Stockman of Michigan.

Opposed to this group were ranked such mainstream conservative Reagan supporters as Arthur Burns, Milton Friedman, Alan Greenspan, George Shultz, and—more elusively—former Treasury Secretary William Simon. Along with many in Reagan's entourage such as Martin Anderson, domestic issues adviser, they saw Reagan captured by zealots, or "hardline ideologues," as *Business Week* termed the Wanniski group.

At issue was the future thrust of the Reagan campaign, Would it be traditional rantings against big government, allowing supporters to argue that Reagan '80 was very much like Reagan '70 in California: a tough-talking right-wing politician on the hustings turned moderate in office, the man who learned how to pull the levers of power, but not too hard? Or would Reagan set off across new, uncharted terrain, preaching the classical supply-side economics that would turn the world of Keynes upside down and provide a bracing tonic for capitalism in the 1980s?

* * *

The most articulate spokesman-strategist among the wild men was Jude Wanniski. Wanniski, formerly of *The Wall Street Journal* and author of *The Way the World Works,* had been the most adroit propagandist for the ideas of Laffer and Professor Robert Mundell of Columbia. Wanniski was the guiding hand behind the Kemp-Roth tax-cut bill. He had advised Reagan and believed firmly that the governor was a convert. . . . A supply-side Reagan, Wanniski thought, could sweep into office in a landslide, whereas a traditionalist Reagan might just sneak past Jimmy Carter, but would not spark the populace with dreams of better times instead of the tightened belts of an age of austerity.

At the end of March Wanniski began to feel that his faction was starting to lose the battle for Reagan's mind. In some desperation he decided to be—to use his favorite word—audacious and go public wherever he could. In the journalistic sector his allies, Evans and Novak, were staking all on the supply-siders. In a long interview with us—reprinted in the *Washington Post* and several other papers across the country—he sketched in the dimensions of the battle. His forthrightness later got him into considerable trouble with Reagan's top advisers. Some said that Jude "had finally done himself in." He hadn't.

"What," we began by asking him, "is the difference between the Reagan of 1976 and the Reagan of 1980?"

Wanniski: "The Reagan of 1976 did not have the concept of the Laffer curve, [which is] the law of diminishing returns applied to tax policy. You can raise a tax rate to a point where individuals are so discouraged from producing because government takes so much out of their production that they produce less, and then the government gets less revenue as a result. That's all the Laffer curve is about. Between 1976 and 1980, that's the whole difference in a nutshell, the idea that you can make the economy bigger and more efficient without having to divide things up. In 1976, Reagan got into difficulties with his $90 billion spending-cut plan which is really shifting spending and tax resources to state and local governments because people jumped on him for collapsing the social safety net.

"Now he understands that there's a way to move the economy to a higher level of efficiency and productivity without first throwing the widows and orphans out into the snow. That's the phrase I use. The traditional conservative Keynesian method suggested that we can reduce the level of activity of the central government, but we have to wrench away all these expenditures from the federal budget, and, somewhere down the line, after we go through the threshhold of pain and sacrifice and austerity, we will be able then to get back to the kind of economy we had years ago."

"So how did Reagan meet the Laffer curve?"

"In one sense Reagan has always understood this. Somebody in December worried about Reagan and Kemp coming together, and said, Will a 68–69-year-old guy really fasten onto these new ideas? How can an old dog learn new tricks? I remembered reading in Reagan's book, *Where's the Rest of Me?* his biography written in 1965, how he understood the disincentive effects of high marginal tax rates on the motion picture industry.

"So now, how exactly does he meet up with the Laffer curve? Well, he meets up with it through us, Laffer himself, and Wanniski, Jack Kemp, and Jeff Bell."

"Where are the milestones since 1976 in the political application of Laffer's ideas?"

"Nineteen-seventy-six was when I met Kemp and we then redesigned his tax program. We threw out all the stuff he had introduced in his jobs-creations act of 1974 to 1975 and put together a simple tax bill, cutting tax rates roughly by one-third in personal incomes. So that was a milestone, because as soon as Kemp did this, it was so simple that we began attracting support in the House of Representatives. Instead of having nine co-sponsors, he winds up in short order getting 95 co-sponsors. Then the press starts writing about Kemp, and he gets interviews, and the whole idea is discussed. Then I write *The Way the World Works,* where I call the Laffer curve the Laffer curve. I give it the name. One chapter of it goes into Irving Kristol's magazine, *The Public Interest,* and that is circulated. People talk about the Laffer curve as something that is simple enough for policy-makers to fasten upon and something where Jack Kemp can go from one member of the House of Representatives to another and take out a paper napkin and draw the curve. So if you talk about milestones, it was critical that we get all the complexities of the idea—and this is classical economics that we are trying to revive—boiled down to a few simple pictures."

"Give us a simple picture of your views."

"The problem is stagflation. This is the problem that hits the Western economies for the last dozen years and all the Western economists—those who are Keynesian and those who are monetarist are all operating on the demand model—the law of supply and demand. And there is no simultaneous equation that can solve unemployment and inflation at the same time in their model. The reason being that the only individual who exists in the demand model is the consumer who either has too little money in his pocket with which to demand—that's unemployment; or he has too much in his pocket with which to demand—that's inflation. So the strategies of the Keynesians and the monetarists all come down to, How do we get money out of their pockets—when there's inflation; or, How do we get money into their pockets—when there's recession. There's no way of dealing with the two problems at once, except in the Marx Brothers movie —*A Day at the Races,* I think—where Harpo is putting money into the guy's pocket and Chico is taking it out the other end.

"So then we have Laffer-Mundell coming along and saying it's not demand that moves the economy, it's supply. Supply is the limiting factor. There's no way that the government can affect the demand of individuals other than by thwarting it. Every individual on the face of the planet will demand as much as he or she can possibly consume. Take an individual. He has unlimited cravings to consume in the few years he has on earth. We all want to live like Frank Sinatra, to move from place to place in our own private jet plane. The demand is unlimited. What limits us as individuals is our ability to supply our own talents in the marketplace in order to exchange for the jet planes and everything else that we want. The ability and the time. So that's why we are called supply-siders. We want to maximize the individual's ability to fulfill his potential. When we see an unnecessarily high tax rate imposed on the individual by the Keynesian trying to take money out of his pocket, we say, Hey look, that's not doing any good for the economy. Get the level of tax rates up to where you're financing the government debt and providing for goods and services, but don't do it in a way that holds that individual back.

"In the simplest model, you have individuals come into the marketplace to transact with each other, and this is true today as it was 3,000 years ago. Now I come into the market and I see all these wonderful things that I want. And in order to get them, I have to go home and figure out what I can bring to the market to get these goods. I have to go and get these goods. I have to go and figure out a way to supply goods to the market. The only thing the government does is to provide for the security of the marketplace. It keeps the bandits out. It makes sure people don't come in and sell tainted bread and wine that will poison us. It provides for the mails and an army and navy and so forth.

"The only recessions that occur, occur because the government suddenly introduces a barrier to commerce that keeps you and me from transacting our goods. An unnecessarily high tariff, or a tax, or a regulation, or it begins to manipulate the money, the currency. That's another thing we ask the government to do: produce a currency that is both the medium of exchange, a unit of account, and a store of value, so we can work today and translate our production into a paper asset that we can change back into goods when our kids are ready to go to college or when we are ready to retire.

"Now the demand-modelers come along and recommend the way to increase or to decrease prosperity, when there's a recession or a surplus of goods. The Keynesians say we should tax goods away from those people who have them and give them to those people who do not have them. They say the problem in the economy is insufficient purchasing power. Either you tax them away from this group and give them to that group, or borrow them from this group by issuing bonds. That's deficit finance. The Democrats and the Keynesians have had that packet, working off a recession through taxes or deficit finance. The monetarists have said, Hey look, why work all of those resources through the central government, through taxes or deficit finance. There's a far easier way to do it, through the private sector. Increase the money supply through the banking system, increase the amount of bank credit and we will not have to make the government bigger. This is why the monetarists have tended to be more conservative, Republican, and the Keynesians, more liberal and Democratic, just depending upon their tastes in how to manipulate demand, whether it should be done through the public or the private sector.

"This is why we, the supply-siders, object as violently to the Friedmañ-ites as we do to the Keynesians."

"Does Reagan really believe in supply-side economics?"

"Yes. Reagan loves the stuff. John Sears, before he left, kept telling Kemp that he should spend more time on the campaign trail with Reagan, because whenever he spent a day or two with Reagan, Reagan came alive. When Kemp leaves, Reagan subsides. He is now at the point where he is getting better and better all the time."

"On economic policy then, it's basically you and Kemp?"

"And Laffer."

"Is there an opposing camp?"

"The opposing camp is an official board of advisers. It includes Arthur Burns, Milton Friedman, Caspar Weinberger, George Shultz, Alan Greenspan. It's a force that has to be reckoned with. They are more or less in a position of arguing caution."

"You are the wild men?"

"We are the wild men."

"Do you think Reagan can beat Carter?"

"Easily. Carter can get as many votes as he got in 1976 and still lose in a landslide, because the electorate is going to be given the first supply-siders it's had."

"What happens when the press gets a bit specific, as when they asked him on Issues and Answers *about the 30 percent tax cut and he covered up?"*

"That was just confusion, because he wasn't briefed. That was one of the points Sears made when he departed. The biggest problem is getting Reagan briefed."

"But supposing Reagan takes a couple of clouts. The press puts some fellow like Leonard Silk on the Laffer question, and there are some moderately technical questions, and the old boy will maybe stick his foot in the trough a couple of times, and there'll be a fuss about Reagan blundering. So then the other camp, the official advisers, will come to the governor and say, This Wanniski-Laffer-Kemp stuff is a bit off the wall. Let's get back to the old verities, i.e., the status quo, the old time religion."

"I wrote a three-page memo this morning to Reagan. I told him questions he was going to be asked and in the last paragraph I said to Reagan, No matter what sort of a box you get yourself into, one thing you've got to remember is Be Stubborn. Even if you're confused, you still think this is the right thing to do. That's all the electorate is going to watch for, that you are absolutely determined in the face of all critical questions."

"But Jude, here's how it will go. They'll say, How can you possibly pay for the defense system you are calling for, Governor Reagan?"

"Out of the bigger economy."

"And they'll say, Governor Reagan, it seems to be some sort of magic you're calling

for here. And your answer would be that the old man has to hang onto the rope, no matter how the winds buffet him?"

"Look at the *Business Week* interview. Reagan really handled it well. Even on *Issues and Answers,* he got to the point where he didn't know what they were talking about, so he switched to Proposition 13 in California."

"He went into a neutral corner?"

"He went into a neutral corner. Our argument is that the voters know what the problem is. The most they have to be persuaded is that this guy is serious and he's not going to change his mind or do nothing once he's elected."

"Let's pretend it's the best of times. Reagan has won the election and there's even a Republican Congress. The world is waiting. What's the first things Reagan does?"

"His program in 1981 would contain at least the following elements if he remains a keen supply-sider: a 30 percent reduction in marginal income tax rates at 10 percent a year; indexing the tax system to offset future inflation; elimination of the gift and inheritance taxes; abolition of the windfall profits tax on the domestic petroleum industry; reform of the central bank to restore a convertible dollar—gold exchange rate."

"Will welfare and social programs be cut?"

"No. Social programs are left in place. 'The safety net,' we call it. Government spending is reduced via economic expansion that makes people ineligible for welfare, unemployment, food-stamp benefits, etc., by virtue of having good jobs and good incomes."

"Let's say you put supply-side economics into operation. How would it enable my life to be any easier? Take any one who doesn't want to work for government, but wants to go on their own, making a living, be their own man, run their own thing. How will supply-side economics help me?"

"Take some really industrious young black on the South Side of Chicago who has the idea of opening up a fast-food chicken restaurant. Just examine him and all the problems that he faces before he can serve his first customer. And it's not only the tax rates, it's the level of wealth of the whole economy that is at issue. If you could—it sometimes sounds like trickle-down economics—if you have the most talented and creative and energetic individual in your whole economy, somebody who's J.P. Morgan, who is discouraged by the high tax rates on his own income and therefore spends more of his time playing polo and sailing his yacht, and less of his time trying to figure out more efficient ways of financing enterprise through the whole top of the system, then there have to be more people underneath him to do the same amount of work and as a result the capital of the country is used up before any smidgen of it gets down into the South Side of Chicago where this guy only needs $1,200 in order to get into business. So there's an interconnection all the way up to the top. It's not just a zero-sum game where you can say, We can solve this guy's $1,200 problem by credit controls, by instructing the banks that they cannot lend to J.P. Morgan, but to lend it to him. That decreases the efficiencies that J.P. Morgan brings to the whole system. If you can find

ways to take people in the country who are productive and get them to
give five minutes a week more of their intellectual energy to the economy,
which means five minutes less to playing polo, then these efficiencies will
work their way down as well. You have to raise the level of wealth of the
whole economy, then this guy has his $1,200. He still faces the Board of
Health of the City of Chicago. He wants to hire a kid and the government
says, No, you have to pay him $3.65 an hour minimum wage. The Board
of Health says he has to have three toilets within 12 feet of the fried
chicken grill. He has to go out and hire lawyers, he has to go out and hire
accountants. It's a big deal just to open up a little fried chicken restaurant.

"Let me give you an idea of what we are talking about. In Spain in the
17th century, they had the idea that wealth and prosperity lay in ac-
cumulating gold. So they had all the universities producing the cream of
Spanish manhood to make them navigators, scientists, and pilots. They
would take the best craftsmen to make ships. They would load all these
people on the ships and travel across the Atlantic, with soldiers and sailors,
and go to the New World. There, they would encounter hostile Indians
who had possession of some small amounts of gold, do battle with them
and a lot of Spanish lives would be lost. But they'd still overcome the
Indians, get their gold, put it on the ships, take it all the way back to Spain,
and then they would dig holes in the ground and bury the gold. All of that
goes on, and if you stand back and look at the net result, nothing has
changed except that some gold that was in that part of the world now is
in this part of the world. Meanwhile, you have expended 10 or 20 or 50
years' worth of the best children that the women could bear and could
have educated going to this totally fruitless enterprise. Because people
thought that wealth was gold.

"And now we have armies of lawyers and accountants and bureaucrats
in the federal government duelling with lawyers and accountants and
managers in the private sector over various directives and rulings and tax
laws and Nobody Producing Anything. And these are the cream of our
whole country! The top of the class of Harvard Business School, of Stanford Business School. All of them involved in wars over things that really
do not contribute."

"What is productivity?"

"Productivity is doing the same work with less effort. I wrote a memo
to Governor Reagan this morning, saying, Carter will boast that he increased the number of jobs since he took office, that there are more jobs
now than there were in 1977 when he was inaugurated. But he should not
be able to boast about this. The only reason there are so many jobs now
is because his economic policies have forced so many people to go to work
to make ends meet. If you'd had correct policies followed in 1975, 1976,
and 1977, you would have maybe 10 million fewer people working today.
The object of economic policy is not more work; it's less work. We are in
the process of destroying capital now as a result of forcing so many women
because of the inflation, because of the contraction in the economy, to go

out and work, rather than stay home and help their children with the reading lessons and drilling them on the times tables. . . ."

"You say productivity is determined by the marketplace. If I make widgets and no one wants to buy them, I would be deemed by the marketplace to be essentially nonproductive. Now, supposing I was a madam running a brothel, and the economy turns down and my middle-class clients can't afford to come by. So my business is failing and my girls are nonproductive in the marketplace. Enter President Reagan, the economy picks up, the tax rates are lower, the middle-class clients have more money in their pockets, come to the brothel, and therefore the girls bring in more money. Now are they being more productive? Are they and the brothel contributing to higher productivity, which we all want?"

"Anything in the economy that satisfies the tastes of individual Americans, individual citizens, is productive. Prostitution is productive. What you will see happening, the more the institutions of government are arranged in a way that will permit people to fulfill their potential, their legitimate potential, is less prostitution, less drugs, less pornography, even abortion. All of these come as a result of the impoverishment of the economy. If you had a real expansion of the economy, in the sense that people will fulfill their own potential at every level, the pressures of people to seek to equilibrium in their own lives, either through deadening their senses or through eliminating an unwanted child through abortion—these pressures fade away."

"So you are saying that Reagan's social policies—anti-ERA, a revulsion against women going into marketplace to make up the family budget, anti-abortion—these attitudes stem not from bigotry or theological puritanism or whatever . . ."

"No. They're a reaction against the forces of Malthusian darkness."

"So you are saying that the forces of darkness are in fact the liberals—pro-ERA, pro-abortion, and so on."

"It's not a matter of Keynesians or Friedmanites. The impulse goes back thousands of years—to those who believe in progress and those who do not. If you believe in progress, then you see a whole set of social attitudes developing because you are expanding opportunities for individuals, even though individuals are multiplying like mad."

"Let's take this regulation/deregulation thing and look at some small airline. Suppose some commuter pilot says he won't land because there's fog, and the boss says, Look, godammit, we're here to make money. You go ahead and land, and he does, and it crashes. Now, at that point, would you protect the marketplace?"

"Oh no, absolutely not. If you commit me to the idea that we're going to have continual contraction from this year, say to the year 2000, then I will revert to Marxism and total regulation and control, because I know that when you have a shrinking pie, there will be business guys and smart guys swarming all over the economy, cutting corners constantly at my expense, to try and make ends meet."

"But in the expanding economy of the 19th century, you had children dragging coal carts along in the mines, right?"

"In an expanding economy, the individual expects more. He will move from the entrepreneur who is cutting corners to the entrepreneur who is not cutting corners. In an expansion, you have less need for regulation. If you provide an environment that is conducive to opportunity and growth, then competition will result in more safety and health and more concerns for the environment, but not without vigilance by the collective, maintaining watchdogs."

"But what about big business institutions which are just as evil as the central government? In other words, to achieve supply-side economics, don't you have to get involved in curbing big-business institutions which are interlocked with big government?"

"I don't find government to be evil, or corporate America to be evil, except insofar as they come up with the wrong answers as to what is good for the whole people. Bankers, by their very nature and training, are put here on earth to get their loans paid back. When you suggest to them that they will get their money paid back easier by lowering tax rates, they don't want to believe it. They would rather believe that it is much easier to get the money paid back by raising the tax rates.... An example: I went down to Puerto Rico in the spring of 1976 to talk to Teodoro Moscoso, the chief economist in the Hernandez Colon administration. The unemployment rate was 20 percent. The economy was in a tailspin. I asked Moscoso, Why in God's name, when this economy is reeling in recession, do you put on a new tax rate? He says, Well, the bankers in New York said it would be a good thing to restore confidence in the economy. I said, Oh Mr. Moscoso, if you went to the bankers and said you've taxed your people to the limit, that the only way to pay off the bonds you owed them was to sell a third of the people of Puerto Rico into slavery, they'd say, Don't tell us. Do it.

"Now we go beyond the shores of the United States to the International Monetary Fund.

"At the Reagan sessions in January, I sat there like a bump on a log, listening to the discussions: how the CIA is no longer effective, how our intelligence agencies are no longer effective, and how we have to do something. All these military people. So I suggested that all we really have to do is to hire one guy to keep track of the traveling schedule of the IMF. And wherever the IMF goes, you know, in six months there's going to be a revolution."

"What are the leading objections to your tax ideas?"

"That the first effect is to put more money into people's pockets. ... The first thing that happens is that a worker, say in Toledo, Ohio, winds up getting an extra $4.12 in his paycheck (after a tax cut). He rushes out with that $4.12 and buys some scarce good, and therefore puts upward pressure on the price and we have more inflation. Now, even Herb Stein and the other Keynesian economists say that, maybe in the long term, people will run around in such a way as to build more plants and equipment to produce this scarce good that costs $4.12. But in the interim, they say, you have this inflationary effect. For the economy as a whole, they see that all you are doing is deferring a tax. If the government is going to give $4.12 to the worker by lowering the tax rate, and it has the same level of expenditures, it must finance $4.12 with a bond. That means sometime in the future the Toledo worker will have to pay another $4.12 in taxes. In other words, it washes out over time.

"What we're saying is that the lower rate, in and of itself, will cause the whole economy to expand. The tax base will broaden, and even the Toledo worker will begin to observe that the liabilities of the government will be spread over a broader tax base and that therefore the claims on his future taxes will drop to $3.81. He will then be able both to consume and to save."

"Is there any proof of this?"

"This is all theory. . . . All we're saying is that there is an extra effect in the economy by having a lower rate which encourages people to produce more, that encourages capital and labor to come forth with greater production.

"One of the first insights I had was when I asked Laffer, How can these incentives be instantaneous? Won't we have to wait three years for them to occur? Laffer said, How long does it take you to reach over and pick up a $50 bill in a crowd. Aah! That's how quick it is, If the incentive is there, the production is there."

How ironic to read some of those lines about "the safety net" today! But this was the philosophy that enabled Ronald Reagan to stare an unemployed worker unflinchingly in the face in the spring, summer, and fall of 1980 and tell him that the Republicans, not the Democrats, were the advocates of growth and would put him back to work. This, plus a 4 percent real decline in living standards in the last two years of the Carter administration, was what gave Reagan the edge.

What had the Democrats got to offer in return?

* * *

There was one Democratic challenger to Jimmy Carter who had the intellectual agility and resourcefulness to meet the supply-sider challenge. But Governor Jerry Brown, in his early forays into New England in late 1979, had to cope with the mockery of the press, which called him "Governor Moonbeam," and the apparently unshakable conviction of a significant slice of the electorate that he was inconstant on the issues: against Proposition 13, for Proposition 13. . . . "If you look at the budget, what do you find?" Brown would tell his college audiences. "Welfare, warfare, and interest on the debt. That's the big picture of the USA and I think it is a very sorry one. I say, let's balance the budget and pay our bills as they come due."

Brown tried to make a synthesis out of environmentalism, fiscal and budgetary prudence, antinuclear polemic, and drumbeating for high-tech expansionism. The resultant brew was welded into a slogan his supporters used to have stenciled on their t-shirts: "Serve the people, protect the earth, explore the universe." (The last injunction referred to Brown's continuing enthusiasm for space colonies, a notion as dear to him as Communist expansionism was to his fellow Californian, Ronald Reagan.)

Brown saw the usefulness of what Wanniski called "simple pictures." "A person who makes about $10,000 a year," he would say, "will contribute over ten years $100,000 to the GNP. If that person develops cancer and is given a quality care cancer treatment, in the space of one year he might contribute $100,000 to the GNP in terms of the medical services and equipment used to treat him. How absurd to have an increase in the GNP dependent on someone getting cancer." There is, Brown would correctly add, no quantification in the GNP for improvements in the quality of life.

Brown stood at the left end of the government/business/labor synthesis being urged by parties as various as Felix Rohatyn of Lazard Frères, *Business Week,* Edward Kennedy, and even John Anderson. It was Brown who originally popularized the phrase "reindustrialization"—a notion dismissed by the supply-siders as "fascism."

"I think," he told us as his campaign bus wound through New Hampshire, "we're going to have to find out if we can take the Japanese and German experience and re-create it in the United States. We'll have to draw a new compact with labor and business and environmentalists and consumers, under the aegis of the public sector. I think this will happen because the stalemate will force this kind of public sector leadership, this new social and political compact. . . . The only way to create a governing coalition is to involve groups that are presently being excluded and over time, redraw the social compact. As the dead ends and paralysis become more obvious, then the nation will have to include more people in the coalition in order to get anything done."

But 1980 was not Brown's year. Not least because, against all his calculations, Senator Edward Kennedy entered the race, permanently injured his challenge by a disastrous interview about Chappaquiddick with Roger Mudd on CBS, but remained till the convention in August 1980 as the lightning rod for Democratic dissatisfaction with Jimmy Carter. It was not easy to pinpoint exactly why the Kennedy campaign was almost always off-key. It became customary to find the reason in Chappaquiddick and the Mudd disaster; and in the groundswell of unity for Carter during the hostage crisis.

But the real problem for Kennedy was that the Right had seized the ideological initiative and he was often trying to guard his flank by announcing that he too was a foe of regulation, with substantial achievements in red tape cutting in the airline and trucking industries. At the same time he ran with his head over his shoulder, looking back to the New Deal, to Harry Truman, to JFK and the New Frontier, to the Great Society as part of the "unfinished agenda." He evoked them all, and more. He reminded audiences that life (at least in terms of interest rates) was better four years earlier under Jerry Ford. And if this was not odd for a Democratic candidate, in the next breath Kennedy was calling for an end to "twelve years of Republican White House rule." The implications were confusing. If life was better under Ford, why not vote Republican? But then, Carter according to Kennedy was also a Republican and had made matters worse. So why vote Republican? This sort of thing led people to forget Camelot and ask, What in God's name was Kennedy talking about.

In imperial majesty at first, in two vast jets and in earthbound caval-cades that stretched across the country like a freight train, Kennedy trav-eled the nation in search of the constituency that had once seemed so assured. He offered the uplifting theme of leadership and faced the rejec-tion of those who thought him too vague. He attacked the Shah and was accused of being a traitor. Chastened, he tried hard issues and proposals in his January Georgetown speech after Iowa. He called for wage and price controls, gas rationing, and a UN commission on the Shah and Iran.

He began to win. But the constituency was one defined as much by Carter's mistakes as Kennedy's own virtues, a refuge for those despairing of the president. By midspring Kennedy was concentrating almost entirely on the economy, switching rather laboriously from attacks on high interest rates to an increasing emphasis on help for the victims of hard times.

Through endless eighteen-hour campaign days, he seemed like a man suspended in a political vacuum, calling almost hourly for debates with a president who would never appear, but too circumspect to attack directly one of the most foolish and dangerous acts of the Carter presidency—the rescue bid in Iran. Kennedy began to receive the field rations of the under-dog and gallant loser: commendations for courage and steadiness of resolve in a time of trouble. The most clichéd moral of them all: expiation for Chappaquiddick.

In Otober 1979: Everybody for Kennedy. By April 1980: Anybody but Carter. The uncrowned king of the Democratic party had become a life raft. People lined up behind Kennedy not because they liked him but because they could not stand the president.

In May Kennedy was sitting in a UAW meeting hall in Anderson, Indiana. He was surrounded by auto workers, many laid off from the local Delco-Remy battery plant. Kennedy talked seriously and to the point about limitations on social security death benefits, truncated unemploy-ment benefits, the need for health care, the pain of relocating in search of a job.

Kennedy spoke briefly of his personal point of view toward health care, in words that hung oddly in the air: "We've got a very good health-care program for members of Congress, and we ought to be able to do as well for the American people. Health is something that is important to my family. I was in the hospital for seven months with a broken back. I have an asthmatic son . . . and a son who also had cancer on him . . . and a sister who is retarded . . . a father who had a heart condition for six or seven years. It would just have bankrupted any family. Sickness is enough of a burden on any family without bankrupting it as well."

Here was a good example of the Kennedy effect. These UAW workers were not listening to just another politician trying for the common touch with a confidential slice of family history. They were listening to one of the best-known sagas in American life. They were not just looking at a man who broke his back. They were looking at the last of the Kennedy brothers, who was miraculously pulled from a plane crash by their very own senator, Birch Bayh. The family was not saved from bankruptcy because of a good health plan for members of Congress, but because the Kennedys are millionaires.

Everyone in the room knew this, and the candidate knew that they knew it. The effect was not one of intimacy but heightened formality. Kennedy stays a man apart, through circumstance, through history.

"You just get the impression," says Rolfe Tessem, an ABC cameraman who had been with Kennedy since October, "that you are looking through a glass wall. Everything gets filtered." No matter where he was or what he was doing, the same old questions rushed in: is he smart, is he dumb, is he lazy, does he really want to be president, does he hate his wife, does she hate him, did he kill the girl, but finally, Who Is He? People did not know. They couldn't fix him in any time or any place, which was probably why so often the speeches—eloquent, just, and passionate—hung in the air, armies of noble words searching for a battle in which no one wanted to engage.

They said that Ted, like his brothers, was marvelous with crowds. A Boston-Irish pol at heart. But you had only to look at Ronald Reagan to appreciate just how uncomfortable Kennedy often was with people. There was a formal reserve you associate with a priest moving among parishioners: of the people yet apart from the people. True always to the forms of the institution. No voter particularly minds vulnerability in a politician. But Kennedy's vulnerability took on the form of the unknown: what happened at Chappaquiddick? In 1979 Kennedy decided that he could be invulnerable even to this. He was wrong. Voters had not forgotten that he got away with it in 1969 and thought he could get away with it again in 1980.

Kennedy's campaign, even after the comeback in the New York primary, was all coda—right through the bogus "open convention" battle in Madison Square Garden in August. He was left with the farewell speech on the fundamentals of liberalism, which left not a dry eye in the house from people who had fought, and who no doubt will fight, to keep him from the Democratic nomination.

* * *

The sleight of hand, executed by the Kemp faction, had been to adorn the visage of Republicanism, red in tooth and claw, with the lineaments of social justice and thus give the old actor his latest role—the savior of the common man.

By the July Republican convention in Detroit the great gamble was being made: Would economic prescriptions barely understood by many of Reagan's closest spokesmen and hotly contested by many of his most important advisers survive as the engine of the Republican juggernaut?

The prescriptions which triumphed in Reagan's mind and in the party platform amounted to the bald assertion that life will improve for all, growth be assured, inflation controlled, production enhanced, and jobs increased and made secure through big tax cuts and a ferocious assault on government regulation.

The party platform ratified in Detroit provided the idiom of the ideological shift:

"To those individuals who have lost their jobs because of the Carter recession, we pledge to insure that they receive their rightfully earned unemployment-compensation benefits.

"The Republican Party recognizes the need to provide workers who have lost their jobs because of technological obsolescence or imports the opportunity to adjust to changing economic conditions. In particular, we will seek ways to assist workers threatened by foreign competition."

The platform wrapup was an absolute reversal of the policies normally associated with a Republican government (and was of course largely annulled immediately after the election). They had had the life-enhancing uplift of New Deal rhetoric: "We propose to put Americans back to work again by restoring real growth without inflation to the United States economy. . . . We must replace the Carter administration's promise of hard times and austerity—one promise which has been kept—with Republican policies that restore economic growth and create more jobs.

"The Democratic Congress and the Carter administration are espousing programs that candidate Carter in 1976 said were inhumane: Using recession, unemployment, high interest rates, and high taxes to fight inflation. The Democrats are now trying to stop inflation with a recession, a bankrupt policy which is throwing millions of Americans out of work. They say Americans must tighten their belts, abandon their dreams, accept higher taxes, less take-home pay, fewer jobs, and no growth in the national economy.

"We categorically reject this approach. Inflation is too much money chasing too few goods. Shutting down our nation's factories and throwing millions of people out of work leads only to shortages and higher prices."

The most astounding reversal of all was the sea-change whereby the Republican party, for so many years the vital organ of protectionist policies, now came up roaring for free trade, while the Democrats teetered toward tariff walls, with the UAW leading the way.

The audacity of all this was breathtaking, and would require nothing less than a miracle from the Almighty God to whom the convention prayed almost without cease. (Sample, from the Monday prayer breakfast for 1,000 delegates: "For a greater respect for human life in our country and for the protection of all life, especially for the unborn, let us pray to the Lord.") The same platform that implied reduced revenues from taxation called for the largest defense increases since World War II. The same platform that spoke with words of understanding and mercy to the poor called also for attrition in federal efforts to help them, with the proposition that Reagan's tax-cut boom would hurtle a poor black into vigorous self-made prosperity before he had time to crash bankrupt and unhelped into the poorhouse and the grave.

A few weeks later the Democrats emerged from their convention, "united" behind the Carter-Mondale ticket. They had a problem. Under Carter the Democrats had sponsored removal of regulation from the oil and gas industry, and having preached shortage for four long years, found themselves wallowing in a worldwide glut of oil and gas, retailed—courtesy of Carter—at the highest prices in history. This was Reagan's free market in action.

Under Carter the Democrats had rushed to the aid of floundering big business, had embraced traditional conservative solutions to inflation by accepting unemployment as the option and Volcker's high interest rate policies at the Federal Reserve. Under Carter the Democrats were promising a 27 percent hike in military spending by the end of his second term. Under Carter the Cold War had been revived, the Soviet invasion of Afghanistan termed "the greatest threat to peace since the Second World War," and the SALT II treaty shelved.

The Democratic party, post-Madison Square Garden, was not split. It was lying on the floor in fragments, in a disintegration of purpose, ideals, and ideas entirely of its own making. Short of calculations about the future membership of the Supreme Court, just how many arguments were there to vote for such a party and such a leader?

* * *

The Left did not have a happy time of it in 1980. Switched between loyalty to the Kennedy bid and the appeal of Barry Commoner's Citizens party, coherence of purpose was never apparent. And of course ultimately, in the Marxist analysis proffered by such as Paul Sweezy and Harry Magdoff of the *Monthly Review,* there was nothing—aside from a long-range struggle for socialism—to urge anyway.

Here, in a talk with us back in the spring of 1980, is how Sweezy and Magdoff saw the situation.

"What's happened to the economy? Why isn't it working?"

Magdoff: "There was a long wave of prosperity which came around the Second World War. It took on different forms in different countries, but there was a certain similarity in pattern. Then this long wave of prosperity tapered off, but the economy was kept going by an enormous increase in liquidity, both in the form of a huge flow of U.S. dollars abroad, and by continued expansion of debt, where the most outlandish forms of speculation in terms of consumer debt and business debt become accepted. So: basic stagnation in the economy and an economy which is operated on the expansion of money."

"What was the basis for the long wave of prosperity?"

Magdoff: "For the United States, it was one underlying factor: you had a long period during the Depression when the housing supply had worn down, consumer durables had worn down, industrial machinery had worn down. Then you get a war. During the war, automobile production and residential construction are constricted, except as needed for war purposes. You have wage and price controls. And for all their weaknesses, you have for the first time a working class with a large reserve in savings. You have corporations with idle capacity, and you have demand. So you have an enormous injection of demand with the money to pay for it, to develop housing, automobiles. With that, you get the suburbs, extension of the cities, the highway system, and so on."

"What caused the decline?"

Sweezy: "You don't need any special causes to explain the slowdown. What you need are causes to explain the periods of upsurge and buoyancy, because the natural tendency of the system is to slow down and to stagnate. When the economy is monopolized to the extent that it is, there is always the potential to make a hell of a lot more profit than can be invested."

"After the war, there was a global investment boom, but these things are always overdone. So, whenever you want to date the decline—it actually comes to the fore in 1974, 1975—there is a sudden discovery that there is a huge excess capacity in steel; there is a huge excess capacity in chemicals. Shipbuilding practically overnight falls down to half of where it was, unemployment goes up throughout the capitalist world. In the advanced capitalist countries (the OECD countries), there are now about 20 million unemployed.

"This is the way the system would be if it didn't have these special stimuli coming from automobiles or railroads or wars or imperialist expansion. The logic of the system is that throughout its history it has required an extremely dynamic environment in order to sustain relatively long periods of expansion and relatively short recessions.

"I just think that period is over with. The prospect ahead is for continued stagnation, not necessarily on the scale of the 1930s, because there are all sorts of demand-sustaining institutions—transfer payments, social security, unemployment insurance, and the military. But keeping up the level of the economy to, say, 8 to 10 percent unemployment still involves the possibility of a continuation of inflation. You would probably have to go to something like the 1930s, with 15 to 25 percent unemployment, in order to break this inflationary spiral. So now you've got the worst of both worlds. You've got the end of the boom, you've got the continuation of stagnation and inflation. And what it's going to lead to, God knows."

"Well, in these circumstances, doesn't it make sense for business to favor a candidate like Anderson, who is calling for some measure of planning in the economy?"

Sweezy: "I think pressures in that direction might grow. But it isn't at all obvious that the political structure of this country is such that a more or less unified policy can be imposed on the whole society. The system is so fragmented in terms of corporate struggles—the executive, legislative, and judiciary; states; localities; the federal government. The whole thing was planned long long ago to keep any real power from developing at the center which could impose itself on the society as a whole. That's very deeply ingrained. Each one of these sectors has a vested interest. . . . So far, labor is the weakest, so it takes the rap, and hasn't fought back very much. But one wonders whether this will go on indefinitely."

"Do you think things will rapidly get worse?"

Sweezy: "All the forces that have produced the present situation are continuing to work. They aren't going to stop. They aren't going to go away. At some stage, if this keeps on, as it has over the last few years, something is going to give. I think you have to go back and look at the 1930s. The New Deal didn't happen all at once. The Depression hit bottom in 1932 and 1933. The president came into office in 1933 on a very conservative program. It was not until the closing of the banks just after Roosevelt took office that they got so scared that they were prepared to use special powers. And still, the first recovery program was very conservative. . . . Then things began to happen at the grass roots."

"What kind of programs are needed now?"

Sweezy: "The problem is not, 'Is Something Needed?' Of course it's needed. Rebuild the cities. Housing is in crisis. You could easily put down a program that would use all the productive resources of the country. That's not the point. Are they going to make a profit out of it? Who's going to make the profit? Who's going to make a loss? That's the way the system works. There's no point in talking about need unless as after the Second World War, when there were a hell of a lot of people with a lot of money who needed houses in the suburbs, who needed highways to get from one to another, and all those needs could easily be taken care of. Nobody lost and everybody profited."

"In terms of the election, do you think there is any sort of substantive debate going on on economic policy?"

Sweezy: "Kennedy is the only one who seems to be raising issues about controls. So in that sense, yes."

Magdoff: "Look, there can't be a debate, because we're in a situation where there is only one way to stop inflation, and that's a major depression, and a hope that it won't take too long and they'll be able to reshuffle things sufficiently through the depression to get us on an even keel. There's nothing you can do. All you can do is to decide whether you protect this part of the population or that part of the population. We're in a society where inflation lives on inflation. The society lives on inflation. We've been this way for decades, and it's not just us, it's the whole capitalist system. There used to be a period where some of the advanced capitalist countries had a slower inflation rate than we had; where the German managers were smarter, or the Japanese were more effective. But it's been spreading all over the world, so the point is not that there may be a more ingenious or competent management, but that there are some very basic issues involved."

Sweezy: "The whole bunch of these advisers to all the candidates don't understand inflation. Charles Schultze [chairman of the Council of Economic Advisers] used to, but the exigencies of politics overtook him. He couldn't stand to play the role he's in now if he followed the obvious lines on inflation he'd laid down in 1959. He said then that any society which is so dominated by rigid or administered prices—he doesn't say monopoly, but these prices would not be so without monopoly and a lot of government regulations bearing on prices—in any such society where prices are fundamentally only variable up, you don't even need an overall increase in demand to get inflation. All you need is a shift from one sector to another. Suppose, with prices in sector A at such and such a level, demand shifts to sector B. Prices in sector B will go up, but in sector A they will not go down.

"This shifting around, which will always occur in a dynamic economy, will raise the general price level, which will raise the cost of living. Real wages will have to go up, and higher wages will mean they are going to have to raise their prices. So there is an internal mechanism which is going to produce inflation. You could stop it by a drastic curtailment of the money supply, but you don't need any autonomous increase in the money supply, you don't need any overall increase in demand, you don't need any general increase in the degree of monopoly. All you need is a shifting around, back and forth."

Magdoff: "Consider the level of international involvement that has developed in this postwar period. It isn't just a question of profits for some corporation with twenty branches all over the world. It's our monetary system. It's our banking system. It's the loans we've made, in the recycling of the petrodollars, these tremendous loans from private banks to the Third World countries. We are so much intertwined with a world international financial system that the ability to design a program which both protects our position internationally and also puts some lid on inflation is full of paradoxes. For example, this crazy rise in interest rates has become a war of interest rates between countries, and they have to do it, because they are beginning to feel the pull of the unbalance of payments. This is something that's not generally recognized, but it's part of the problem. Running the economy on a day-to-day basis, from the government's standpoint—to the extent that they do run it—is a hell of a complicated thing."

"Now you were saying when we sat down that supply-side economics [i.e., creation of more capital for investment to stimulate the economy, advocated by Reagan and his advisers] is irrelevant. Why do you say that?"

Sweezy: "What it is designed to do, as I understand it, although it does seem a little unbelievable, is the following: they increase profits, and these people are going to rush off and make investments which will increase productivity and therefore bring supply up and prices down."

"You stimulate the businessman's lust to rush into the marketplace, to produce and compete, by lowering the tax rates."

Sweezy: "That's it, so they'll have more left over to invest. But the problem is that they've got enough to invest. A lot of big corporations have more than they know what to do with. So really, all this is a program to increase the total amount of cash flow. Absolutely nobody, I am sure, could produce any information, any evidence whatever, that this would have any effect of the kind which it is supposed to have."

"What it seems to boil down to is this: take money out of welfare or some social expenditure and put it in a semi-conductor plant in Texas. That's what a Reaganite would say."

Magdoff: "Of course that's what they all say. That's what a lot of economists say. But what sense does it make? There was a listing in *Business Week* of some of the large corporations, which keep 25 or 35 percent of their assets in cash. When you buy Treasury Certificates or commercial paper, you make your 15 or 20 percent on it. They're having a ball. They're not investing in factories. . . .

"Look, capitalists invest where there is a chance to make good profits and where there's some security for their investment, as well as for profits. The capitalist does that when he sees there is an adequate market, which is the basis for investment. When there isn't a market, they don't invest. No matter how much money they have, they're not going to add another mill here or another factory somewhere else."

"At this point, do you really think there is a separation between the state and the corporate sector?"

Sweezy: "The function of the state is to see that the environment, the conditions, the atmosphere, and so on are such that corporations can prosper. But you can't do that all the time. There are fights among the corporations as to who is going to have the most influence over the state. You can't say corporations are identical to the state. You can certainly say the state exists to do its best to make an environment and a system in which corporations can flourish. Of course, that way of putting it is not theoretical enough for some Marxists. . . .

"There are fierce struggles within the corporate system. [The question is] Who is going to get on top and knock their heads together and bring out some coherent program for society as a whole? It certainly isn't going to be any candidate of any party on the horizon now. U.S. society is not the kind that can somehow be subjected to a straitjacket. Japan, of course, is much more successful in that respect than any of the others. As far as that model is concerned, I don't see any sign of it happening here. Our history does not give any good indication of it."

"How do you define the working class?"

Sweezy: "Seventy-five percent of the country. . . ."

Magdoff: "People who work for wages. . . ."

Sweezy: "A broad definition: everybody who doesn't have a source of income except wages, or whose other source of income is nominal. So that means you are dealing with 75 or 80 percent of the population."

Magdoff: "The divisive forces within the working class are enormous.

At periods, this was overcome. It was overcome in the thirties. You really had class war going on in this country. My point is, sure there are divisions, and management is operating [to pit them against one another]."

"But you would argue that these divisions erode if, as you say, things 'really got going.' Do you see any movement of this sort visible now?"

Magdoff: "Do I see it coming? No."

"Take this whole question of productivity. The usual line is that the American worker is indolent; he's not producing; he's not working hard enough."

Magdoff: "Who says that they're unproductive? The whole thing is built mostly out of thin air."

Sweezy: "Phony statistics."

Magdoff: "Productivity has a very specific meaning, and can only have a specific meaning, and that is the difference between two periods, in how much labor is required to produce a given basket of goods. You've got to be able to identify the basket of goods; you've got to be able to identify the people. When you're dealing with commodities, it makes a certain amount of sense. It takes so many workers to make a notebook of this sort in my hand; it took so and so many a year ago. Then you've got a meaningful measurement, but what do you do with products that are changing? Take, for instance, the automobile. They throw in new electronic devices. They add, they subtract. It's not the same automobile. And what's been happening is that to measure things of that sort, they use some arbitrary number that is unrelated to either quantity or quality in any real sense. This is nothing yet. The real problem arises when they take in the whole field of services. Now you're in a society where the amount of labor that's being used in producing goods has been going down, relatively, with increase in productivity. The new jobs have been created in the service sector. And it's not just a service sector to serve the people. It's to sell, to push, to advertise. Now what the hell does productivity mean there?"

Sweezy: "Or even in a useful field like teaching, what does it mean to have an increase in productivity? You double the size of the class and probably get a quarter of the education."

Magdoff: "Motor vehicle dealers, people who sell cars, amount to 833,-000 people. People manufacturing automobiles amount to 793,000. The economy becomes more and more of a service economy, with more and more effort put into selling, advertising, pushing, speculating, buying and selling real estate, buying and selling stocks, commodity speculation, and all the clerical work that goes with it.

"So, we are bound to get a decline of productivity, if you're getting into more and more of a service industry type of society, where you push more and more. Does that mean labor is less productive here? It just isn't so. Throughout the history of capitalism, as far as manufacturing is concerned, there's been a steady, persistent increase in productivity, output per worker, to the extent that we can measure it. It doesn't increase every year exactly the same percentage. Sometimes it goes up 3 percent a year, sometimes it goes up 2.7 percent a year. In periods where there's a stagnation, productivity doesn't go up as much. But it goes up! Manufacturing's been going up all this period. The only possible argument they have is that for some years it's been at a slower rate than in previous years. What the hell does that mean? How do you measure the productivity of a fireman? Or a person handling social security payments? . . . It doesn't make any sense. But this is all included. It's become part of the regular mythology. Editorialists write about it, speeches are made. . . ."

Sweezy: "The reason is perfectly obvious, because it's grist for this whole supply-side mill."

Magdoff: "Look at the subway strike. Take away the 20-minute rest period, they say, and you'll increase the productivity. Here are 1978 figures taken from the *Fortune* listings. . . . I haven't got my calculator but I'll give you a rough idea. General Electric: If you take the profits after taxes and divide by the number of employees, the profits are $3,000 per employee. Now you take Siemens in Germany. Not exactly identical, but in the same area. There, it's a $1,000 in profit per worker. In Phillips, it's around $900 per worker. Now, it could be that the productivity is lower, but one sure thing is the profits are higher."

"I remember you writing somewhere that the Eastern European countries had no inflation problem."

Sweezy: "That was a couple of years ago. As they get increasingly into the international system, the inflation infection seeps through."

"What did they do to control it?"

Sweezy: "They've planned total output and total incomes and the money supply and all the rest of it. They don't do it perfectly, but they keep inflation under some sort of control."

Magdoff: "I just want to put in a footnote on the extent to which they themselves are using the market as a rationing device. In order to exert discipline both on the working class and on consumption patterns, they get away from planning and rely more and more on rationing, and impose discipline through prices. They permit increases in prices, certain kinds of goods within their country, as a way of stimulating certain types of production. This is the market technique which often contributes to a certain type of inflation pressure."

"So one of the claims for the Eastern bloc—full employment, along with stability on the inflation front—is beginning to erode?"

Sweezy: "These seem to be the only legitimate claims such societies have to existence. If they start giving that up, too, I don't know what you have left."

Magdoff: "There's a difference. They have inflation, but nothing like this."

"You argue for socialism in the Monthly Review. *Given the limits of socialist education here, what are you asking people to understand?"*

Sweezy: "You mean, why are we saying such obviously unrealistic and utopian things? . . . I guess because we think it's a long-range proposition and if people don't start to learn now, they'll be that much farther behind in ten years."

Magdoff: "Within this framework, if Keynes were sitting here, or Harry White were sitting here, there's nothing the smartest guys could do to rescue this situation."

But conversations such as this one were scarcely typical of most mainstream press commentary. All the usual vices of the press are magnified in a political campaign, and 1980 was no exception. The list of issues which escaped serious scrutiny is a large one, commencing with the conservative onslaught on SALT II and the propaganda barrage for increased arms spending. (Richard Burt, *The New York Times* correspondent covering these areas throughout President Carter's term, took a job with Secretary of State Haig early in 1981.)

The diminution of the investigative zeal which marked the early and mid-1970s contributed to the paucity of vigorous coverage. The network of industries and interest groups backing Reagan—and rewarded in the wake of his victory—remained virtually immune from any fierce probing, with only desultory examination of Reagan's "kitchen cabinet" network of California millionaires.

At a very elementary level, journalists covering the campaign learned to like Governor Reagan and to tolerate his tranquil brand of ignorant demagogy without undue protest.

* * *

Journalists on the campaign trail spend much time discussing the merits of campaign managers, on whom they are of course dependent for much of their information. And campaign managers are Machiavellis of calculation and foresight when their candidates are winning; forgotten when their candidates are not. The press uses the managers, the managers use the press, and both parties are dependent on the equipage of a modern campaign: the plane, the television camera, and the computer.

"I remember, when covering Hubert Humphrey in 1972, one of the maddest campaigns in my life," John Lindsay, veteran *Newsweek* reporter, reminisced in October 1980, "we flew one day from San Diego up to San Francisco to go to a lunch in Chinatown, and then to run through Chinatown. Hubert would run with a whole group, a whole battalion of local TV station people running behind him. Halfway through this, I grabbed one of Humphrey's guys and said, 'What the hell are we doing here? Even the lunch wasn't very good. But to fly all the way from San Diego to here —he's not saying anything, he's not talking to anybody, he's just running through Chinatown.'

"The guy said, 'It'll be all over the six o'clock news tonight.' I said, 'What? That Humphrey can run through Chinatown?' He said, 'No. That's what it will show, but it will reveal him to be a very active, vigorous man, and anyway, the only asset we have in the campaign is the airplane. We have no money for anything.' It was true. The only thing the Humphrey people had going for them was the campaign plane. The only reason they could put the campaign plane in the air was because we were there: us and the Secret Service. That, to me, symbolizes our problem today. Without the plane, there is no campaign."

Lindsay was right, of course. Movement is the message, as recorded by the thirty-odd cameramen, soundmen, producers, and reporters from the three networks who followed each major candidate, controlled the schedule, and packaged some action each day for a minute or so of national consumption each evening. In the field were the foot soldiers. Back at headquarters were a handful of men and women determining what actually got on—hence just how much the national audience would see of Jimmy Carter, Ronald Reagan, and maybe John Anderson. This entire production is today governed by one act: the assassination of John Kennedy in Dallas in 1963.

The shooting of the president of the United States that year was the single most important event in framing the coverage of a modern presidential campaign. From then on, and accelerating after the assassination of Robert Kennedy in 1968, campaigns became what John Lindsay accurately describes as "a national body watch." The main reason, after all, why the cameras of all networks now follow every step of every candidate through every public instant of his day is not because the candidate might choose to pick his nose halfway down Main Street, but because he might get shot.

The TV cameras share the body watch with the Secret Service, and the two custodial enterprises share much of the cost of the plane. Television requires that the candidate move from one visually interesting site to another. The Secret Service supervises the actual movement. Where the candidate goes, and what he says when he gets there, are dictated by political common sense and the computer.

The computer churns out the poll, and the poll determines all. In the old days, candidates sailed through campaigns with traditional navigational aids: a word with this or that political boss, an "important endorsement," a debate, a speech to one special-interest group or another. And, as might be expected with such imperfect technology, the candidate was occasionally fetched up in a shipwreck on unforeseen rocks. Such was the case in 1948, when dead reckoning told Republican candidate Thomas Dewey that his course was surely set for the harbor of victory. He was wrong. Harry Truman, contrary to all expectations, made the safer landfall.

Campaign navigational aids have changed vastly. In 1948, computer polls would have showed Dewey that he was going wrong, why and where, long before the horrible surprise of that postelection dawn. The modern poll allows for instant replay and—in the hands of sophisticates —for correction in midcourse. In the spring of 1980 amid the hostage crisis, Jimmy Carter was playing the Rose Garden strategy, saying that the hostage crisis required him to stay in the White House. Wife Rosalynn was dispatched in his place. Then pollsters saw an ominous change on their computer printouts. The Rose Garden strategy was dead. The voters thought Carter should be out on the road. Rosalynn was recalled, the president announced the hostage crisis was "manageable," and he was on the road himself.

There's more to polls than simple candidate management. Back to Lindsay: "Just to show what spear carriers we've become for TV, the writing press now reveals to the American reader, without the slightest embarrassment, four different polls by four different institutions showing four different things without any effort to explain what's going on. There's got to be a puzzled person out there somewhere who asks, 'How can CBS, *The New York Times,* this poll group and that poll group all come up with different figures, all wildly beyond the error factor they say is inherent in their own program?' One says Carter is leading, the other says Reagan is leading. One says Anderson is having a distinct impact on Carter's vote, the other says it's minimal. They all come out in the same story, and no one sits back and says, 'Now look, this is the reason for it.' It's all a mirage."

Not quite a mirage. The polls conducted by the candidates are, as noted above, useful navigational aids allowing for instant replay and a change in direction. The polls sponsored by the big media organizations (CBS–*New York Times,* ABC—Harris, and NBC–AP) partly fulfill this function but have a wider role. They are, in and of themselves, pure media events designed to sustain interest in the twelve-month body watch otherwise known as a presidential election. They are also triggers for the press corps. Remember the Reagan-Anderson debate? The day after, the press was inclined to declare Reagan the main beneficiary of the encounter. Then came the results of the ABC–Harris poll, which stated that Anderson had come out ahead by six points. A few days later, exhilaration in the Anderson camp was crushed by the NBC–AP poll, which gave less favorable readings. Then came the *coup de grâce* by CBS–*New York Times,* which put Anderson decisively behind. Cynical press coverage of Anderson mounted, and as he sank yet lower in subsequent polls, he ran into deeper financial crisis. Anderson had been trying to borrow money from the banks, using his standing in the polls to argue that his candidacy would draw more than 5 percent of the vote on November 4 and hence qualify him for federal funding, out of which the banks could be repaid. Poll status and consequent shortage of money went hand in hand in a downward spiral.

The use of polls by the media can present a candidate with devilishly tricky problems. The prevailing myth is that all reporters are objective and fair. But the poll is a fine example of just how subjective and unfair the game really is. The same question asked in different ways elicits different responses. Take, for example, "Would you vote for John Anderson?" and "Would you vote for John Anderson if you thought he could win?" Polled answers to the first question made him a loser; to the second, a near winner. Then came the spiral. The reporters objectively announced that, according to the latest poll, John Anderson was a loser. The woeful countenance of the loser was spread across television. The next poll showed him even lower. He began to lose nightly news transfusions. And so it went. Plane, camera, computer: coordinates of modern democracy.

* * *

Ronald Reagan survived the fall campaign because at that time, in their heart of hearts, not enough people thought he would blow up the world; because of the hostage crisis in Iran; because the Democratic, not the Republican party became infected with the toxin of Hooverism; because the electorate was indeed—just as Reagan suggested—worse off in 1980 than it was in 1976. So Reagan not only survived. He triumphed.

And he triumphed too because ideological consensus in the academies, the press, and the Congress tilted decisively to him in all the central assumptions of his appeal: that the Russians were in the process of attaining military superiority and were intent on global subversion and expansion; that big government had got too big; that the economy was in crisis; that a momentous reorientation away from the tenets of the New Deal was in order.

It was only after January 20 that it began to become rapidly apparent what redirection Reagan and his advisers actually had in mind. But by then, of course, campaign rhetoric had served its purpose.

THE 1980 EARTHQUAKE: REALIGNMENT, REACTION, OR WHAT?

Walter Dean Burnham

I

Election analysts have long recognized that some elections are more important than others.[1] These infrequent "critical" elections involve major and durable realignments of power blocs, the shape of public policy, and the basic structure of coalitions in the electoral marketplace. Such realigning elections have occurred in the United States during the Jacksonian Era, in 1860, around 1896, and during the New Deal.

In recent years the question has been hotly debated as to whether critical realignments—at least in their classical form—have not become extinct.[2] Those who take such a view point to the overwhelmingly massive evidence for *dealignment* in the American electorate. This dealignment is directly associated with the near-collapse of the intermediary role of political parties in shaping voting decisions in recent decades, and the resort by more and more voters to other cues (notably those provided by public relations imagery and television) to their vote—that is, if they vote at all. More generally, dealignment is associated with the exhaustion of historical alternatives to the structures of power that dominate American economy and society today. That is to say, it is associated with the supposed inevitability of the modern interventionist political-capitalist state, and the impossibility of the two leading alternatives to it—social democracy on the Left, and a return to neocapitalist orthodoxy on the Right.

It is the most obvious thing in the world that a conclusive answer to the analytic problem of the 1980 election—realignment, dealignment, or simply a huge deviation?—cannot be provided just now. The future character of the American electoral market will be determined by what the Republican winners of the 1980 election do with their victory. It can be flatly asserted, however, that the 1980 election, whether realigning or not, is the most important such political event since the New Deal realignment itself. Not even the 1948 election provided the country with so big a shock as the one just past; and—it goes without saying—1948 will have had almost trivial policy consequences compared with those in immediate prospect. The global results are already well known.

First, an elected incumbent president was defeated in his bid for re-

98

election for the third time in the twentieth century. Moreover, this was no narrow loss. At the height of the Great Depression, Herbert Hoover won only 39.6 percent of the total popular vote, and 11.1 percent of the electoral vote, in his 1932 bid for reelection. In 1980, Jimmy Carter did little better: 41.2 percent of the total popular vote, and 9.1 percent of the electoral vote. Even in two-party terms, the magnitude of Carter's loss (44.7 to 55.3 percent for Ronald Reagan) was almost as large as the margin by which Adlai Stevenson was defeated by Dwight D. Eisenhower in 1952.

Second, the man chosen to replace him was not just another Republican. Ronald Reagan was and is the charismatic prophet of the now-dominant Right. He is clearly the most conservative president elected since Hoover won office in 1928. As we shall see, this does not remotely imply that any huge proportion of the electorate voted for him on ideological grounds: but we can anticipate many ideological consequences.

Third, the size of Reagan's final victory was predicted by no one, including any known polling organization. But even this shock pales in comparison with the enormous Republican victory in the Senate elections. Prior to November 4, even the most sanguine Republicans assumed that they might gain four or five seats in the Senate. In the end, the gain was twelve—the largest since 1946, and in a presidential year the largest since 1920. As a result, the Republicans have won easy control of the Senate, and there are good reasons to suppose that they may keep this control for quite a while. With extreme conservatives like Senators Thurmond, Hatch, Garn, and Helms now chairing the Senate's committees, the policy change in the 97th Congress will not be incremental; it will be a severely jolting experience.

Fourth, the relative magnitude of the Republican gains in the House of Representatives was more restrained, since the structural considerations in modern House elections—in particular the electoral insulation of most incumbents from electoral tides elsewhere—did not vanish into thin air. Still, the modal preelection projection had been for a Republican gain of between a dozen and twenty seats; again, no one foresaw a gain of thirty-three, or a margin of 243 Democratic to 192 Republican. If most Democratic members won reelection, such key majority-party leaders of the 96th Congress as John Brademas of Indiana and Al Ullman of Oregon went down to defeat. The party margin is now close enough to make it probable that a conservative coalition will take over policy control of the House on a great many issues. The prospect is for unified conservative control of the entire federal government for the first time since 1953—indeed, one suspects, for the first time since 1929.

This is the more likely since the Democratic leadership is more demoralized, in greater disarray, than in living memory. It is almost not too much to say that an entire generation of older Democratic Senate liberals perished in the electoral earthquake of 1980. In the House, it would seem very likely not only that southern conservative Democrats will coalesce with their Republican brethren on many policy issues, but that others—convinced that liberalism has been repudiated—will shift ground to the Right in the interests of perceived self-preservation. Ascending from the wreckage of 1980 is an already endlessly repeated theme: The Democratic party has run out of ideas, it has no common purpose, it must rediscover some reason for existence. This conventional wisdom, as we shall see, has a great deal to recommend it. Indeed, in retrospect this is a very peculiar "majority party." If it retains a lead over the Republicans of 45 to 25 in party identification, it finds itself almost always "underproducing" victories in the electoral market. This is particularly true of presidential elections. In the generation since 1952, there have been eight of these elections: four Republican landslides (1952, 1956, 1972, 1980), one Democratic landslide (1964), and three extremely close elections, two won by Democrats (1960, 1976) and one by Richard Nixon (1968). The eight-election mean (on a two-party percentage basis) has been 47.7 percent Democratic, 52.3 percent Republican. By now, this is just about enough—despite the huge sloshing around from election to election which characterizes the modern period—to say that at the presidential level, at least, the country has something approaching a normal Republican majority as a matter of fact, if not as a matter of party identification.

Virtually no one anticipated a result so fundamental or so astounding. It is more than usually necessary to make the attempt, even so early after the fact, to place this earthquake in its context and to evaluate its implications. We turn first to an evaluation, in greater detail, of what actually happened.

II

Turnout. Probably the first question to ask in any election analysis is who voted and who did not. On the basis of virtually complete information, turnout in 1980 continued to fall for the fifth time in a row. At 54.0 percent of the voting-age population, national participation reached the third lowest level since the creation of a national party system and a democratized presidency in 1828. This, however, does not do full justice to the subject. Throughout most of our twentieth-century political history, the southern states followed an exclusionary policy directed against blacks, with the result that that region had much lower turnouts than the country as a whole. Only with the passage of effective voting-rights legislation in 1965 did this gap begin to close. By 1980, it had virtually disappeared for two reasons: continuing relative improvement in southern turnout, and continuing participation declines in the rest of the country. To get some sense of the true magnitude of the participation problem, it is useful to make a long-term regional separation in turnouts, expressed as percentages of the total potential electorate. This is provided, for the period 1824–1980, in Table 1.

TABLE 1

The Appearance and Disappearance of the American Voter: Turnouts by Region and Nationally, 1824–1980

PRESIDENTIAL TURNOUT RATES

YEAR	North and West	Border*	Non-South	South†	National	
1824	25.5%	35.0%	27.1%	27.4%	27.2%	
1828	60.6	68.4	61.6	42.6	57.3	
1832	64.8	62.7	64.6	30.1	57.0	
1840	82.0	77.4	81.5	75.2	80.2	
1844	80.2	79.8	80.1	74.3	78.9	
1848	74.5	70.2	74.0	68.2	72.7	
1852	73.7	59.9	72.0	59.4	69.4	
1856	82.9	66.7	81.0	72.0	79.2	
1860	84.6	73.3	83.3	76.3	81.9	
1864	80.8	43.2	75.9	(Civil War)	75.9	
1868	86.4	58.5	82.8	71.5	80.9	
1872	75.3	66.6	74.0	67.0	72.3	
1876	87.0	78.7	85.8	75.3	83.3	(Last Reconstruc-
1880	87.6	77.4	86.1	65.1	81.0	tion election)
1884	84.8	76.6	83.7	64.3	79.1	
1888	86.3	83.7	86.0	63.8	80.8	
1892	81.5	78.5	81.1	59.2	76.1	
1896	85.6	89.3	86.1	56.9	79.5	
1900	82.3	85.7	82.7	43.4	73.7	
1904	76.6	76.7	76.6	29.0	65.6	
1908	75.6	79.2	76.1	30.8	65.8	
1912	67.1	71.4	67.6	27.8	59.0	
1916	68.1	76.6	69.1	31.7	61.7	
1920	53.6	63.6	54.9	21.7	49.2	(General Wom-
1924	57.4	58.3	57.5	18.9	48.9	an Suffrage)
1928	66.7	64.5	66.4	23.5	56.9	
1932	66.3	65.7	66.2	24.3	56.9	
1936	71.8	68.0	71.4	25.0	61.0	
1940	73.7	67.4	72.9	26.1	62.4	
1944	66.8	56.4	65.6	24.5	56.3	
1948	62.8	54.2	61.8	24.9	53.4	
1952	72.1	66.3	71.4	38.4	63.8	
1956	69.8	64.2	69.2	36.6	61.6	
1960	73.6	66.0	72.8	41.4	65.4	
1964	69.6	61.5	69.0	46.4	63.3	
1968	66.6	59.8	66.1	51.8	62.3	
1972	61.7	55.1	61.1	45.7	57.1	
1976	58.8	54.5	58.5	48.8	55.8	
1980	57.3	54.0	56.9	50.0	55.1	

*Border states: Kentucky, Maryland, Missouri, Oklahoma, West Virginia.
†Southern states: Alabama, Arkansas, Florida, Georgia, Louisiana, Mississippi, North Carolina, South Carolina, Tennessee, Texas, Virginia.

Note: Throughout, aliens are excluded from the population-base denominators on which these estimates are based. This is not the case with most contemporary (post-1960) reporting of turnout as percentage of the total voting-age population including aliens: hence the discrepancy with the 55.1% figure for 1980 and the 54.0% (voting-age population) mentioned in the text.

If, as is often argued, realigning elections are closely linked with out-pourings of new voters and significant increases in the turnout rate, then 1980 does not qualify on this criterion. Instead, we must ask ourselves what, if anything, this election has in common with those of 1920 and 1924. For taking the non-southern states as a whole, participation rates in 1980 are barely higher than the all-time lows reached in 1920, and are distinctly below the levels set in 1924, hitherto the second lowest rate ever reached in the past 150 years of presidential elections. Surely there is no comparison so far as sex differences in turnout are concerned. These were massive in the years just after woman suffrage in 1920—the spread seems to have been on the order of 30 percent or so. Today, this difference has wholly disappeared. There may, however, be other similarities, and to such speculations we shall return. For now, it is worth noting as a practical matter that the results look rather different if one takes the candidates' percentage of the total citizen electorate as the benchmark. Of the total vote cast, Carter won 41.0 percent, Reagan 50.7 percent, and Anderson and others 8.2 percent. Of the total potential electorate, however, the results are Carter, 22.6 percent; Reagan, 28.0 percent; others, 4.5 percent; the "party of nonvoters," 44.9 percent. Without in any way attempting to deny the magnitude of Reagan's victory, it is worth observing that his share of the potential electorate is not much larger than the share of Republicans among party identifiers in the electorate as a whole, and is rather *less* than the 28.2 percent Wendell Willkie received in 1940 while going down to a landslide defeat at the hands of Franklin D. Roosevelt.

Some argue that nonvoting in the United States is also a nonproblem from an analytic point of view. I cannot agree. In the short-term sense that only people who vote are likely to have their preferences counted, or in the equally short-term sense that landslides and "mandates" will be evaluated—and have practical policy consequences—only in terms of the vote actually cast, the argument is obviously correct. But it is also banal. Ever since the early years of this century, the most conspicuous comparative difference between the United States and other advanced industrial societies has been the much higher levels of abstention here than there. It has also been clear for many years that the "party of nonvoters" in the United States is concentrated among the poorest and most dependent social classes.[3] There is a huge "hole" in American participation much more sharply class-stratified than any recent election between Republican and Democrat. As I have long argued, this "hole" seems inseparably linked to another crucial comparative peculiarity of the American political system: the total absence of a socialist or laborite mass party as an organized competitor in the electoral market.[4] Evidence for this proposition has been presented elsewhere, and the point is glaring enough on the face of the participation data presented by the Census Bureau's surveys to require no further elaboration here.[5]

Moreover, there is specific reason to suppose that in 1980 there were sharp candidate-preference differences between those who voted and those who did not; and particularly between those who had exerted themselves to register and those who did not. These data, taken from the final preelection CBS/*New York Times* poll, demonstrate this point, while reflecting as usual a much closer balance between the two leading candidates than actually existed in the end (Table 2).[6] Even discounting for the apparent gap of more than five percentage points between this poll's aggregate result and the overall outcome, it seems nearly certain that the relative partisan differential of about ten percentage points between registered and nonregistered adults remained. Indeed, since we lack postelection information about any change in nonregistered preferences, it might well have been more than 10 percent in the end.

Viewed overall, it is perhaps not too surprising that a relatively unpopular conservative Republican candidate could win about 28 percent of the potential citizen electorate. What is shocking is the collapse of Carter's position and that of the Democrats generally. What kind of a "majority party" is it whose incumbent president wins the support of scarcely a fifth of the electorate? Clearly, if Reagan was relatively unpopular, Carter by election day had become extremely so. As we shall see, there are important reasons for supposing that more than one key to the conundrum of 1980 can be found in the Democratic party itself, and the dynamics within it which gave us Jimmy Carter as its presidential candidate in the first place.

Demographics and Attitudes: Where Was the Swing Concentrated? How "Ideological" Was It? In a landslide "surge" such as occurred in 1980, we can reasonably expect that most groups in the population will have joined in the swing toward the winning party or candidate. This is what happened. It is patent from the remarkable survey data given us by

TABLE 2

Two-Party Data on Candidate Preference, Stratified by Turnout Category among Adult Population (1980)

CATEGORY OF ADULT	TWO-CANDIDATE VOTE		
	% *Carter*	% *Reagan*	*Lead*
Registered voters (71% of sample):			
Most likely to vote (top 25%)	47.1	52.9	5.8 R
Middle group (50%)	49.95	50.05	0.1 R
Least likely to vote (bottom 25%)	52.8	47.2	5.6 D
Adults by registration status:			
Registered (71% of sample)	49.4	50.6	1.2 R
Nonregistered (29% of sample)	59.4	40.6	18.8 D
Total adult population (100%)	52.3	47.7	4.6 D

The New York Times just after the election that the usual underlying group differentials in party support remain, but also that in some respects they have been curiously eroded, to the net advantage of Ronald Reagan and the Republicans. In what follows, we should observe that analysis is couched in two-party (or two-candidate) terms. This implies the judgment —one I believe to be well-founded—that the much-touted "Anderson difference" turned out in the end to approximate zero. This candidate, running as a solo centrist Independent, was ultimately unable to define a stable constituency for himself. His support, originally in the mid-20s, finally fell below 7 percent as his initial supporters drifted, apparently in more or less even proportions, to one or the other of the major candidates.

The full array of this survey is presented in Appendix Table A.[7] Here we highlight some of its more salient findings.

Partisanship. There were a few groups in the electorate whose support for Jimmy Carter, on a two-candidate basis, was actually larger in 1980 than in 1976. One of the most striking examples was among liberal and moderate Republicans, who showed a negative Republican swing of eleven and three percentage points, respectively. This suggests a pale last glow of a much more powerful movement among such Republicans the last time a conservative Republican ran, the movement against Barry Goldwater in 1964 which produced such remarkable results as a better than 2-to-1 Democratic victory in Vermont, which had never before gone Democratic. But such movements among the residual self-identified liberals in the GOP were much more than offset by Democratic defections of 8 percent among moderate Democrats and 9 percent among conservative Democrats, along with a 9 percent decline in Carter's support among moderate Independents. At the end of the day, Reagan had won 28 percent of self-identified Democrats and Carter only 12 percent of self-identified Republicans. Independents as a whole broke 36 percent for Carter, 64 percent for Reagan, an overall decline of 8 percent in Carter's share of this crucially important category of voters. For what it may be worth, we note that this gross result closely approximates that of 1952 on this dimension as well as on the whole: Eisenhower won 27 percent of Democratic identifiers, 66 percent of Independents, and 96 percent of Republicans.

Group Preferences: Demographics. In terms of class structure variables and age, Reagan's major gains over Ford in 1976 came in what might be called "middle America," by almost all criteria. People in the middle-income bracket (family income of $15,000–24,999, 30 percent of the sample) swung most heavily Republican (7 percent). Blue-collar workers swung most heavily in the gross occupational classifications used in this survey (8.5 percent)—in fact, producing a Reagan lead of 1 percent. On the educational front, the largest swing away from Carter was among those who had some college (12 percent), followed rather closely by those with high school education or less (8 percent). People with college degrees shifted only from 45 percent Democratic in 1976 to 41 percent in 1980. Labor union households showed a larger swing than nonunion households; in-

deed, Carter's 4 percent lead over Reagan was the poorest showing in this
core Democratic group of any candidate in modern times except for George
McGovern in 1972. Finally, voters who fell within the age bracket 30–44
swung Republican much more heavily than any other age group, in sharp
contrast to 18 to 21-year-olds, who were as a group *more* Democratic in
1980 than their older brothers and sisters had been in 1976. It seems clear
from all this that, taken as a whole, Reagan's very considerable gains
among middle-income, middle-educated, younger-middle-aged voters
were not compensated by any Carter gains among the groups where he did
best in 1976: younger, better-educated, and more affluent voters.

But there are three extremely salient demographic cleavages in 1980
which make this election stand out, and which require a fuller discussion:
race, sex, and religion.

As to race, it is not too much to say that blacks were among the chief
losers of the 1980 election: 84 percent for Carter in 1976, they were 85
percent for him in 1980. Whites, on the other hand, shifted from 48
percent to 40 percent Democratic, and Hispanic Americans from 76 percent to 60 percent. In many important respects, blacks and Carter had a
peculiarly close relationship. The social and economic policies of the
American Right, with its stress on pure achievement standards (as the
white middle class interprets achievement) and on "supply-side" economics, has little to say to the interests of blacks or any other group which has
a strong dependence on or linkage to the state. As a group, they are more
nearly isolated now than they have been since at least the beginning of the
civil rights revolution in the 1950s. If the country really does go conservative as a long-term proposition, they lose, just as the subordinate classes
and races of the Third World countries lose.

So far as sex is concerned, one of the chief truisms of American politics
has always been that—at least so far as major-party candidates are concerned—there is very little difference in voting behavior along such lines.
By comparison with, say, sex-related differences in voting Communist or
Christian Democratic in Italy, they remained moderate in the American
elections of 1980—but only by such a comparison. For the gap between
men and women increased to 8.5 percent, the largest ever recorded. Similarly, while the male vote shifted fully ten percentage points from 1976
to 1980 (51 percent for Carter to 41 percent four years later), the female
shift was only 1.5 percent (51 to 49.5). What are the explanations for this?
Basically, there are two rivals in the field. The first, deriving from pretty
universal historical experience in non-American situations, stresses a generalized propensity for women to be more conservative than men whenever politics is so structured that major-party choices have a conservative-
radical polarity.[8] Implicit in such an explanation is the view that there is
a *macho* quality among male voters which is sometimes tapped—in the
American case, notably where what might be described as androgynous
candidates present themselves to the electorate. Presumably, such an explanation might be advanced to account for Eisenhower's particular

strength among women in 1956 ("reassuring, grandfather-figure"), and McGovern's exceptional weakness among men in 1972 (32 percent among men, 38.6 percent among women). Were we to extend this line of argument to the Carter-Reagan race in 1980, the nexus would be found in a much greater female than male sensitivity to the risks involved in electing Reagan to the presidency—notably the supposed risks, which Carter stressed so much in his campaign, of thermonuclear war. Alternatively, it might also be said that men were especially repelled by Carter's record in office, and perhaps precisely by his image of humility and long-suffering in the face of extreme provocations such as the Iranian hostage situation.

Obviously, much more information will be needed before one can pass on such rather sweeping "gestalt" issues. But it does seem that the major alternative explanation finds some direct support from the data of this survey. Women in favor of the Equal Rights Amendment (ERA)—22 percent of the entire sample—gave Carter 63 percent of their vote. On the other hand, women against the ERA (17 percent of the whole sample) split for Reagan by a 31–69 percent margin. There can be little question that, overall, Reagan's opposition to ERA contributed in no small part to the drag on his appeal to women. And it may be inferred—circumstantially at least—that the so-called war-peace issue made an important contribution as well. In any event, this sex-related polarization, if modest, is one of the most striking differences between 1980 and preceding elections. If we turn to the famous "typical voter" developed by Scammon and Wattenberg, the 47-year-old wife of a machinist living in Dayton, Ohio, we must remain doubtful as to whether she voted for Carter or Reagan in the end. Her husband, on the other hand, probably voted for Reagan.

The question of religion in the 1980 election is a much more complex matter. This is a year, more than any other since the quite different religious battles of the 1928 or 1960 elections, in which high-intensity religious groups have come to the center of the political stage. The pervasiveness of religious cognitions in American political life is yet another—and very important—comparative peculiarity of this country in the cosmos of advanced industrial societies. Two of the candidates in 1980 were personally "born-again" Christians (Carter and Anderson), while the third expressed a very traditional American religiosity and was the favored candidate of such new ecclesiastical Right groups as Moral Majority. The whole matter deserves more extensive treatment in its own right, and we have made an effort to do this in Appendix A. For the moment, we will confine our remarks to the demographic side of things.

Briefly put, the Democratic party's liberal wing has become associated with issues such as abortion on demand which are anathema to a minority of Roman Catholics and some evangelical Protestants. Carter's "mistake" in the March 1 vote at the UN on Israel, coupled with his brother's "Libyan connection" and the administration's generally critical attitude toward the Begin government, placed Jewish voters in a classic situation of cross-pressure. Carter suffered relatively staggering losses among both groups, with Catholics shifting from 55 percent to 44 percent, and Jews from 65 percent to 54 percent of two-candidate preferences in 1976 and 1980, respectively. To some indeterminate extent, the Catholic shift can probably be read as being linked with the increasingly solid position of most Catholics in "middle America" somewhere, with an additional minority thrust contributed by "right-to-life" Catholics seeking a constitutional amendment to outlaw abortion on demand. The Jewish debacle—clearly the lowest Democratic margin among Jews since 1932, if not before—is a more straightforward expression of anxiety and suspicion of Carter's intentions vis-à-vis Israel. Still, it should be emphasized here that we are speaking only of *decisively large minorities* among Jews and other groups, not "Jews as a whole," "Catholics as a whole," and so on. If the anti-Carter swing among Jews was large at 11 percent, it was just as large among Catholics; and in the end Carter did win a two-candidate majority of the Jewish vote. On the other hand, it is the shift of decisively large minorities which decides the outcomes of elections and which, if permanent, can lead to outright political realignment.

Attitudes and Life Situations. The Carter years were associated with the decay of the American empire abroad and the deterioration of the political economy (and many Americans' posttax, postinflation real income) at home. The visible symbols were the endless Iranian hostage imbroglio on the one hand, and rampant inflation and high unemployment on the other. For some years, a massive attitudinal shift has been underway toward support for higher levels of defense spending and a tougher national line against the USSR. Similarly, the work of Edward Tufte and others who analyze political economics in the age of the political-capitalist state have stressed a great deal of aggregate sensitivity in the electorate to economic conditions.[9] The "misery index" (a crude additive model of unemployment and inflation rates) at one point in early 1980 reached 28, the highest value since the collapse of the laissez-faire system in 1932. Later, it settled down to a more modest figure, somewhere in the 20–24 range. But this was more than high enough, in retrospect, to arouse suspicions that the incumbent would be decisively rejected by the voters. The great American middle classes are being relentlessly squeezed by adverse international and domestic change. To an exceptional extent, this campaign was fought out in terms of a debate—much more implicit than explicit, but nonetheless central—between those who believe, with Reagan, that revitalization of "the American dream" in the 1980s is possible and those who, with Carter, believe that privation and a historically revolutionary decline in mass expectations are inevitable.

The relatively few attitudinal-situational items in *The New York Times* survey convey something of what was apparently going on within the electorate. Of all the 1976–1980 shifts recorded, the most massive were those associated with respondents' judgments as to whether over the past year their family finances had become better, were about the same, or had grown worse. It is quite characteristic of our economically disordered time that only 16 percent of the sample believed their finances were in better shape, as compared with 34 percent who saw themselves as worse off and 40 percent who saw little or no change from 1979 to 1980. If those in the "better off" category gave Carter a 59–41 percent lead over Reagan and those who responded "the same" split evenly (50–50), the large minority who believed themselves worse off gave nearly a 3-to-1 lead to Ronald Reagan (28 percent Carter, 72 percent Reagan). Viewing the change from 1976 to 1980 in terms of incumbent party-candidate rather than Democratic and Republican in both elections, it is rather striking that Carter did somewhat better than Ford among the "worse-off" group, and strikingly less well among the "better-off" group (incumbent up 5 percent in the first category, down 11 percent in the second). The overall profiles do not look so very different: the dramatic difference is that the proportion of those who regard themselves as "worse off" has grown steeply from about one-fifth of respondents to more than one-third.

When respondents were asked to say whether they regarded inflation or unemployment as a more serious problem, two rather surprising things happened. First, despite the great hue and cry which has surrounded the issue of inflation in the past year or two, only 44 percent of respondents chose that as the more important problem; 39 percent were more preoccupied with unemployment. This, without doubt, reflects the aftermath of the stagflation recession which the Carter administration engineered in late 1979. Even more striking is that defections from Carter—not only in absolute but in relative terms—were concentrated among those for whom unemployment was the most important problem. Among those selecting inflation, Reagan won 67 percent, up only two points from Ford's 65 percent showing in 1976. Among those worried about unemployment, on the other hand, the decline in Carter's support was fully nineteen percentage points (from 75 percent in 1976 to 56 percent in 1980).

This kind of question is recognized to tap important class-related differentials in the American population. Put it its crudest, people who worry most about unemployment are much more likely to believe themselves or their families at direct risk than people who worry most about inflation—in short, vastly oversimplified, working-class versus middle-class respondents. The candidate gap was fully forty percentage points in 1976; by 1980, it had dropped to twenty-three. The reason for this, I believe, is twofold. First, Carter's essential economic policies were Republican policies—though obviously of an old-guard, Establishment character rather than the New Right, capitalist-populist economics favored by many in the Reagan coalition. Such policies could hardly appeal to the core elements of the northern ex-New Deal Democratic coalition. This was, after all, precisely the point of Edward Kennedy's primary challenge to Carter. Kennedy put the matter too extremely, and not very politely, when he referred to Carter as "Ronald Reagan's clone"; but he did touch an essential reality of this administration and of this election.

It would not be impossible in this context, after all, to arrive at a semi-Downsian judgment of what happened in 1980 along this dimension. Jimmy Carter, elected out of nowhere and coming to the fore in the hard vacuum of the "majority party in disarray," owed little and gave less to the core elements of this unwieldy coalition in the industrial states. Only when 1980 came along and he was required either to retire or seek reelection did Carter, opting for the latter, suddenly rediscover the historic virtues of the Democratic party as one concerned with jobs and with the welfare of the ordinary person. The map of his primary losses to Edward Kennedy tells much of the story. Why, apart from considerations of traditionalism in party or group identification, should a working-class voter continue to support the most conservative Democratic president for his time since Grover Cleveland left office in 1897? If the election was in some important sense between anger at Jimmy Carter and fear of the great unknown which Ronald Reagan evoked, anger eventually won. When the returns from Flint, Michigan, are in, we shall probably learn that participation declined steeply and that, among those who still voted, there was a brisk shift toward Ronald Reagan. In view of the city's current unemployment rate of 21.5 percent of the labor force, why should those not be the electorate's dynamic movements in 1980? One is almost tempted to make two final observations as we begin to leave the trees and contemplate the whole forest. In the first place, if a president who leads the so-called party of the people works on behalf of others across his four-year term, he cannot expect that "the people" will work for him on election day. In this respect, Anthony Downs's discussion of the causes and effects of rational abstention may repay another reading. Second, in the country of the blind, the one-eyed man is king. There is nearly total policy and intellectual disarray within the Democratic ranks today. The Republicans offer, on the other hand, an apparently coherent alternative, a plausible way out of the quagmire.

An Ideological Election? Our detailed journey through the electoral terrain of 1980 suggests pretty strongly that at the level of the mass electorate, it had become a question of throwing Jimmy Carter and the Democrats out with whatever alternative was available. In a room with only two exits, people will surge toward one, wherever it leads, if the other is blocked in some way. Very much of the 1980 shift, it seems to me, can be linked to a negative, highly general, public rejection of a failed incumbent administration. This is likely to occur when the levels of pain and anxiety in the electorate are pretty high, and when the "ins" are held responsible by decisive minorities of voters because they are "ins." Our *New York Times* survey underscores this point. Fully 38 percent of Ronald Reagan's supporters gave as their chief reason "it is time for a change," a situation very reminiscent of 1952. By contrast, only 11 percent of these Reagan supporters gave as their primary reason "he's a real conservative," a figure which compares with the 15 percent who gave no reason at all. Moreover, fully half of this "time-for-a-change" group were unwilling to cite any other reason (whether party identification, leadership, judgment, experience, or "conservatism") for their choice. A simple profile of the two broad Reagan groups permits certain inferences which fall well within the mainstream of modern survey research explanations of the vote (Table 3).

What comes out, overall, is a group which seems markedly more weakly socialized, probably lower in the class structure, less conservative, more Democratic, and significantly less enthusiastic about the final choice than the other (residual) category of Reagan supporters. It would be futile as well as premature to make guesses about the levels of cognitive constraint within the 1980 electorate as a whole compared with earlier years, or to assert that there was no ideological component in the choice patterns of voters. There certainly seems to be no doubt that issues and issue voting played a major role in the outcome. But as one looks more closely at these issues, they appear to converge on economic distress, foreign policy anxiety of a generalized kind, and a personal rejection of Jimmy Carter (and, one assumes, the Democrats) as the incumbent target of wrath. It has never before happened in modern times that the Republicans have been able to take the offensive on bread-and-butter economic issues. Their being able to do so contributed decisively to their victory. In the end, it seems reasonable to conclude that the Reagan-Republican landslide victory of 1980 was forged in the crucible of a more pervasive and intense public discontent than anything seen in modern years. It was very probably not an "ideological" election at the grass roots, but rather a case of "throw the rascals out." It would therefore correspond well to V. O. Key's observation that the public voice in such episodes is both powerfully loud and, at the same time, indistinct. But, whether ideological or not at the grass roots, the election will be put to ideological ends by those who won it.

TABLE 3

Differences between Reagan Supporters, 1980

| VOTER CATEGORY | TYPE OF SUPPORTER | | |
	"Time for a Change"	All Other	Differential
Conservatives	34	42	−8
Favoring Equal Rights Amendment	39	29	+10
Democrats	27	19	+8
Age group 18–44	60	45	+15
Decided final week of campaign	29	16	+13
Support for Reagan:			
Strong	27	51	−24
Favor, but with reservations	42	29	+13
Voting mainly against the			
other candidates	27	11	+16
DK, NA	4	8	−4

The Geography of the Vote. Voters, of course, live not only within social groupings, but in definite geographical locations. At least a word about these aspects of political geography is in order. Obviously, residence can be stratified in the standard survey pattern: big-city, smaller-city, suburban, and rural residence. As we would expect, Reagan was weakest among big-city dwellers, followed by small-city residents and then by suburbanites and rural voters. But electoral geography also permits a more extensive view of strength, weakness, and long-term change in a major-party coalition. Indeed, certain probabilities about the near future emerge which are not quite so visible in any other way, particularly when 1980 and its immediate setting are evaluated in terms of long-term demographic change.

We begin with Map 1, which shows the Democratic percentage of the two-party presidential vote in the 1980 election. Several points are noteworthy about this electoral geography. The most striking of all is the shift of a political Mason-Dixon line from its old North-South position to an East-West position. A line drawn along the 96th meridian of longitude bisects the United State remarkably cleanly. East of it, a few states can be found which fall in the bottom two quartiles, including suburban Connecticut, New Hampshire, and New Jersey, and fast-growing Florida. To the west of it, with the sole exception of Hawaii, is solid Reagan country. It is in particular in the Plains and Mountain states that Reagan won by enormous majorities.

In the southeastern quadrant of the country, one doesn't quite know whether to be surprised that Jimmy Carter lost everything but Georgia, or that so many of these losses were by phenomenally close margins. Had the Reagan swing been only one percentage point less than it actually was, Carter would have won the electoral votes of Arkansas, Mississippi, Tennessee, Alabama, Kentucky, South Carolina, and Massachusetts (71 in all). Still, the pre-1976 voting behavior of this region suggests the magnitude of the problems facing any non-southern Democrat in appealing for its electoral votes. As for the northeastern quadrant—broadly, the Snow-belt center of aging cities and industries—Carter's loss to Reagan was on the whole not of enormous proportions. In relative terms, this area of the country has now rather decisively emerged as the most steadily Democratic of all. This is hardly surprising, for here older ethnic, racial, and trade union concentrations are linked to a concentration of economic decline as well. Even if not in the special circumstances of 1980, it is here if anywhere that the compensatory interventions of the political-capitalist state are most likely to be welcomed, and most likely to be widely felt to be necessary. Conversely, the presence of robust population and economic growth on one hand, and the relative absence of indicators of decay and dependence on the other, make the Sunbelt in the West and in parts of the South prime targets for a continued growth of Republican-conservative dominance.

Map 2, showing the comparative magnitude of the 1976–1980 swing,

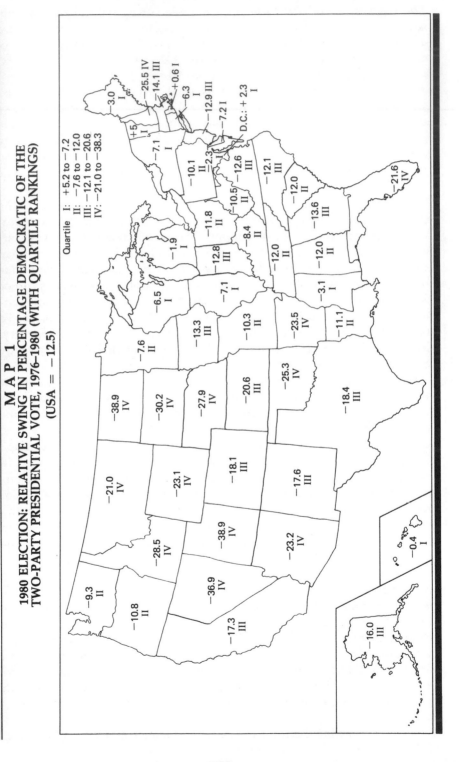

MAP 1

1980 ELECTION: RELATIVE SWING IN PERCENTAGE DEMOCRATIC OF THE TWO-PARTY PRESIDENTIAL VOTE, 1976–1980 (WITH QUARTILE RANKINGS)

(USA = −12.5)

Quartile   I: +5.2 to −7.2
         II: −7.6 to −12.0
        III: −12.1 to −20.6
        IV: −21.0 to −38.3

paints the same picture. It suggests, moreover, that the pro-Republican swing is concentrated in the areas where the Reagan percentage was largest; and, conversely, that it tended to be least in places where Carter did best in 1980. In other words, the regional differentials—already quite evident in the distribution of the 1976 vote—became significantly more extreme in 1980. Once again, the key regional differential lay between a growing West and a declining Northeast, with the South occupying what is probably a temporary and unstable proximity to the Northeast dependent on the fact of Jimmy Carter's candidacy.

This pattern is, if anything, even more sharply delineated when the long-term Democratic trend from 1952 to 1980 is considered (Map 3). For the country as a whole, this trend has been nearly zero, though partisan swings have ranged back and forth from a Democratic maximum of 61.5 percent in 1964 to a Republican maximum of 61.8 percent in 1972. Regressing the percentage Democratic of the two-party vote across this time period for each state yields a regional differentiation which, to an almost incredible degree, is a mirror image of the sectional polarization marking the critical election of 1896. The bottom quartile (most pro-Republican trend) is concentrated in two core areas, the intermountain West and the states of the Deep South. The top quartile (most pro-Democratic trend) is similarly concentrated in two places: the far Northeast (New York and New England), and the upper Midwest, centered around Minneapolis.

It is not difficult to tease out the very broad regional implications of these trends. There were a number of major contributing factors in the sectional polarization of 1896. Clearly the most important was the fact that the states in the northeastern area of the country were part of the imperial or "metropole" heartland during the age of primary industrial development. In no small part, the 1896 election was fought over the terms and beneficiaries of this industrial-capitalist development. The Republican party then was the only organized commitment to the political logic of industrial capitalism which made sense in either intellectual or coalitional terms. Eighty-five years and a million intervening variables later, a profound reversal of fortunes has revealed itself. Sometimes referred to as the contemporary struggle between Yankees and Cowboys, between Snowbelt and Sunbelt, emerging political conflict is becoming organized around energy-surplus/energy-deficit issues, and around the rapidly accelerating decay of the old industrial heartland as international economic competition grows.

The gross boundary between the top and bottom halves of the nation on this long-term trend line broadly etches the difference between those parts of the country which have acute and obvious urban decay problems and those which do not; between those parts of the country which are absolutely or relatively losing population, and those which are not; between those parts of the country whose surplus energy "taxes" in an age of expensiveness are high and those whose are not; between those parts of the country where blacks and unions are relatively well organized, and

MAP 2
1980 ELECTION: PERCENTAGE DEMOCRATIC OF TWO-PARTY PRESIDENTIAL VOTE AND QUARTILE RANKINGS
(USA = 44.7%)

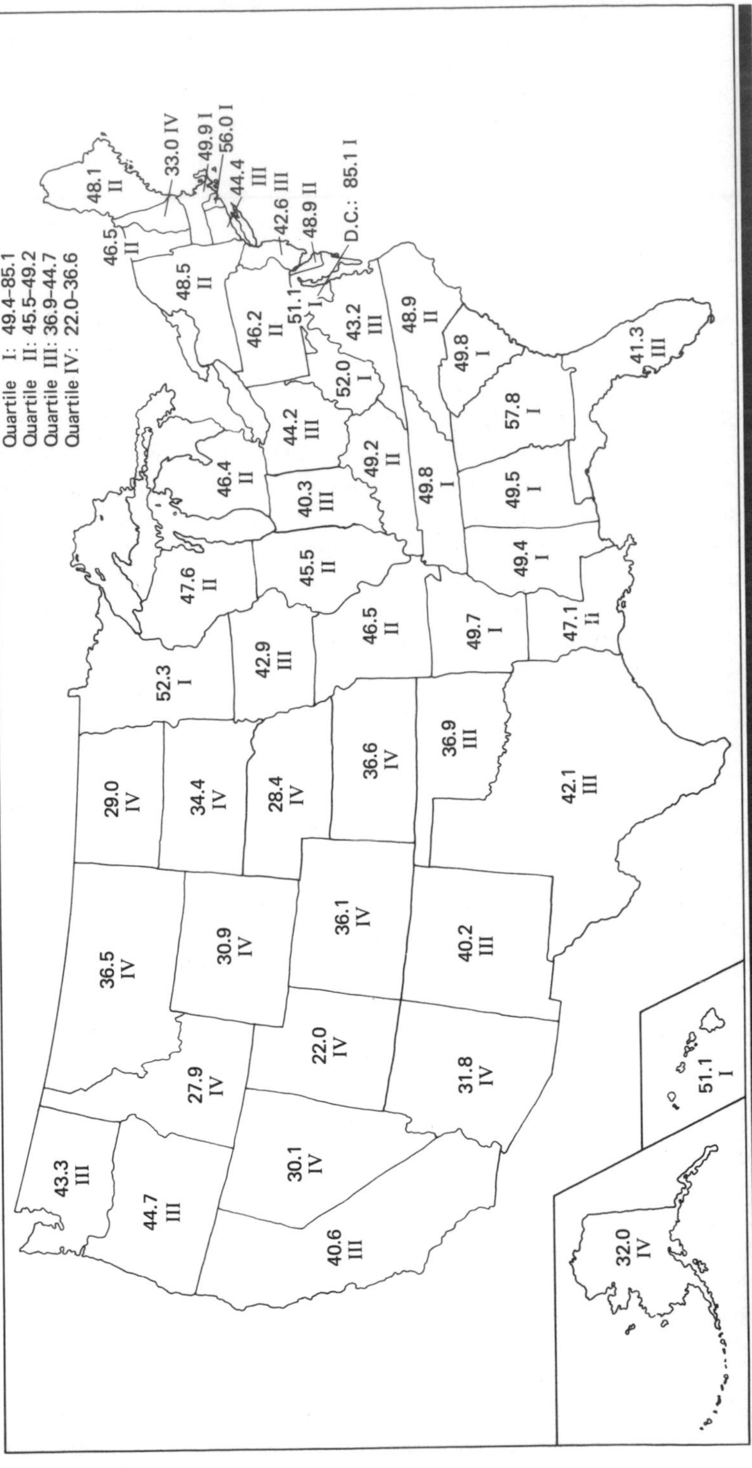

Quartile   I: 49.4–85.1
Quartile II: 45.5–49.2
Quartile III: 36.9–44.7
Quartile IV: 22.0–36.6

48.1 II

33.0 IV

49.9 I

56.0 I

44.4 III

46.5 II

42.6 III

48.9 II

D.C.: 85.1 I

48.5 II

51.1 I

43.2 III

48.9 II

46.2 II

52.0 I

49.8 I

41.3 III

46.4 II

44.2 III

49.2 II

57.8 I

40.3 III

49.8 I

49.5 I

47.6 II

45.5 II

46.5 II

49.7 I

49.4 I

52.3 I

42.9 III

47.1 II

29.0 IV

34.4 IV

28.4 IV

36.6 IV

36.9 III

42.1 III

36.5 IV

30.9 IV

36.1 IV

40.2 III

27.9 IV

22.0 IV

31.8 IV

43.3 III

44.7 III

30.1 IV

40.6 III

51.1 I

32.0 IV

those where they are not. The highly visible "sagebrush rebellion" resembles nothing quite so much as a revolt by those who are personally and situationally successful against the burdens imposed on behalf of those who are not. If Ronald Reagan's main stock in trade in the 1980 campaign was to preach the hope and optimism that "the American dream" is not dead after all, it would be likely to be a particularly compelling argument for the active voters of those parts of the country where it had never seriously come into question in the first place.

And who can doubt that the entire demographic movement described between the 1970 and 1980 censuses points squarely in a pro-Republican direction? There is the continuing heavy movement toward the Southwest and Florida, sure to be reflected in the 1982 reapportionment scheme for the House of Representatives. There is a most striking relative movement away from metropolitan areas as a whole and toward rural and small-town areas, many of which had until 1980 not reported a population gain of note in more than fifty years. And, of course, within metropolitan areas the decline of the central cities has accelerated. The population becomes daily more deconcentrated—a problem which may well haunt us in the future if we ever need to go to World War II style gasoline rationing, but which for the moment represents a major area of growth for Republicanism and conservatism. Speaking only from a New England perspective, we may well say in this regard that, as New Hampshire goes, so goes the nation.

A Note on the Senate Election. We return for a somewhat more detailed discussion of the senatorial earthquake of 1980, a more remarkable event if possible than the presidential election itself. This discussion is quite deliberately focused on the spatial distributions of Map 3 and their implications. Only twice from the end of World War II until 1980 has a party lost twelve Senate seats without any corresponding gains: in 1946, bringing a temporary Republican ascendancy, and in the Democratic landslide year of 1958. Moreover, at *no* time since the upheaval of 1932 has either party lost as many as nine incumbents in a general election. The normal course of events is such that *some* countertrend races occur somewhere in the thirty-odd Senate contests every two years. The exceptions correspond to years in which a very strong thrust toward one party is evident: since World War II, in 1946, 1948, 1958, 1964, 1966—and 1980. The "supershift" cases—where there are no countertrend elections and where a net shift of at least five seats occurs—are more infrequent still: the 1946–1948 pair, 1958, and 1980.

It is much more often than not that "supershift" years have enduring consequences for the balance of power in the Senate. The most conspicuous case in modern times is that of 1958, which replaced partisan parity by a Democratic majority. That majority was to survive for more than twenty years. Whether the 1980 Republican upsurge will prove equally durable is, of course, impossible to say. We do know that the profile which is up for election in 1982 presents some exceptional Democratic targets for

MAP 3
REGIONAL DIFFERENTIALS IN SECULAR PARTY TREND, 1952–1980:
TERM OF REGRESSION LINE (BASED ON % DEM. OF TWO-PARTY VOTE) AND QUARTILE DISTRIBUTION
(USA 1952–1980: Y_c = 47.88 − 0.03X)

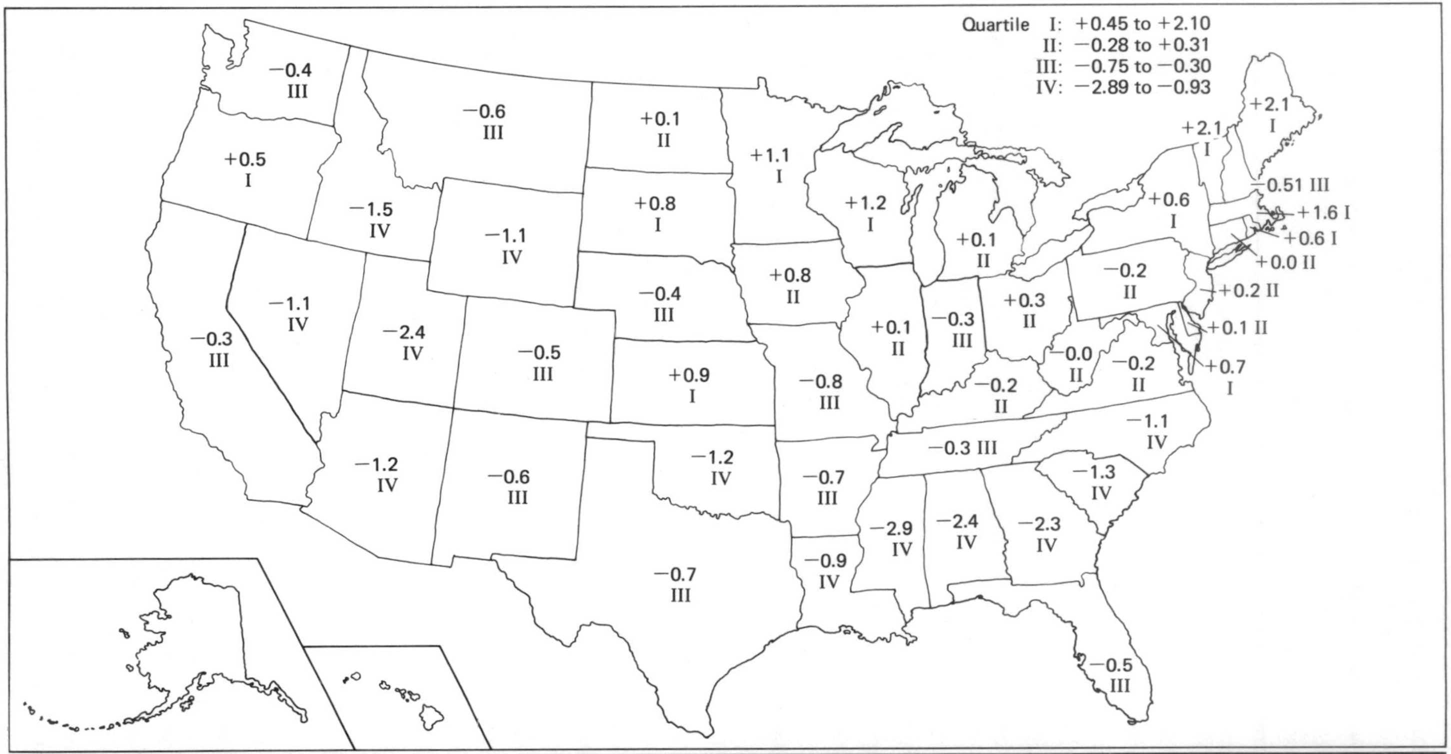

Quartile I: +0.45 to +2.10
         II: −0.28 to +0.31
        III: −0.75 to −0.30
         IV: −2.89 to −0.93

Republicans and comparatively few Republican targets for the opposition. But we know other things as well.

The most widely remarked feature of the 1980 Senate elections was the wholesale defeat of old Democratic liberal senators who had been around for many years: Nelson of Wisconsin, Culver of Iowa, Bayh of Indiana, McGovern of South Dakota, Church of Idaho. But underlying these defeats, and the even more remarkable Republican gains in the South, was what can only be described as a resurgence of Republicanism as such. The contrast between what happened in 1980 and Richard Nixon's "lonely landslide" of 1972 could hardly be more striking. In that year, despite Nixon's overwhelming lead, the Democrats actually made gains in the Senate. If one Democratic incumbent was defeated and three open seats held by Democrats went Republican, four Republican incumbents lost their bids for reelection and two formerly Republican open seats were won by Democrats. But there is more to the story even than this. As we have seen, the popular vote margins for Reagan in the southeastern states were tiny, and Carter easily won Georgia. Yet Republican Senate candidates were elected in the Democratic open seats in Florida and Alabama, while conservative Democratic incumbents were ousted in Georgia (in the teeth of Carter's local victory) and North Carolina. It is not entirely clear what "coattails," if any, may have been involved. But these elections —even more than the more famous ones in the North and West—reflect a powerful and probably autonomous, if convergent, *Republican* tide.

Consider again Maps 1 and 3. A long-term Republican trend which has been proceeding for decades at the presidential level now seems to have caught up with Democratic senatorial candidates—incumbents and open-seat contenders alike—for essentially the first time in postwar political history. The South in particular seems in movement from solid Democratic to predominantly Republican. If in 1946 and 1952 all twenty-two senators from Dixie were Democrats, by 1980 the balance had become eleven Democrats, ten Republicans, and Harry Byrd of Virginia, a Republican in everything but name. The movement in the sparsely populated Mountain states (including Alaska) has been scarcely less dramatic, and is now approaching completion. Without attempting too long a look ahead, it seems accurate to say that the Democrats cannot look forward to better than parity at best with the Republicans in the Senate for the foreseeable future. Whether we will eventually see a more or less "solid" Republican South and West in the Senate remains to be seen, of course. But such has been the trend, and it does not take much contemplation of the fact that the Senate is an unapportioned body—in which Alaska counts as much as California—and the fact of such shifts to lead to the suspicion that the Republicans may be in command of the Senate for quite a while to come. This, if so, will be one of the more important revolutions in modern American political history. As 1958 began a long era of liberalism in public policy, with the Senate often leading the way, so 1980 marks its obvious close. One thing is absolutely certain in all this: An entire generation of older Democratic liberal leadership has gone under in the earthquake of 1980; if past upheavals are any guide, we can expect that it will take quite a long time for the party to pull itself back together again.

WHAT DOES IT ALL MEAN?
REFLECTIONS ON THE 1980 ELECTION
AS A HISTORICAL MOMENT

Now that we have conducted our preliminary *tour d'horizon* of the 1980 battlefield, the time has come for an effort at synthesis. American elections have a notably heteroclite character. Not only are they structurally complex events on an order of complexity found nowhere else; they also project analytic perspectives which differ widely according to the level at which the analysis is pitched. The amount of disagreement among presumably competent scholars as to what is really out there in the electoral market remains distressingly high. The long-protracted debates over voter rationality, the extent to which American voters display cognitive competence in relating themselves to political stimuli, and the significance and extent of issue voting, are all symptomatic of this problem. What is even worse is the fact that no decent bridges have even now been built to connect many of these levels.

Consider the problem of the density of ideological thinking in the American electorate, particularly as it relates to the programmatic consequences of the 1980 election—consequences which will be more extremely conservative than anything the country has seen for fifty years. As we have observed, there is fairly good reason to suppose even this early that a very substantial part of Regan's voters—far more than necessary to elect him (or Carter for that matter, had one-third of them switched to or stayed with him in the end)—were not reacting personally in terms of an ideological *Weltanschauung.* From evidence of the recent past, indeed, it is not at all likely that ideological or near-ideological strata in the electorate constituted more than at most one-fifth of those who voted, even by a relatively relaxed definition of ideology.[12] Yet many political activists (including many who are not Republicans, like Senator Tsongas of Massachusetts) believe that this election was the clearest conservative mandate in a generation. Nor are such observers wrong. They are certainly not wrong as a matter of subsequent policy fact, since President Reagan and the 97th Congress will certainly fashion conservative public policy in a quite abrupt break with the recent past. But they are also not wrong, in a certain important sense, so far as the mass electorate is concerned.

This paper is scarcely the place to attempt any definitive bridge-building in an area of scholarship (voting analysis) which is today in considerable intellectual disarray. What follows is a mere suggestion of an explanatory scheme which might help to reconcile such apparently divergent arguments as those we have just stated. It is based upon two primary propositions about voters in general. The first of these is that voters take their world pretty much as they find it. This can in some empirical situations involve adherence to political parties dedicated to radical-revolutionary or reactionary-counterrevolutionary overthrow of the existing political, economic, and social system. For their world contains historical, ecological, demographic, and economic "givens" which make such responses to it both rational and highly ordered. But in the American case in particular, the uncontested hegemony of liberal capitalism in the political-cultural domain has systematically excluded any such alternatives to an existing state of affairs, at least since the Civil War. Indeed, the more one looks at American politics as a whole in a comparative context, the more it becomes, as it were, a politics of *ceteris paribus.* Had all other things been equal; had no serious "struggles in the state" ever developed; had radically divergent political subcultures associated with class, nationality, and other struggles under conditions of capitalist socioeconomic modernization never broken out; had the typical pattern of secularization in the religiocultural domain never materialized with the spread of science, technology, bourgeois social relations, and urban-industrial economic relations —had all these things never happened in the cosmos of advanced industrial societies with democratic political systems, they would look much more like the United States than they actually do.

Why should this be so? The basic rationale for undestanding American politics—alluded to by European observers of the American scene from Crèvecoeur in the eighteenth century through Tocqueville and Bryce in the nineteenth and Münsterburg, Siegfried, and others in the twentieth— achieved classic synthesis in Louis Hartz's study, *The Liberal Tradition in America,* [13] as amended by the concept of "fragment society" which Hartz and his associates subsequently developed. We may put this argument in terms favored by the Italian Marxist theoretician Antonio Gramsci. Hegemony is an invariable and essential ingredient in the reproduction of relations of domination and subordination in all class societies, and is "carried" and propagated by intellectuals organically linked to the dominant mode of production. This hegemony in the cultural domain is, accordingly, propagated in one way or another by all the society's communications media, including the church (or, as in the United States, the churches, more than 350 of them), the school, the press, the conscript army (as in pre-1914 France, for instance), and other primary institutions. But the crucial difference between the United States and most if not all other advanced industrial societies with democratic political regimes is that in this country alone, *hegemony has been effectively uncontested.*

The basic thrust of Hartz's comparative argument is that there has been one and only one dominant intellectual-cultural tradition to be reproduced by the media instruments of hegemony, the tradition of individualist-liberal capitalism. The underlying comparative historical reality which made so remarkable a thing possible can be summarized in four words: no feudalism, no socialism. Throughout the vast bulk of American political history, two essential ingredients for state-building were missing. First, there were no organized social solidarities in conflict with each other over capitalist modernization. In other words, there were no "struggles in (or over) the state" between traditionalist manorial nobility on one side and the king and bourgeoisie on the other; hence no stage of incipient or actual royal absolutism; and subsequently, no effectively organized struggle between an ascendant capitalist ruling class and an alienated proletariat. Second, from the end of the Napoleonic world wars until the destruction of Europe's international power position in World War II a century and a quarter later, there was no permanent or serious military pressure—no credible, much less deadly, international threat—with which the Americans had to contend.

A full analysis of these and many other contributory variables cannot remotely be attempted here; we note only in passing the following summary observations.

1. The United States has a constitutional regime which is of almost incredible antiquity and cumbersomeness. This "Tudor polity," as Samuel P. Huntington calls it, seems frozen in a time which elsewhere disappeared centuries ago.[15] It is an unconsolidated state; a "system of multiple cracks"; a system which was precisely and accurately called by one of its creators, James Madison, a "feudal constitution." It has survived so long and with so little fundamental change solely because—as both Hartz and Huntington recognize—it rests, as did English constitutional arrangements under Elizabeth I, on a *consensus rei publicae*.

2. Empirical studies of contemporary American political culture have pretty conclusively demonstrated that this uncontested hegemony has been received and internalized by most Americans.[16] Of course, this does not reach the level of ideology in most cases. To the contrary: as Hartz rightly observes, where there is no organized conflict over the fundamentals of collective existence in society or economy, what elsewhere would require ideological clarity for its defense tends to recede here below the level of consciousness to become "prejudices" or "inarticulate major premises." If Robert Lane's analysis of the problem is accurate, one effect of this mass reception—and more important of the many serious barriers to the development of any coherent view rivaling individualist-liberal capitalism in the culture—appears to be an atomization of response to stress in the average American's personal life. This includes an introjection of guilt or blame for the inevitable *relative* failure in this culture's terms which he or she experiences.

3. As the Constitution is archaic and nondeveloping from a comparative point of view, so the culture as a whole appears not to have passed nearly so far along the path toward *secularization of outlook* as could be anticipated, granted the overall modernity and "superdevelopment" of the American political economy. This matter is addressed at greater length in the Appendix essay, "Social Stress and Political Response." We will

confine ourselves here to two observations. First, a diffuse and pervasive religiosity is much more important a component in the reproduction of America's uncontested hegemony than seems commonly appreciated by social scientists. This religiosity is heavily derived from the traditions of *dissenting Protestantism* which was brought to these shores by the founding population in the seventeenth and eighteenth centuries. Second, a completely characteristic American pattern of reaction to severe cultural stress has been the periodically recurring religious *revival movement,* usually of ultra-evangelical Protestant character. These episodes have come and gone in waves from the time of Jonathan Edwards in the mid-eighteenth century to that of Billy Graham, Oral Roberts, and others in the mid-twentieth. This pervasive reliance on religious modes of countering the effects of social stress on the individual will in itself tend to "crowd out" such wholly secular alternatives to "the liberal tradition in America" as Marxism. With a dominant emphasis on the personal salvation of the individual, the Christian religiosity of the American political culture reinforces the *social compartmentalization* of the individual's response to stress and failure in his or her own personal milieu.

4. As Americans have not been able after all to escape history forever, the collapse of the free market economy in 1929 produced intolerable social conditions, and hence the rise of the interventionist political-capitalist state. Unless we join in the heroic assumptions of neo-Victorian economic conservatives about the causes, consequences, and cures of this epochal collapse, the probabilities are that the political-capitalist state has come to stay. Opinion data consistently make the point that Americans are in the main eager to get the particularized benefits coming to them personally which this state offers. But they also make it clear that, as such, it is not well loved among most Americans.[17] As an empirical matter, the post-New Deal political order has seemed to offer opportunities for capital accumulation and for the promotion of social harmony and welfare. Not the least important of the ingredients of the latter was the damping down of the capitalist business cycle's destructive effects. But, essentially, its justifications have been empirical only—and, almost always, couched in the form of propositions that it makes capitalism work better, that it makes a continuation of the "American dream" possible. At no time has the American political-capitalist state been presented intellectually as an alternative to the basic values of individualist-liberalism and of capitalism in the culture. Rather, its claims to legitimacy rest upon the ultimately more aleatory grounds that it is supposed to be an improvement, almost in the sense that a road construction project is an improvement.

As we have suggested, the bulk of the American electorate have taken the world as they have found it. If the political-capitalist state enjoyed widespread support for so long, if the Democratic party was the normal majority party after 1932 and even after 1945, the explanation surely lies in two dimensions. First, the new state seemed to "work" empirically for many years. High levels of individual aspirations not only continued, but were realized on a mass scale after 1945. Second, conservatives and Republicans suffered for a very long time from their class and ethnocultural narrowness of outlook. The Democratic coalition enjoyed such long-term ascendancy as it had precisely because "the nature of the times" seemed to permit Americans to have it both ways: to gain the benefits of the political-capitalist state without having to pay excessive costs, and to enjoy the pleasures of continually rising affluence and—for many—rising social status as well. In such a world, it seemed that only cranky ideological perfectionists and corporate oligarchs would be likely to decry the passing of relatively simon-pure laissez-faire. Similarly, the acute long-term problems involved in attempting to process the policies of the political-capitalist state through a feudal constitutional structure were widely unappreciated; so was the problem that, in some fundamental sense, the political-capitalist state as such enjoyed only at most derivative legitimacy in the culture.

Of course, the reasons for this happy state of affairs, ultimately, lay outside partisan politics or the activities of policymakers. Broadly speaking, there were two uniquely favorable historical conjunctures, and they were closely connected. The first was the Great Boom of 1945–1970, the longest and most affluence-generating economic boom in the whole history of American capitalism. The second was the emergence of the American empire on the shattered ruins of the international balance of power which had existed since the end of the Napoleonic wars. This empire was (and is) in deadly rivalry with its Soviet counterpart: but in fact, outside the carapace of Soviet bloc states, it long enjoyed world ascendancy in economic, military, and geopolitical terms.

From a domestic point of view, this world historic change in the international position of the United States had a most important consequence. If there had been little enough purchase within the traditional American political culture for a mass-organized Left-radical critique of an existing liberal-capitalist order before World War II, the rise of Soviet-American rivalry put a quietus to it—very possibly for good. Conflicts which in the history of European political development had been vertically structured within each polity were now increasingly "exported" into the *international* arena. At one pole stood the "super-Marxist" power, the USSR; at the other, the "pure-capitalist" power, the USA. On the domestic level, this ideological and power rivalry between empires was to provide a conclusive reinforcement for uncontested hegemony in the United States. As the claims of the Third World for *international* redistribution of resources (from "us" to "them") came to be heard more and more loudly, this fixative became still more fixed substantively, even if some token concessions were made by American policymakers for practical reasons. The uproar over the Panama Canal treaty in 1979 owed no small part of its intensity to a growing reaction within American public opinion against such claims. This reaction was further amplified in recent years by the rise of OPEC and the Iranians' seizure of the American embassy in Tehran.

Most Americans (at least those in the active electorate these days) have profited from the empire's existence, and from America's economic preeminence within it. One suspects that, however obscurely, they have sensed that they have profited from it. Anxiety over its decline—reflected in direct economic costs, such as in the price and availability of oil and other scarce resources, and in growing Soviet military and geopolitical power—clearly had a great deal to do with Ronald Reagan's election in 1980. In this regard, one of the findings of *The New York Times* poll should be repeated here: 54 percent of the respondents agreed with the statement that the United States should take a more forceful line against the USSR, even if this increases the risk of war; only 31 percent disagreed. Of those agreeing with the statement, 70 percent voted for Ronald Reagan and 30 percent for Jimmy Carter. Of the less than one-third who disagreed with such a "forward strategy," only 36 percent voted for Reagan, compared with 64 percent for Carter. Unfortunately, this question was not asked in 1976. But there can be little doubt that, as is the case with attitude questions dealing with the adequacy of our defense spending, there has been a sharp movement toward a harder international line in our public opinion over the past four years. Clearly, this is what Ronald Reagan promised to deliver if elected; almost certainly, this is what will be delivered: 1980 is the election in which the empire strikes back.

If loss of control over the international environment has prompted a patriotic, nationalist response with considerable religious overtones in some quarters, loss of economic growth has dramatically disclosed the shaky foundations of the political legitimacy of late capitalism that welfare programs and transfer payments to economically dependent sections of the population have developed. The only way to pay for so expensive a state is to achieve and maintain sustained economic growth. If growth stops, the economy and society acquire a zero-sum character, as Lester Thurow has recently pointed out. At some point along the way, the state will appear to grow intolerably expensive to those who must pay for its activities through taxation and inflation. As living standards decline and an expensiveness threshhold is reached, revolts against the state's domestic expenditures grow exponentially. Protest movements from Mogens Glistrup's party in Denmark to Howard Jarvis's Proposition 13 in California attest to this. And Ronald Reagan, without any doubt at all, tapped a sensitive nerve when he argued that the problem is not that the people have been living too well, but that the government has been living too well.

In the peculiar American situation, the disappearance of the surplus as the competitive position of American capitalism has deteriorated in the world has thrown the leadership of the Democratic party into massive intellectual confusion. It has done more: it has disclosed that the political-capitalist state with which the Democratic party is so closely identified no longer "works." But this had been its chief, if not sole, claim to legitimacy. Stripped of this claim, its managers and defenders must inevitably wind up in intellectual and policy disarray. To move toward a social-democratic position is literally unthinkable for many or most of them, and the only coherent alternative is that represented by the resurgent Republicans. In the specific situation facing the United States at the moment, everything favors the use of the contemporary state's capital-accumulation and imperial-defense functions to the exclusion, more or less, of its social-harmony and welfare functions.

The whole point of any zero-sum game (like chess, for example) is that people who win do so in direct proportion to the losses of others. The whole point of post-1945 "growthmanship" in political economics had been to prevent zero-sum games from dominating politics because of their cumulatively destabilizing character. As we move toward zero-sum conditions, it is difficult to see how Democrats can embrace the full range of capital-accumulation strategies which are basic to the program of "reindustrializing America." Were they to do so, they would have to abandon huge numbers of ordinary Americans, making the organized representation of interests in an industrial class society even more ineffective than it now is. As we have indicated, one important proximate reason for Ronald Reagan's victory over Jimmy Carter was that Carter had in fact gone a very long way in this direction. By doing so, as an incumbent, he handed the "economic issue" over to the Republicans—the first time in modern history that has happened.

One may indeed wonder, if this analysis is at all correct, how, when, and under whose auspices the Democrats will rediscover a common sense of identity, purpose, and intellectual understanding of their world. If social democracy is excluded a priori as an alternative, political capitalism no longer delivers the goods, and they can't really merge outright with the Republicans and Milton Friedman, what can they do? They can, of course, wait for Ronald Reagan and his allies to fail and, if they do fail, pick up the pieces as a desperate electorate turns to the opposition. But of course, it is possible that they will not fail. And even if they do, the stark alternatives remain: capitalist revitalization, social democracy, or a revived political-capitalist consensus. In the meantime, one can only repeat the words of the psalmist: when the trumpet gives forth an uncertain sound, who will gird himself for the battle?

And what of the voters in all this? We have spoken to some extent of the proposition that they take their world as they find it. In America, that means a pretty stable structure of experiences and expectations derived from living in capitalist society. It also means concrete choices in concrete historical circumstances. These choices are, of course, shaped by uncontested hegemony in the cultural domain, reinforced by the fixative which international competition between Marxist and capitalist, between "poor" and "rich," between "south" and "north," provides. Within this largely deterministic matrix, voters also attempt to do a second thing: to express their interests through the political process.

Expressing interests is, in the first place, a matter of the level, density, and structure of political consciousness. Such consciousness is overwhelmingly a variable, not a constant. I very much doubt that there is any such general phenomenon as *the* nature of belief systems in mass publics. It is by no means surprising to find that, if Anthony Downs's spatial model of party competition cannot be squared with the ways most Americans act in elections, the same model seems to work parsimoniously and effectively to account for Italian voting behavior.[18] We come very close here to the threshold of the old debate in leftist circles about "false consciousness" versus consciousness of presumably some other kind. This issue can, I believe, be finessed here. It is perhaps enough to make the point that— even in David Truman's terms—potential interests will not become actually realized interests with any effect at all on the political process unless or until they achieve some form of *effective organization.* It is very probable that a full articulation of conscious political interests in a population requires an underlying structure of opposition on some fundamental issue of collective existence—be it religion, nationality, social class, or something else. The fundamental characteristic of a *ceteris paribus* politics based upon uncontested hegemony in the cultural domain is that many interests will never be perceived at all, much less organized in the electoral market; and that all will be more or less skewed toward what the system supported by this uncontested hegemony can provide. It is precisely because the United States has such a politics that there is no remote possibility of creating Gramsci's "modern prince," the party-as-collective-intellectual, within it.

As Lee Benson and others have pointed out, this state of affairs does not lead to a disappearance of interest conflicts, but rather to their more or less infinite expansion and proliferation. Crucial swing voters in both the middle and the working classes shifted to Reagan in 1980 because they were directly hurt or threatened by Carter's economic policies, policies which called for sacrifice, constraint, and unemployment without ever remotely suggesting why such sacrifices were called for, or what to do to make the burden of sacrifice more equitable. Crucial swing voters among American Jews were repelled by what they saw to be Carter's policies toward Israel. Evangelical Christians apparently swung toward Reagan in protest over the growing moral laxity they saw in American society. And so it goes.

Still, the overriding issues of this election were almost certainly economic and imperial-maintenance issues, with the former the more important. Perhaps the most durable interest most American voters have is the maintenance of the "American dream" itself: the promise of a better life, and particularly the promise of a better life for one's children. By all comparative standards, such a dream has been predicated on hugely optimistic assumptions, and such general social optimism has been at a heavy discount in recent years. Maintenance of the voter's personalized aspirations cannot be understood as an interest objective apart from the implicit assumptions surrounding it. These, quite literally, are not debated or reflected upon, but are matters of course: a healthy growing capitalist system at home and overwhelmingly convincing strength internationally.

What all this means at the end, it seems to me, is that in the specific historical conjuncture of 1980, the election was decided by a coalition of voters of highly diverse specific interests, but also of a common interest. With social democracy invisible and the Democrats' political-capitalist message increasingly seen as part of the problem rather than the solution, there was only one place for the voters in this coalition to go. Ronald Reagan promised above all that the "American dream" could be revitalized. Perhaps even more important, he projected a boundless faith and optimism that the traditional ways could work; and in this, stood in sharp contrast to a Carter whose message appeared to be gloomy, pessimistic, and confused.

We should stress at the end, as at the beginning, that nearly half of the American electorate did not participate at all in this election. These nonvoters are concentrated at the bottom of the class structure. There is a high probability that any potential interests they might possess cannot achieve organized expression so long as uncontested hegemony survives. It would seem more than reasonable to suppose that debates between the defenders of a confused and degenerate political capitalism on one side and the resurgent advocates of social and economic conservatism on the other are simply irrelevant to a great many of them. As the debate is overwhelmingly a typically American middle-class debate, one could well suppose that others who are not exercised by one or another variant of the "American dream" but have literally no alternatives would rationally abstain. They would do so for exactly the reasons that Anthony Downs laid down twenty years ago—namely, that in such conditions the individual's party differential is zero.

The congressional turnout rate in Shirley Chisholm's poverty-stricken district in Brooklyn was 18 percent of the estimated potential electorate in 1980, and the presidential turnout there could not have been more than a few percentage points higher. Clearly this is an extreme case but, like many others, reflects a more general problem. What relevance, after all, would a choice between a Carter and a Reagan possibly have to any potential political interests which the overwhelming majority of adults in this district might possess? Heavy and class-skewed abstention rates are the inevitable consequence of this *ceteris paribus* politics. They will endure as long as hegemony remains uncontested (in other words, as far into the future as anyone can see), and they will probably become more and more extreme as conservatism moves into the ascendant. Whether at some point this stable—and by now nearly oligarchic—equilibrium of forces in American politics will become unstable is, of course, a perennial question. It cannot be dealt with here. It is enough to observe the obvious—that our whole electoral politics rests upon a huge and growing political vacuum at the bottom of the social structure. There are, of course, many ways by which people in such a vacuum can express their interests in politics. By no means are all of these ways electoral, or even institutionalized in any form.

Taken as a whole, the 1980 election may perhaps best be read as a classic electoral case of conservative-revitalization politics. The mazeways of a great many Americans have been seriously disturbed both economically and culturally. The decay of empire and economy, taken together, has created optimal conditions for skilled conservative political entrepreneurs to offer the most consoling and least disturbing way out of the impasse. This quite literally involves a return to the "good old days" when the exactions of the state did not press so heavily on the individual, when the economy was delivering the goods, when the empire was strong and our position within it unchallenged, and when "proper" standards of social and cultural morality were maintained without much question. Rhetorically, at least, the Reagan campaign promised something of a return to two supposedly golden ages: the 1950s internationally, the 1920s domestically.

We need scarcely assume that abnormally large numbers of voters necessarily believe these conservative utopias can be reached in fact, or that "conservatism" as a specifically ideological matter thoroughly saturated the electorate or the swing voters who gave Ronald Reagan his victory. No, the reality is probably not far removed from the picture of the American electorate which was painted by the authors of *The American Voter*, [19] perhaps amended somewhat by the portrait to be found in *The Changing American Voter*. [20] Nor was large-scale "ideological voting" necessary for a conservative outcome. In the most fundamental sense, the 1980 election was a *landslide vote of no confidence in an incumbent administration*. Some of these landslide votes of no confidence (such as 1894 and 1932) have signaled the arrival of critical realignment. Others, such as 1920, 1952, and in a relatively hidden way 1968, did not. All of them reflect, however, major breakpoints in the flow of American political history. They all reflect the temporary or permanent bankruptcy of a preceding ruling coalition, its leadership and its policies; and the exceptionally high levels of pain within the electorate associated with such bankruptcy. The election of 1980 was such an event, albeit much more complex and diverse in its impact than some of our earlier examples. It very probably opens the door into a new phase of our political history.

How long that phase lasts depends on what Ronald Reagan and his allies do with their victory, and perhaps even more on the pressures imposed by the real world at home and abroad. If their conservative hypotheses hold up under the rigorous reality testing which is about to take place, something approximating an older critical realignment may well be in prospect. If not, we will have to consider the grim possibilities implicit in the eruption of a full-fledged crisis of the regime as a whole. For this would be a situation where social democracy is an excluded alternative a priori, liberal political capitalism has been discredited, and the new conservative incumbent leadership also fails to meet the expectations of the American public. To a degree quite unusual in American political history, an enormous part of this country's political future depends on what happens next.

NOTES

1. The literature on critical realignments in American politics has by now become voluminous indeed. See, for instance, the extensive bibliography included in the most recent collection of essays on the subject, Bruce A. Campbell and Richard J. Trilling (eds.), *Realignment in American Politics* (Austin: University of Texas Press, 1980), pp. 329–352.
2. The view that a classic type of critical realignment was occurring in the late 1960s was most forcefully presented in Kevin Phillips, *The Emerging Republican Majority* (New Rochelle: Arlington House, 1969). The opposite position can be found in Walter Dean Burnham, "American Politics in the 1970s: Beyond Party?" in William N. Chambers and Walter Dean Burnham (eds.), *The American Party Systems*, 2nd ed. (New York: Oxford, 1975), pp. 308–357.
3. See my essay, "The Appearance and Disappearance of the American Voter," in Richard Rose (ed.), *Electoral Participation: A Comparative Analysis* (Beverly Hills: Sage Publications, 1980), pp. 35–73.
4. Originally in Walter Dean Burnham, "The Changing Shape of the American Political Universe, *American Political Science Review,* 59 (1965) pp. 7–28.
5. The Census Bureau surveys on registration and voting participation in American elections begin with 1964, and have been issued biannually ever since. The most completely reported of all is that for 1972, *Voting and Registration in the Election of November 1972,* Series P-20, No. 253 (October 1973).
6. *The New York Times,* November 3, 1980, p. 14.
7. Data reworked into two-party format from survey reported in *The New York Times,* November 9, 1980, p. 28.
8. The comparative data on sex differences in voting behavior are very extensive. See, for example, Herbert L. A. Tingsten, *Political Behavior* (London: King, 1937), pp. 10–78; and for recent Italian experience, Samuel H. Barnes's essay in Richard Rose (ed.), *Electoral Behavior: A Comparative Handbook* (New York: Free Press, 1974), especially pp. 191–192.
9. See especially Edward R. Tufte, *Political Control of the Economy* (Princeton: Princeton University Press, 1978); and Douglas A. Hibbs, Jr., "Political Parties and Macroeconomic Policy," *American Political Science Review,* vol. 71 (1977), pp. 1467–1487.
10. Anthony Downs, *An Economic Theory of Democracy* (New York: Harper & Row, 1958), pp. 260–278.
11. *The New York Times,* November 9, 1980, p. 28.
12. See, for example, Norman H. Nie, Sidney Verba, and John R. Petrocik, *The Changing American Voter* (Cambridge: Harvard University Press, 1976), pp. 110–122. An extremely important theme of this work—particularly in light of the 1980 results—is that, as greater levels of cognitive constraint have come into being, there has been a distinct and marked rightward shift in opinion distribution. See the discussion on p. 371.
13. New York: Harcourt, Brace, 1955.
14. Louis Hartz et al., *The Founding of New Societies* (New York: Harcourt, Brace, 1964).

15. Samuel P. Huntington, *Political Order in Changing Societies* (New Haven: Yale University Press, 1968), pp. 93–139.
16. See, for example, Robert E. Lane, *Political Ideology: Why the American Common Man Believes What He Does* (New York: Free Press, 1962). This work is not precisely the fruit of a large-scale scientific sample survey, but more than makes up in depth what it lacks in statistical breadth.
17. See Lloyd Free and Hadley Cantril, *The Political Beliefs of Americans* (New Brunswick: Rutgers University Press, 1967).
18. Compare, for example, Donald E. Stokes, "Spatial Models of Party Competition," in Angus Campbell et al., *Elections and the Political Order* (New York: Wiley, 1966), pp. 161–179, with Samuel H. Barnes, *Representation in Italy* (Chicago: University of Chicago Press, 1977), pp. 97–115. There is no particular reason to suppose that either discussion inaccurately portrays the electorate to whom it refers.
19. Angus Campbell, Philip E. Converse, Warren E. Miller, and Donald E. Stokes, *The American Voter* (New York: Wiley, 1960).
20. Norman H. Nie et al., *The Changing American Voter.*

APPENDIX TABLE A

How They Voted: Two-Candidate Preferences in 1980 and 1976, by Category of Voters

VOTER CATEGORY	% OF SAMPLE	1980 D	1980 R	1976 D	1976 R	REP. SWING
Partisanship						
Democrats	43	72	28	78	22	6
Independents	23	36	64	44	56	8
Republicans	28	12	88	9	91	−3
Political Tendency						
Liberals	17	68	32	73	27	5
Moderates	46	47	53	52	48	5
Conservatives	28	25	75	29	70	4
Party and Tendency:						
Liberal Democrats	9	83	17	88	12	5
Moderate Democrats	22	70	30	78	22	8
Conservative Democrats	8	56	44	65	35	9
Liberal Independents	4	63	37	69	31	6
Moderate Independents	12	37	63	46	54	9
Conservative Independents	7	24	76	27	73	3
Liberal Republicans	2	28	72	17	83	−11
Moderate Republicans	11	14	86	11	89	−3
Conservative Republicans	12	6	94	6	94	0
Democrats for Kennedy in primaries	13	73	27	x	x	x
Politically active Democrats	3	79	21	x	x	x
Politically active Republicans	2	5	95	x	x	x

APPENDIX TABLE A (Cont.)

VOTER CATEGORY	% OF SAMPLE	1980 D	1980 R	1976 D	1976 R	REP. SWING
Region						
East	32	48	52	52	48	4
Midwest	20	45	55	49	51	4
West	11	40	60	47	53	7
South	27	46	54	55	45	9
Race						
Black	10	85	15	84	16	−1
Hispanic-American	2	60	40	76	24	16
White	88	40	60	48	52	8
Sex						
Men	51	41	59	51	49	10
Women	49	49.5	50.5	51	49	1.5
Women for ERA	22	63	37	x	x	x
Women against ERA	15	31	69	x	x	x
Religion						
Catholic	25	44	56	55	45	11
Jewish	5	54	46	65	35	11
Protestant	46	40	60	44	56	4
Born-again white Protestant	17	36	64	(53)	(47)	(17)
Age						
18–21	6	51	49	49	51	−2
22–29	17	50	50	53	47	3
30–44	31	41	59	50	50	9
45–59	23	42	58	48	52	6
60 and over	18	43	57	47	53	4
Family Income						
Under $10,000	13	55	45	59	41	4
$10,000–14,999	14	53	47	56	43	3
$15,000–24,999	30	42	58	49	51	7
$25,000–49,999	24	36	64	37	63	1
$50,000 and over	5	28	72	x	x	x
Occupation						
Professional-managerial	40	37	63	42	58	5
Clerical, sales, other white collar	11	47	53	46	54	−1
Blue collar (manual labor)	17	49.5	50.5	58	42	8.5
Agriculture	3	31	69	x	x	x
Unemployed, looking for work	3	61	39	66	34	5
Education						
High school or less	39	49	51	57	43	8
Some college education	28	39	61	51	49	12
College graduate	27	41	59	45	55	4

A P P E N D I X   T A B L E   A   (Cont.)

VOTER CATEGORY	% OF SAMPLE	1980 D	1980 R	1976 D	1976 R	REP. SWING
Labor Union Status						
Labor-union household	26	52	48	60	40	8
Nonunion household	62	39	61	44	56	5
Respondent's Family Finances						
Better than a year ago	16	59	41	30	70	−29
About the same as a						
year ago	40	50	50	51	49	1
Worse off than a year ago	34	28	72	77	23	49
Family Finances and						
Party Identification						
Democrats						
Better	7	83	17	69	31	−14
Worse	13	55	45	94	6	39
Independents						
Better	3	56	44	x	x	x
Worse	9	24	76	x	x	x
Republicans						
Better	4	19	81	3	97	−16
Worse	11	6	94	24	76	18
Most Important Problem						
Unemployment	39	56	44	75	25	19
Inflation	44	33	67	35	65	2
Attitude Toward USSR						
More forceful, even						
If It Increases						
risk of war: Agree	54	30	70	x	x	x
Disagree	31	64	36	x	x	x
Attitude Toward						
Equal Rights Amendment						
Favor ERA	46	56	44	x	x	x
Oppose ERA	35	28	72	x	x	x
When Respondent Decided						
about Choice						
Knew all along	41	48.5	51.5	44	56	−4.5
During primaries	13	33	67	58	42	25
During party conventions	8	40	60	52	48	12
Since Labor Day (early						
September)	8	36	64	50	50	14
In the week before						
the election	23	45	55	51	49	6

Source: *The New York Times,* November 9, 1980, p. 28.

APPENDIX A
SOCIAL STRESS AND POLITICAL RESPONSE:
RELIGION AND THE 1980 ELECTION

One of the most notable features of the 1980 election has been the emergence of high-energy religious "particles" directly into the electoral arena. To a great extent, this was foreshadowed in 1976 and in 1978—in 1976 by the very considerable importance Jimmy Carter and others attributed to his status as a born-again Christian, and in 1978 by a number of spectacular single-interest campaigns aimed at senatorial incumbents who favored abortion. The religious flood reached something of a full tide in 1980, with the launching by Jerry Falwell and other evangelical ministers of Moral Majority into the electoral market, and with the entry of the Catholic Archdiocese of Boston against pro-abortion congressional candidates in Massachusetts. Perhaps it should also be noted that all three major candidates in 1980—Carter, Reagan, and Anderson—profess having been "born again."

Since at least 40 percent of probable voters in 1980 profess to have had a personal experience of Jesus Christ, the latter convergence is perhaps not to be wondered at. For the United States is, certainly statistically, God's country to a quite remarkable extent.

It is a commonplace of studies which center on social modernization that the transition to advanced industrial society has typically been strongly associated with secularization of belief systems and cognitive perspectives concerning human existence. Whether this is in some transcendental sense a "good" or "bad" thing is beside the point of this argument. It is enough to point out that secularity and socioeconomic development have long been understood to be positively related. In most primitive societies, for example, magical incantations are used to dispel evil when volcanoes erupt or the sun is eclipsed, for it is clear to the population that "the gods are angry." Such perspectives are matters of life and death for their believers; they look quaint, whimsical, or primitive to the populations —or at least the more or less educated classes—of Europe and North America. More generally, as nineteenth-century popes like Pius IX and Leo XIII clearly understood from their own perspective, the arrival of modern science, liberalism, and industrial capitalism has been very hard on traditionally articulated structures of religious belief and social interactions grounded on religious belief.

Viewed as a cross-sectional matter, then, the proposition suggests itself that the higher the level of development in a given society (the closer it is to the "advanced industrial society" end of a developmental continuum), the smaller will be the fraction of its population for whom religious beliefs are of great importance. Conversely, the closer the society is to the "underdeveloped" (presumably traditionalist) end of the continuum, the larger will be the fraction of its population for whom religious beliefs are highly salient aspects of their existence. One convenient measure of the latter is provided by a 1976 Gallup international survey, which asked respondents in a number of countries a series of questions about their religious beliefs. One of these questions asked them to say whether their religious beliefs were very important, fairly important, not too important, or not at all important.[1] The fourteen countries or regional areas included in this survey ranged on this dimension from India (81 percent saying their religious beliefs were "very important") to Japan (12 percent in this category). A useful composite measure of development (date around 1973) is presented by J. P. Cole in his study, *Geography of World Affairs*. [2] This consists of country scores on the first principal component of a multivariate analysis incorporating twenty-two "development variables" in all.[3] The data are presented in Chart 1 on page 135.

Two things are immediately visible on inspection. First, the overall relationship is not only as posited, it is nearly linear and extremely strong. If the two North American "fragment societies" are excluded, fully 96 percent of the variance in the percentage responding in the "very important" category is explained by the composite development variable. Second, the United States in particular does not fit the main sequence at all, and Canada fits poorly. This is reflected in the regressions: when Canada is added, 11.5 percent of the variance explained is lost, and when the United States is also added, the total variance explained declines by 43.5 percent. Put another way, if the United States fit the main sequence line with a development score of 45.6, the percentage of its respondents in the "very important" religious belief category should approximate zero instead of the actual 56 percent. Or, with a 56 percent score on the religious belief dimension, its development level should be about 2.5 rather than 45.6— roughly comparable, therefore, with the development levels found in Chile, Mexico, Lebanon, or Portugal.*

---

*For the reader who is not mathematically inclined, regression analysis refers to a series of statistical techniques whose application quantifies the relationship between two or more variables. Multivariate analysis and multiple regression refer to the application of such techniques to three or more variables. Such quantification for two variables, X and Y, can often be expressed in the linear form $Y = a + bX$, where the functional relationship between X and Y is that of a straight line. The fit between predicted Y values along this line and the actual data or observed values is rarely exact, but a measure of the relative usefulness of predicting Y as a function of X may be derived from contrasting the magnitude of error of such prediction with the magnitude of error of predicting Y values on the basis of the mean (average) of all observed Ys. This interval measure is actually a measure of the proportional reduction of error achieved by the regression, and is derived in the following fashion. For any observed value Y_i, the regression equation will furnish a predicted value $\hat{Y}_i$. By convention, the difference between Y_i and $\hat{Y}_i$ is called "unexplained" deviation, the difference between $\hat{Y}_i$ and the mean is called "explained" deviation, and the difference between Y_i and the mean is called "total" deviation. The proportional reduction in error provided by the regression may be expressed as the ratio of the sum of the squares of all such "explained" deviations to the sum of the squares of all "total" deviations.

This ratio of explained variation to total variation, commonly denoted r^2, is the basic coefficient of determination. Its value ranges from zero to one. Assuming the relationship

Such an extraordinary "outriding" cannot fail to present us with a general contextual variable of the utmost importance for comparative analysis. Surely, for example, the notorious lack of rapport or understanding between Chancellor Schmidt of West Germany and President Carter finds some of its explanation in the fact that most Europeans—and particularly its secularized elites—have nothing in their social experience which makes it readily possible for them to comprehend American religiosity, especially in its "born-again" form. One may even suspect in this regard that (like most American intellectuals in places like Cambridge, Massachusetts) the European attitude is not merely one of incomprehension, but of the kind of condescension the "modernized" tend to have everywhere for the "premodernized."

There is, of course, more to the story than mutual irritations at summit conferences. In European electoral politics, *secularization has been an essential precondition for the emergence of leftist parties, and therefore for the entire matrix of developed alternatives in the electoral market.* This proposition is true in Catholic and Protestant countries alike, and is both sufficiently general and sufficiently powerful a finding of comparative electoral analysis to require no elaborate documentation here.[4] As to how much religious consciousness may be read as more or less "true" or "false" consciousness, compared with class analysis and socialism, is a question which need not detain us here. It is enough to say that one very strongly tends to "crowd out" the other. The teachings of the popes from Pius IX to John Paul II—that one cannot be an "integralist" Christian and a Marxist at the same time—correspond at the level of mass electoral behavior to a very important truth of comparative politics. The failure of leftist—or even laborite—party political alternatives to develop and stay the course in the American electoral market has long been understood to be one of the key problems when it comes to studying this system in comparative perspective.[5] Explanations for this American curiosity have varied widely, from "frontier theses" to arguments stressing American affluence and the persistence of a single, hegemonic "liberal tradition" in the American political culture.[6] Surely each of these explanations accounts for part of this phenomenon. But the more one studies the history of American electoral politics, the stronger seem to become heterogeneous ethnocultural patterns as constraints on the development of such alternatives. Among these, the extraordinary persistence of religious commitments as such must be regarded as an autonomous constraint of profound importance. They bespeak a general cognitive consciousness profoundly alien to such alternatives in the electoral domain.

Why should religious perspectives have retained so exceptional a

---

between X and Y to be linear, an r^2 value approaching zero indicates little reduction in error through the use of the regression, and consequently a weak relationship between the variables. Conversely, an r^2 value approaching unity indicates a strong relationship between the variables.

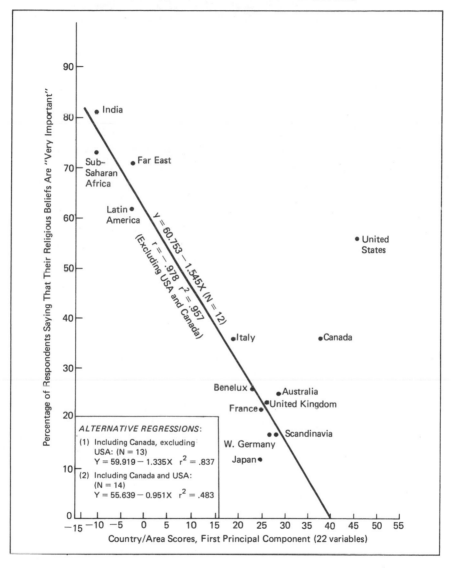

CHART 1
RELIGION AND DEVELOPMENT:
RELATIONSHIP BETWEEN 1976 GALLUP RESPONSES SAYING
THAT RELIGIOUS BELIEFS WERE "VERY IMPORTANT"
TO RESPONDENTS AND COUNTRY SCORES ON THE FIRST
PRINCIPAL COMPONENT OF A
MULTIVARIATE DEVELOPMENT ANALYSIS

Percentage of Respondents Saying That Their Religious Beliefs Are "Very Important"

- India
- Sub–Saharan Africa
- Far East
- Latin America
- United States
- $Y = 60.753 - 1.545X \ (N = 12)$
- $r = -.978 \ r^2 = .957$
- (Excluding USA and Canada)
- Italy
- Canada
- Benelux
- Australia
- France
- United Kingdom
- Scandinavia
- W. Germany
- Japan

ALTERNATIVE REGRESSIONS:
(1) Including Canada, excluding USA: (N = 13)
$Y = 59.919 - 1.335X \quad r^2 = .837$
(2) Including Canada and USA: (N = 14)
$Y = 55.639 - 0.951X \quad r^2 = .483$

Country/Area Scores, First Principal Component (22 variables)

Sources: Religious beliefs: *Gallup Opinion Index* (AIPO), "Religion in America 1976." Developmental Index: first principal component based on 22 development variables, J. P. Cole, *Geography of World Affairs* (London: Penguin, 1979). Situation as of 1973.

dominance here? It would take us too far afield to attempt any extensive analysis of this question at this point. Clearly, the very size of the country, the exceptional ethnic and racial heterogeneity of its citizenry, and the "liberal tradition" as a kind of *lingua franca* regulating exchanges among this diverse population at as low a political temperature as possible, all make a significant contribution to it. More generally, the analysis of "fragment cultures" undertaken by Louis Hartz and his associates seems a promising way to approach the problem.[7] For such explanations stress, rightly, the crucial importance of detaching a founding population from a larger matrix; isolating it thoroughly from any serious external influences or pressures over a very long time; and leaving it in charge of socializing widely heterogeneous bands of newcomers into the dominant myths and symbols of the political and social culture. Nor can one forget that this "state of nature" is also to at least some extent a state of artifice. That is to say, the export of class conflict into the international arena via Soviet-American imperial rivalries in the domain of ideas as of interests has done a great deal by itself to make religious activity a respectable and desirable concomitant of American nationality, and to create a situation in which agnosticism, atheism, and skepticism are denied such respectability. The point is stressed by a sociologist of religion who had unimpeachable conservative credentials, Will Herberg. In *Protestant, Catholic, Jew* Herberg stresses the extent to which—especially by the Augustan Age of the 1950s—the three major religious traditions in America had converged, as it were, on a celebration and "divinization" of the American way of life.[8]

So far as the founding culture argument is concerned, it is well known that the United States was largely founded by people who had, or later acquired, a religious perspective which was shaped by one or another sect of dissenting Protestantism. In this regard, one aspect of the Gallup international 1976 religious survey seems of considerable interest. In Western Europe, 35 percent of Catholics as compared with only 22 percent of Protestants gave a "very important" response. But in the United States, those so responding were 68 percent of Protestants and only 60 percent of Catholics: an American increment of 46 percent among Protestants, compared with 25 percent among Catholics.

So far as the "crowding-out" argument is concerned, we may wish to identify the American social groups among whom the "very important" response is highest. They include, in order, nonwhites (72 percent), people of grade-school education (70 percent), housewives (68 percent), and Protestants (68 percent), the latter constituting 61 percent of the entire sample. Except for housewives, such people in Europe would be particularly fertile ground for socialist entrepreneurial activity in politics—Protestants because of greater secularism of attitude, nonwhites and grade-school educated because of their modal position in the class structure.

If American religiosity has always been something of a "brooding omnipresence" in our political skies, it has not always been a front-and-center phenomenon in our political conflicts. Viewed over time, the most striking thing about this dimension is that it comes and goes in a wavelike pattern. There have been many, many religious revivals—all of them of evangelical Protestant character, demanding "rebirth," "commitment to Our Lord," and so on—from the time of Edwards and Whitefield in the mid-eighteenth century to the crusades of Billy Graham and Oral Roberts in the contemporary era. Issues directly associated with Protestant social *angst,* apart from such revivals, have regularly spilled over into the political arena in moments of exceptional cultural stress. These have historically included the rise of millenarian and social reform movements in the Greater Puritan Diaspora of the northern states (1840–1860), out of which Mormonism came and conquered Utah; surges of nativist ferment directed explicitly against the pope and his immigrant minions (1844–1860; the 1890s; 1918–1930); Prohibitionism (1850s, 1880s, and our "noble experiment" nationally under the Eighteenth Amendment, 1919–1933); and, following World War I, the meteoric rise and fall of the Ku Klux Klan as a national, rather than a purely southern, phenomenon (1918–1925).

Such episodes may be variously considered as to their causes, or as to the truth of their critiques of opponents. Leaving the purely religious revivals aside, the politicization of religious *angst* has been intimately associated from the beginning with evangelical Protestant response to disruptive large-scale secularizing changes in society and economy. As H. L. Mencken recognized, such social strains were at the vortex of the infamous Scopes "monkey trial" in 1925—a legal case which characteristically involved assessment of the truth or falsity of the Biblical account of creation on one hand, and the Darwinian theory of evolution on the other. Being the kind of society it is, social conflicts which elsewhere might give rise to traditionalist conservative or socialist parties are cognized here in religiomoral terms. They come and go as "prairie fires," and form on the whole useful indices of direct socioeconomic pressure on traditional value systems and interests.

Contemplation of the post-1960 social scene in the United States, amplified by such political actions as that taken by the Supreme Court in the 1973 abortion case, permits a rather quick understanding of some of the forces at work behind the rise of Moral Majority and other religiopolitical activity in 1980. Homosexuals have "come out of the closet." The nuclear family is seriously eroded, as current divorce rates and the proportion of single-parent families in the population makes clear. Crime is up, the empire is down. And, in the specific case of abortion, an issue is nationally politicized about which there is little or no room to compromise, and which energizes not only the traditional evangelical Protestant constituency, but the Roman Catholic Church as well. Widespread perceived loss of values is rather acute. Traditional mazeways are disrupted, and recourse is had to revitalization strategies.[9]

This is dominantly an individualist political culture. The tendency toward individual atomization in such a culture is always relatively consid-

137

erable. Such tendencies grow during periods of mazeway disruption. Revitalization becomes a matter of *individual* salvation and rebirth, rather than collective struggle. To the extent that it is accomplished, of course, the individual becomes rebonded to an affective community larger than himself or herself, or the nuclear family; but he or she remains an individual. Moreover, to the extent that religion is assimilated to the traditional American way of life as Herberg claims that it is, it is inevitable that such revitalization movements will include an across-the-board attack upon the enemies of Light—that, for example, among some evangelicals, opposition to the Panama Canal treaty or Salt II will become virtually *de fide,* along with the Biblical account of creation.

In contemplating the longer-term future of "political religion" in America, two perspectives should perhaps be kept in mind. The first is that, its optimistic name to the contrary, Moral Majority comes nowhere near having a majority of Americans in its support. Secularization, as we have said, has not passed America by; indeed, it has markedly accelerated in recent years, and this acceleration has produced the inevitable politicoreligious revivalist response. One can expect, on past form, that this too will pass away in another "wave," and will be the more likely to do so if and when, as many expect, serious disruptions develop in the American political economy during the coming decade. In conjunction with that, it should also be stressed that no action lasts very long in politics without a reaction—and that one value in our dominant liberal tradition which will be invoked to stop the forward march of political evangelism is the ancient attachment to the First Amendment's command that church and state be kept separate.

On the other hand, there is much reason to suppose that these religious prophets in politics will continue to lead substantial minorities in protest against secularism and cosmopolitanism of all kinds. Such minorities count for much in American politics at all times, and especially when, as at present, the political system is seriously blocked and its traditional integrative institution, the parties, have disintegrated. In such a time, veto-group politics can and does run rampant, paralyzing efforts to forge coalitions remotely capable of governing the country. Thus, the swamping of all American politics by Moral Majority does not seem in prospect. But the snarly, intemperate, and blocked character of politics in an age of single-interest hyperpluralism seems likely on the whole to become more and more deeply entrenched as permanent fixtures of our politics for the foreseeable future. Moral Majority and its opponents will make, in all probability, significant contributions to this happy state of affairs. Meanwhile, many very serious issues confronting the country will be ignored in the electoral market or, if raised at all, will be presented in a religious-revivalist intellectual framework which in truth is born out of its proper time.

But whatever happens, the "brooding omnipresence" of religious perspectives in American life is likely to be with us for a very long time. In a recent article, Theodore Caplow and Howard M. Bahr report the findings of a survey they administered to high school students in Muncie, Indiana. This study was a self-conscious replication of a pioneering survey given to the town's high school students more than fifty years earlier by Robert and Helen Lynd in their classic study, *Middletown*. [10] Naturally, some "modernizing" change, as it were, can be detected in comparing these students with their grandparents. But if, in 1924, 72 percent of the high school students chose the literal interpretation of Genesis as more accurate an account of the origin and history of mankind than the theory of evolution, 50 percent of such Middletown students made the same choice in 1977. The authors' conclusion is striking, but then so are the findings of this survey:[11]

> What are we to make of these results? It appears that in this one middle-sized midwestern city some of the religious, political, and social attitudes of the post World-War I era have persisted with remarkable tenacity. . . . We certainly cannot assert that the values expressed by Middletown adolescents are typical of their peers throughout the United States or that the long-term trends discerned in Middletown can be generalized to any larger aggregate. What we do report is that in this one midwestern community, selected originally for its lack of unusual features, we have not been able to find any trace of the disintegration of traditional social values. It is hard to believe that the young people of even one midwestern community are as strongly imbued with religion, patriotism and the Protestant ethic as their grandparents were at the same age, but that is what the data seem to be telling us.

The authors phrase these remarks with admirable attention to the usual academic qualifications. But to the extent that this microcosm might replicate a larger world—and the extraordinary salience of religious perspectives in this country compared with others at the "developed" end of the spectrum suggests as much—we can expect that our electoral politics will continue to be suffused with a religious dimension closely interwoven with patriotism and the Protestant ethic. We can also presumably expect that the waves of surge and decline in the explicitly political orientation of evangelical religion will continue indefinitely as a recurrent fixture of our political life.

NOTES

1. Gallup Opinion Index, Report No. 130, *Religion in America,* 1976, p. 8.
2. London: Penguin, 1979, Table 8.7, pp. 209–210.
3. These twenty-two variables include such staple items as per capita gross national product (in U.S. dollars), percentage urban of the total population,

daily food consumption in calories per inhabitant, population under the age of 15 as percentage of the total population, and life expectancy at birth. The whole list is presented in Cole, Table 8.4, p. 204.

4. This phenomenon is implicit throughout a great many of the country studies reported in Richard Rose (ed.), *Electoral Behavior* (New York: Free Press, 1974). See, for example, the analysis for Italy in this volume (Samuel H. Barnes), p. 214. With 38% of respondents overall preferring the Left parties (PCI, PSU, and PSIUP in 1968), the first "branching" involves a split between those respondents who do not attend church regularly ($N = 1011$) and those who do ($N = 972$). Of those who do not, 58% preferred the Left; of those who do, 17% preferred the Left.

5. This problem forms one of the chief motivations behind Louis Hartz's analysis of the American political culture in his classic, *The Liberal Tradition in America* (New York: Harcourt, Brace, 1955). The work of Seymour M. Lipset over the years has also been pervaded by preoccupation with this issue. See also the broad-ranging collection of essays in John H. M. Laslett and Seymour Martin Lipset (eds.), *Failure of a Dream? Essays in the History of American Socialism* (New York: Doubleday, 1974).

6. The frontier thesis is most elaborately developed by Walter Prescott Webb, *The Great Frontier* (Austin: University of Texas Press, 1963). The affluence hypothesis, stressed by Werner Sombart in 1906 (see Laslett and Lipset, op. cit., pp. 593–608), receives particular emphasis in David Potter, *People of Plenty* (Chicago: University of Chicago Press, 1957). For the "liberal tradition," see Hartz.

7. The term "fragment society" (or "fragment culture") was coined by Louis Hartz to describe societies settled by Europeans outside the European "metropole." See Louis Hartz (ed.), *The Founding of New Societies* (New York: Harcourt, Brace, 1964).

8. Will Herberg, *Protestant, Catholic, Jew* (New York: Doubleday, 1950). This book, of course, was written in the heyday of the Eisenhower-era consensus and the publication of Dale Carnegie-like homilies on "peace of mind" or "peace of soul" by Norman Vincent Peale (Protestant), Fulton J. Sheen (Catholic), and Joshua Loth Liebman (Jewish). Needless to say, criticism rather than pure celebration was to become an important part of American religion during the period from the escalation of the Vietnam war in 1965 through Watergate and Nixon's resignation in 1974.

9. For a full discussion of this line of analysis, see Chalmers Johnson, *Revolutionary Change* (Boston: Little, Brown, 1966).

10. New York: Harcourt, Brace, 1929.

11. Theodore Caplow and Howard M. Bahr, "Half a Century of Change in Adolescent Attitudes: Replication of a Middletown Survey by the Lynds," *Public Opinion Quarterly*, 43 (1979), pp. 1–17, at pp. 16–17.

DOMESTIC STAGFLATION AND MONETARY POLICY: THE FEDERAL RESERVE AND THE HIDDEN ELECTION

Gerald Epstein

As Jerry Ford left the White House he handed Jimmy Carter three envelopes, instructing him to open them one at a time as problems became overwhelming. After a year, Carter opened the first envelope. It said, "attack Jerry Ford." He did. A year later, Carter opened the second envelope. It said, "attack the Federal Reserve." He did. Three years into his term, and even more overwhelmed by the economy, Iran, Afghanistan and so forth, Carter opened the third envelope. It said: "prepare three envelopes."

Paul Volcker, *January 1981*

Ever since Richard Nixon's preelection machinations in 1972, it has been widely believed that presidents manipulate the economy to get reelected. Social scientists have developed an entire theory of "electoral business cycles" to describe this manipulation.[1] The theory usually assumes that voters are myopic—they care about the direction in which the economy is moving the year before the election and tend to forgive sins committed two or three years earlier. It suggests that a president who wants to be reelected ought to create high unemployment levels in the first two years of his term to give himself room to reduce unemployment as the next election nears. This conforms with the common empirical finding that in assessing presidential performance in economic affairs, what voters care most about is how fast their income is growing the year before the election. The faster it grows, the more popular the president is likely to be.

Whatever the validity of electoral business cycle theory, Jimmy Carter, the consummate office seeker, did not follow its prescriptions.[2] In fact, he seems to have reversed them. From 1977 to the middle of 1979, the economy experienced one of the longest peacetime expansions in its history. Real GNP grew at an annual average rate of 4 percent, and unemployment fell from 7.7 to 5.8 percent. But then the decline set in. In 1980, the growth rate of real income dropped to zero, workers' real weekly earnings fell by almost 3 percent, and unemployment skyrocketed back to 7.5 percent. Inflation, whose containment had been a major announced ad-

Jonathan Jacobson provided excellent research assistance. I would like to thank William Sweet, Carl Van Duyne, and Michael Wattleworth for providing useful material, and Raghbendra Jha and John Sheahan for helpful comments on an earlier draft. I would especially like to thank Thomas Ferguson, Joel Rogers, and Mark Breibart for extensive discussions on the material presented here.

ministration objective, was still almost double digit on election day. Not since Herbert Hoover had a president presided over an election-year economy that behaved so diametrically opposite to what social science and common sense would suggest to be the outcome of a reasonable reelection strategy.

What happened?

Popular commentary explains Carter's failure to manipulate the 1980 economy as a simple function of the doubling of OPEC oil prices in 1979. Since a large percentage of aggregate consumption goes to direct and indirect purchase of energy, spectacular price rises for that commodity have an almost immediate inflationary impact throughout the national economy. Rising energy costs have the additional effect of draining consumption from other sectors of the economy, thus reducing the demand for goods. As a consequence, production slows and unemployment rises. Such an explanation of simultaneous inflation and unemployment is misleading, however. Even before the 1979 OPEC action, a series of domestic and international problems was developing that would critically affect the election. Single-minded attention to rising energy costs captures only part of the story.

The common explanation focuses on the president as the most important actor shaping the national economy. In the case of Jimmy Carter, such a focus is misplaced. Central to understanding the Carter administration's economic policy is a recognition of the degree to which the president deferred to the Federal Reserve in the shaping of that policy. Accepting presidential manipulation of the economy as a framework of analysis misses this outstanding feature of the Carter years. To the extent that anyone was in charge of the national economy, it was not the president, but the Federal Reserve. It is the Federal Reserve which has the formal power to manipulate interest rates and the money supply—crucial determinants of inflation, unemployment, and the value of the dollar. Moreover, it can do all this without presidential or congressional consent, and in this way is insulated from the pressures of electoral politics. Jimmy Carter appointed Paul Volcker to be chairman of the Federal Reserve; when the dust settled it was Volcker who remained to tell jokes on the Carter presidency.

But if the Fed can claim independence from electoral politics, its enormous authority makes it a crucible for other and equally important struggles for power. Exploring the institutional dynamics and constraints operating on the Federal Reserve not only shifts attention to the more relevant actor in the formation of national economic policy, but also brings into view all the larger conflicts now shaping the American political economy as a whole. It highlights as well a final irony of the Volcker joke. During the last two years of the Carter presidency not even the Federal Reserve could control the national economy. Wild vacillations in the economic climate triggered abrupt changes and policy reversals at the Fed. Unhappily for Jimmy Carter, no one was in charge.

Consider the following chronology of major Reserve Board policy initiatives during the period:

On November 1, 1978, the Federal Reserve increased the discount rate by a full percentage point, the largest increase to date. The purpose, according to the Fed's chairman, G. William Miller, was to "call a halt" to the year-long decline in the foreign exchange value of the dollar. But after a short recovery, the dollar lost much of the ground it had gained.

Just a year before the election, Paul Volcker, the new chairman of the Fed, announced a major shift in its policy. Henceforth, he said, the Fed would control the growth in the money supply and let the market determine interest rates, regardless of how erratic they might become. Bringing the money supply under control, he said, would be necessary to fight inflation and speculation, and protect the dollar.

But on March 14, only six months later, the Federal Reserve was again forced to take dramatic action. The Fed announced a sweeping new battery of credit controls and restrictive policies to reduce the money supply. Over the next thirty days, the money supply did decline at an annual rate of over 14 percent, the largest monthly decline since the Great Depression. But from June to November it skyrocketed back up at an annual rate of over 15 percent. The prime rate jumped to almost 20 percent in April and plunged to 11 percent in July. The dollar followed right along.

In August, when Congress and the Reagan camp were in the midst of a frenzy of tax cut promises, Volcker made it clear that, in line with Carter's position, the Fed would not support such a cut. Citibank's Leif Olsen remarked, "Volcker's a strong man in the President's camp right now." But Volcker's marching orders came from elsewhere. On September 26, less than six weeks before the election and over the strenuous complaints of the Carter administration, the Fed lifted its discount rate by a full percentage point, driving the prime rate upward again.

By election day, unemployment had risen to over 7.5 percent, the inflation rate was almost 10 percent, and workers' real wages had fallen almost 3 percent from the year before. Stagflation, the coincidence of low economic growth and high inflation, remained. At no time since the Great Depression has the Federal Reserve followed such a contractionary monetary policy in an election year, exercised its power over the financial sector to such a degree, and yet seemed in so little control of the economy.

How can one explain the confluence of such great political power and economic impotence in the context of the hidden election of 1980?

The Fed's power and problems result, in part, from an implicit "deal" within the political system. As problems mount and the necessary solutions become increasingly unpopular, Congress and the president attempt to escape blame by letting the independent Fed act. But this deal is only part of the explanation. The Fed also has its own views of what is necessary, and it uses its independence to impose them on the rest of us. At the same time, the Fed's independence is highly contingent. The Fed needs allies to protect it from the political process when its policies do not seem so necessary to those in Congress, the White House, or the streets. For both historical and structural reasons, the financial community is such an ally. But allies rarely come for free.

Thus the Fed is being asked to solve increasingly intractable macroeconomic problems, wants to shape those solutions to fit its own view of the world, and needs to satisfy its political constituency—all at the same time.

These imperatives present a basic dilemma that neither simple monetarist solutions to tighten monetary policy nor dramatic supply-side policies to cut taxes can repeal. They therefore hold the key both to an understanding of macroeconomic policy in the hidden election, and the problems which won't go away when Reagan gets his turn.

STAGFLATION AND THE HIDDEN ELECTION

Jimmy Carter's inability to find a solution to stagflation virtually eliminated his reelection chances, and Ronald Reagan faces the same prospect if he fails to fashion a cure. To understand Carter's failure and the imperatives facing Reagan, the roots of stagflation must be investigated. And although the causes of stagflation are not fully known, any analysis is doomed if it does not attempt to understand the implications of one central fact: the decline of United States power in the world economy since World War II. In the late 1940s, the United States produced 60 percent of the Western industrialized world's manufactures and 40 percent of the world's goods and services. By the late 1970s, both shares had been cut in half, and United States' manufacturing exports fared even worse. In 1953, almost 30 percent of Western industrial countries' manufactured exports were from the United States; by 1976, the United States share had shrunk to 13 percent.[3]

Yet there is no simple connection between this decline and the economic and political crisis we now face. Though cries of American impotence were loudest in the 1970s, production and manufacturing export shares have stabilized or even increased in the last ten years. Ronald Reagan looks to Dwight Eisenhower for inspiration, but the largest proportion of the American decline occurred during his administration. Almost two-thirds of the reduction in United States' manufacturing production and export shares occurred in the 1950s, with almost half taking place between 1955 and 1960.

The paradox of a partially stabilized international position in the face of massive domestic and international instability can be resolved if one understands, to put it crudely, that the chickens have come home to roost. The reduced position the United States finally reached by the late 1960s rendered unstable institutional arrangements that depended so heavily on overriding American power and were so crucial to domestic prosperity and political stability in the twenty years after World War II.[4] The breakdown of the Bretton Woods system in 1971 and the OPEC price increase of 1974 were the critical events that consummated that fall. For the United States and the world economy to restore stability and growth, international and domestic restructuring of these arrangements is required. Yet persistent attempts by the United States to maintain its outmoded international role and the inability of anyone else to set up a new order not only help to explain the recently stabilized American international position, but have also precluded the restructuring that is actually required.

As a result of the failure to reconstruct an international order, domestic restructuring has become both much more important and much more difficult. The domestic implications of international stability are certainly complex, but to put it simply, the changed nature of the world economy, the American role in it, and the domestic pressures that result have boxed the United States into a corner. Both inflation and stagnation create problems. But inflation has become the only way to fight stagnation; and stagnation has become the only way to fight inflation. The combination—stagflation—represents an unhappy compromise of powerful forces and interests. It is a compromise that probably cannot last long, as the machinations of the recent election and the instability of the political coalitions associated with it suggest.

The inflationary consequences of fighting stagnation, and the stagnating consequences of fighting inflation, result from problems endemic to the way capitalist economies have always worked. The recent increase in the political power of labor at home and abroad, the current structure of the international monetary system, and the formation of the OPEC cartel have exacerbated the problems virtually to the point of crisis.

Throughout the history of capitalism, sustained economic expansion has created problems. The major one is that expansion eventually leads to tight labor markets as pools of unemployed labor dry up. Tight labor markets, in turn, reduce the threat of dismissal, almost inevitably leading to increased wage demands. More strikes and greater militance on the shop floor often also result, and both lead to lower productivity. Since manufacturers' profits depend on getting high output while paying low wages, all three factors squeeze profits as full employment is maintained. If firms can raise prices, they solve one problem but create another. By raising prices, manufacturing firms can protect their profits. If they do, however, the inflation that results from full employment affects others adversely, especially financial interests. Sustained full employment presents a dilemma, then. If prices do not increase, manufacturing profits are squeezed.[5] If prices do increase, wealthy bondholders and the financial community—Keynes's rentier interests—are harmed. Inflation becomes the way to fight stagnation, but it is a way that places strains on financial markets and political conditions.

As economic expansion is maintained and manufacturers respond by raising prices and inflation, the powerful groups that are hurt, and the financial markets, which function poorly with high and variable rates of inflation, begin to require recession and unemployment to restore decorum to the labor market and to create slack in other markets to reduce inflationary pressures. A recession can be created if Congress can be induced to raise taxes or to reduce government spending. But if groups in society and the bureaucracy are able to protect themselves from budget cuts and tax increases, then contractionary fiscal policy is not a real option.

A recession can also be created if the Federal Reserve tightens up on the money supply and raises interest rates.[6] This reduces the availability of money and increases the cost of credit, reducing borrowing, sales, and economic growth. But tight monetary policy is particularly onerous for manufacturing interests. Tight money means higher interest rates and therefore higher costs for firms that borrow.

But whether monetary or fiscal policy is used, decorum in the labor markets is restored at a cost. High unemployment lowers sales and reduces profits. The longer it takes for unemployment to reduce wage demands, the costlier a recession is to manufacturing interests. In addition to raising prices and calling for contractionary macroeconomic policy, manufacturers have a third alternative. They can invest in new technologies that reduce their reliance on labor. But if the Federal Reserve is maintaining high interest rates to stem inflation, then this avenue of relief from the profit squeeze is undermined as well.

Indeed, the longer the recession and the tighter the monetary policy necessary to bring it about, the less likely a restoration of the conditions for profitability and long-term growth. Private investment, on which productivity growth and the accumulation of profits ultimately depend, is hindered by the high interest rates and excess capacity that induced recessions create. To make things worse, partly because of the increased power of labor, monetary policy and contractionary fiscal policy seem to be less and less effective in reducing wage increases and inflation. Tight money thus seems to lead to stagflation—it generates excess capacity and unemployment and lowers investment and productivity growth without putting much of a dent in inflation.[7] The ability of the government to satisfy demands for lower inflation without imposing heavy costs on manufacturing interests is now greatly undermined by the fact that cutting government spending or increasing taxes are politically difficult courses. So financial institutions and markets turn to the Federal Reserve for relief. But the ability to control the course of the economy has been further undermined by the resistance of workers to cuts in wages even in the face of high unemployment. Stagnation thus comes to be the only way to fight inflation.

The configuration of the world economy in the wake of reduced American power and the unstable structures resulting from the failure to reconstruct a new order greatly exacerbate the inflationary consequences of expansion as well as the costs of stagnation. These problems in turn result from and exacerbate political conflicts of the highest order.

The machinations involve a host of characters: nation-states, classes within nations, and groups within classes. Ultimately these characters must be understood within the structure of the institutions they created, struggled over, and progressively undermined in the course of the postwar era. No international institution gives a better vantage point from which to understand this evolution and the problems created by its breakdown than the Bretton Woods system created by the allies at the end of World War II and officially dismantled by Richard Nixon in 1971. On the domestic front, few institutions have been a more important terrain for the struggle over Bretton Woods than the Federal Reserve. The contest over the Bretton Woods system, together with the reduced ability of the United States to control the world price of oil, put the problems of expansion and stagnation into their proper context, and lay the basis for understanding the macroeconomic dilemmas of the hidden election and beyond.

Bretton Woods created a system of fixed exchange rates based on the use of the dollar as the principal international currency. The United States pledged to buy dollars with gold at a fixed price. After the war, the United States produced goods and services Europeans and the Japanese needed to rebuild their shattered economies. As a result of both factors, foreign central banks were willing to accumulate and hold dollars in their foreign exchange reserves. The dollar became the major reserve currency of the international system. It was an arrangement that conferred considerable benefits on some actors within the international system, but not without considerable costs to others.

The primary benefit of the reserve currency role was that the United States could run chronic balance of payments deficits. In principle, it could have run a deficit by importing more goods and services than it exported (a trade deficit), or it could have invested more dollars abroad than foreigners invested in the United States (a capital account deficit). From the end of World War II until 1970, the United States exported more goods and services than it imported. But between 1950 and 1971, when Bretton Woods broke down, net United States financial outflows exceeded net exports (exports minus imports) in every year but three.[8] The United States was able to run these deficits without the value of the dollar declining because foreign governments were willing to buy up the excess dollars flowing abroad, preventing the excess supply from driving down the dollar's value.

The French referred to this ability of the United States to run chronic balance of payments deficits—buying up factories by simply printing money—as the "exorbitant privilege." The standard view of the American acquisition of that privilege is expressed well by James Tobin, a member of the Council of Economic Advisers under President Kennedy: "The United States did not seek this privileged role; it arose by accidental evolution rather than by conscious design."[9] C. Fred Bergsten, assistant secretary of the Treasury for international affairs under Carter, takes a strikingly different view:

> In effect, the United States used the IMF as a multilateral cover for its national dominance—which of course also had the merit for other countries of providing a cover for their impotence, and some actual protection against the United States. It decided to handle the issues unilaterally, and usually did so quite generously and quite well. However, in the process it created a system based on the dollar and U.S. hegemony rather than on the IMF and international cooperation. . . . Achievement of key currency status does require a choice by the dominant country, at least to the extent of rejecting the possible alternatives, and it is a mistake to say—as many commentators and officials do, for understandable if erroneous political reasons—that the United States did not seek the reserve currency role, but had it thrust upon us.[10]

The benefits from the exorbitant privilege were not distributed equally over time or across groups. The institution of fixed exchange rates helped to create international stability, which was conducive to international trade, economic growth, and the fight against communism in Europe and Japan. In the process, United States' direct investment grew at a steady rate of 10 percent per year from 1950 to 1960. The rate of growth of this investment was higher in Europe than elsewhere: there it grew at 13 percent per year, a pace which was especially upsetting to the French.[11]

The ability of the United States to run chronic deficits because of the key role of the dollar facilitated the ability of the multinational corporations to expand around the world buying land and factories and hiring cheap labor without the government having to impose *excessive* austerity on the domestic population in order to reduce imports. That, in turn, helped to maintain the domestic political conditions for multinational expansion. But these conditions could not be maintained forever. In the 1950s, Yale economist Robert Triffin was already pointing out a fundamental weakness in the Bretton Woods system: the rest of the world needed dollars to carry out international finance and trade, but the only way in which the dollars could be provided was by the United States running balance of payments deficits. Those deficits, however, would eventually undermine the world's confidence that the dollars would be redeemable for gold or goods at reasonable prices. As its foreign investments multiplied and the United States began importing more from abroad and producing a smaller proportion of the world's output, the value of dollars held by central banks came perilously close to the value of the United States' gold stock. One dramatic danger was that foreigners would demand gold for their dollars, as provided in the Bretton Woods agreements. Indeed, between 1957 and 1960 over a quarter of the American gold stock was bought by foreign central banks, mainly the French.[12]

By 1959, the United States had lost over 60 percent of the share of manufacturing exports it had won along with World War II. With less demand for dollars with which to buy goods, and with private and official confidence in the ability of the United States to maintain the value of the dollar waning, substitutes for intrinsic value had to be found to convince others to hold onto dollar reserves. For the next ten years, the major financial question facing American policymakers, including the Federal Reserve, was how to maintain the Bretton Woods system despite the declining relative power of the United States.

Arthur Schlesinger reports that, upon entering the White House, the two things that worried John Kennedy the most were nuclear war and the balance of payments.[13] (He does not say in which order.) As Kennedy took office in 1961, the unemployment rate was almost 8 percent. The Council of Economic Advisers was committed to reviving the growth of the domestic economy and was willing to reduce the role of the dollar in international affairs, if that was what it would take. To revive economic growth, the council preferred a policy mix of low interest rates to stimulate investment and government budgets balanced at full employment. But as James Tobin, a member of Kennedy's council, put it: "A really aggressive monetary expansion was not in the cards because of the balance of payments."[14] A loose monetary policy would have lowered interest rates. With interest rates lower at home than abroad, investors would have sold dollars to buy foreign currencies. The outflow of dollars, in turn, would have worsened the balance of payments, placing another nail in the coffin of Bretton Woods. As the chairman of the Fed, William M. Martin, explained: "Even if indeed an occasion arose when we could preserve the international role of the dollar only at the expense of modifying our favored domestic policies—even then we would need to pay attention to the international repercussions of our actions."[15] But eventually, the Bretton Woods system and the high interest rates used to protect it became especially onerous for domestic manufacturers.

In principle, a number of policies could have been undertaken that would have reduced the need for tight money to protect the balance of payments and Bretton Woods. One solution was to devalue the dollar. That would have increased the cost of imports and reduced the cost of American goods to foreigners, thus helping to restore the competitive position of the United States at home and abroad. Dollar devaluation faced a host of obstacles, however.

For one, Europe and Japan were enjoying the high dollar exchange rate that made their goods cheaper in American markets and American goods more expensive in their own. In 1950, for example, the dollar cost of Japanese goods was half as high as that of American goods, and German, French, Italian, and British goods were three-quarters as expensive.[16] By the mid-sixties their cost advantage had eroded, and they would have been reluctant to let a dollar devaluation erode that advantage any further. On the American side there was strong opposition to devaluation, particularly from financial interests. They believed devaluation would lead to inflation. If the dollar falls in value, that increases the cost of imports and allows domestic producers to raise their prices in tandem. The reasons financial interests tend to oppose inflation are worth looking at with some care, since some interesting divisions among them will arise.

The standard textbook maxim holds that debtors gain from inflation while creditors are hurt. This follows since debtors are able to repay creditors in dollars worth less than those they borrowed. If, however, inflation is expected, or even if it is not expected but can be quickly adjusted to, lenders are likely to extract higher interest rates to compensate for the reduced value of the dollars repaid. The shorter term the loan, the more flexible the credit arrangement, and the more power they have to alter contracts, the less creditors are harmed by inflation. As part and parcel of the conventional wisdom, it is commonly believed that, being creditors, banks dislike inflation. And, in fact, investment banks, which engage in long-term credit activities, have a good deal to fear from high and variable inflation—which, it appears, have gone hand in hand. When interest rates increase because of expectations of increased inflation, bond prices fall since the returns the owners of the bonds receive are lower than they could get on the open market. The drop in bond prices lowers the value of the bonds. Bondholders, quite naturally, become reluctant to take similar risks in the future. In general, when inflation is high and variable, interest rates and bond prices fluctuate as well.

As a result, buying, selling, and underwriting long-term debt becomes a risky and less profitable business. Small commercial banks and savings and loans, because of government regulations, narrow market position, and few resources to devote to innovation, have relatively little flexibility in changing interest rates as inflation and market interest rates vary. They also tend to be harmed by high and variable inflation. Large multinational commercial banks, on the other hand, operate in a broad range of domestic and international markets and have great financial resources for innovation. They are therefore able to adjust quite quickly to an inflationary environment. They have, however, more subtle and complex problems with a large devaluation, which I describe below.

Finally, many feared that devaluation would actually destroy the Bretton Woods system. Since many countries held much of their reserves in dollars, devaluation could have cost them dearly. It would have disrupted economic and political relations among the major industrial powers, and harmed American interests as well. One way out of the impasse was to find a way to reduce the reliance of the international monetary system on the dollar. That would allow the United States to pursue a looser monetary policy without worrying that an excessive dollar outflow would undermine the very basis of the system; in the extreme, it might allow devaluation without disrupting the entire system. Proposals to reduce the reliance of the international monetary system on the dollar had been suggested periodically, especially during times of dollar weakness. Two recurring ones were the creation of a world money that could at least partly satisfy the need of central banks for reserves, thereby reducing their reliance on the dollar; and a substitution account, which would create an asset dollar holders could substitute for their dollars without having to sell them on the foreign exchange market. That would avoid exchange market instability and could help preserve Bretton Woods without requiring United States' monetary policy to be as restrictive as it would have to be otherwise.

Proposals to create an international currency under the auspices of the IMF were introduced throughout the 1960s. The first substitution account plan was proposed at the IMF annual meeting in Washington in September 1962. The so-called Maudling plan would have allowed central banks to deposit unwanted currencies in a mutual currency account, in exchange for international money whose value would be guaranteed in gold. Thus, any participating country worried about the future value of the dollars it was holding could get a gold-based guarantee of that currency's value without having to sell the dollars for gold. The initiative received no support from the official community gathered in Washington. Robert Roosa, an investment banker and undersecretary of the Treasury under Kennedy, would have no part of it.[17] Roosa's opposition was no aberration. Throughout the early sixties, American financial institutions and the Treasury Department fought tooth and nail all proposals that would reduce the reserve currency role of the dollar, including those that called for the creation of an international currency and for a substitution account. Those who proposed a reduction in that role had a well-defined view of the basis for this opposition. James Tobin, a scarred veteran of these battles within the Kennedy administration, described the view in the following terms:

> The reluctance of U.S. financial circles to accept a solution that recognizes the decline in the reserve-currency status of the dollar seems to be based on a misunderstanding. It is feared that such a solution will also displace the dollar from its role as the principal medium of exchange in private international transactions. This would lose New York and the country some financial business and income, and the nation would no longer enjoy the ability to finance payments deficits from the yearly increment of private foreign demand for dollar working balances. . . . But no one is proposing to create an international money for private circulation. There the dollar will remain unchallenged. . . . Indeed, any international monetary reform that removes the danger of a run from dollars into gold can only strengthen the world's private demand for dollars.[18]

But Roosa was not convinced. In a famous debate on this point, Roosa admitted that reducing the reserve currency role of the dollar without harming American financial institutions might be possible, but he quickly added: "Separating the transactions (private) roles from the Reserve currency role would be as delicate as separating Siamese Twins."[19]

Moreover, the major multinational banks knew that their fate was tied up with world economic growth and international trade in general, and the fate of American multinational corporations in particular. Banks make money by financing the production and trade of their customers. Small

American banks were more or less confined to financing domestic production in the 1950s and 1960s, so their primary concern was with domestic growth and trade (as long as growth was not inflationary). But large international banks had a global reach: their concern was that the open trading system of Bretton Woods, which contributed to world economic growth, be maintained. They had a special interest in the growth, profitability, and expansion abroad of American multinational corporations, for here they had an edge on their domestic and foreign financial competition. The major advantage that large American commercial and to some extent investment banks had over domestic and foreign competitors under the Bretton Woods system was their familiarity and close relationships with American multinational corporations that moved abroad. Laws that prohibit interstate branching in the United States in order to protect small domestic banks have until recently been notoriously difficult for large banks to break. There were few laws against American banks setting up branches overseas, however, especially in the unregulated offshore markets. Eastern banks were better able to serve their large corporate customers if they moved from the East Coast to London than if they moved from New York to Texas. Large established banks knew that their futures lay with the growth of the multinationals. This growth in turn depended on the companies' having access to profitable opportunities abroad, and the resources to pay for them. One way to get such resources, of course, was by maintaining the reserve currency role of the dollar.

But by the late 1960s, the costs in tight money and high interest to maintain the system, and the system itself, greatly reduced or even eliminated the "exorbitant privilege" accruing to broad sectors of the American business community. The major problem was that the longer Bretton Woods was maintained, the longer the fixed dollar exchange rate was overvalued. That meant that imports remained cheap and exports remained relatively expensive, harming domestic manufacturing interests. In 1950, Japanese products were half as expensive as American products; in 1970 they were still one-third cheaper. In 1950, German goods cost 72 percent of American goods; in 1970, they still cost only four-fifths as much.[20] It is common to blame cheap foreign labor for the fact that the competitiveness of American manufacturing was eroded at home and abroad. But the high interest rates used to protect the balance of payments, which inhibited borrowing, investment, and expansion by domestic manufacturers, and the overvalued exchange rates were the real culprits. The desire to preserve the reserve currency role of the dollar and to avoid the inflationary impact of devaluation had led the Fed and the Treasury to fight proposals for dollar devaluation and the reduced role of the dollar that might entail.

In 1966, President Johnson stepped up the Vietnam war spending while refusing to risk popular disaffection by increasing taxes to pay for it. The increased spending, then as now, led to a major dilemma for the Fed. Monetary policy in 1966 almost caused a collapse of the housing market in California and the savings and loan associations connected with it. The tax surcharge in 1968 was not sufficient to fight inflation and restore decorum in the labor market, which had to contend with 4 percent unemployment or less for two years in a row. Martin maintained tight monetary policy in 1969 and early 1970, and $4 billion flowed into the United States from abroad, but the credit crunch almost created a financial panic.[21]

When Arthur Burns was appointed chairman of the Federal Reserve by Nixon in 1970, he reversed the tight money course. In August 1971, President Nixon officially dismantled the Bretton Woods system by refusing to convert dollars into gold and by devaluing the dollar. It is commonly believed that Nixon abandoned Bretton Woods because he was forced to do so by international creditors, who were demanding more gold than the U.S. government had. However inevitable Bretton Woods' collapse, the American government had some control over its timing. Nixon abandoned Bretton Woods when he did in order to devalue the dollar, restore American manufacturing's international competitiveness, and avoid the stagnating effects of tight monetary policy on the domestic economy.[22] Nixon had appointed Arthur Burns to the Fed to help facilitate this process. But the long-term attempt by the Fed and the Treasury to maintain the outmoded role of the dollar and its international position might well have already done its damage. As C. Fred Bergsten, Carter's assistant secretary of the Treasury, put it before he took office:

> Since it was such financial concerns which permitted the dollar to become overvalued by 1971 and cause significant losses of jobs for Americans, perhaps the Treasury Department and the Federal Reserve Board, rather than U.S. trade negotiators, should be accused of "selling out U.S. interests to the foreigners."[23]

The roots of the decline of the U.S. domestic manufacturing sector and productivity growth might well be sought, then, in the effects of the Bretton Woods system and the policies undertaken to maintain it.

Federal Reserve concern with the welfare of banks in general and their international expansion in particular was not new in the 1960s. From its inception, the Federal Reserve has had a very close—one might say intimate—relationship with the financial community in the United States. The standard textbook explanation of the founding fathers' rationale for creating the Fed is straightforward:

> The Federal Reserve System was created by Congress in 1913 to avoid the banking crises that had periodically plagued the United States economy —the most recent of which was the panic of 1907.[24]

But the explanation, while partially true, is highly misleading. The Fed was created not only to alleviate banking panics, but also to keep the money supply out of democratic control, to facilitate the cartelization of the banking system by the largest banks, and last, but far from least, to help large American financial firms compete better with European ones. Although these goals were not perfectly embodied at the inception of the system— nor are they fully realized today—they have been the system's driving force throughout its history.

Following the panic of 1907, large banks developed various proposals for a central bank. But large and small banks were bitterly divided over proposals for reform. Generally, smaller banks were apathetic or deeply opposed to any central system, fearing that it would be controlled from New York. For their part, large banks, and especially those in New York, wanted a centralized system, one they could control, one that would stop their relative decline in power domestically, and one that would provide policies which would enhance their ability to compete in international financial markets. These proposals emerged at a time of great social agitation in the United States. The Socialist party, liberal reformers, and Bryan Democrats, among others, were pushing for broad social changes, not the least of which was the dismantling of the large Eastern "Money Trusts" and for more public control over the money supply.

The fear of more radical reforms and the particular interests of large bankers led to a compromise between the large and small banks by which the new monetary authority would be decentralized. There would be regional reserve banks subject to the control of a central Board of Governors located in Washington and appointed by the president, rather than one central bank controlled by bankers. The Federal Reserve Act signed by Wilson toward the end of 1913 provided for as many as twelve regional banks, leaving the Board of Governors in Washington, however, with little formal power. In a common assessment, Galbraith concludes that "The regional idea had, in fact, triumphed and the real authority lay with the twelve banks."[25] This view is misleading, however. The real power in the early days of the system lay with the New York Federal Reserve bank and the large Eastern interests it represented. Under the powerful leadership of Benjamin Strong, the New York Fed won most of the internal battles bitterly contested by Washington.

Despite the compromises, Benjamin Strong and other important early figures in the Federal Reserve understood the importance of the new bank. As Strong put it in 1915: ". . . if all such prejudices, political and sectional, against New York and its bankers can be overcome by such measures as have been adopted in the Federal Reserve Act, I should feel that the work now being done has been well repaid."[26] And while political protection of bankers was a goal well served by the establishment of the Federal Reserve, promoting New York's international role was an equally important objective. As Carter Glass, who was instrumental in the creation of the system, told a Washington audience:

The proponents of the Federal Reserve Act had no idea of impairing the rightful prestige of New York as the financial metropolis of this hemisphere. They rather expected to confirm its distinction, and even hoped to assist powerfully in wresting the scepter from London, and eventually making New York the financial center of the world. Eminent Englishmen with the keenest perception have frankly expressed apprehension of such a result. Indeed, momentarily this has come to pass. And we may point to the amazing contrast between New York under the old system in 1907, shaken to its very foundations because of two bank failures, and New York at the present time, under the new system, serenely secure in its domestic banking operations and confidently financing the great enterprises of European nations at war.[27]

But the big bankers in New York and elsewhere did not get everything they wanted from the Federal Reserve. To gain support for the system, membership was made voluntary, and the government maintained control over the appointments to the board in Washington. The division of authority between New York and Washington, the ability of state banks to stay out of the system, and the ultimate power that Congress, in principle, could exercise meant that big bank control over monetary policy and big bank control over the banking system were not guaranteed.

After the debacles of the 1930s, power within the Federal Reserve System was largely transferred from the regional reserve banks to the Board of Governors in Washington through a series of legislative and administrative reforms. This shift is commonly seen as representing the virtual elimination of banker control over the policies of the Federal Reserve and the consolidation of a central bank under public control. The real story is more complex. Recent evidence indicates that the movement actually represented the triumph of Midwestern and California banks over the New York financial interests for representation *within* the policymaking structure of the Federal Reserve. The shift broadened the interests represented in the Fed and reduced the debilitating battle for power between New York and Washington by centralizing control in Washington.[28]

Such centralized control and broadened interests also meant that longer-range views of what was necessary to protect the financial integrity and profitability of American financial institutions on a domestic and international scale were more likely to inform Federal Reserve policies. But the contingent nature of the Federal Reserve's independence from Congress and the executive, and the important political power of small banks in Congress, meant that the Fed would not always be able to follow the policies necessary to maintain the longer-run interests of the financial community. The Federal Reserve needed the support of the financial community to preserve its independence from the government. But that support has a price, which often has to be paid in terms of the narrow interests of its supporters.

Milton Friedman is one of the few economists who understands this problem, on one level at least. He believes that the best way to fight inflation and maintain the conditions for stable economic growth is for the

Federal Reserve to control the money supply. But for most of its life the Fed has chosen to try to control interest rates (credit conditions) instead. Friedman attributes this decision to a simple fact:

> An independent central bank will almost inevitably give undue emphasis to the point of view of bankers. . . . In the United States, for example, the Reserve banks technically are owned by their member banks. One result is that the general views of the banking community exercise a strong influence on the central bank, and since the banking community is concerned primarily with the credit market (interest rates), central banks are led to put altogether too much emphasis on the credit effects of their policies and too little emphasis on the monetary effects of their policies.[29]

Friedman goes on to say that in the United States, in principle, "the central bank can make the amount of money anything it wishes." But the dilemma of banker influence is deeper than Friedman recognizes. The Fed's dependence on bankers for its political independence means that the Fed is unable politically to impose the burdens of long-run monetary control on its political constituency, even if it *chose* to control the money supply. The problem is that whenever the Fed tries to control one form of money, financial institutions create another form that is not subject to the Fed's control. Financial institutions create new moneys like credit cards, because it is profitable for them to do so. In principle the Fed could prevent such innovation, but only at the expense of financial profits. And when it creates policies that harm those, it must pick its fights carefully and from a position of strength.

The ability of the Federal Reserve to control the money supply in the long run is also undermined by the international integration of financial markets. The Eurocurrency market is just one example of an international institutional innovation that creates a new kind of money, Eurodollars, which hinders the Federal Reserve's control of the money supply. This dilemma is very deep and goes to the heart of Milton Friedman's famous tenet that, to control inflation, the Federal Reserve should pick a particular money supply and cause it to grow at a constant rate. If the Fed cannot *control* the money supply, then the political process will have to find some other means to protect financial institutions and markets from the inflationary consequences of expansion.

The breakdown of Bretton Woods in 1971 and the advent of flexible exchange rates in 1973 altered the situation, as did the dramatic increase in oil prices and accumulation of OPEC wealth that soon followed. *They both increased the need for and benefits from inflation and they both undermined the ability to stop it without generating stagnation.*

As I suggested earlier, full employment leads to a profit squeeze for manufacturing corporations by increasing the militance of workers. Manufacturers can respond to the profit squeeze in a number of ways. One is by raising prices to protect profits. But for that to work for manufacturers in general, a number of conditions must hold. First, the Federal Reserve must increase the money supply. This results from a simple fact: if more money is not available to buy all the output produced at the higher cost, then some of the output will not be sold.[30] Higher unemployment and lower sales and profits will result. Federal Reserve–created inflation might be one way to fight the profit squeeze brought on by sustained full employment, and indeed for this reason the Fed is routinely pressured to expand the money supply, thus maintaining inflation. But for inflation to maintain manufacturing profits in the face of lower productivity or higher wage demands, a second condition must be satisfied. Firms must be able to raise prices faster than workers raise their wages. There is in fact strong evidence that in the United States, increases in the rate of growth of the money supply *do* increase manufacturer profits, primarily because wages do not keep up with prices.[31]

One further condition is required for higher prices to solve the problems posed by sustained full employment: firms must be able to raise prices without being undercut by foreign competition. Under the Bretton Woods system of fixed exchange rates, however, this condition could not be met. If domestic manufacturers tried to raise prices, foreign competitors could undersell American manufacturers at home and abroad.[32] The difficulties firms had in passing on higher wage costs partly explains why so many wanted a dollar devaluation and a shift to floating exchange rates, even if that meant the destruction of the Bretton Woods system. Floating exchange rates can protect domestic manufacturers from the detrimental profit effects of maintained expansion. As costs go up, firms can raise their prices. If such price rises are sufficiently widespread, the dollar will depreciate. The fall in the value of the dollar will increase the costs of imports, thus protecting domestic firms' markets in the United States while making American exports cheaper, protecting their markets abroad.

This competitive edge can be maintained, however, only if nominal wages do not go up with the dollar depreciation, even though the depreciation-induced inflation erodes workers' real wages. The Fed is thus faced with a dilemma. If it tightens monetary policy to reduce the inflation caused by a devaluation, profits and sales will be reduced. If it allows the devaluation-induced inflation to erode workers' real wages and restore the profitability of manufacturers, financial interests and markets will be harmed. If the workers attempt to maintain their real wages by increasing their wage demands, the dilemma becomes exacerbated. If workers' wages go up and manufacturers raise prices, that will cause the dollar to devalue even more. The economy may fall into a vicious circle of devaluation, inflation, devaluation that might be extremely difficult to break.[33] As long as workers' wages lag sufficiently behind prices, however, manufacturers can benefit from devaluation and the inflation that results.

Thus the breakdown of Bretton Woods and the advent of floating exchange rates loosened the strait jacket on American economic growth that had become ever tighter during the late 1960s. But the breakdown

157

also meant that expansion might become more inflationary as it led to dollar depreciation. At the same time, although dollar depreciations were useful in restoring the international position of American exports in the world economy, they could do so only if workers' wage demands could be held in check and if the inflationary consequences were not too unsettling to American financial interests.[34] In the longer run lurked a more dangerous possibility. In the face of the reduced share of American production in the world economy, attempts to maintain the role of the dollar might re-create the old Bretton Woods dilemma. American economic expansion might have to be called to a halt to prevent massive instability on the foreign exchange markets and the breakdown of the international financial system. It was such concerns that led ultimately to the Fed's halting of the 1976–1979 U.S. economic expansion. On the other hand, paradoxically, floating exchange rates, along with the pricing policy of OPEC, and major increases in the labor force help explain why the Fed allowed the expansion to go on as long as it did.

The fact that OPEC priced its oil in dollars and held much of its accumulated wealth in dollar assets created new opportunities as well as dangers for American financial and manufacturing interests. Oil price increases meant that other countries needed to use more dollars to buy OPEC oil, and OPEC would hold more dollars in assets. Both factors helped to maintain the international position of American financial institutions in the short run. Moreover, the pricing of oil in dollars gave other countries an incentive to let their currencies appreciate against the dollar, since that reduced the cost of oil to them in their own currencies. This in turn helped to restore the competitiveness of American manufacturing. By the middle of 1980, the average unit labor costs in the United States were lower than those in Japan, Germany, France, and the United Kingdom; and in 1978, the cost of an average basket of goods in Japan, Germany, and France was 27, 35, and 14 percent higher than in the United States.[35]

But the OPEC cartel posed grave dangers as well. Increases in OPEC oil prices meant that the real standard of living in the United States had to fall if oil imports were to be maintained. Corporate profits, wages, or government spending would therefore have to fall in turn. Again, for manufacturers, inflation was the preferred solution. If they could raise their prices to compensate for the higher cost of oil and workers could not raise their wages commensurately, then workers' real wages would fall to pay for OPEC oil. All other things being equal, financial institutions would have opposed this solution. But two factors mitigated this opposition. First, after the initial OPEC price rise, OPEC acted somewhat like American workers. It failed to increase its oil prices to keep up with the cost of the goods the West sold it. By inflating, the United States was able to reduce the real cost of OPEC oil, and the amount of wealth the West transferred to the OPEC countries. Most sectors of American business wanted to minimize the wealth that escaped their control. Large accretions of wealth usually imply large accretions of power, which the business community, the American government, and the Federal Reserve were anxious to prevent. As Anthony Solomon, president of the New York Federal Reserve, put it in a recent speech:

> Our objective should be to take out of OPEC's hands the ability to force real oil prices higher, to unblock OPEC restraints on oil production, and to retain in our country the money that would otherwise be paid as tax to OPEC members in the form of higher oil prices.[36]

Second, in order to pay for OPEC oil, all interests desired an export surplus, which a controlled depreciation of the dollar could bring about. But a strategy of inflating away OPEC's wealth and controlled exchange depreciation could only work for so long. Decisions by the OPEC countries to hold fewer dollars in their reserves as their value fell—or, worse yet, to stop pricing oil in dollars—could cause downward pressure on the external value of the dollar. The simple existence of this possibility could, in times of general instability, cause massive speculation against the dollar and turmoil in international financial and commodity markets that was greatly worsened by expansion and attempts at controlled depreciation.

The difficulties the United States had in bringing about a controlled depreciation and creating an export surplus to pay for OPEC oil were greatly heightened by increased international competition with Europe and Japan in the wake of the American decline and as a result of the power of the European working class. In the United States, as I suggested, workers' wages do seem to lag behind prices. There is strong evidence that in Europe, however, wages do not lag behind by nearly as much, if at all. Why this differential relationship holds is not completely understood. But whatever its cause, it is of great importance. Expansionary policy in Europe is more likely to lead to exacerbated inflation as wages quickly catch up with prices, without a reduction in the wage share of income. In virtually all European countries, the share of wages in manufacturing income increased between 1964 and 1978. In Germany, it went from 63 to 71 percent; in France, from 52 to 54 percent; in Italy, from 64 to 72 percent; and in the United Kingdom, from 70 to 84 percent.[37] There is good reason to believe that slow economic growth became a consensus policy in Europe in the 1970s partly because of the increased labor share and the inability of expansion to reduce it.[38] Indeed, there is some evidence that the strategy may have worked. During the second oil price increase in 1979, European workers' real wages were eroded much more quickly and to a much greater extent than they had been in the wake of the first price increase.[39]

Equally important, Europeans wanted to reduce the transfer of wealth from them to OPEC. They therefore wanted to reduce oil consumption by lowering economic growth. And, equally significant, they also wanted to generate an export surplus to pay for OPEC oil. The nature of the labor markets in Europe, the governments' response to them, and their desire for an export surplus all affected the ability of the United States to expand in the mid-1970s without undermining the dollar and creating inflationary pressures.

From 1976 to 1978, the failure of Europe to grow rapidly and increase its imports meant that the United States balance of payments deficit and downward pressure on the dollar were greatly exacerbated. Aware of the problem, Carter's economic advisers and the Fed's Miller kept cajoling Europe to grow faster. But the relative militancy of the working class in Europe and export imperatives constrained the ability of American capitalism to satisfy its manufacturers' demands for growth without undermining American and international financial institutions and markets. Thus, when their costs finally outweighed their benefits, financial institutions finally demanded an end to growth, inflation, depreciation, and the exchange market instability induced by them. Because of historical institutional ties, and because the government is often politically incapable of reducing government spending or increasing taxes, financial institutions turned to the Fed for relief. But the ability of the Fed to fight inflation and protect the dollar is being seriously undermined just as the need for it to do so increased. The relative impotence of the Federal Reserve means that all sectors of American business now require new methods to fight inflation.

A great deal of evidence suggests that contractionary macroeconomic policy cannot reduce inflation in the United States without at the same time creating serious dangers. It seems, for one thing, that Marx's reserve army effect is becoming less and less powerful. Contractionary monetary policy results in large amounts of unemployment with relatively little reduction in wages and prices.[40] This increases manufacturers' demand for inflation, but reduces the Fed's ability to satisfy the financial demands to stop it. In the recession of 1920–1921, for example, wage inflation fell by 37.4 percent and price inflation by 56.8 percent. In contrast, during the severe recession of 1973–1975, wage inflation *increased* by 2.9 percent and price inflation by 8 percent. This is the extreme case, but the same general pattern emerges for milder cases as well.[41] One simulation of an econometric model of the economy showed that contractionary monetary policy would take until 1985 to reduce the inflation from 10 to 4 percent, but the unemployment rate would have to increase to over 10 percent.[42] It seems highly unlikely that any political coalition could withstand that kind of austerity. Margaret Thatcher is attempting just that in the UK, and serious strains are showing after only a year.

The reasons for the reduced ability of unemployment to discipline workers are not completely understood, but a number of factors are probably involved. The use of Keynesian policy in the past to reduce the duration and severity of unemployment, and the expansion of social programs to reduce its pain, have probably reduced the willingness of workers to take wage cuts even in the face of unemployment.[43] Even the benefits accruing to financial institutions from Fed inflation fighting are called into question. The very solvency of financial and nonfinancial corporations begins to be undermined the higher interest rates go and the tighter credit becomes. Both inflation and economic expansion tend to reduce the liquidity positions of corporations. This results partly from the fact that inflation increases the tax advantages of using debt, partly because in a boom corporations are willing to take more risks, and partly because long-term debt becomes relatively more expensive the higher and more variable its inflation. In 1976, the ratio of liquid assets to current liabilities of nonfinancial corporations was 38 percent. By 1980 it had fallen by a quarter, to 28 percent, its lowest point ever. Over the same period, the ratio of long-term debt to short-term debt increased by a similar proportion.[44] If the monetary authority attempts to stop the expansion by tightening the money supply and reducing sales, firms may find it difficult or impossible to pay back their debts. As Rapping puts it, the Fed can pull on a string, but only at the risk of breaking it.[45]

The OPEC oil price increases have enormously exacerbated the international financial dangers of attempting to fight inflation by creating a recession. In 1979, American banks had outstanding over $55 billion in loans to Third World countries.[46] Many of these were made to help finance oil imports. After the first major oil price increase in 1974, there was much speculation in the financial press on the ability of the private banking sector to take deposits of OPEC wealth and lend them to countries who needed to borrow in order to buy back OPEC's higher priced oil without a rash of bankruptcies ensuing. But most major American banks assured everyone that they could handle the job, and they did with minimal help from the IMF. This time around, however, it is virtually impossible to find a banker or bank regulator who thinks the banks can do it alone. As Volcker put it:

> Although there is still some leeway, it seems to me, for reasonable increases in bank lending to these countries, one potential danger in the recycling process that we must avoid as far as possible is the overloading of the commercial banking system. . . . If we urge [the Third World] to make real adjustments, they, in turn, will expect us to keep our markets open to their goods.[47]

If the banks are going to be repaid, the United States or other industrial countries will have to import billions of dollars of goods from these countries. Importing such amounts will be virtually impossible politically and economically if economic growth is not sustained. Protectionist pressures almost inevitably build if high levels of unemployment and low profits are maintained for long periods of time. Other countries would probably respond in kind. If trade wars are exacerbated, financial battles will be hard to win.

The roots of stagflation in the United States can now be discerned. Sustained economic expansion generates reduced productivity, higher costs, and demands for inflation; OPEC and domestic oil price increases generate demands for inflation; and dollar devaluations increase demands for inflation—all to transfer wealth from American workers without eroding corporate profits. But inflation undermines financial markets and causes the dollar to depreciate. The latter in turn can generate great instability on foreign exchange markets because the dollar is still the linchpin of the international financial system, despite the great reduction of American power. Demands for relief from the "rentiers" pour in to the Fed, but while the Fed is able to generate high unemployment, before it can make a major dent in inflation it relents for fear of creating financial crisis. In the meantime, investment has been discouraged by high unemployment rates and tight money, which means that in the next round, productivity is damaged and the basis for noninflationary growth is undermined.

The standard economic theories no longer seem to hold much promise of solving the stagflation problem. Milton Friedman's view that the Federal Reserve should just reduce the money supply does not seem tenable. In the medium run such attempts can only damage powerful interests in the economy, and call into question its financial and political stability. In the long run, such control is virtually impossible. Yet Keynesianism, the major alternative, has been discredited. Economic expansion creates inflationary excesses, which, we have seen, also harm powerful interests and pose serious dangers. It is small wonder that a new theory, supply-side economics, which promises to sustain economic growth without exacerbating inflation, was embraced by the winning presidential candidate. It is also little wonder that that administration's promises can be fulfilled only if a noninflationary method to cut government social spending and workers' real income is discovered. Otherwise the Fed will have to rise to the occasion as it has in the past, to stem the "inflationary" excesses of government. Its ability to do so, however, is hardly a foregone conclusion.

MONETARY POLICY IN THE HIDDEN ELECTION

Economic policy during the Carter years can be greatly illuminated with the help of the framework outlined in the previous section. During the Carter years, three different men were chairs of the Federal Reserve. The circumstances surrounding their appointments illustrate the contingent nature of the Federal Reserve's independence and the difficulties of maintaining that independence if the appropriate political constituency is not cultivated. The problems faced by the three, Arthur Burns, G. William Miller, and Paul Volcker, also suggest the difficulty of satisfying any constituency when the macroeconomic problems become increasingly intractable.

Despite the vulnerability of the Fed, however, the Carter years also show that its relative independence means that it is to the Fed that financial institutions and the president must turn for relief when the political process is too stymied to take charge. But the Carter years also show that increased international competition between the United States and Europe and Japan, the power of OPEC, the need to satisfy the demands of its financial constituency, the integration of international financial markets, and the power of labor at home and abroad greatly undermine the ability of the Fed to restore conditions of profitable expansion in the United States, much less help incumbents get reelected.

Jimmy Carter failed to reappoint Fed Chairman Arthur Burns in December 1977. The business press speculated that the reason was that Burns, the man of impeccable conservative credentials, having served as chairman of Eisenhower's Council of Economic Advisers (1953–1956), counselor to President Nixon (1969–1970), and head of the Federal Reserve beginning in February 1970, was on a collision course with Carter. Carter, the Democrat, had inherited a 7.4 percent unemployment rate from Gerald Ford and hoped to get it down. Burns would not go along, so he was fired.

The reasons for Carter's failure to reappoint Burns are considerably more complex. One would be simplifying only slightly by saying that Carter wanted to appoint someone who would fit in with the multinational business decor of his administration.[48] For his part, Burns had abandoned his natural constituency, large bankers, and had alienated small bankers as well. Moreover, he was implicated in the massive recession of 1974–1975. Having lost support on all sides, when Carter chose not to reappoint him in December of his first year in office there were few cries of dismay, and no financial panic. Moreover, Burns's reputation as a tight-fisted monetary conservative was misleading in any case. As Rapping puts it:

> [Burns] was the ultimate pragmatist: talking and acting conservatively by day and running the printing presses by night. Burns was a closet inflationist rather than a great liquidationist in the tradition of Andrew Mellon, Treasury Secretary in the early 1930's. . . . Burns did not pursue the Mellon policy quoted so vividly by Herbert Hoover. "Liquidate labor, liquidate stocks, liquidate the farmers, liquidate real estate. . . . It will purge the rottenness out of the system." . . . With the advantage of historical perspective, Burns bowed to necessity as a more ideological and less pragmatic conservative might not have done.[49]

Burns's role was hardly benign, however. There were dramatic swings in the money supply during the early part of his tenure at the Fed from 1970 to 1974. The increase in rates of growth of both the nominal and real money supply during the two years from 1970 to 1972 is spectacular, as is the decline in the year and a half following. The latter preceded the worst recession the United States has experienced in the postwar period.

There has been a great deal of speculation concerning Burns's motivation in the extraordinary monetary expansion of 1970–1972. Much of it has centered on the suggestion that Burns was trying to engineer Nixon's reelection.[50] Rapping's implicit view that Burns was attempting to forestall a major financial panic resulting from the tight policies inherited from Martin is undoubtedly correct. But the policies to stabilize the financial markets in the wake of the Cambodian invasion in the spring of 1970 and the Penn Central collapse in the fall cannot account for the massive increases in the money supply over the next two years. Of more importance here was Burns's attempt to keep interest rates low during Nixon's wage and price controls in 1971–1973. As chairman of Nixon's Committee on Interest and Dividends, Burns was worried that Congress would attempt to control interest rates. He hoped to insulate the banks, and to avoid putting them in the undesirable position of experiencing a credit squeeze, on the one hand, or raising interest rates and bringing down congressional wrath on their heads, on the other. More important, however, was Burns's concern that rising interest rates would reduce political support for the wage controls which formed the basis of reestablishing American international competitiveness after the devaluation of the dollar in August 1971. A representative passage appears in the Federal Open Market Committee meeting in September 1972:

> Chairman Burns [commented that] it was clear that the Pay Board would find it extremely difficult to lower the wage guideline if consumer prices, profits, and interest rates were rising rapidly and if the Committee on Interest and Dividends [of which Burns was Chairman] responded to pressures to relax the dividend guidelines. Assuming, however, that over-all developments were of a kind that permitted the Pay Board to lower the wage guidelines, subsequent sharp increases in interest rates might well create problems.[51]

If wages increased after the devaluation, export profits would fall; if export producers raised prices, exports would not become competitive on world markets. In order to keep interest rates low, the Fed had to keep expanding the money supply in the face of strong demand for credit as the economy boomed.

The Fed's role in the major recession of 1974–1975 is more difficult to assess. Though Burns has been blamed for the severity of the recession, the role of monetary policy was considerably less clear. The two major difficulties facing the Fed during the first OPEC price hike were its inability to forecast the effects of the hike, and its inability to forecast the effects of its monetary policy on the economy. The first was a general problem facing all the institutions attempting to deal with the massive disruption following the quadrupling of oil prices and the oil embargo. The second problem was the Fed's alone.

The difficulty facing the Fed was one manifestation of the general problem it has in controlling the money supply: the relationship between the amount of money it puts into the economy and the effects of that money on the economy is subject to erratic shifts. These shifts are due to the invention of new kinds of money over which the Fed has no control. Prime examples of new money are credit cards and money market funds (which are like checking accounts) created by brokerage houses. When new money is created, it will affect the amount of spending in the economy. If the Fed does not know how much has been created, it does not know how much money it should create through its own policy. Such a major shift occurred during 1973–1974. In fact, its cause is still not completely understood. But the shift created massive uncertainty for the Fed, which made it difficult to make policy and extremely difficult to judge its intentions from the effects of its policy. It is undoubtedly true that the Fed was not willing to let inflation run rampant. But it probably ended up with a much more restrictive policy than it bargained for, and contributed much more to the major recession than it intended.[52]

The widespread perception that the Fed had major responsibility for the recession, however, generated bitter congressional criticism. In March 1975 Congress passed a joint resolution calling on the Fed to reduce interest rates, to announce annual growth targets for the money aggregates, and to appear periodically before the appropriate congressional committees. While the congressional oversight of monetary policy has little direct impact on policy, passage of the bill represented movement toward less independence for the Fed. The effects of the great contraction bear most of the responsibility for the passage of the congressional oversight. But Burns's premature attempts to centralize the Fed, even further reducing the powers of the Regional Reserve banks and the smaller banks they represent, undermined the Fed's traditional base of support in Congress, which might have been able to fight off the attack. Burns, for example, apparently attempted to use Reserve Bank budgets and staffing limits as a means to affect the research of the Reserve Banks. And on one occasion he tried to prevent and then alter the testimony of Reserve Bank presidents before the House committee on banking and currency.[53]

So when push came to shove, Burns had lost allies on all fronts. He was implicated in the destruction of the Bretton Woods system, which disrupted the relations between the United States, Japan, and Europe, alienating the multinational business community; he was blamed for the recession; he had allowed the independence of the Fed to be eroded; and he had alienated small bankers as well. As it happened, Burns did not attempt to slow the growth rate of the economy. Except for some threatening increases in the federal funds rate in the fall of 1977, Burns pursued a middle course. During 1977, the economy grew at an annual rate of 5.3 percent and employment grew by 3 million people. The rate of growth of real hourly earnings declined, raising both the share of profits in income slightly and the after-tax rate of profit as well. Toward the end of the year, the depreciation of the dollar became worrisome, especially since the trade deficit was not improving. But that was to turn around early in 1978.

Miller took over from Burns in March 1978 and proceeded to ensure that the recovery would not falter. "I'm going to be concerned with keeping the economy going and not having a recession. I am going to run it for human beings," Miller said in December.[54] Real per capita spendable income did increase by 3.8 percent in 1978, the fastest rate since 1973. But that resulted from more people working, not higher hourly wages. During the year, real compensation per hour declined even though productivity increased by almost 2 percent. Indeed, the vast expansion of the labor force in the midst of relatively small increases and even declines in real wages goes a long way toward explaining the ability of the United States to sustain growth over the long 1976 to 1979 period. The increase in the labor force resulted not only from demographic factors, the baby boom, and social factors such as the increased desire of women to work outside the home; it also resulted from the need of extra workers to find paying jobs to support their families in the wake of slower economic growth of the late 1960s and early 1970s. This increase in the potential "reserve army" was critical to the ability of the United States to expand without running into the barriers of worker militancy and higher wage demands. Between 1976 and 1980, employment in the United States grew by 11 percent, while in Japan the figure was 5 percent and in Germany 3 percent, the next two largest increases among industrialized countries.[55]

And the expansion was having its intended effect on OPEC's surplus. OPEC's current account surplus declined by $20 billion, the largest decline since 1975. The 1978 reduction resulted primarily from the deterioration in OPEC's aggregate terms of trade (which are the price of its exports relative to the costs of its imports). During 1978, OPEC as a group experienced an 11 percent decline in its terms of trade relative to 1977. Of the total 15 percent increased cost of imports to OPEC, over half reflected the depreciation of the dollar against major currencies; the rest stemmed from inflation in the industrial countries. The terms of trade facing OPEC in the fourth quarter of 1978 were 23 percent less favorable than they had been in 1974. OPEC's surpluses also fell partly because oil exports declined because of conservation measures by Europe and Japan. Exports also declined because European economic growth had not recovered since the 1974–1975 contraction. While real GNP in the United States was growing by 5.3 percent in 1977 and 4.4 percent in 1978, the European countries were growing at 2.3 and 3 percent, compared to their 1963–1972 average of 4.5 percent.[56]

Despite Europe's failure to grow as rapidly, dollar depreciation was finally also having its intended effect on the U.S. trade balance. It improved by $5 billion in 1978. But in September 1978, concern for the dollar finally began to take its toll in the Fed's decision-making body. In September Henry Wallich, one of the Fed's major spokesmen on international monetary matters, dissented on the side of tightness for the first time during the Carter administration. From September 1977 to September 21, 1978, the dollar fell by more than 56 percent against the Swiss franc, 42 percent against the yen, and 19 percent against the German mark. The Fed raised the discount rate toward the end of September as a first step to strengthen the dollar. In October, Carter unveiled a new "anti-inflation" program, including voluntary wage and price controls, in an attempt to prevent workers' wages from catching up with the depreciation-induced inflation that two years of economic expansion had created. The exchange markets were unimpressed, however. The dollar fell almost 2 percent the last few weeks in October.

The dollar was declining despite an increase in American interest rates, an improvement in the trade balance, and a rate of inflation that was in the middle ranges of European inflation rates. The view taken by the administration and numerous economists was that the dollar was undergoing an irrational speculative attack, a view which has an important element of truth. Free markets that have as their object the accumulation of profit are not likely to be stable when the world has nothing solid on which to base expectations. Uncertainty breeds speculation.

The uncertainty was generated, however, by real factors of great significance. First was the recognition that OPEC was not likely to continue playing the fool to the American game of using inflation to erode its wealth. Second, Europe was creating the European Monetary System (EMS), partly in response to the dramatic declines in the dollar over the previous year. Some feared that the EMS would lead to a currency bloc competing with the dollar as a reserve currency, and therefore for holdings of OPEC surpluses. Finally, European countries were less reluctant to support the dollar as they began to see the benefits from appreciating currencies, both in terms of lowered inflation and in terms of increased profits for their financial institutions.

To prevent the position of the dollar from eroding further, the Fed and the Treasury, on November 1, made it clear that, after almost a five-year hiatus, they would again begin to defend the dollar's role. The Fed raised the discount rate by a full percentage point, the largest amount ever, increased reserve requirements on large banks, and sold bonds denominated in yen and marks to sop up excess dollars in the foreign exchange markets. The measures temporarily staved off the speculative fervor. But in December oil exports were halted from Iran, and OPEC announced a 14.5 percent increase in the price of crude oil to be phased in over the next year. The OPEC price increase and the revolution in Iran exacerbated the Fed's problems, which had been mounting in any case. At the beginning of 1979, the Federal Reserve and the international team within the administration and their allies were badly divided on the proper course of action. Within the Fed, Paul Volcker, president of the New York bank, dissented for the first time in March and April, calling for tighter policy. Wallich joined him.[57]

Meanwhile, Blumenthal and Miller were openly fighting. In April, as the dollar continued to fall, Blumenthal was calling for tighter policy, while Miller expressed "satisfaction" with the current degree of restraint.[58] Miller received support from welcome quarters. As the controversy swirled, David Rockefeller, chairman of Chase Manhattan Bank, gave a rare on-the-record speech at the bank's annual Washington dinner–press conference on April 18, 1979. Rockefeller said: "Miller 'correctly' had opposed 'dramatic' changes in Federal Reserve Policy. . . . The New York bank executive noted that at the end of the last expansionary period, tightening produced a 'harmful crunch.' " Presumably he was referring to Burns's policy in 1974.[59] To make sure there was no mistaking his concern, however, Rockefeller reportedly "Praised the administration's November 1 dollar support program. 'It has demonstrated to dollar holders that this country is prepared to support the dollar.' "[60] Since the dollar was still holding up against other currencies in April, a majority of the Fed and Miller did not want to risk a credit crunch as long as inflation was helping to reduce real wages to pay for oil. In 1979, real wages fell by $45 billion, enough to pay for the higher cost of imported oil.[61]

During the summer, in an attempt to rescue his reputation and the election from the jaws of OPEC, Carter reorganized his cabinet. Having fired born-again interest hawk Blumenthal, Carter needed someone whose very presence could maintain the confidence of the foreign exchange markets. Worried that a feverish dollar speculation could undermine the whole international system, Carter had hoped to prop up the dollar with psychological warfare on the exchange markets in lieu of real warfare on the electorate. The president turned to Paul Volcker, president of the New York Federal Reserve, a former undersecretary of the Treasury who had been involved in the monetary negotiations of the early 1970s, and a former vice-president at Chase Manhattan. Volcker became chairman of the Fed in August. Miller, whose credibility on the exchange markets had been sacrificed to the economic expansion, became secretary of the Treasury. The expansion had gone on, apparently, a bit too long. Roosa exclaimed that "Volcker is absolutely the right man and I'm delighted."[62]

Reputation is quickly depreciated. The money supply continued to grow at a rapid pace, as American banks borrowed billions of dollars from their banks in the Eurodollar markets. In September, silver and gold prices skyrocketed and the value of the dollar dropped substantially, despite intensive intervention by the United States on the foreign exchange markets. By the end of September, all proceeds from the sale of the yen and mark bonds the previous year had been exhausted, and foreign exchange borrowed from the Germans was running out. At that point, the Germans were apparently approached to see if they were willing to extend more credit so that the Federal Reserve could continue carrying out its dollar support operations. But the Germans proved uncooperative. Morgan Guaranty reports:

> The discussion apparently ended with agreement by the German and U.S. authorities that continued heavy central bank intervention alone was not the answer to the dollar-mark problem. Instead, more fundamental action

to curb inflationary pressure in the United States was needed to arrest the dollar's decline against the mark and to curb speculation in gold and other commodity markets.[63]

Since the European central banks were unwilling to intervene heavily in the exchange markets, Volcker rushed back from an international monetary conference to a secret meeting in Washington. On October 6, the Fed announced a series of restrictive measures, including a percentage point hike in the discount rate to a record 12 percent (now almost an anachronism), an increase in reserve requirements on a range of managed liabilities, and most important of all, a new monetary management technique.

Volcker chose a meeting of the American Bankers Association to unveil his new policies. "Whatever the Fed had in mind," Volcker said, the Fed's moves "Weren't designed to make your life as bankers easier."[64] But the big bankers did not seem to be complaining. Willard Butcher, president of Chase Manhattan, said: "It will tend to deepen what has been seen as a relatively shallow recession but is a price worth paying. Inflation is a terrible cancerous disease that takes radical action."[65] However, the disgruntled president of a small Southwestern bank said: "Once again the banking system has been called upon to make sacrifices while other segments of society roll merrily along."[66] Just as small bankers are hurt most by inflation, their inflexibility means they lose more when the Fed takes dramatic action. By reducing the money supply, the Fed reduces the resources at the disposal of small banks. Large banks, on the other hand, are often able to get resources anyway by borrowing from large corporate customers. Neither do small banks benefit from the international effects of the Fed's policies, since they tend not to participate in international lending.

One policy change was of special significance. Volcker announced that the Fed would stop trying to control interest rates to stabilize the money supply. Instead, it would let interest rates fluctuate and try to control bank reserves directly. The Fed claimed this policy would give it more direct control over the money supply, but its real motivation was different. The Federal Reserve needed to take dramatic action that would calm the nerves of the money and commodity markets. Moreover, it knew that, if it were to maintain the value of the dollar and the health of the financial markets, the Federal Reserve might well have to take contractionary policies which would drastically increase interest rates. Yet interest rates are highly visible and politically dangerous for the Federal Reserve and the banking community as a whole.

When interest rates were so politically sensitive during Nixon's wage and price controls, and Burns would not raise the Federal Reserve discount rate to help the banks raise their primes (see below), some major banks invented a prime free of human intervention. The prime rate, they said, would be set by a formula which would tie the prime to their cost of funds.

"We married ourselves to the market—for better or worse," said E. E. Palmer of Citibank.[67] But the prime rate still went up faster than it came down when the cost of funds varied, raising questions about the sanctity of the marriage.

The Fed's desire to marry the market and insulate itself from political pressure during the election year (and in general) undoubtedly played an important role in the decision to target bank reserves rather than interest rates. But letting interest rates fluctuate wildly to reduce political opposition probably created more problems than solutions for the Fed. Some studies have shown that widely fluctuating interest rates create uncertainty and discourage investment. Moreover, fluctuating interest rates create risks for those investing in dollar-denominated assets that could hurt the value of the dollar even further in the long run. By October, the Federal Reserve and the credit markets were running the economy. *The Wall Street Journal* reported in November:

> The Carter administration has made little comment since it formally endorsed the new policy. One policy maker commented that the President would like to put a little distance between himself and the Fed but will not outrightly criticize that body fearing it could hurt the dollar on the foreign exchange market.[68]

Even the opposition could not attack the Fed. In an interview with *Business Week* in October, Kennedy was asked whether he approved of the Federal Reserve's recent steps. He replied:

> One of the leading problems in the country at present is inflation. The steps the Fed has taken are not steps that I would differ with, although we have to monitor this action extremely closely over the next several weeks to see whether it will put us over the brink and into a more serious recession.[69]

Meanwhile, in December, Lelan Prussin, vice-chairman and world banking chief of Bank of America, reported that the Fed's moves are "working fine. Credit demand has slowed, aggregates are declining, and there's much more discipline."[70]

In January 1980, OPEC crude oil prices increased 9.5 percent, and the second phase of domestic decontrol of oil prices went into effect. By March, *domestic* oil prices had doubled from a year earlier and OPEC prices had more than doubled.[71] The economy officially went into a recession, probably brought on by the October 1979 policies.[72] But the Consumer Price Index went up at an annual rate of 17.5 percent, significantly greater than the 12.6 percent increase of December. Productivity took a mysterious drop in the last quarter of 1979 and first quarter of 1980, wages began to rise rapidly, and unit labor costs began to increase at a rapid pace. Interest rates began rising as well, partly in response to the expectation that, in the wake of Iran and Afghanistan, military spending and inflation would take off.

By the end of February, influential Henry Kaufman, general partner of Salomon Brothers, an investment bank, was widely quoted as believing that a national inflation emergency should be declared which included a

> temporary wage and price freeze or a simple mandatory controls program provided they were joined with cuts in government spending and limits on government and private borrowing.[73]

In an article in *The New York Times* on February 27 entitled "Price Controls Gaining Friends," Leonard Silk reported:

> A growing number of critics contemplating 18% inflation, possible destruction of the bond market or even an end to the democratic system, as *Business Week* warned, have become convinced that controls might be necessary . . . with the only alternative being a major and prolonged recession, controls have become more and more acceptable except to a few tenured academic economists.[74]

But Paul Volcker, in testimony before the Senate banking committee, said that controls would not be useful against inflation. He warned that they would "divert attention from what really needs to be done," reduction in American dependence on OPEC and cuts in government spending.[75] Kennedy came out for a six-month freeze on wages and prices, and calls for consideration of controls came from Robert Byrd and William Proxmire. Yet on February 26, Carter called controls "counterproductive," and said he did not see any prospect at all of supporting them.[76] Those are the words of someone opposed to controls and someone who is planning to implement them but does not want panic price and wage increases to undermine them before they are in place.

There are some indications that a number of Carter's political advisers were recommending controls. Controls could have saved Carter from a spiraling inflation and recession at election time. *The New York Times* was even speculating that controls would return soon after Kennedy was no longer regarded as a threat. But as Representative Weiss (D, NY), a leading proponent of controls, reported in late February:

> Sentiment is shifting [in Congress] but it is still very slow. The Republicans have done a very good job brainwashing the Democrats, convincing them controls don't work.[77]

Even the financial community was divided. On March 6, Leif Olsen, chairman of Citibank's economic policy committee, wrote in *The Wall Street Journal* in an article "Fear Rules the Credit Markets" (presumably a reply to Salomon Brothers' Kaufman):

The fear that grips the credit markets will lead to self-destructive advocacy of wage, price and credit controls it has traditionally and wisely opposed in the past. . . .[78]

By this time, Walter Wriston, president of Citibank, had endorsed Reagan. And Citibank was worried that credit controls would be slapped on, costing it millions of dollars in loan interest.

On March 4, *The New York Times* reported that John Dunlop, the Harvard professor who had directed the administration's Pay Committee, composed of business and labor leaders, had made a bid to increase the scope of the committee to include such issues as "capital formation, trade policy and credit policy," which Congress seemed unable to deal with. Instead, Paul Volcker and the Federal Reserve took control again.

Wage and price controls might have saved Carter. But he did not want to seem to vacillate, and his major economic advisors were opposed to controls. Congress was unlikely to support controls for good reasons: oil prices were a major driving force behind inflation, and controls could not affect them. Moreover, wages were not keeping up with inflation as it was, so if controls were to help stop inflation, they would probably only have hurt business profits. In the end, Carter had only the Fed to turn to. And turn he did. On March 14, Volcker announced new measures to put an end to the "fear" that had gripped the bond markets. He announced that the Federal Reserve would implement the president's credit controls. The controls placed limitations on the extension of new consumer credit through credit cards, and put reserve requirements on money market funds. Money market funds were not subject to interest ceilings and had bid away billions of dollars from savings and loans and commercial banks. The controls were slapped on despite the fact that the rate of growth of consumer credit had been falling for virtually the entire previous year.[79] A congressional investigation later contended that credit controls had helped many banks raise terms on credit cards, on which they had been losing money. They had been reluctant to change the terms themselves for fear of losing out to the competition. Regulations like these often serve to help financial institutions coordinate their pricing, while at the same time performing a macroeconomic function for the Federal Reserve.

Over the next month, interest rates and the dollar skyrocketed. The money supply took a nose dive. Between April and June, real GNP fell at an annual rate of almost 10 percent, the largest quarterly decline on record. And along with it, interest rates and the dollar plunged. The prime rate fell from a high of almost 20 percent in April to 12.5 percent in July. Other interest rates fell even more. The press reported that the economy was in a free fall, and the Federal Reserve madly attempted to reverse itself. In June, the money supply grew at an annual rate of almost 14 percent, and at 11 percent in July.[80] But by that time unemployment had taken off; by July it was at 7.8 percent. The Fed was reluctant to reverse itself too quickly, however, since the dollar had lost much of the ground it had gained. Anthony Solomon, former undersecretary of the Treasury, who had replaced Volcker as president of the Federal Reserve Bank of New York, cautioned against too precipitous a decline in interest rates and the dollar.[81]

For its part, the administration was letting the government budget become more expansionary. The high employment deficit, which measures how expansionary the government budget is, moved from $2.2 billion in 1979 to over $21 billion from April to June 1980 and to $20.7 billion from July to September. Part of this expansion resulted from technical procedures involved in measuring the deficit, part from increased unemployment and other payments associated with the recession. But on the basis of the available evidence, it seems unlikely that the administration was trying to impose contractionary policy; it probably was attempting to pump up the economy. Meanwhile, congressional Democrats and Republicans were competing to see who could come up with the quickest tax cut proposals in the face of the perceived economic free fall. Carter cautioned them against ill-conceived proposals, especially those directed toward individuals. He came up with his own plan, "the economic revitalization program," which stressed corporation tax cuts, including those for the declining sectors of steel and auto. Volcker warned that tax cuts, especially personal ones, were inflationary in the current environment, and suggested that he would not accommodate them unless government spending were reduced. If Volcker raised interest rates sufficiently, he could nullify their expansionary effects.

After a 21.6 percent increase in the money supply in August, the Fed reduced the rate of growth of the money supply in the two months before the election. In the last week in September the Fed tried to tighten up even further. On September 26 it raised the discount rate by a full percentage point again. As Volcker put it later:

> We had to recognize that the already precipitous decline in interest rates might be misread as a fundamental reversal of policy . . . a lessening of our resolve to fight inflation. Such a false interpretation could only have undermined the ultimate success of that effort . . . [and] could have complicated our task further by undermining confidence in the dollar on foreign exchange markets . . . as it turned out . . . that . . . was avoided.[82]

But by September, Carter was fighting for his life. He and his advisors complained that the Fed's discount rate hike was unnecessary. Fuel was added to the fire when the commercial banks, led by Reagan supporter Walter Wriston's Citibank, began raising their prime rates. They jumped from 11 percent in September to 13.5 percent by the end of October. Even Volcker began to worry that such massive increases in the weeks before the election stretched the limits of political etiquette. In his own defense, and apparently in a politically safe jab at Wriston, Volcker explained: "There's a tendency for markets to jump and I wonder if they haven't jumped too far." But by October, it was simply a waiting game. The overall unemployment rate had risen to 7.6 percent, virtually as high as it had been when Carter had beaten Gerald Ford four years earlier. The blue-collar unemployment rate was a full percentage point higher at 10.8 percent, and the black unemployment rate had risen from 12.7 percent in 1976 to over 14 percent in October 1980. And inflation was still 5 percent higher.

After a respectful pause during October, the Fed began to respond again to the real underlying pressures. Between November and the end of December, the prime rate skyrocketed to 21.5 percent with a 2 percent increase in the discount rate leading the way. This time Carter was not complaining. But the newspaper headlines blamed high interest rates for the failure of auto sales to recover. The old conflicts were not about to fade away with Jimmy Carter, nor are they likely to in the face of the supply-side mystification and wishful thinking of the Reagan team.

MACRODILEMMAS: THE HIDDEN ELECTION AND BEYOND

The three main economic problems facing the American economy are the declining growth of productivity, the massive increases in oil prices, and the increased international competition facing important sectors of its industry. I use the term "American economy" advisedly: These are problems that affect the vast majority of American citizens, but big business is using them to mobilize support to solve its own difficulties.

The major economic problem facing the big business community is how to increase the profitability of major American financial and nonfinancial institutions without continuing to impose burdens on each other, and at the same time without undermining political stability at home.[83] The more the burden can be placed on the Third World, OPEC, Europe, and Japan, the less they have to put on small business and workers at home. While shifting some of the burden to foreigners is a necessary part of any viable strategy, the reduced power of the United States in the world economy and increased competition from abroad means that restructuring at home is unavoidable if the stagflation impasse is to be broken. And to conduct that restructuring, a policy of economic and political obfuscation and further reduction of democratic control over the economy will have to be pursued. Increasing the power of the Federal Reserve is a prime component of this strategy.

On the domestic side, the success of that restructuring will depend on the ability of corporations to get the government to force consumption and real income losses on the majority of the American people without resorting to inflation, which undermines financial markets and the international monetary system. Already the business press is pointing out that "breaking inflationary expectations" will be one of the major problems facing the Reagan administration. These expectations are simply workers' waking up to the fact that almost 8 percent of their incomes have been lost in the last two years, with the expectation that they might be able to make some of it up. Increasing productivity is the key to the domestic strategy of increasing corporate profits and the international competitiveness of American business without imposing significant costs on the financial sector. If productivity increases, and workers' wage demands do not match that increase, manufacturing profits can increase without a resort to inflation and international competitiveness can be improved without having to rely on the depreciation of the dollar. Reducing taxes to corporations and the wealthy are further ways to redistribute income. But if tax cuts are not matched by increases in productivity or reductions in government spending, then inflation results, imposing the old dilemmas once again.

Arthur Laffer's supply-side economics, which was embraced by Ronald Reagan, appeared as a possible way out of this dilemma. According to Laffer's argument, individual income tax cuts would restore the individual initiative high taxes had muted. If people were subjected to lower tax rates, so the theory went, they would work more, save more, and invest more. All this, according to Laffer, would increase production and productivity. The biggest miracle of all was that supply and income would go up by so much as a result of these cuts in tax *rates* that the actual amount of taxes collected would actually stay the same or increase. Thus, the government budget would not have to be cut at all to avoid increasing the deficit or fueling inflation.

At one level, Laffer's supply-side economics is simply an attempt to redistribute income toward the rich. In the fifties, only one-third of the government budget was spent on transfer payments. By the early 1970s, two-thirds of the government budget consisted of transfers. The after-tax, after-transfer distribution of income is virtually the same now as it was at the end of World War II. But without these and other government programs, the distribution of income would have been considerably less equal. Tax cuts directed toward the rich and cuts in spending programs designed to help the poor are a thinly disguised exercise to reverse this.

Even on its own terms, however, there is at least one basic problem with supply-side economics: it has no foundation in fact. The pillar on which there seems to be the most evidence concerns savings. Supply-siders say that reducing taxes will increase saving and investment. There is little evidence that more saving produces more investment; the sequence is more likely to be the reverse. But what is at issue here is whether increases on the returns to saving will even increase saving. Stanford economist Michael Boskin published a very influential article in 1978 which, contrary to much previous evidence and conventional wisdom, purported to show that high returns to saving did in fact increase the amount saved. But many economists have complained that they have tried but failed to replicate his results. One even sent his results to Boskin, asking him for comments on the paper. After more than a year and a half, he still had not heard from him, nor had he been able to get his paper published. The implicit argument in Boskin's paper that taxes should be lowered for wealthy savers remains in the public domain as justification for tax cuts for the rich.

Laffer's supply-side economics also assumes that increasing wages after taxes will increase the labor supply and raise productivity. But the experience of the 1970s suggests that the stick works much better than the carrot to increase labor hours, and in any case, such increases are unlikely to help restore productivity growth. As I suggested earlier, between 1976 and 1980 employment in the United States increased by a phenomenal 11 percent. That increase of the "reserve army of labor" was significantly responsible for the ability of the 1976–1979 boom to last. Moreover, that expansion was at least partly due to the need of families to increase the number of wage earners simply to keep their standard of living at a constant level. And although the expansion helped to maintain the boom, it also created problems. While the ratio of investment spending to GNP remained at almost the same level between 1974 and 1979, as it had between 1959 and 1969 (as opposed to many commentators who argue that the United States does not save and invest as much as it used to), the rate of growth of the ratio of the capital stock to hours worked fell from a 3.3 percent rate during the earlier period to only 0.2 percent during the 1974–1979 period. The decline was not as significant in manufacturing as it was for the business community as a whole, but it was significant there as well. Generally a decline in the amount of capital that workers use reduces the amount of output each can produce. And although the reduction does not explain all the productivity decline, it is at least as and probably much more important than government regulations, taxes, and spending.[84] The reduced productivity that results from increased supplies of labor does not bode well for the ability of supply-side economics to stop inflation without lowering real wages.

Even the wealthy advocates of supply-side tax cuts embodied in the Kemp-Roth bill doubt its ability to slow inflation. They have suggested a return to the gold standard to go along with it—a monetarism that sticks. The essence of a gold standard is that the supply of gold will determine the money supply. Not trusting the political will or desires of the Fed, advocates favor rule by the market rather than by politics. The gold standard would supposedly maintain discipline on the economy and bring the money supply and inflation under control. If a gold standard were established in combination with tax cuts for wealthy individuals and a reduction in government spending for the poor, rich rentier incomes could not be eaten away by inflation and the United States would become a virtual individual rentier paradise, or so the thinking goes.

But the bulk of corporate America, including the large financial community, is more concerned with the stability and growth of their institutions on a world scale. Tax cuts, they say, should be for corporations, not for individuals. Individuals are just as likely to increase consumption as to increase saving. Monetary policy should be firm, but flexible. For them, Paul Volcker would probably be better than a gold standard. As undersecretary of the Treasury during the dollar troubles of the early 1970s, among American negotiators Volcker was reportedly the last to abandon convertibility of the dollar to gold and the most insistent on returning to gold at the earliest opportunity. If Volcker can maintain the relative autonomy of the Fed, he can be Reagan's gold standard, but a more flexible one to salvage the financial structure from a debt recycling or tight money collapse. The preferred strategy of the financially oriented supply-side Republicans is to couple corporate tax cuts with tight monetary policy and cuts in social spending.

Faced with a situation in some ways similar to the one confronting the economy today, the Kennedy administration devised a corporate investment tax cut to stimulate investment that was being discouraged by high interest rates maintained by the Fed to protect the dollar. The motivation is the same this time around. The mix of tight money and a corporate tax cut is designed to protect the dollar, as were the taxes in the early sixties; they are also designed to squeeze the housing industry, despite vast increases in family formation expected over the next decade. By reducing resources devoted to housing "consumption," corporate supply-siders hope to redirect resources devoted to excessive housing to the corporate sector to help offset the detrimental effects of tight money on manufacturing corporations. While they insist that only resources devoted to excessive housing speculation will be transferred, such fine tuning seems highly unlikely.

The major battle on the domestic side will involve the attempt to slash social spending to make way for corporate tax cuts and high defense spending. If this attempt is not successful, then Volckerism—tight monetary policy—will have to step in to stem the inflationary tide. But that can only lead back to the stagflation impasse. Redistributing income at home might help to alleviate problems facing business and might even generate some greater investment and productivity gains. But further domestic and international action will have to be taken to protect American business from international competition, to preserve the role of the dollar, and to protect the integrity of the international financial system in the wake of OPEC.

A prime example of the response of American business and its protectors to increased foreign competition is the financial community's new turn toward domestic restructuring with the help of the government and the Federal Reserve. In the spring of 1980, as the Federal Reserve was desperately trying to get the money supply, interest rates, and the dollar under control, it was winning a major political battle in Congress. On March 5, eleven days before the Fed's March action, the Senate and House resolved their differences on major financial reorganization legislation in a "whirlwind conference.' "[85] Just a few days before, staffers on the Hill were bemoaning the difficulty of reaching agreement on the major differences between the House and Senate versions.

On March 31, President Carter signed into law a "far reaching" banking bill he had singled out as a key component of his new anti-inflation program. At a White House signing ceremony, Carter called the legislation a "significant step in reducing inflation" and a "major victory for savers.' "[86] Senator Proxmire, chairman of the Senate Committee on Banking, Housing and Urban Affairs, referred to the bill as the most significant banking legislation since the passage of the Federal Reserve Act of 1913. The legislation that generated so much excitement was the Depository Institutions Deregulation and Monetary Control Act of 1980. In essence, the bill represents the culmination of a sixty-year struggle by the Fed to bring all depository institutions under its jurisdiction. Seemingly unrelated, but in fact of integral importance, the bill makes major strides toward pushing thrift institutions (savings and loans and mutual savings banks being the most important) into direct competition with commercial banks. The effects of that competition may well be to render appropriate one opposition senator's name for the bill, "The Depository Institutions Abolition Act."[87]

The Fed pushed the bill as being necessary to bring the money supply under control. The bill will in fact help, since it will give the Fed more control over and better information about all banks in the system. However, the significance of the bill lies less in the reserve requirements which will be imposed on all depository institutions than in the intense domestic financial competition it will allow. The large banks' pressure for the bill and its ultimate importance can be understood only in the context of the increased domestic and international competition which large American banks have felt since the early 1960s and the increased danger of international transactions since the OPEC price increases of 1974 and 1979. Both have heightened the urgency with which the large American financial institutions and their regulators have pushed for restructuring domestic financial competition.

The small commercial banks represented by the Independent Bankers Association of America (IBAA) and the small thrift institutions represented by the U.S. League of Savings and Loans Associations were adamantly opposed to the bill. Speaking of an earlier version of the bill in the House and Senate, a representative of the IBAA said: "Nothing is acceptable in either of those bills. . . . The way the bills are structured, there's nothing in it for us." Indeed, the small banks, having significant power in the House, were able to stop Federal Reserve attempts to make reserve requirements mandatory, even after the House Banking Committee had supported the Fed. "People tend to listen to what their community banker says," one financial community lobbyist said. "They have a very good feeling for what's happening in the community and their connections are very good." The small bank lobby seemed so strong, in fact, that the

Federal Reserve backed down considerably. It was even willing to accept a bill that would have substantially reduced the number of commercial banks under the Fed's control if the erosion in Federal Reserve membership were at a slower rate than the Fed was predicting.

Yet by March the power of the small banks and thrift institutions in Congress had been virtually broken. With the financial markets on the verge of panic, Paul Volcker and the Federal Reserve were more and more seen as the only hope. As a result, Jimmy Carter and Paul Volcker were able to take another giant step down the path traveled by J. P. Morgan and Benjamin Strong toward a centralized banking system that could better compete with the centralized banking institutions of Europe, Japan, and the OPEC countries.

The competition facing large American banks both at home and abroad has been substantial in the last decade. Money market funds offered by brokerage houses have attracted billions of dollars in deposits away from the nation's commercial banks and savings and loans. On the loan side, the commercial paper market, by which corporations bypass the banks and lend directly to one another, has become a significant competitive factor. Even more worrisome has been the influx of foreign banks into the United States. Until recently, these banks were not subject to Federal Reserve requirements. Moreover, they were not prohibited by the federal government from setting up full-service branches across the states, while American banks, generally, are not allowed to engage in interstate branching. The growth of these banks in relation to the large American banks has been rapid. Between November 1972 and May 1977, the assets of foreign banks increased 175 percent, while assets for the large American banks increased only 40 percent. Concomitantly, the share of the foreign banks in large bank business in the United States increased from 5.2 percent in November 1972 to 10.4 percent by May 1977. Seventy-five percent of foreign bank corporate loans were made to domestic borrowers.[88]

One of the most obvious manifestations of the increased competition facing American banks has been the erosion of one of their main methods of fixing interest rates—the so-called prime rate convention. The prime rate is the rate of interest the large banks charge their most creditworthy customers. Essentially, the prime rate is a signaling device by which the large banks fix prices. Such price-fixing can work as long as the political process and the competition tolerate it. Since the early 1970s, both conditions have been significantly changed. Political toleration depended on the willingness of the Federal Reserve to protect the price-fixing by shielding prime rate changes with similar changes in the Fed's discount rate. Market toleration depended on the relative absence of competitive sources of corporate loan funds.

The importance of Federal Reserve support for the prime rate convention can be most clearly seen from the differences between two similar events: prime rate changes under the Martin Fed during President Johnson's wage-price guideposts of the early 1960s and prime rate changes during the Nixon wage and price controls under the Burns Fed. In December 1964, several banks boosted their prime rates, but in response to pressure from Johnson they rescinded the boosts two days later.[89] By the fall of 1965, the members of the Martin Fed who were most concerned about the detrimental effect of the economic expansion on the balance of payments wanted to tighten monetary policy. They wanted to increase the discount rate to signal to the international currency markets that the Fed was serious. There was, however, another consideration in their desire to raise the discount rate. As Sherman Maisel, a member of the Board of Governors during this period, tells the story:

> But a more critical factor was the desire to aid the banks in breaking President Johnson's stranglehold on the prime rate. As part of his general desire for low interest rates and his guidepost policy, President Johnson had forced banks to maintain a low prime lending rate. Since the banks wished to avoid a political battle with the President, some Board members felt that it was up to the Federal Reserve to oppose him in order to avoid a threatened inflationary increase in bank credit.[90]

The discount rate was raised, the prime rate was raised, and there was a political battle. But this time, the rates stuck.

During Nixon's wage and price controls, however, Burns was primarily concerned to keep the prime rate down in order to protect the wage controls from political pressure. As a result, the large banks abandoned the prime rate convention based on following the signals given by the Fed. A number of the banks created formula primes, rates set by "the market," not by the banks. Although the convention had not been murdered by political battles of the early 1970s, it had been badly wounded.

The death blow will be dealt by the market. Corporations can borrow from one another and from foreign banks, in the United States or in the Eurodollar markets. The ability of the banks to make the prime stick, even when they have the political will to establish it, has been seriously undermined. As market interest rates began their rapid descent after the March 1980 action, the banks tried to keep the prime rate from falling as rapidly as their cost of funds, despite their pretense of setting their prime on the basis of a formula which marks up the rate over the cost of funds. The high prime was maintained in an attempt to create some pricing discipline in the banking industry. But according to a Federal Reserve study, the large New York banks could not maintain the cartel: in the first six months of 1980, more than two-thirds of all loans were made at rates well below the prime.[91] The political process will probably engage in contributory manslaughter. Representative Henry Reuss, chairman of the House Banking Committee, recently attacked "prime-rate falsies fashioned by the major banks that would shame the nation's brassiere industry," claiming that banks charged small customers the prime "falsie" and above, while giving cut-rate deals to the large corporations.[92]

Competition in the United States has been accompanied by even fiercer competition abroad. The share of the top 50 American banks in the banking business of the world's top 100 banks has declined steadily since 1969. In 1969, the largest 50 American banks made 40 percent of the top 100 world banks' loans; in 1979, their share was cut to 21 percent.[93] These data refer to both domestic and international banking business. The data on international business alone (loans made and deposits accepted outside the home country) mirror these overall figures. In 1974, the American banks accounted for 45.7 percent of the world's international banking loans and other claims; in 1979, they accounted for 30.3 percent. The largest drop occurred between 1977 and 1978, as the dollar was rapidly depreciating, when the United States' share declined by over 16 percent.[94]

The decline in the share of bank lending has been most dramatic among the OPEC countries.[95] Between December 1977 and June 1979, the share dropped by almost a third to 35 percent. The other largest drop occurred in the loans to non-oil-exporting Third World countries. Here the share dropped from 54 percent in December 1976 to 48 percent in December 1977 and to 38 percent in June 1979. Among the Third World countries, the decline has been particularly steep in Latin America. The only non-oil-exporting countries where American banks increased their share of lending were Chile, Colombia, South Korea, the Philippines, Thailand, and Egypt.

The drop in the share of bank lending to oil-exporting countries has been accompanied by a decline in the share of OPEC bank deposits that have accrued to American banks from 42 percent in 1975 to 36 percent in 1978.[96] The share deposited in overseas branches of American banks has stayed constant, however, which means that the decline has occurred in deposits held in American banks in the United States. There is some evidence that this trend has substantially accelerated since 1978—some have attributed the decline over that period to the freeze of Iranian assets in November 1979.[97] These figures suggest that the fear that rapid American inflation would lead OPEC countries to diversify out of dollars might well have some basis in fact. Along with the decline in the share of international lending has come a decline in the share of profits the largest American banks derive from their international business. Whereas from 1970 to 1975 the share of profits accruing to the top ten banks involved in international lending was over 45 percent, it had dropped in 1979 to 37 percent. The growth rate of international earnings declined substantially for every bank among the top ten between 1970 and 1975 and 1975 and 1979.[98]

Increased competition partly accounts for the decline of American banks in international lending. Another factor is that international lending has become riskier. By December 1977, the nine largest American banks had lent out to non-oil-exporting Third World countries over 180 percent of their capital accounts, which are supposed to serve as a buffer in case of default.[99] The exposure of the large banks had not declined by June 1979, and has probably increased since then. While the risk associated with commercial bank lending to the Third World has remained high, and in the past year has undoubtedly increased, the profitability of lending to oil-importing countries has declined due to increased competition among multinational banks. The percentage by which loans are marked up over the cost of funds was lower at the end of 1979 than it had been before the first oil price hike in 1973, and only half as high as it had been in 1976.[100]

Increased competition always concerns corporations, and bankers are no exception. Through the years, bankers have tried to find means to reduce competition among themselves. One major way is to try to coordinate pricing policies. An especially interesting attempt was made at a recent international banking meeting by Wilfried Guth, managing director of Deutsche Bank in Frankfurt.

Guth decried the long, sad story of reduced profitability of international lending:

> After the Herstatt crisis, [interest] spreads recovered from an intolerably low level. . . . Since then we have experienced an almost uninterrupted decline in margins. . . . In situations like this we tend to give the blame to the market. But who is the market? Must we say in paraphrasing Sartre: The Market—that is the others (the other banks?) . . . So why did we let the market dictate what we didn't want?[101]

The culprits are not hard to discover. "We all know what the main reasons for this are . . . our very keen competition. Undoubtedly these trends have been reinforced by the continuous appearance of ambitious newcomers to the market who are eager to acquire leading positions by offering favorable rates." What is the solution to this unhappy state of affairs? Guth suggests that perhaps the bankers' profit calculations have been faulty: "I can merely guess that by applying all defensible cost saving calculations, one would arrive at a minimum average acceptable margin somewhere around 1%. . . ." Praising the power of science, Guth concludes: "Thus simple mathematics again demonstrate the need for a wider range of margins than ones we have manoeuvred ourselves into." Almost as an afterthought, he adds: "I am, of course, aware that our distinguished friends on the borrowing side will not appreciate this statement. . . ." But, as Guth noted at the outset, especially when there are hungry newcomers, banks have extreme difficulty cooperating. Signals from central bankers might help. Volcker has suggested that "Higher spreads and shorter maturities may well be necessary to induce lenders to assume the greater risks in lending."[102] Wallich has been even more vociferous. "I've said a million times, spreads are totally inadequate."[103]

Central bankers are, of course, concerned with more than commercial bank profits. Their concern is with the stability of the international financial system. But a coalition of interests forms around both, especially when the foreign newcomers are to blame. However, just as price fixing could not stabilize the economy during the Great Depression, merely fixing spreads will not solve the recycling problem.[104] Larger problems require larger restructuring, an issue to which we will return.

As domestic and international competition step up, the large banks turn to the Fed and the government for relief. The passage of the Depository Deregulation and Monetary Control Act is only the first victory by the large banks in their attempt to centralize, or as *Business Week* puts it, "rationalize" the banking industry.[105] The Carter administration conducted a two-year study analyzing the possibility of reducing restrictions on the movement of banks across state lines. Although the study was essentially finished well before November, the administration delayed releasing it until after the election, obviously concerned about its political impact on small bankers and their friends. The study calls for the phasing out of antibranching laws over a number of years. This will enable large banks to buy out smaller commercial banks in other states as well as set up branches in states in which other large banks already have a dominant market position.

The Fed has given provisional approval to the establishment of "free banking zones" in which bank activities financing or gaining deposits from international business will not be subject to reserve requirements and other lending restrictions that apply to domestic banking. It is not at all unlikely, however, that banks engaging in domestic business will be able to get around the legislation. If such activities were not subject to Fed control, however, the Fed's control over the money supply might well be further eroded. The creation of an international free banking zone will make a minuscule ripple of instability, however, compared to the dangers involved in the evolution of international trade and financial competition in the context of the vast redistribution of wealth and power from the Third and Western worlds to OPEC.

If such dangers are to be avoided, it is necessary (but certainly not sufficient) to resolve two related issues among the advanced capitalist countries. The first is the instability in the international financial markets which is endangering international finance and trade while inhibiting domestic economic growth. The second issue is the vast debt owed by the Third World and Eastern European countries to Western banks. These debts require that the industrialized countries continue to grow and import or find some other means to ensure that these banks are repaid. As it turns out, a joint solution to these problems is being fashioned by the United States government and the Federal Reserve. But the attempts by the Fed and the Treasury to maintain the international financial role of the United States, and the desire of Europe and Japan to expand theirs, will make any coordinated action to salvage the international financial system difficult. In many ways, the problems plaguing the system are further manifestations of those plaguing Bretton Woods: the American share in world production has dropped from 40 percent in 1950 to only 20 percent in 1979, but the dollar is still used as the world's major reserve currency.[106] In 1979, at least 65 percent of the world's official foreign exchange reserves were held in dollars. Thus there is a major discrepancy between the greatly reduced economic importance of the United States and the relatively large role of the dollar. The issue that arose in the 1960s arises now in even starker form: the inability of the international financial community to move to a new system might well result in major financial instability or in the necessity of a tight United States monetary policy. Such a policy could impose heavy burdens on the American economy and world economic growth.[107]

For the Fed, the immediate implications of this failure now, as in the 1960s, is that a tight monetary policy is required to protect the value of the dollar. But as before, the willingness to negotiate a reduction in that role might help to stabilize the system and free up domestic monetary policy. A substitution account is again being considered to facilitate that process. A substitution account would allow central banks to deposit excess dollars acquired from years of U.S. balance of payments deficits, rather than selling them on the exchange markets. The substitution account issue was raised in 1978 by Johannes Witteveen, managing director of the IMF. At the IMF's annual meeting in Belgrade in 1979, before the October "revolution," finance ministers and central bankers were able to agree for the first time to propose an account based in the IMF at the upcoming IMF meetings in April 1980. When April arrived, the United States, Germany, and Japan suddenly withdrew their support, and the plan was shelved.

One basic stumbling block in the negotiations concerned the allocation of the costs of the account. If European, Japanese, and OPEC central banks were to be convinced to exchange dollars for some other asset, then the return and risk they received on that asset had to be at least as desirable to them as what they would have been able to achieve on their own. The negotiators had to determine who would bear the interest costs and who would guarantee the value of the assets exchanged for dollars.

The negotiators had also to determine the benefits that would accrue to them and their constituencies from establishing the account. Negotiators from the Treasury Department wanted to stabilize the international currency markets and protect the value of the dollar without at the same time allowing any other particular country or group of countries to achieve a major reserve currency role. As Bergsten, Carter's assistant secretary of the Treasury for International Affairs, recently put it:

> My own view is that a world monetary system based on several reasonably important national currencies might be subject to substantial risks and uncertainties. . . . Lest there be misunderstanding, let me make clear that I am not advocating an effort to preserve excessive preeminence for the dollar . . . I am suggesting . . . that we should seek consciously to promote the use of the Special Drawing Right (SDR, the IMF created money) as an alternative to the use of national reserve currencies.[108]

When the dollar was stabilized by other means and events, however, the attraction of the fund for the U.S. would quickly fade.

Germany and Japan, on the other hand, had an interest in the account as long as they had an excess of dollars, and as long as they did not want to create another monetary system that would exclude American participation. By April, however, both conditions had been eroded. In December 1978, the European Economic Community agreed to establish the European Monetary System, which came into force in March 1979. In principle, if not in fact, the EMS represented an alternative to the transformation of a world monetary system under the auspices of the IMF. The creation of the EMS directly reduced European support for the substitution account. The creation of the European Currency Unit (ECU) in conjunction with the EMS involved a substitution account of sorts. Members of the EMS deposited 20 percent of their gold and dollar reserves with the EMS in return for ECU. Thus, the Europeans reduced their holdings of potentially unwanted dollars without creating exchange rate instability. Although this might have helped to stabilize the dollar in the short run, in the longer run it represents a European solution over which the United States exercises little control. Finally, as a result of the oil price increases in 1979, European countries began running balance of payments deficits and needed dollars to pay for oil, further reducing their desires for a substitution account.

For its part, the United States negotiators refused in April 1980 to ask Congress to support guarantees for the value of the account that prospective central bank depositors demanded.[109] It seems safe to say that in an election year, Congress would have been reluctant to guarantee billions of dollars of reserves, especially when much of them were owned by OPEC countries. The United States instead decided to push the IMF to use its member-donated gold stock to provide the backing. The non-oil-exporting Third World countries were particularly opposed to this, however. They correctly see the IMF's gold as partly belonging to them, and even in the best of circumstances many were suspicious that the creation of the fund would limit their choice of reserve holdings in order to allow the United States to continue running balance of payments deficits.[110]

In any case, at least a short-term solution had already been found for the dollar problem that did not depend on the agreement of the Congress or the Third World: Paul Volcker and the Fed had raised interest rates enough to stabilize the dollar. Japan's and Germany's deficits also helped stabilize the dollar, at least in the short run. In the face of the renewed strength of the dollar, financial interests within the United States and the U.S. government were no longer certain that the risks associated with the formal establishment of an internationally controlled account were worth the benefits. If the Fed could independently guarantee the value of dollar reserves without giving up the perceived unilateral benefits associated with the maintenance of the dollar as a reserve currency, there was no point in supporting the account. The cost, of course, would not be legislated by Congress, but would be borne nonetheless by manufacturing profits and the unemployed.

Another reason that the United States withdrew its support of the substitution account is that, apart from Volcker and the Federal Reserve helping to guarantee the value of the dollar, the IMF is indirectly establishing recycling facilities which, in a sense, use the IMF's gold to back an informal substitution facility. The IMF is planning to issue bonds denominated in IMF's unit of account—the SDR—and will use the proceeds to lend to countries having balance of payments problems. That will reduce the amount of dollars in the system relative to the amount of wealth, thereby reducing the risk to dollar holders of a dollar sell off. It will also, of course, reduce the risk to commercial banks, who will have the IMF bear some of the risk of lending to the Third World. Thus, bypassing Congress, the Fed will implicitly guarantee the value of the dollar. Through the recycling facility, the IMF will implicitly use the IMF's gold to guarantee the dollar wealth of the countries that lend to it—presumably OPEC countries—without an explicit agreement from the Third World countries to allow gold to be used for a substitution account.

Congress cannot be bypassed entirely in the international debt underwriting game. Both the IMF and the World Bank are asking member countries for increased contributions. Virtually all the major governmental-financial personnel have urged Congress to supply the funds. A. W. Clausen, former president of the Bank of America, named by President Carter to succeed Robert McNamara as president of the World Bank, was asked in a recent interview how he would convince a conservative Congress to come up with the money. Clausen replied: "I will say to them, and I know many of them, that I am a banker and that in my professional judgment we have no choice but to support this approach. The Marshall Plan worked, . . . and if we don't produce this expanded level of support —comes the revolution. It's as simple as that."[111]

Extended financing will not be the only method the IMF and World Bank use to ensure that Western banks are repaid and the revolution is avoided. "Adjustment" and "surveillance" are the key terms here. Adjustment of deficits means that the Third World countries will have to reduce domestic consumption in order to export enough products to pay back their debt. Surveillance is the mechanism used to try to ensure that the standard of living within these countries will actually be reduced. As Paul Volcker puts it: "I believe it is especially important under the circumstances for the IMF to play a strong role. The role of the fund is important not only because that institution has sizeable financial resources but mainly because through the good offices of the IMF there is a better chance to achieve the right mix between adjustment and financing." But Volcker insists:

> If we urge them to make real adjustments rather than borrowing excessively in the years ahead, they, in turn, will expect us to keep our markets

open to their goods. . . . If the industrial countries all try hard to improve their trade balances . . . the only outlet would be even larger deficits for the developing countries. . . . The traditional notion is that a successful industrial country ought to have a current account surplus. I am not against surpluses, but . . . [w]e have to avoid the view that only surpluses are acceptable because some countries will have to be in deficit. . . . [I]t is clear that we cannot make long-run progress collectively if we are forced to repeat the 1977–78 cycle of large U.S. current account deficits and a quick reversion to surpluses in other major OECD countries.[112]

In other words, the Europeans must open their doors to Third World imports.

Volcker spoke these words in March 1980, as he was driving American interest rates up to 20 percent, forcing the Germans to raise theirs. A few months later, C. Fred Bergsten was hailing before an international group the new turnaround in balance of payments surpluses and deficits: "Our export volume has been rising twice as fast as world trade for two and a half years. On the other side of the equation, Japan and Germany have moved into substantial deficit in 1979 and 1980 . . . [which is a] major achievement of the international adjustment process."[113] As Bergsten suggests, U.S. attempts to maintain its international role in the face of its reduced power have been successful, but the international turmoil created in the process might show the victory to have been a Pyrrhic one.

CONCLUSION

The need for a basic restructuring in the domestic and international economy is accompanied and made more difficult by a similar need in the realm of mainstream economic doctrine. Conventional economic thought has offered no solution to the basic problem facing the current international system—namely, the need to maintain economic growth, but the inability to do so.

While the two main schools of received economic wisdom differ in important respects, their common terrain is their most important and vulnerable characteristic. The critical promise of the Keynesian revolution is that proper government policy can maintain full employment and economic growth, thereby protecting the capitalist order from both the Left and the Right. Monetarism contends that if government and the Federal Reserve would simply end misguided Keynesian policies, full employment and growth would be achieved by the private market on its own. On the desirability of government intervention, monetarists and Keynesians vigorously disagree. On the ability of capitalism to sustain full employment, however, they are one.

While both Keynesianism and monetarism promise sustained economic expansion, the new role played by monetarism in recent years belies their ability to honor the pledge. In these inflationary times, monetarism has become the theory of discipline. For many years following the Great Depression, it was widely held that monetary policy was impotent—only fiscal policy mattered. Later, the neo-Keynesian synthesis, hailed by Richard Nixon himself, recognized that money mattered indeed. Though the revival of monetarism in academic circles owes much to Milton Friedman, its success is primarily a recognition that the Federal Reserve could and would use tight money to thwart economic expansion when it found it necessary to stop inflation.

Yet as Margaret Thatcher tries her experiment of reducing the money supply in England, generating the highest level of unemployment since the Depression, monetarism is even losing its appeal as a disciplinary tool. In advanced capitalist economies, contractionary monetary policy primarily reduces output and profits, not inflation, as the monetarists had suggested. And the Keynesians, for their part, have still not figured out how to maintain economic expansion in an internationally integrated financial system based on a declining currency in the face of working-class power. Out of this theoretical wasteland emerged Arthur Laffer's supply-side economics, which offered some ray of hope for noninflationary expansion. But it is pure mystification, and is increasingly coming to be recognized as such.

In this vacuum, it becomes all that much easier for those in power to try to fashion a cure that attempts to do what they know how to do best, armed with only faith that it will cure the ills of the system. Corporate supply-side economics is the strategy to which Reagan will turn. Corporate tax cuts and attempts to cut social spending rather than personal tax giveaways to the rich are the wave of the future. But for the strategy to have some chance of curing the stagflation impasse, a number of conditions must be satisfied.

On the domestic side, success will depend on the ability of the administration to force consumption, social service, and real income losses on the majority of the American people without resorting to inflation.

In the international sphere, success depends on using the offices of the IMF, and perhaps more blatant methods, to convince Europe and Japan to open their markets to the Third World, get debt-ridden Third World countries to reduce their consumption so they can repay their debt, and force OPEC to maintain oil production at a reasonable price. But with the reduced power of the U.S. government abroad and its impaired legitimacy at home, it is unlikely that it can muster the political power necessary to impose these burdens, short of that which comes out of the barrel of a gun.

Short of that solution or of some miraculous mustering of political power at home and abroad, Paul Volcker and the Federal Reserve will have to take charge again to stem the inflationary "excesses" of government. But Volckerism, like Thatcherism, can only inflict harm on the domestic economy; and because the United States is still so important internationally, Volckerism would be far more dangerous.

NOTES

1. See, for example, David G. Golden and James M. Poterba, "The Price of Popularity: The Political Business Cycle Reexamined," *American Journal of Political Science,* 24 (November 1980), 696–714; Edward R. Tufte, *Political Control of the Economy* (Princeton, N.J.: Princeton University Press, 1978); and the reference cited there.

2. Golden and Poterba, among others, cast doubt on the view that presidents have manipulated the economy. Tufte provides support for the theory. All data are from the *Economic Report of the President 1981,* unless otherwise indicated.

3. The data in this paragraph and the next are from Stephen V. O. Clarke, "Perspective on the United States External Position since World War II," *Federal Reserve Bank of New York Quarterly Review,* 5 (summer 1980), 22; and William H. Branson, "Trends in U.S. International Trade and Investment since World War II," NBER Working Paper No. 469 (1980), pp. 22–23.

4. The same sort of argument is made in the interesting article by Leonard Rapping, "The Domestic and International Aspects of Structural Inflation," in James H. Gapinski and Charles E. Rockwood, eds., *Essays in Post-Keynesian Inflation* (Cambridge, Mass.: Ballinger, 1979). See Fred Bloch, *The Origins of International Economic Disorder* (Berkeley: University of California Press, 1977) for an extremely useful analysis of Bretton Woods and international monetary politics generally. I have drawn heavily on both of these.

5. Raford Boddy and James Crotty, "Class Conflict and Macro-Policy: The Political Business Cycle," *Review of Radical Political Economy,* 7 (spring 1975), 3. See this article for the best discussion of this conflict. See Thomas E. Weisskopf, "Marxian Crisis Theory and the Rate of Profit in the Post-War U. S. Economy," *Cambridge Journal of Economics,* 3 (1979), 341–378, for an excellent empirical investigation of the profit squeeze in the postwar United States.

6. R. E. Rowthorn, "Late Capitalism," A Review of Ernest Mandel's *Late Capitalism, New Left Review,* July–August 1976, and R. E. Rowthorn, "Conflict, Inflation and Money," *Cambridge Journal of Economics,* 1 (1977), 215–239; and Samuel Bowles and Herbert Gintis, "The Crisis of Liberal Democratic Capitalism," mimeo, analyze monetary policy and inflation in a framework similar to the one used in this paper. Sam Rosenberg and Thomas E. Weisskopf, "A Conflict Theory Approach to Inflation in the Postwar U.S. Economy," *American Economic Review* (May 1981) also use a similar model, except theirs assumes that the money supply will accommodate all inflation generated by conflicts over income shares. The argument here is that, while that might be true in the long run as international markets and innovations supply the money that is required to finance transactions, in the medium run, central banks have enough control over the money supply to affect the inflationary process. As a result, a theory of monetary policy is required to explain when inflation will be allowed and when the central bank will generate unemployment to stop it. James R. Crotty and Leonard A. Rapping, "The 1975 Report of the President's Council of Economic Advisers: A Radical Critique," *American Economic Review,* December 1975, pp. 791–811, and Rapping, "The Domestic and International Aspects of Structural Inflation,"

also take into account the domestic and international financial imperatives on monetary and fiscal policy.

7. See the studies referred to in notes 41 and 42 below.
8. Clarke, op. cit., p. 23.
9. James Tobin, *National Economic Policy* (New Haven, Conn.: Yale University Press, 1966), p. 124.
10. C. Fred Bergsten, *The Dilemmas of the Dollar* (New York: New York University Press, published for The Council on Foreign Relations, 1975), pp. 111–112.
11. Branson, op. cit., pp. 77–80.
12. Clarke, op. cit., p. 27.
13. Bergsten, op. cit., p. 81.
14. James Tobin, *The New Economics One Decade Older* (Princeton, N.J.: Princeton University Press, 1972), p. 14.
15. Quoted in E. Ray Canterbery, *Economics on a New Frontier* (Belmont, Calif.: Wadsworth, 1968), pp. 155–160. This book is the source of much useful information on economic policy in the Kennedy-Johnson years.
16. Clarke, op. cit., p. 32.
17. See "The Proposed Substitution Account in the IMF," *Midland Bank Review,* winter 1979, pp. 21–24.
18. Tobin, *National Economic Policy,* op. cit.
19. See Bergsten, op. cit.
20. Clarke, op. cit., p. 23.
21. Ibid., p. 27.
22. See Bergsten, op. cit., and Crotty and Rapping, op. cit., pp. 791–811.
23. Bergsten, op. cit., p. 311n.
24. Raymond Lombra, James B. Heredeen, and Raymond G. Torto, *Money and the Financial System.* (New York: McGraw-Hill, 1980), pp. 396–397.
25. John Kenneth Galbraith, *Money: Whence It Came, Where It Went* (Boston: Houghton Mifflin, 1975), p. 140. Much of the analysis in this section draws heavily on Gabriel Kolko, *The Triumph of Conservatism* (New York: Free Press, 1963).
26. Quoted in Kolko, op. cit., p. 251.
27. Ibid., p. 254.
28. See Thomas Ferguson, *The Fall of the House of Morgan: Critical Realignments and Industrial Sectors* (New York: Oxford University Press, in press).
29. Milton Friedman, "Should There Be an Independent Monetary Authority," in Leland B. Yeager (ed.), *In Search of a Monetary Constitution* (Cambridge, Mass.: Harvard University Press, 1962), pp. 236–238.
30. In the short run, a greater value of transactions can be financed with the existing money stock.
31. See Maurice D. Levi, "Money and Corporate Earnings," *Journal of Money, Credit and Banking,* February 1980, pp. 84–93. Levi studied the effects of the money supply on the before-tax earnings of nonfinancial corporations in the 1964–1975 period. There are several ways in which money supply changes can affect corporate earnings. One is by reducing the real value of the corporation's debt. A second is by reducing the real value of workers' wages. Levi found that increases in the money supply increase real, before-tax earnings briefly. *Accelerations* in the money supply increase corporate earnings for a longer period of time. He hypothesized that this resulted from lags in the adjustment of wages to prices, citing evidence that there are equal numbers of net debtors and creditors among nonfinancial corporations so that the debt relationship ought to cancel out in the aggregate. After-tax profits are of ultimate interest, however. It seems that apart from the wage process, the major tax effects of inflation are of two kinds: one, historical costing of capital goods increases taxes since it costs more to replace goods than it cost

to buy them; the other is tax deductibility of interest costs on debt which go up as interest rates increase during inflation. In the aggregate, they seem to balance out. See Franco Modigliani and Richard A. Cohn, "Inflation, Rational Valuation and the Market," *Financial Analysts Journal,* March–April 1979, pp. 24–44; and James Tobin, "Stabilization Policy Ten Years After," *Brookings Papers on Economic Activity,* 1 (1980), 19–71.

32. See Crotty and Rapping, op. cit., pp. 791–811. Inflation was still of some help to them. See Levi, op. cit., pp. 84–93. Levi ran his tests after flexible exchange rates had been operating for only a few years, so he could not directly test the argument made here that manufacturing corporations are helped more by inflation under a flexible exchange rate system than under a fixed rate system.

33. See Tobin, "Stabilization Policy," op. cit., pp. 19–71; and Rudiger Dornbusch, "Exchange Rate Economics: Where Do We Stand?" *Brookings Papers on Economic Activity* I (1980): 143–185.

34. There is a distinction between real and nominal exchange rates, interest rates, and money supplies. Monetarists tend to assume that the Federal Reserve cannot affect the real components in the long run. There is ample evidence, however, that the Fed can affect these for significant periods of time, at least in the United States. See Dornbusch, op. cit., pp. 143–185, and Tobin, "Stabilization Policy," op. cit., pp. 19–71.

35. Clarke, op. cit., p. 32; and International Monetary Fund, *Annual Report 1980,* p. 26.

36. Anthony M. Solomon, "United States and the World Economy," *The Federal Reserve Bank of New York Quarterly Review,* 5, 2 (summer 1980), 5.

37. See Jeffrey Sachs, "Wages, Profits and Macroeconomic Adjustment: A Comparative Study," *Brookings Papers on Economic Activity,* 2 (1979), 269–332.

38. Increased labor share also reduces profits and might reduce investment, leading to slower economic growth.

39. See *Economic Report of the President 1981,* pp. 184–189.

40. See Sachs, op. cit., and Bowles and Gintis, op. cit.

41. See Sachs, op. cit., p. 81.

42. Tobin, "Stabilization Policy," op. cit., p. 67.

43. See Bowles and Gintis, op. cit. Another reason why firms might be reluctant to reduce wages and would rather lay off workers is that they have developed finely crafted wage differentials to legitimate the hierarchical nature of the firm. They might, therefore, be reluctant to upset these differentials by changing wage scales when demand falls off in response to contractionary policy.

44. For seminal discussions of financial instability created by economic expansion, see work by Minsky—for example, Hyman P. Minsky, *Keynes* (New York: Columbia University Press, 1975) and "The Federal Reserve: Between a Rock and a Hard Place," *Challenge,* May–June 1980, pp. 30–36.

45. Leonard Rapping, Review of "Reflections of an Economic Policy Maker," *Challenge,* November–December 1979, p. 9. In the 1950s and 1960s contractionary monetary policy worked in the first instance by causing a contraction in the housing industry. The political power of the savings and loan and construction industries won a number of regulatory concessions which partially insulated the housing industry from tight monetary policy. That, in turn, has placed more of the burden of tight money on other industries in the war against inflation, but that pattern does not seem to always hold. In the recession of 1980, housing was hit extremely hard, as it had been in the 1960s.

46. See William Sweet, "Third World Debts," *Editorial Research Reports,* II, 4 (July 25, 1980), 544.

47. Paul L. Volcker, "The Recycling Problem Revisited," *Challenge,* July–August 1980, pp. 12, 10.
48. See Thomas Ferguson and Joel Rogers, "Miller of the Fed," *The Nation,* August 12–25, 1978.
49. Rapping, review of "Reflections of an Economic Policy Maker," op. cit., pp. 65–66.
50. See Tufte, op. cit., and Alan S. Blinder, *Economic Policy and the Great Stagflation* (New York: Academic Press, 1979), chap. 8.
51. See William Poole, "Burnsian Monetary Policy: Eight Years of Progress?" *Journal of Finance,* May 1979.
52. Blinder, op. cit., chap. 8.
53. Jerry L. Jordan, "Discussion: The Political Economy of Arthur Burns," *Journal of Finance,* May 1979, pp. 496–498.
54. *Fortune,* December 31, 1978.
55. *Economic Report of the President 1981,* p. 30.
56. Morgan Guaranty, *World Financial Markets,* December 1978.
57. See Federal Reserve Bank of St. Louis *Review,* March issues, for much useful information on the internal dynamics of monetary policymaking.
58. *The New York Times,* April 20, 1979.
59. *Washington Post,* April 19, 1979.
60. Ibid.
61. Tobin, "Stabilization Policy," op. cit., p. 32.
62. *The Wall Street Journal,* July 26, 1979.
63. *World Financial Markets,* October 1979.
64. *Business Week,* October 22, 1979.
65. *U.S. News and World Report,* October 22, 1979.
66. *Business Week,* October 22, 1979.
67. *Business Week,* April 1, 1972.
68. *The Wall Street Journal,* November 20, 1979.
69. *Business Week,* October 22, 1979.
70. *The Wall Street Journal,* December 13, 1979.
71. *Survey of Current Business,* October 1980.
72. See Ray C. Fair, "Estimated Effects of the October 1979 Change in Monetary Policy on the 1980 Economy," NBER Working Paper No. 538 (August 1980).
73. *The New York Times,* February 22, 1980.
74. *The New York Times,* February 27, 1980.
75. *The Wall Street Journal,* February 26, 1980.
76. *The Wall Street Journal,* February 27, 1980.
77. Ibid., February 25, 1980.
78. Ibid., March 6, 1980.
79. See *Federal Reserve Bulletin,* August 1980, p. 630.
80. Mlb, seasonally adjusted.
81. Information in the next two paragraphs is taken from the *Economic Report of the President 1981.*
82. *Federal Reserve Bulletin,* December 1980, p. 951.
83. There is a great deal of disagreement about the degree to which the profitability of nonfinancial U.S. corporations has declined in the 1970s relative to earlier recent periods. A good number of studies suggest that both before-tax and after-tax rates of return are lower in the period following the middle 1960s (see Martin Feldstein and James Poterba, "State and Local Taxes and the Rate of Profit in the Post-War U.S. Economy," NBER Working Paper 1980, for example). However, other studies suggest that the after-tax return has remained more or less constant. (See, for example, Modigliani and Cohn, op. cit., pp. 24–44.) What is indisputable, however, is the fact that real

after-tax corporate profit growth rate has declined from 2.8% a year for 1959–1969 to 1.6% for 1968–1979; more dramatically, however, stock prices, in real terms, have tumbled in the last ten years; they are about half their historic peak level in 1968. For no other ten-year period, including the Great Depression, have stocks performed so poorly. This poor performance has harmed the wealth of stockholders and the ability of corporations to raise funds for investment in the stock market. See William C. Brainard, John B. Shoven, and Laurence Weiss, "The Financial Valuation of the Return to Capital," *Brookings Papers on Economic Activity*, 2 (1980), 453–511.

84. The major thing to understand about the 2.5 percentage point decline in productivity growth as between the 1948–1965 period and the 1973–1979 period is that there is virtually no agreement as to what accounts for it. Numerous studies come up with widely different answers to the question, and most careful studies suggest that the decline remains essentially a puzzle. The position taken by the Council of Economic Advisers under Carter in view of this intellectual vacuum is that, even if a decline in investment did not cause a decline in productivity growth, an increase in investment can improve productivity. Of course it's important to realize that increases in productivity won't necessarily reduce inflation. Once again it becomes a question of holding the rate of growth of wages below productivity increases if both profits and inflation are to be substantially improved. See *Economic Report of the President 1981* and earlier years.

85. Information in the following paragraph is taken from the *Congressional Quarterly*, April 12, 1980.

86. *Federal Reserve Bulletin*, June 1980. See the article in this issue for detailed information on the provisions of the bill.

87. *Congressional Quarterly*, July 7, 1979.

88. Henry S. Terrel and Sydney J. Key, "The Growth of Foreign Banking in the United States: Analytical Survey," in *Key Issues in International Banking*, The Federal Reserve Bank of Boston, 1977, pp. 56–58.

89. Randall C. Merris, "The Prime Rate," Federal Reserve Bank of Chicago, *Business Conditions*, April 1975, reprinted in Thomas Havrilesky and John T. Boorman, *Current Perspectives in Banking* (Arlington Heights, Ill.: AHM Publishing Corporation, 1976), p. 75.

90. Sherman J. Maisel, *Managing the Dollar* (New York: Norton, 1973), p. 76.

91. Thomas C. O'Donnell, "What Went Up Comes Down—But Slowly," *Forbes*, June 23, 1980, pp. 33–34.

92. Ibid.

93. Compiled from various issues of *Fortune Magazine*.

94. Salomon Brothers, Bank Stock Department, "Lending to LDCs: Mounting Problems," April 2, 1980.

97. *Euromoney*, July 1980.

98. Salomon Brothers, "United States Multinational Banking: Current and Prospective Strategies," June 1976; and Salomon Brothers, op. cit.

99. Volcker, op. cit., pp. 3–14.

100. Ibid.

101. "The Problems Raised by the Growth of International Banking Lending," presentation at the International Monetary Conference, American Bankers' Association, New Orleans, June 1–4, 1980.

102. Ibid., p. 13.

103. *The Wall Street Journal*, July 2, 1980.

104. See Gabriel Kolko, *Main Currents in Modern American History* (New York: Harper & Row, 1976), and Gabriel Kolko, "Intelligence and the Myth of Capitalist Rationality in the United States," *Science and Society*, summer 1980, pp. 130–154.

105. *Business Week,* March 24, 1980.
106. See Clarke, op. cit., p. 22. If ECU are counted as part of the world's foreign exchange reserves, the share of reserves held in dollars fell from a high of over 86% in 1976 to 65% in 1979. If, on the other hand, the ECU substituted for dollars are counted as dollars and those substituted for gold are eliminated from the total foreign exchange holdings, then the dollar share in 1979 is almost 78%, which would still comprise a drop of 9 percentage points. The most dramatic change over the period, however, is the decline of sterling, from the currency with the second largest share in 1973 to the fifth largest, and the dramatic rise in the use of the German mark and the Japanese yen as reserve currencies. The pattern of increased use of the dollar around the time of the first OPEC price increase in 1974 is reflected in official holdings as well. But this second OPEC price rise did not induce a similar rebound. Though an increase in the use of the dollar might appear in later statistics, the creation of the ECU and the active attempts of the Germans, Swiss, and, to some extent, Japanese to make their currencies into reserve currencies will make it less likely that the OPEC increase by itself will resurrect the dollar this time around.

The relative maintenance of the dollar's share in international reserves in the face of a decline in the United States' share of world production might mask substantial changes in the composition of reserve holdings among different countries. In particular, those who worry about the stability of a multiple reserve asset system seem to be primarily concerned with Third World and oil-exporting countries diversifying out of dollars. But data on such diversification are difficult to come by. Detailed data on holdings by particular countries outside the major European countries are not available after 1977, and as suggested earlier, these data are strongly influenced by the high demand for dollar reserves following the first OPEC price rise. However, one can calculate the minimum probable holdings of dollars by assuming that the Group of 10 Countries plus Switzerland hold all their reserves in dollars and then figuring what proportion the rest of the world holds. If this experiment is performed, one discovers that in 1979 the share of dollar holdings in the rest of the world is 60.3% if the ECU is excluded and 37.6% if the ECU is included as foreign exchange reserves. This, of course, is a bare minimum. The Group of 10 Countries and Switzerland probably hold around 90% of their reserves in dollars.

The investment and commercial bankers had warned that the breakdown of the Bretton Woods system and the advent of floating exchange rates would lead multinational corporations and central banks to reduce their holdings of dollars, increase their use of other currencies, and, through the "Siamese twin" effect, would lead to a reduction in the market share of U.S. financial institutions. They also warned that an international financial system based on the use of more than one currency (a multicurrency system) and floating exchange rates would be unstable and costly.

We have seen that the market share of U.S. banks in international finance has indeed fallen. That reduced share has been accompanied by a reduction in the use of the dollar relative to other currencies in both private and official capacities. The dollar's share fell from 78% of the total banking claims in 1974 to 68% in 1979. The drop in the share of international bonds denominated in dollars is even greater, from 63% of the total in 1974 to 42% in 1979. The share of dollar-denominated bonds increased somewhat during the heavy financing associated with the first OPEC price increase in 1974–1976, but dropped off afterward. The same phenomenon occurred in the

Eurocurrency Market. But the long-run trend appears to be a decline.

107. See Rapping, "The Domestic and International Aspects of Structural Inflation," op. cit., and Block, op. cit., for a similar argument.

108. C. Fred Bergsten, "International Monetary System in the 1980's," in Bergsten, *The World Economy in the 1980's: Selected Papers of C. Fred Bergsten, 1980* (Lexington, Mass.: D. C. Heath and Co., 1981), pp. 23–37.

109. H. Johannes Witteveen, *Annual Report of the Group of Thirty* (Consultative Group on International Economic and Monetary Affairs, Inc., 1980), p. 3.

110. I. S. Gulati, "New Substitution Account Proposal," *Economic and Political Weekly,* April 19, 1980, pp. 743–748.

111. *Euromoney,* December 1980.

112. Volcker, op. cit.

113. Bergsten, "International Monetary System in the 1980's," op. cit.

CHINATOWN: FOREIGN POLICY AND ELITE REALIGNMENT

Bruce Cumings

Later on, as I comprehended better the many-layered design of Mao's conversation, I understood that it was like the courtyards in the Forbidden City, each leading to a deeper recess distinguished from the others only by slight changes of proportion, with ultimate meaning residing in a totality that only long reflection could grasp.

Henry Kissinger, *White House Years*

In our own time we have no choice but to engage with the ch'eng. . . . *The next step—to go toward victory, to win with the* ch'i—*is at once more complex, more subtle, and more demanding.*

Richard Nixon, *The Real War*

First one up the China wall intervenes in Ethiopia against the Soviets.

Zbigniew Brzezinski, 1978

Why do the three architects of American foreign policy in the 1970s speak Chinese? And what does this ostensibly discredited gang of three have to do with foreign policy in the 1980s? Each of these men has been condemned to purgatory by established liberal opinion. In the wake of William Shawcross's revelations about Cambodia, Stanley Hoffman of Harvard and Anthony Lewis of *The New York Times* hinted at charges of criminality, and said Kissinger should never again hold high office. During the 1980 campaign, Lewis also called repeatedly for Carter to purge Brzezinski. As for Nixon, the calumny heaped upon him by liberals since 1946, not to mention August 9, 1974, would fill volumes and dwarf even Deng Xiao-ping's pillorying of Mao. Yet, our gang of three (with their many allies) have etched the 1980 Cold War consensus. Or so I will argue.

A straightforward essay on foreign policy debate in the recent presidential campaign would be brief indeed. It could be summarized as follows: do you want the M X missile, the Trident sub, the Rapid Deployment Force, the "stealth" bomber, the cruise missile, counterforce targeting strategy leading to a first-strike capability, the China card, containment in the "arc of crisis," and a 5 percent increase in defense spending; or do you want all the above plus the neutron bomb, the B-1 bomber, antiballistic missile systems, civil defense capability, and an 8 percent increase in defense spending? This was Carter versus Reagan. Or perhaps you prefer an earnest, sincere, conflicted, and decent idealist who raises all the tough questions (without answering them): John Anderson, the Jimmy Carter of 1976 revisited. Those candidates outside the new consensus (Barry Commoner, Ed Clark) were found in the netherworld of independent television and local radio talk shows. In the face of this desultory debate, therefore, one has to probe beneath the surface to hidden currents and conflicts, and to the purged or pilloried gang of three. In other words, to understand our foreign policy you have to do "Washingtonology."

You may think you know what you're dealing with, but believe me, you don't.

Noah Cross to Jake Gittes in *Chinatown*

For a brief, fleeting moment in the late 1960s and the 1970s the turmoil of the times opened the way to radical insight—that is, insight that penetrates to the roots of our crisis. Roman Polanski, a Pole who later fled to Paris on statutory rape charges, and whose wife was slaughtered by that gang of five (the Mansons) that unfortunately symbolized the counterculture for so many complacent Americans, made a film during this period called *Chinatown.* Ostensibly a nostalgic detective yarn, the deep meaning of the film reversed East and West and turned American politics on its head. Asia, Hegel, Marx, and other nineteenth-century thinkers told us, had a peculiar mode of production characterized by huge water-control projects and a lack of private property, leaving a stupefied mass at the mercy of successive despots: the Asian satrap found in the delivery of water the source of ultimate power. Our Chinatowns, successive generations of Americans believed, were populated by inscrutable deviants given to Tong wars, nefarious conspiracies, sleazy double-dealing, mayhem, and general depravity. Asians, whether here or there, lacked the requisites of freedom and civility.

Polanski's film takes us to Southern California, where a hegemonic despot (Noah Cross, played brilliantly by John Huston) manipulates water supplies and Los Angeles politicians toward the end of great wealth and power. Having owned the public water system for Los Angeles in the past, he gave it up to "public" control: that is, he put his son-in-law (who thinks "life begins in the sloughs and tidepools") in as water commissioner. The despot also manipulates his daughter (Faye Dunaway) and his other daughter (sister/daughter to Dunaway) toward the end of male dominance and the preservation of incestuous secrets. Despotism, water control, nepotism, incest: it is the Asiatic Mode of Production in our backyard. In the climactic final act, set in Los Angeles' Chinese community, Jake Gittes, the detective (read "investigative reporter") who has discovered all these truths, is led away from the murderous scene by his colleagues: "Forget it, Jake, *it's Chinatown.*"

Vietnam was our Chinatown. Unlike any previous experience in America's involvement with the world, it briefly lifted the veil on our imperial behavior. In so doing it tore the fabric of consent underpinning foreign policy. A restoration of consensus required what the Maoists call a "reversal of correct verdicts." Now, given that the verdict was correct (this was not "a noble war"), the initial method was a forgetting: amnesia. If the forgetting could then be combined with a healing, foreign policy elites could get on with the business of defending imperial interests. Jimmy Carter was our healer. But before coming to him, there is a more central figure to be considered: our Noah Cross.

THE HELMSMAN: RICHARD NIXON

As much as any figure alive today, Nixon has been at the center of postwar American politics. With Watergate and the tapes, we should know more about this man than any other president. His quirky, elusive, secretive personality has been probed in many studies, yet there are few serious appreciations of his centrality to our time. Perhaps this is because in the cycles of his seven crises we are always sure at each point that we have got rid of him: after Hiss, after the 1952 campaign scandal, after the 1960 defeat, after the 1962 press conference where he *told* us we wouldn't have him to kick around any more; above all after 1974, when his defeat seemed so complete that liberals felt a pained sense of loss because they would *not* have him to kick around any more. His outrageousness (another way of marking his distance from the consensual midpoints established by Eastern elites) also encourages a lack of attention. Nixon symbolizes the Chinatown of our politics: Americans don't like to believe that their leaders are "tricky," not clean-shaven, given to mudslinging, to swearing like a trucker, or to appearing before news conferences as vaguely catatonic. They don't like a leader who has to say "I am not a crook"; who refers to "the Jews" as "you know, they're arty, they're leftwing"; who says as he goes to meet an Italian leader, "I don't give a shit about the Italian lira"; or who refers to State Department officials as "impossible fags." They don't like a president whose national security advisor refers to him as "a little crazy, you know."[1] For this and many other reasons this leader (some would say "despot" and he would say "sovereign") who emerged from our last frontier in Southern California has gone remarkably unstudied. He has been *in* our world but not *of* it, something he understands better than anyone else. He is the insider as outsider. Clark Clifford once remarked that Nixon "was the first American president since the war who didn't have to worry about Richard Nixon." As it happens, he is also the last: one of Ford's first acts was to pardon this man to keep him out of jail; Carter labored amid a growing clamor for Nixonian foreign policy.

No politician has had a career more linked to China than Nixon. He came to prominence in the "who lost China" debate, red-baiting his opponents and pursuing Alger Hiss with dogged thoroughness. In the 1950s he was the leading hawk, along with John Foster Dulles, in talk of unleashing Chiang Kai-shek and having nothing to do with "Red China." In the 1960s he ventured to the heartland of his enemies, New York, and sought to bolster his Eastern credentials. By 1967 he had hit on an opening to China, recognizing both the consequences of the Sino-Soviet split and his own unique position in American politics, making it possible for him to trump the liberals like Kennedy and move toward China.

This personality we all know. But how do we explain his centrality? It is because Nixon, so alien to what Americans like to think about their country and their leaders, is a paradigmatic example of the transformation of United States foreign policy and the rise of the national security state in the postwar era. From its earliest days the Cold War led to behavior abroad that could not be justified by traditional morality; protected by two great oceans, most Americans had known nothing of war and intervention. For most Americans our policies went from the morality of the early postwar period to the immorality of the Vietnam period (this involved its own convenient forgetting of Korea, Iran, and Guatemala). Nixon's forte was amorality. Even in the earliest days of his lathered pursuit of Hiss, one can find that peculiar combination of shrewd, intelligent, and studied method directed toward indecent ends. In the period 1968–1974 Nixon introduced to an America that had been insulated from its acts abroad the concept of amoral realism, and the Cold War returned home.

A vice to many, amoral realism was virtue to the thousands (millions?) of bureaucrats who, since the Great Leap Forward in defense spending of 1950, drew their paychecks from the Pentagon, the armed services, the intelligence agencies, or the corporations and academies that serve the national security state. This bureaucratic accretion bulked very large in the growth of the American state and perpetuated its interests by reference to constant foreign threats. Amoral realism (we could call it the Nixonian accretion) is the appropriate ideology for those with an interest in permanent imperialism; it is the perfect guide for those who have introduced into our language the euphemisms of nuclear "exchanges" (that is, holocaust), pacification (that is, war), intelligence "communities," "protective reaction" (that is, aggression), and so on. The national security apparatus is the organizational expression of the executive power that has grown by leaps and bounds as America connected with the world. It all persisted through the amnesia and healing of the period 1974–1980; here is Nixonism without Nixon.

Nixon thus personified the amorality and the dogged permanence of the national-security types. But he was more than that: he was, as president, a dynamic executive who did more to change our foreign policy than anyone since Dean Acheson. Constantly underestimating Nixon, most analysts have missed this. In the two critical decisions of his presidency that, more than any others, revolutionized postwar foreign policy, Nixon was the helmsman. On China, he was the architect and Kissinger was his engineer[2]—something even the endlessly self-promoting Kissinger acknowledges in his memoirs. In the days of the Johnson-Nixon transition, an aide quoted Kissinger on his talks with the president-elect at the Hotel Pierre: "Nixon wants to reorganize China."[3] In the 1971 New Economic Policy, Nixon was the architect and John Connally was his engineer. Yet after his removal from office, Nixon found his only welcome in Peking.

Richard Nixon is our Deng Xiao-ping: hounded from office twice for trying to "reverse correct verdicts," Deng was never down for the count. Neither was our survivor. In his new book, a new Nixon appears: one who speaks in Mao-style epigrams, or in Chinese; one who raises the specter of a new Communist threat in all parts of the globe save China. It is as if, scorned first by Eastern liberals and then by the whole nation, Nixon sought refuge in his perennial China connection; it is for him the source of his place in history, and the auspices of his resurrection.

THEORIES OF THE THREE WORLDS

Maoist strategic thought since the 1930s has conceived of our planet as divided into three worlds. By the 1960s this had evolved to a conception of a first world of superpowers (the United States and the USSR), a second world of advanced capitalist and socialist states (East and West Europe and Japan), and a third world of emerging nations seeking independence from both other realms. The hidden currents of the 1970s can be understood by examining two other three-world theories, that of Nixon-Kissinger and that of the Trilateralists. The palpable failures of both conceptions by the late 1970s in turn open the way to comprehending the new consensus of 1980, and the general lack of serious foreign policy debate in the campaign.

Richard Nixon recognized in the late 1960s that the Sino-Soviet split had made room for a new geopolitics. A conspiracy disguised as two states, straddling the Eurasian land mass, had become two states in barely disguised conflict. A transnational sphere, the socialist bloc, had come unstuck; since these were nations, it was possible to understand their differing interests, base American policies on them, and pursue an amoral balance of power politics. With a political career founded on a shrewd amorality, it is not surprising that Nixon was among the first of politicians to grasp the new reality. Having based his academic career on balance of

power reasoning, it is equally unsurprising to find Henry Kissinger attracted to the Nixonian conception.

The Sino-Soviet conflict emphasized the truth that both China and
the Soviet Union were *regional* powers, and that each could be used in the
containment of the other: containment of communism by communism.
The delinking of the two socialist giants made linkage possible for the
United States. That is, Nixon could pursue a triangular diplomacy with
the great luxury of having more leverage over China and Russia than
either had over him. Although there was much talk of "linkage" in Soviet-American relations during the Nixon years, what Nixon achieved was
not the pressure derived from linking Soviet activities the world over,
but the room for American maneuver that came from separating the Soviet problem from the China problem, and the separation of both from
the second and third worlds. Problems that had for a generation been
seen as connected were separated. As triangular diplomacy emerged full-
blown in 1971 and 1972, Nixon and Kissinger discovered that they
could have a free hand in dealing with our allies in the second world and
our enemies in the third world by dealing separately with China and
Russia. They could talk to Mao and Chou while pursuing aggressive war
in Vietnam and Cambodia; Kissinger says the opening to China was "a
major defeat for Hanoi." In summit meetings in Moscow in 1972, Nixon
learned that neither the mining of Haiphong, coming just before the
summit, nor the secret deals with the shah (to recycle petrodollars for
massive amounts of weaponry, thus turning Iran into a regional *gendarme*)
would deter Brezhnev from pursuing détente.[4] Nor would either Communist power come to the defense of a beleaguered Chile, where Nixon had
devised policies to "make the [Chilean] economy scream" and to overthrow Salvador Allende.[5] Amid all this, détente proceeded and SALT took
on "a life of its own."

Thus, what one had in the Nixon years was a process of *detachment,*
not linkage. China detached from Moscow, both detached from Hanoi;
the allies detached from the threat of monolithic communism and therefore vulnerable to American economic pressures. The three worlds could
be dealt with independently. In the first world of superpowers, the flowering of détente approached a two-power condominium, something implicit in much of Kissinger's academic writing. Nixon probably had the
shrewder conception: telling the Soviets they were an equal global power
and the two superpowers would rule the world, while hamstringing and
containing the Soviets through the China connection and regional powers like Iran, thus reaffirming the basically regional character of Soviet
power. In the second world we could stick it to our allies, amid sharp
West-West economic competition. In the third world we had a free hand
for the general free-for-all that characterized Soviet-American competition in this realm—or what Kissinger politely called "setting the limits of
diversity."[6]

THE NEP: GREAT DISORDER IN THE SECOND WORLD

The wind in the bell tower heralds a storm in the mountains. There is great disorder under heaven and the situation is excellent. . . .
As a result of the emergence of social-imperialism, the socialist camp which existed for a time after World War II is no longer in existence. Owing to the law of uneven development of capitalism, the Western imperialist bloc, too, is disintegrating.

Deng Xiao-ping, *1974*

Among the other things that Nixon shares with Chinese leaders is that they like Charles de Gaulle. For Nixon's Walter Mitty, grandiose conception of "the sovereign," De Gaulle was perfect. For China, De Gaulle was the great leader who, in the early 1960s, resisted American pressure by launching an independent military force and an opening to China. Much more than Nixon, Mao understood the disintegrative effects of De Gaulle's policies, which led Western Europe from alliance to national economies in competition with each other. Perhaps dimly aware of declining American hegemony over the second world, but sharply aware of market competition from Japan and West Germany, Nixon acted.

On August 15, 1971 (V-J Day), Nixon announced "a declaration of economic war."[7] He imposed a 10 percent surcharge on imports, a 10 percent reduction in foreign aid, and the suspension of dollar convertibility into gold. For the Japanese, this was the second "Nixon *shokku*" (the first being China); in fact, along with the China opening, it was the second profound shock that Nixon dealt to the world at large and to elites at home. Using John Connally, an archetypal nationalist, as his battering ram, Nixon outraged Eastern establishment free-traders and moved sharply away from a generation of internationalism abroad, founded on the principle that world capitalism needed a central authority to make it work.[8] Now the hegemony was retreating to nationalism, greatly furthering the disintegrative trends already in motion. Nor did the NEP deal solely with economic relations; it ran the gamut from political relations (refusal to consult allies) to calls for "burden-sharing" in the defense of the free world.

In spite of Nixon's shrewd, amoral nationalism in the three worlds, his policies failed—less because of the conception than because of a general and largely irremediable decline in American hegemony. Détente in the first world, as Mary Kaldor notes, had "a corrosive effect" in the second world.[9] Without a strong Soviet threat and amid sharp economic competition, the Allies were freer to maneuver and strike their own deals. Thus, by the mid-1970s, it was apparent that West Germany had pursued a deep and economically beneficial détente with Moscow, and Japan had done the same with Peking. Both had moved faster than the United States. At home, détente encouraged a period of domesticism, as Americans felt less threatened by the world at large; the postwar anti-Communist consensus was further shredded as Americans watched Nixon drink *mao-tai* with Chou; and détente spawned its own opposition, as hardliners regrouped around a ritualized Soviet threat. One may therefore take it almost as a principle that détente polarizes at home and abroad, whereas superpower confrontation unites at home and abroad. In times of détente the Allies and the American people get off the mark, out of control.

Nixon's conception of détente mixed with containment also failed. By 1975—a key year in shifting American policies—the Soviets had, in Nixon's words, "leapfrogged" over the boundaries of containment. Speaking also of "wide flanking movements" and a breaching of "the third front,"[10] Nixon argues that Soviet or Cuban-Soviet African involvements in the mid-1970s (Angola, Mozambique, Somalia-Ethiopia) and subsequent activities in Indochina and South Asia in the late 1970s have somehow broken the rules of the game, so that we now face "the most powerfully expansionist nation the world has ever known," and our choice is "between surrender and suicide—red or dead." Now even "the big enchilada" (Watergate fans need to know that this is Saudi Arabia and not John Mitchell) is threatened.[11] What Nixon fails to mention is that the Soviets were in fact *continuing* the rules of the game in Nixonian détente: free-for-all in the third world. They also sought to move from regional to global power. Since the Soviets had given us a free hand in Indochina, Iran, Chile, and elsewhere, and had tolerated the activities of our Cubans in Vietnam —that is, the South Korean expeditionary force that saw more than 300,000 soldiers active there over a seven-year period—by what reasoning would the United States suddenly decry similar Soviet activities?

Nixon's own third world policies also failed, rather miserably. He avers that "we had won the [Vietnam] war militarily and politically" by 1973,[12] but in fact, of course, we had lost it, and not even the Kissinger-Nixon figleaf could cover the sorry spectacle that occurred in April 1975. Following on that debacle was an even greater one, the failure of our armed-to-the-teeth regional *gendarme* to hang on to power in Iran. Nixon chooses to blame all this on the "arrogant carping" of the "best and the brightest," and "the failures of America's leadership class," by which he means the Eastern establishment that never accepted him. Having symbolically detached himself from "the presidency" during Watergate, treating the office as if it were unrelated to his depravity and something to be preserved through his continuing presence in it, he now detaches himself from the debacles and crimes of his foreign policy. Arguing that we lost Iran because we "set higher standards of conduct for our friends than for our enemies" (think about that one), Nixon in fact illustrates what Christopher Lasch has said about the men of the Nixon years: they were "fatally removed from American life."[13] Most Americans cannot stomach a foreign policy in which we do battle with the standards of conduct characteristic of many of our friends (the Shah, Somoza, Park Chung Hee), let alone those of our enemies. The saga of "Richard Nixon removed from office" was one of a man so removed from common morality that the only question was which crime to remove him for. By the time the American people were seemingly done with him in 1974, he had done more to destroy consensus than all the "carping" of all the "best and the brightest" put together. In his wake came a new theory of the three worlds, hoping to put Humpty-Dumpty together again.

THE THREE WORLDS OF TRILATERAL POLICY

The Chinese view of bipolar disintegration and great disorder under heaven in the early 1970s had an uncanny resonance with the assumptions that informed the Trilateral Commission, that combination of David Rockefeller's money and Zbigniew Brzezinski's brains that emerged in reaction to Nixon's NEP and the general deflation of American power. The Trilateral vision asserted that this erosion of influence and control was less deleterious than might be thought, if the Western powers and Japan were to recognize the sources of their real strength: their central positions as the most advanced economies in the world. The emphasis was on economic-system disintegration, not power-bloc dissolution; the remedy was not national and social revolution, as the Maoists had it, but market-economy solidarity leading to restoration and revival, reformation rather than transformation, or a return to what one Trilateral study termed the "belle epoque" of the immediate postwar era.[14] Here was the new internationalism of the 1970s.

In the first world, Trilateralism would move away from the strategic centrality attached to Soviet-American relations of the Nixon years; but like Nixon, grain deals and technology transfers would be continued to enmesh the Soviet Union further in an advanced world system dominated by the Trilateral nations. Trilateralists were pronounced in their belief that through such means, the Soviets would be confined and dependent on the West and Japan.[15] The lure of a big socialist market simply sweetened the idea.

In the second world, the emphasis would be on collegiality rather than confrontation: Japan, Germany, and the United States would work toward common policies, transnational economic planning, and general solidarity that would eliminate the threat of anarchy in the world monetary system, protectionism in world trade, and the specter of "neo-colonial *chasses gardeés*" between the Trilateral countries and "the regions to the south of them." China would be treated like the Soviet Union: a nation to be tamed and welcomed in, once bureaucratic conservatism had replaced revolutionary socialism, which was taken to be the general path trod by socialist nations.[16]

In the third world, the policy would be accommodation, not intervention—a necessity, given the unprecedented accumulation of power represented by the OPEC actions of 1973. The substitution of Andrew Young for the oppositional Daniel Moynihan as UN ambassador subsequently symbolized this shift perfectly. In place of Nixon's economic nationalism came the code word of the mid-1970s, "interdependence." From the world's policeman, the United States would change to custodian or "night watchman." In place of the values of freedom and liberty, Zbigniew Brzezinski argued, would be the value of equity: in this manner, America would no longer find itself in "a hostile world."[17] An emphasis on human rights would restore the United States as a moral force abroad, and provide a counterpoint to and a healing salve for the Nixonian combination of amorality and immorality. All in all, the Trilateralists had written, as Ferguson and Rogers say, "a general program for achieving a liberal integrated world economic system, secure from protectionist disruption and domestic upheaval."[18]

Jimmy Carter, first discovered by David Rockefeller in 1971 and welcomed into the Trilateral Commission in 1973,[19] proved to be the ideal candidate to serve the healing function. A Sunday School teacher, rhetorical populist, and face-up honest man, his election symbolized the American yearning to have moral policies at home and abroad. Some twenty-five Trilateralists became members of the new administration,[20] and the first year of foreign policy embodied a thorough rejection of Nixonian three-world strategy. In the first world, the Soviet connection was deemphasized, and in place of the horse-trading Nixon-Kissinger SALT negotiations, Carter tabled a proposal in March 1977 that severely upset the negotiating process in its call for much more thorough arms control. In a major speech in May 1977 Carter announced that the United States was now "free of that inordinate fear of communism" which had motivated earlier policies. Indeed, we were now coming into a halcyon post–Cold War period, "Era II," in which cooperation would replace confrontation in the Soviet-American relationship.

The "China card," played masterfully by Nixon, was put back in the deck. Secretary of State Cyrus Vance put China policy on the back burner in 1977–1978; his trip to Peking in August 1977 was a disaster, leading Deng Xiao-ping publicly to call it a step backward. Carter administration officials fanned out to the capitals of the second world, seeking to get the Japanese and Germans to coordinate economic policies (the "Three Locomotives" would pull the world economy in their wake), stop proliferating the makings of nuclear weapons, and reach voluntary limits on exports to the American market. In the third world, Carter put pressure on American allies with abusive regimes, such as South Korea, where he pushed for a full withdrawal of the 40,000 American troops stationed there; arms sales to such regimes were to be cut by 10 percent per year.

This set of policies did not last much past early 1978. Trilateralism, or internationalism recrudescent, could not reestablish the so-called *belle epoque* in the face of steady American decline; it could only be an Indian summer of the "halcyon days" of postwar hegemony. An empty husk, it withered within a year.

THE TWO-LINE STRUGGLE IN THE CARTER ADMINISTRATION, 1977–1980

Mao Tse-tung thought that the conflicts wracking China in the 1960s could be captured by the phrase "struggle between two lines." Every unity, Mao said, contains two contradictory opposites; the opposing tendencies are often hidden, only to burst forth with sudden energy: "one divides into two." The hidden conflict in China appeared in the early 1960s only in allegorical tales directed at Mao; in 1965, Mao had one member of the Gang of Four publish salvos in a counterattack that now is taken as the opening of the Cultural Revolution. China-watchers in the United States came to accept the reality of two lines in conflict, but puzzled over what to call them: Maoists v. Dengists? Moderates v. Radicals?

The Carter administration contained within it two contradictory tendencies in foreign policy. One was represented mostly by a group of younger scholar-diplomats associated with the magazine *Foreign Policy.* This tendency was located in the State Department. The other current was located in the National Security Council. It would be hard to call these currents "moderates v. radicals" or "Brzezinskites v. Vanceists." Let's just call them column A and column B. In 1977, Jimmy Carter chose advisors from each.

Column A included Cyrus Vance, Richard Holbrooke, Leslie Gelb, Paul Warnke, Anthony Lake, Richard Moose, Marshal Shulman, and, at the UN, Andrew Young. Most had been members of the Trilateral Commission. Most had mildly opposed the Vietnam war, at least after the 1970 invasion of Cambodia. Some, like Lake, had resigned national security positions in protest, leading Kissinger to tell Carter that "you seem to hire the people I fire." This "new-boy network," as William Safire called it, represented a new generation of Eastern Establishment liberals (except for Vance, an older charter member): they accepted the Trilateral vision as post-Cold Warriors who had their minds changed by the Vietnam era— although not to the point of burning bridges to high office.[21]

Column B, which we might call the "Brzezinski difference," included preeminently Zbigniew Brzezinski himself; Samuel Huntington of Harvard University (but resident in the White House now and then); William Griffith and Lincoln Bloomfield of MIT, also commuting to Washington; Michel Oksenberg, the NSC China man; and Colonel William Odom, former student of Brzezinski at Columbia dubbed "the hawk's hawk." These individuals, and most others associated with NSC, had been supporters of the Vietnam war throughout; some, like Brzezinski, had made startling changes in their published writing in the early and mid-1970s. This represented less a conversion than a tacking to the wind. All were a new breed of foreign policy technocrat, willing to serve any administration.

Franz Schurmann has argued that in a modern state structure, the executive organization possesses a room for maneuver that is unavailable to the large bureaucracies that populate central government. The bureaucrats occupy a realm of interest, where standard routines and operating procedures and vested interests hamstring and confine all creativity. The executive, however, can function like a creative entrepreneur in the economy, bringing in new ideas and visions without the constraints of great bureaucracies.[22] No one can read Kissinger's *White House Years* without realizing the truth of this formulation. Nixon and Kissinger launched wars against the State Department, had utter contempt for it, and ended up centralizing almost all important foreign policy decisions in their own hands. The State Department—the "fudge factory," "Foggy Bottom"—is the epitome of the bureaucracy as a realm of vested interest and tedious routine. The national security advisor, on the other hand, has his own personal staff and, above all, daily access to the president. Thus, he is able systematically to accumulate the influence and the critical knowledge necessary to win bureaucratic battles with rivals. This process has led to a truly incredible arrogation of power by unelected, ambitious technocrats working outside the established procedures of foreign policy formulation. In the 1970s, the system produced two foreign-born national security advisors who, like Richard Nixon, were in our world but not of it.

Jimmy Carter, as president, was certainly of our world. He was classically American to his roots and to his soul. This also meant that, as a typical American, he had little experience with foreign affairs, in spite of several years of Trilateral tutoring. What Kissinger has said about American politicians in general was even more true of Carter:[23]

> It is literally the case that you are starting with a *tabula rasa,* and that the position the political leader takes is much influenced by the type of intellectual that almost quite accidentally winds up in his entourage.

Carter even saw himself as a student, listening to all the best advice and getting up early in the morning to cram in the welter of empirical detail crossing his desk. A man with no commitments that he could not be talked out of, within months he was captured by Brzezinski.

Brzezinski was a Polish-born aristocrat, a political scientist from Columbia University whose scholarly work was flashy and trendy and not substantial enough to give him the scholarly credentials of Henry Kissinger. But he did apparently hanker after Kissinger-style power. Richard Falk recalls a meeting in the early 1970s at which someone in jest handed Brzezinski a mask of Henry Kissinger:[24]

Brzezinski immediately put it on and started laughing compulsively. He became quite hysterical and subsided only when the mask was removed a long minute or so later.

Sally Quinn's long, gossipy piece on Brzezinski in *The Washington Post* confirms his penchant for seeking to out-Kissinger Kissinger. He apparently hoped to cap his career by becoming secretary of state in the second Carter administration.[25]

In 1977, Brzezinski, Huntington, and their staffs—along with allies in the Pentagon—began the creation of alternatives to the Trilateral program. Column B came to accept the Nixonian view that Soviet leapfrogging made a new containment necessary; there could be no détente, no Trilateral accommodation, without it. This was not a matter of a handful of people reversing policy; column B drew on strong currents of support outside the administration in the anti-détente forces building all during the 1970s.[26] In the absence of necessary documentation, we have to search out this reversal in the fine print of our dominant newspapers, pursuing a Washingtonology that can reveal the hidden struggle. We are fortunate in having on hand Richard Burt, described by Hodding Carter, former State Department spokesman, as "notorious for being an open wound on the National Security Council. They turn on the arterial flow and he transmits it to *The New York Times*"; when Burt writes, he said, you can see "Brzezinski's lips move."[27]

Burt himself noted that foreign policy crises in the Carter years seemed "to hasten changes,"[28] an important insight. Crises are to the advantage of those who anticipate them and who are in position to act. They clear away underbrush. Column B seized on real and phony crises eventually to trounce column A.

In 1980, the Carter administration approved three new policies: the famous PD-59, changing strategic nuclear targeting from the old, city-busting Mutual Assured Destruction (MAD) to a "countervailing" strategy of attacking Soviet nuclear installations; the lesser-known PD-51, projecting a tactical nuclear response in the event of Soviet aggression in the Persian Gulf region; and the creation of the Rapid Deployment Force (RDF), designed for conventional deterrence and intervention. All these policies were Nixonian in origin and were elaborated in 1977 by Brzezinski and his sidekick, Samuel Huntington, with Pentagon support from Harold Brown.

A critical aspect of containment in the 1970s era of limits to American power was the threat of tactical use of nuclear weapons to block *conventional* attacks through the containment periphery. James Schlesinger, Nixon-Ford defense secretary, suggested in the wake of the Indochina debacle in 1975 that a North Korean conventional attack might be met with a nuclear response. In 1977, Huntington extended the idea to the Middle East-Persian Gulf region, and the crises of 1980 pushed the policy through. In the wake of Afghanistan, Clark Clifford was dispatched to India, where he remarked publicly that further Soviet aggression would "mean war," which, given limitations on our conventional forces, could only suggest to many observers using tactical nuclear weapons to block conventional advances. In the summer of 1980, according to Jack Anderson, PD-51 became policy.[29]

The PD-59 "countervailing" strategy, suggesting a budding American first-strike capability,[30] had its germination in Nixon's 1971 "World Message"; Schlesinger broached it again in 1974, leading to severe criticism by then-Senator Edmund Muskie.[31] At the end of 1977, Brzezinski and Brown came back to the idea after reading a study by Huntington concluding that "the Soviet Union did not accept the theory of mutual deterrence" —a cardinal principle of the Committee on the Present Danger crowd. Brzezinski sought to push PD-59 through again in the spring of 1979, and alluded to it in a long interview in March 1980, saying that effective deterrence requires "a wider range of options than either a spasmodic nuclear exchange or a limited conventional war." But the policy was not approved until the presidential campaign heated up, in August 1980. The formerly critical Muskie, by then secretary of state, read about PD-59 in his morning newspaper.[32]

A new means of conventional containment, the Rapid Deployment Force (RDF), also had its origins in 1977 planning and also was pushed through in the wake of various crises in 1979–1980. In mid-1977, Brzezinski and Huntington, spurred by concerns about security in the Persian Gulf, "advocated the creation of a rapid deployment force for use in third world crises." Carter approved the general idea in August 1977, but then the plan met opposition from the State Department and the Pentagon. So the administration continued to rely on the Shah as a regional surrogate *gendarme* (the Nixon-Kissinger policy). On New Year's Eve 1977, Carter praised the Shah for creating in Iran "an island of stability" in a troubled region, which was "a great tribute to you, Your Majesty, and to the respect and the admiration and the love which your people give you." The fall of Iran suggested again, however, the virtues of an interventionist RDF; in the wake of the false alarums over Soviet combat troops in Cuba in August 1979, Brzezinski pushed the new policy to fruition.[33] In a little-noted speech in Chicago in December 1979, *before* Afghanistan, Brzezinski said the RDF "will give us the capability to respond quickly, effectively, *and even pre-emptively.*"[34]

The early months of the Carter administration included a variety of initiatives drawn from column A as well, but even these seem in retrospect to have been halfhearted. The cancellation of the B-1 bomber in 1977, for example, now seems to have been a tradeoff with the new "stealth" bomber, under secret development for several years.[35] The Carter human rights policy was no sooner announced than it was directed less to those regimes where Americans have a *direct* responsibility for repression, such as the Philippines and South Korea, and more to the Soviet Union and Eastern Europe. As Marcus Raskin has argued, Brzezinksi saw the United

States as a dynamic power, capable of sending salvos to the East that would disrupt the stodgy bureaucratic facade of Soviet rule and sow dissension among Soviet allies in Europe.[36] The troop withdrawal from Korea also no sooner saw the light of day than it met with furious opposition. General John Vesey, former commander of American forces in Korea, began arguing within Carter circles in late 1976 that a putative North Korean buildup made the withdrawal impossible; soon thereafter, a Carter appointee on NSC told me that "only one person supports the withdrawal, and that is Jimmy Carter." The formal reversal of the policy was finally announced when Carter visited and toasted Park Chung Hee in June 1979. Six months later Park was assassinated, and Carter supported the subsequent emergence of an even more brutal dictatorship.

Arms sales to our allies and friends, which were to have come down by 10 percent per year, began rising immediately. The defense budget, which candidate Carter said he would cut by $5 billion to $7 billion, went from $108 billion in 1977 to $142 billion in 1980. The general reversal from column A to column B did not really become apparent, however, until 1978. Column A "reached its high water mark" in early 1978, and then faded quickly as Russian and Cuban activities in Angola and the Horn of Africa provided the crisis necessary to tip the bureaucratic balance.[37] The "new boys" at State started resigning. Having argued for SALT first, China second, the new boys watched as NSC reversed the priorities: now it would be China first, SALT second.

BRZEZINSKI PLAYS HIS CHINA CARD

China, for Nixon, Kissinger, and most Americans, is a far-off netherworld of inscrutable people and delicious opportunities. The real China is alien, but "China," as an issue and a symbol in American politics since 1945, is familiar and central. China was a mysterious arena in which Nixon could play because he was unassailable on "China." The State Department, however, had lost several career China hands to the China issue, and therefore grew nearly catatonic at the thought of departure from routine policy. But the executive is free to act. Therefore, our gang of three has found throughout the 1970s that China—and "China"—is a great resource to be deployed in struggles with antagonists at State and in the world at large (meaning mostly the Soviets).

Brzezinski remarked in an interview in late 1980 that he had a "shorthand formula" to explain the failure of SALT: "Salt lies buried in the sands of the Ogaden."[38] What does this weird formula mean? It means that Soviet leapfrogging to Africa through its own and Cuba's involvement in the Horn in early 1978 (opposing Somali aggression, of course, but never mind that), provided a minicrisis that enabled the reversal of priorities: China before SALT. In March 1978, Carter gave a harsh anti-Soviet speech, written by Brzezinski, at Wake Forest College, drawing attention to politics in the Horn.[39] In late March, Brezhnev pointedly toured the Sino-Soviet border areas.

Soviet activities in the Horn tilted Brzezinski toward playing the China card, which in turn scared the Soviets. It was during this period that Brzezinski opened "back channel" communications with Peking, and that the fundamental decision to normalize relations with China was made, over the opposition and with the exclusion of the State Department. In May 1978, Brzezinski made a visit to China that was totally different in tone from Vance's visit the previous year. He said the United States had "made up its mind" to normalize. Then he made the remark at the Great Wall quoted at the beginning of this essay. After his return to Washington, some reports suggested that the United States had decided to sell military-related technology to China; Washington also arranged for the sale of a UNIVAC 1100 series computer to China, something that had been denied to the Soviets.[40]

Normalization of relations with China followed on December 15, 1978: the joint statement committed the United States and China to opposition to "hegemony" (Soviet influence) the world over. According to a column B official I talked with, the normalization documents were sent over to the State Department on the morning of December 15; this official remarked, "we smashed those bastards." Almost simultaneously, Vietnam invaded Cambodia—an unprecedented event in the socialist third world, done with obvious Soviet backing. In February 1979, Deng Xiao-ping toured the United States, dropping threats to invade Vietnam; it appears from the available record that Carter administration officials sought to discourage him from doing so. Still, the demurrals were sufficiently tepid that when Deng returned to Peking and invaded Vietnam, the Soviets were able to charge that American officials had colluded with him in this act. For days following the invasion, there were reports of major Soviet troop movements along the Chinese border; but in the event the Soviets stayed their hand and China withdrew from Vietnam having, so it said, "taught a lesson."

In February 1979 a remarkable article appeared, written under the pseudonym Justin Galen. The author was reputed to be close to James Schlesinger. He argued that as China developed militarily, the United States could use it as "a powerful check and balance" on the USSR; normalization had thrown "the old China hands" into "history's trash can," and had been "the toughest message the U.S. has sent to the USSR in the last five years." China already posed a threat that "the Soviets take extremely seriously"; China's capabilities would in the 1980s "improve strikingly," and as long as pragmatists remained at China's helm, "it will be almost forced to maximize its interdependence with Japan, Europe, and the U.S." The overall result would thus be greatly strengthened containment of the Soviet Union. Playing the China card, the author thought, "seems to be the best game in town."[41]

A year later, in the wake of the Afghanistan invasion, Secretary Brown visited China, toured sensitive military installations, and caused much press speculation about a military alliance between Washington and Peking.[42] Within weeks, the Carter administration had agreed to transfer to China a ground station for the Landsat satellite, along with sophisticated computers and taping technology that had military as well as civilian application. Other so-called "dual-use" technology transferred to China included early warning radar, communications gear, and logistical support equipment. China also got most-favored nation trading status, something long denied to the Soviet Union. A week after this "major policy shift,"[43] Leonid Brezhnev met with former French Prime Minister Jacques Chalban-Delmas and seemed almost beside himself:

> Believe me, after the destruction of Chinese nuclear sites by our missiles, there won't be much time for the Americans to choose between the defense of their Chinese allies and peaceful coexistence with us.

Brezhnev said a nuclear arming of China (something no American had suggested, to my knowledge), would lead to "a Soviet nuclear attack on China," giving American leaders "only minutes to decide their options."[44]

Later on in the year, amid the continuing American embargo of grain sales to the USSR, Carter agreed to sell the Chinese 6 to 8 million metric tons of grain for each of the next four years. The final result of China policy thus witnessed a replacement of the Soviet Union American leaders thought they had found in the early 1970s with the China of the 1980s. That is, a socialist country deficient in grain and technology suggests a policy of welcoming the socialist country into the world economy on the assumption that such ties would hamstring it and make it dependent, and would provide a huge socialist market for American exports. The policy failed in regard to the Soviet Union, the world's largest self-sufficient economy. It seems to have succeeded with China, with the added benefit of containing Moscow. But the cost to the stability of the superpower relationship has been profound. It was in this overall context that Franz Schurmann interpreted the Afghanistan invasion not as a thrust at Middle Eastern oil, but as "a resounding message to Washington and Peking."[45] Brzezinski, in turn, could not resist sending his own message by materializing on the Afghan border in February, playing with machine guns and telling the Afghan rebels that God was on their side. Much more fundamentally, in my view, through its actions column B told the Soviets from mid-1978 on that China was more important than SALT. The Soviets responded to American actions in a tit-for-tat way, leading to a dialectical interaction in which SALT II was eventually lost.

By the time the Carter people had fully played their China card it was enough to shock even the hardboiled crew that came in with Reagan. His transition team advisors reported that "they were startled by the depth and breadth of relations with China," including Defense Department studies concluding that the United States should arm China, secret joint intelligence projects, and Chinese contact with some forty American munitions manufacturers.[46]

THE END OF THE TWO-LINE STRUGGLE IN THE NEW COLD WAR CONSENSUS

Both three-world theories of the 1970s—the Nixonian and the Trilateral—failed. Under the ostensible rubric of the general Trilateral program, column B in the National Security Council carved out a different policy and in so doing triumphed bureaucratically over column A in the State Department. Vance resigned in April 1980, having tired of "losing to Zbigniew Brzezinski." But there was a final humiliation in store: two weeks later, Carter referred to his replacement as "much stronger and more statesmanlike" than Vance.[47] At the Harvard commencement on June 6, Vance gave a poignant speech full of Trilateralist echoes; in this unprecedented fashion, at least for a former secretary of state and scion of the Eastern Establishment, we heard the last hurrah of 1970s internationalism.

Edmund Muskie replaced Vance and quite predictably lost every round to column B. He was reduced to complaining publicly about NSC power on at least three occasions[48] and to learning about PD-59 from his morning newspaper.

The triumph of column B policy explains the desultory foreign policy debate of the 1980 campaign. Bert Lance, who ought to know, once remarked that "Carter runs left but governs right."[49] The rightward lurch in Carter foreign policy met a rightist entrenchment in the Republican party, and the result was predictable: both candidates sought to out-Cold War each other. The move Right has provided the basis of newfound consensus, at the cost of squeezing out nearly all alternative foreign policy thinking and most of the "New Boy network."

For most Americans and almost all the media, this is not how the story was told at all. Instead, the new Cold War of 1980 was brought on by Soviet adventurism, culminating in the Afghanistan invasion, which Carter called our "most serious crisis since World War II." The American people have been frightened by arguments that the Soviets have a first-strike capability, are outspending us by 3 to 1 on defense, and are on the march the world over. This in turn has spawned a remarkable new nationalism and bellicosity among the American public at large, compounded by the long frustrations in returning the hostages from Iran. Let us therefore examine this new Soviet threat.

Richard Burt reported the new "consensus" of American intelligence analysts in May 1980 that "in the next few years the Soviet Union could achieve an edge over the United States in every major measure of strategic nuclear power."[90] This judgment represented the coming together of two separate estimates done in 1976 by "team A" and "team B" (their terms, not mine) in the George-Bush-directed CIA. Team B included Richard Pipes of Harvard; Lieutenant General Daniel Graham, former director of the Defense Intelligence Agency; Paul Nitze; William Van Cleave of the University of Southern California; and others. These individuals concluded that the Soviets were moving ahead of the United States in military spending and strength (indeed that they had doubled their spending in the 1970s), and were moving toward a war-winning nuclear capability. Team A apparently demurred, although neither report has been released in full to the press. By the 1980 campaign, the team B analysis had become accepted wisdom among most national security analysts and the bible of candidate Reagan.

Arthur Macy Cox, former State Department and CIA analyst, has argued that a "tragic error" led to the team B conclusions: the Soviets were discovered not to have doubled defense spending, but to have increased the percentage of their GNP devoted to defense—a quite different matter, reflecting more on Soviet inefficiency than on a new threat. Cox states "there have been no dramatic increases," and found a January 1980 CIA estimate that all during the 1970s Soviet defense spending increased annually at the rate of only 3 percent, or at about the American rate.[51] He also noted that Moscow must worry about Peking; Justin Galen estimated that as much as one-third of Soviet defense capability is directed at China.[52] A recent study from the Center for Defense Information argued that the Soviets have had as many losses as gains in recent years, with their influence peaking in the late 1950s (influence in 14 percent of the world's nations) and dropping to the current rate of 12 percent. This report also asks the question "Who lost China?" and reminds us that it was the Soviets.[53]

I believe the Soviet Union is far behind the United States in technological and economic dynamism, and seeks to compensate for its weakness with a big military machine. Its invasion of Afghanistan reflected fears of China and the crumbling of an allied socialist regime; the timing of the invasion is easily explained as a reaction to the triumph of column B in the Carter administration and the knowledge that, in a presidential election year, Soviet-American relations never move forward. The Polish crisis of 1980–1981 is the most glaring indication of Soviet weakness, both in the infirmities and brutalities of the socialist system in the USSR and Poland, and in Moscow's creeping inability to dominate East Europe. The primary difference in the late 1970s from previous periods is the continuing Soviet attempt to move out of regional containment boundaries, and—unlike previous periods going back to 1945—American unwillingness or inability to continue containment.

The Cold War was fought, grew, and seemed to come to an end through three crises. The first was in Europe (Greece and Turkey), the second was Korea (1950), in which containment was applied throughout East and Southeast Asia, and the last was Vietnam, as the United

States stretched its conventional power to the limit and still lost.

Of these three crises, the preferred one for national security elites of our time is Korea. A conventional assault provoked by five years of internecine conflict in a far-off, little-known country provided the wherewithal to force through the world-ranging program of NSC-68, the single most important Cold War document of our era, written mostly by Paul Nitze. Defense spending trebled, the Allies were corralled, consensus at home was assured. If Truman and his generation acted on the 1938 Munich analogy, Nitze and his generation act on the 1950 analogy: in the midst of crisis, the country united to fight a global struggle. That same generation now looks back on 1950 with nostalgia, but also as a guide to our time.

In 1978, *Time* magazine, various newspapers, and Zbigniew Brzezinski began referring to an "arc of crisis" stretching along the southern rim of China and the Soviet Union, through Iran, and around to the Horn of Africa and down to southern Africa. In the wake of Afghanistan, there emerged the "Carter doctrine," which applied containment to the Persian Gulf region. The region had, "an official" (Brzezinski) said on January 25, "been elevated to the status of Western Europe, Japan, and South Korea."[54] Three days later, Brzezinski appeared on ABC-TV and in his best Strangelovian manner referred to South Asia and the Persian Gulf as the "third strategic zone." The first had been Western Europe in the late 1940s; the second had been East Asia in 1950; now we beheld the third drawing of a containment line. In March, Brzezinski referred to the same area as "the third vital strategic zone," which had to be defended against Soviet aggression.[55] The policy led to, among other things, greatly enhanced naval capability in the entire Indian Ocean region; bases in Oman, Kenya, and Somalia; and big arms transfers to the "big enchilada," Saudi Arabia. In July, Brzezinski went so far as to depict border troubles between Cambodia and Thailand and the invasion of Afghanistan as "twin thrusts ultimately directed against Western trade routes in the Indian Ocean," according to Richard Burt's paraphrase.[55] There are others who might object that something else draws American attention to the region: its general turmoil, having little to do with Soviet finagling, and above all its vast oil resources.

Brzezinski is hardly the only one drawing an analogy between the crises of 1950 and 1980. Emma Rothschild has argued that huge defense spending increases spawned by alleged crises suggest a desire "to return to the old economic and technological patterns"; these efforts represent "an instinctive return to the industrial and scientific culture of an obsolete expansion."[57] Paul Nitze, as much as anyone else the architect of the 1950 shift, cites 1950 in a recent *Foreign Affairs* article and goes on to argue that we face possibly the "gravest" threat "at any time since the end of World War II." Therefore:

> Providing for the common defense now requires the kind of priority that it had in 1950, a major adjustment of priorities. . . . We should seek to

end the alienation of the U.S. middle class from the military. . . . [We] should adopt a strategic view of foreign and defense policy . . . [which] takes into account the entire world chessboard and the correlation of forces five and ten years from now.

He argues for the worldwide containment of the Soviet Union, something which our allies, plus China, must join.[58] Nitze is hardly alone; Nixon says many of the same things in *The Real War,* and one hears everywhere that the decade of the 1980s will be fateful for the United States. And in what may be the most despicable commentary produced by any Reaganite (and this is saying something), William Safire argued on February 26, 1981 that El Salvador has become "this hemisphere's South Korea"; like Korea in 1950, this "is a place where we can win." Winning is what?, Safire asks: "Is it supporting a military junta that kills the opposition but by its repressive nature produces more opposition that becomes necessary to kill? If need be, yes—considering the aggressive totalitarian alternative" (presumably he refers to the Catholic Left and the guerrillas in El Salvador).[59]

The record of the 1950 turnaround has, in fact, a quite different analogy with 1980: history is repeating itself (and we hope only farce will follow tragedy). In 1950 Nitze worried over our military strength "becoming dangerously inadequate," and about the mid-1950s when the Soviets would pull ahead if we did nothing; 1954 might be "the year of maximum danger." Critics were silenced within and outside the government, and a handful of critically placed officials pushed the new policy to fruition.[60] Worried congressmen then sound like worried congressmen now. Several of them told Acheson in 1950, "Our foreign policies . . . have been a series of temporary expedients with no long-term, forward-looking design." Acheson responded: "In a very short time we will come into a period of extreme peril. Is it not better therefore for us to plunge all of our energies into hammering on the concept of a unity of our military and economic forces. . . ." At the same meeting, John Foster Dulles called for "a regeneration of spirit" (Nixon's *ch'i*) and "positive action" in the face of the Soviet threat.[61] Acheson and Nitze, with Dulles's help, pushed the new policies through in the wake of the Korean crisis: a civil war, interpreted as a Soviet step toward world domination. George Kennan was the Cyrus Vance of that day, increasingly irrelevant in the formulation of foreign policy; in August 1950 he left the State Department.

Within the United States the crisis in 1950 redrew the boundaries of acceptable foreign policy debate by moving several steps to the Right. As the spectrum shifted, the opening to the Right gave unreconstructed rollbackers an opportunity; on the Left it isolated the "Wallaceites" and critics like I. F. Stone, who found it difficult to get a publisher for his book on the Korean war. The new acceptability stretched from liberal anti-Communists like Hubert Humphrey to bomb-'em-to-the-Stone-Age types like Curtis LeMay. McCarthyism played the major role in redrawing these boundaries.

This consensus held until Vietnam, which shifted the spectrum to the Left once again. Critics who rejected imperial policies became acceptable, and the revisionist view on the origins of the Cold War got a serious hearing on the campuses. A radical critique of American global policy convinced many, but had the more important effect of neutralizing most liberals and excluding the far Right from acceptable discourse. The real hardliners were not the focus of attention; most Vietnam debate was between radicals and liberals, with both of them deeming the far Right beyond the pale.

However convincing at the intellectual level, the antiwar revisionists had only a tiny institutional base and could not sustain the critique to work a real change in American policy. But they made liberals and moderates look over their shoulders to the Left; here was the so-called Vietnam syndrome. The New Boy network at State was made up of such people; they could not wholeheartedly accept the radical critique, but gave it more credence than they did the hardline Right. The result was to confuse them deeply, and subsequently to exhaust their ideas. They could not turn to the Left, because that meant career oblivion. Yet they could not believe the Right.

American liberalism has a tendency to fall away to the Right that is like a physical principle. In the face of alarms about Soviet expansionism, liberals and moderates have been able to mount no effective defense; by 1980 they had been overwhelmed, and many had joined in the rituals of the new Soviet threat.[62] Thus the coming together of 1980, the establishment of virtual consensus on foreign policy by the two major parties, has had the effect of moving the consensual midpoint to the Right, opening the way to a hearing for rightist think tanks like the Hoover Institution and the American Heritage Foundation. The Reagan victory, of course, gave a tremendous boost to this process, but so did the travails of column B at NSC. This, in turn, has established new parameters of acceptable discourse.

Neoconservative political scientists Karl Jackson and Paul Seabury heralded Reagan's electoral victory as "a rare opportunity to create a bipartisan foreign policy coalition." Arguing that "foreign policy has been in a crisis since 1968," through twelve years in which foreign policy elites "have devoured each other's ideas rather than sought a solid consensus," they called for a new, bipartisan national coalition and a new consensus. Who will be included? "Non-McGovernite Democrats," and everyone to the Right.[63] Numerous articles in *Commentary* magazine have argued for the same axis of inclusion: writing of the New Boy network, for example, Carl Gershman argues that "it no longer deserves to be listened to by anyone." Walter Lacqueur, in an article that could be a brief of Nixon's *Real War,* argues that the United States in the 1980s will have to fight a battle on two fronts, and "the domestic struggle may well be the most protracted," because spokesmen for the "discredited orthodoxy" still hold positions in government, the media, and the academic world. Such people still refuse to admit that they were "grievously wrong."[64] Liberal Anthony Lewis, who had called several times for Brzezinski's resignation, referred to Senator Edward Kennedy's list of names for a select commission on foreign policy as covering "the ideological spectrum," defined as stretching from George Ball and Stanley Hoffman on the Left to Richard Pipes and Elmo Zumwalt on the Right. This list "spans the ideological conflict."[65] Actually, the list excludes all the prominent antiwar critics on the Left, most of whom view Hoffman and Ball as power-oriented, and therefore tepidly critical, liberals.

Brzezinski, an architect of the new consensus, could not resist a parting shot to his enemies. In late November he told Richard Burt that "the Democratic Party damages itself when it moves excessively to the left"; he had been systematically opposed by those Democrats who thought he wished "to revive the Cold War."[66] The leader of column B who functioned as a Trojan horse for the right-wing line throughout the administration now presumes to chastise column A for losing the election. And what about that other key Trilateralist, David Rockefeller? His judgment of wind direction was a bit finer than Zbig's; in a little-noted speech in April 1980 in Los Angeles—that is, within earshot of Ronald Reagan—he criticized a foreign policy based on "fuzzily defined moral issues—such as human rights"; he went on: "Of late, I fear, our country has been too didactic with its friends and too weak and vacillating with its enemies"; there had been "zigzag, switch and somersault."[67] In September he materialized in Seoul to meet with the new general who had shot his way into the presidency over at least a thousand dead Korean bodies; a picture featured in most Korean newspapers showed David shaking hands with the general, who in turn looked somewhat dowdy in his new banker's pin-striped suit.[68] By mid-November David was touring Latin America, telling Argentine and Brazilian and Chilean and Paraguayan generals that Reagan's policies will lessen or remove human rights restrictions and be based on such "national interests" as trade and natural resources.[69] Ronald Reagan was so charmed by all this that he welcomed David Rockefeller into his circle of advisors . . . or was it David who welcomed him?

THE REAGAN CROWD AND THE STRUGGLE BETWEEN MODERATES AND RADICALS

The new consensus and the exclusion of the "McGovernites" has called a temporary end to Chinese-style "line struggle" in American foreign policy. In a two-line struggle, Mao said, contradictions were antagonistic. But in conflicts within one line, dispute still existed, but contradictions were nonantagonistic. This is the case with the new administration, but that should not make us think the conflicts are less real. Ever since the election, our Washingtonology reveals a struggle for the heart and mind of the new president. We can call the two sides moderates and radicals: after all, that is the designation in august places like *The New York Times* editorial page.

The radicals and the moderates can be precisely distinguished by their position on the Trilateral Commission, a symbol of the internationalism of the Eastern Establishment. Rockefeller's Los Angeles speech referred to a "drumbeat of inanities" about the TC, coming increasingly from "activists of a conservative but not extremist stripe who ought to know better."[70] In the spring of 1980 Reagan's Florida campaign manager had been highly critical of the TC, and George Bush had to resign his membership in it and the Council on Foreign Relations because of rightist criticism. In Washington State, prominent political scientists were invited to testify in the capitol by state legislators who kept getting calls from conservatives asking if the TC was a conspiracy. As the Reagan campaign widened the boundaries of acceptable discourse rightward, it discovered the widespread idea in right-wing circles that the TC was part of the same internationalist, one-world, pro-Communist banker's conspiracy stretching back through the Council on Foreign Relations to Roosevelt's Yalta sellout and the New Deal. The task of the moderates, therefore, was to ensure that the rightward shift did not go so far as to exclude them as well.

Candidate Reagan did not do much to quiet the fears of the moderates. During the campaign, he trotted out much of his famed "red meat language," designed—or so the moderates will tell us—to sate the appetites of his old right-wing constituency. In his VFW speech in August, Reagan referred to the Vietnam war as "a noble cause," to the Soviet buildup as the greatest "in the history of mankind," and remarked that "We're already in an arms race—but only the Soviets are racing." Two days later, in a Boston address to the American Legion, he referred to the Democrats as "dominated . . . by the McGovernite wing," described the United States as "second to one," and said the American people were sick and tired of leadership that tells us "why we can't compete with the Japanese and Germans, and . . . why we can't contain the Russians."[71] Earlier, in another Chicago speech, Reagan had referred to the ongoing battle with "Godless communism," and urged a "housecleaning" of the State Department and a new "grand strategy" for the 1980s. At other times, he called for funneling weapons to the rebels and blockading Cuba in response to the Afghanistan invasion; referred to the Shah of Iran as "as good an ally as we've ever had"; called for assistance to free peoples in Central America and deplored the Sandinista takeover in Nicaragua; and argued for military *superiority* over the Soviet Union.[72] Some of his red-meat language angered our red friends in China, especially when he called for upgrading relations with Taiwan.

As the campaign progressed, some of the red meat was pulled back. In a tortuous statement on China and Taiwan (August 25), he sought to mollify Deng Xiao-ping. On October 19 he delivered a general pull-in-the-horns speech, talking about making the secretary of state the main foreign policy advisor, committing himself to "rapid growth" in the China relationship, and developing not superiority but "a margin of safety" in dealing with the Soviets. At the same time, Republican moderate stalwarts like Henry Kissinger, former Ambassador Anne Armstrong, former Secretary of State William Rogers, and Senator Howard Baker traveled with the candidate and then went off to give speeches assuring various audiences of the candidate's new-found moderation.

The election brought an immediate impact. The South Korean generals jumped for joy and got ready to execute Korean democrat Kim Dae Jung. Rightists went on the offensive in Central America, leading an American diplomat to state that "a lot of barbarism is being carried out in Reagan's name of which he could never approve."[73] At home, moderate and radical forces launched major efforts to influence the candidate's foreign policies and his cabinet selections.

In order to understand the postelection conflicts, it is necessary to understand the forces competing for Reagan's attention. In Chinese terminology, we find several forces: (1) principled right-wingers, (2) right-wing opportunists, (3) "fake-Left real-Right" types, (4) capitalist-roaders (national), (5) capitalist-roaders (international). In American terms, we find that group 1 is drawn mostly from two sources, the Hoover Institution and the Heritage Foundation; groups 2 and 3 include the multitudinous neoconservatives; group 4 consists of Reagan's friends in his so-called kitchen cabinet; groups 2 and 5 include David Rockefeller, most of the Republican moderates, the American Enterprise Institute (AEI) crowd, and Henry Kissinger.

Through much of the internecine Republican battling of the late 1970s, gearing up for the campaign, two think tanks fought for the allegiance of candidates. The AEI in Washington, D.C., seeking to be a moderate Right Brookings Institution, backed moderates like George Bush. It sought to distinguish itself from the far Right Hoover Institution in Stanford, California. But Reagan's candidacy shifted ballast toward Hoover, from which Reagan has drawn many advisors. The president, Glenn Campbell, was a Reagan appointee on the California Board of Regents and is chairman of a task force on domestic policy. Milton Friedman, Richard Staar, and Peter Duignan were among the Hooverites advising on foreign policy. Hoover's board of overseers includes executives from General Electric, historically close to Reagan; also William Simon, former secretary of Treasury; and John Swearingen, chairman of Standard Oil of Indiana. Duignan exemplifies the strong views of the Hooverites: He once referred to Soviet Ambassador to Washington Anatoly Dobrynin as "an absolute swine," and to Henry Kissinger as having "given up the struggle . . . he was like Chamberlain. He just wanted to survive in our time." Of the Vietnam war, Duignan says: "The great tragedy was that we didn't stay. We lost our nerve and didn't stick to the domino theory." He favors stationing a "quick reaction strike force of 35,000 to 40,000 men in the Sinai," noting that "there are no radical students, lefties, or peaceniks there to bother us." As for communism, Duignan thinks "there is no justification for any communist regime in the world." Reagan has attended informal seminars at Hoover for years and was made an "honorary fellow," the only other two being Alexander Solzhenitsyn and Friedrich Hayek.[74]

The Heritage Foundation presented a victorious Reagan with a 20-volume, 3,000-page blueprint covering the gamut of foreign and domestic policies. Among other things, it argued for "raising defense spending by $35 billion, unleashing the CIA, using food as a foreign policy weapon, [and] restoring congressional internal security committees" (that is, like the House Un-American Activities Committee).[75] The Heritage Foundation was founded in 1974 by Richard Weyrich, a hard-line rightist hit man working with political action committees; $200,000 in seed money came from beer mogul and union-buster Joseph Coors. Trustees of the foundation now include industrialist J. Robert Fluor and the ubiquitous William Simon. Other donors include Justin Dart of Dart Industries, the Scaife family of Pittsburgh, Dow Chemical, and Bechtel Corporation. The foundation claims to have an "academic bank" of 1,000 scholars, opposes the appointment of "Nixon-Ford retreads like Henry Kissinger and George Shultz," and favors appointing John Connally and William Simon.[76]

A third major source of Reagan foreign policy advisors is the Committee on the Present Danger (CPD) founded in 1976 and including most of the "team B" analysts of the Soviet threat for the CIA. The CPD includes an assortment of hardliners and former officials: Richard Pipes, William Van Cleave, William Casey, Richard Allen, John Connally, Eugene Rostow, General Daniel Graham, Fred Ikle, Dean Rusk, David Packard, James Schlesinger, and Paul Nitze, as well as Hubert-Humphrey-aligned neoconservatives like Max Kampleman, William Connell, and Lane Kirkland of the AFL-CIO. Pipes, Van Cleave, and Graham were core "team B" members; Pipes strongly believes that the Soviets seek nuclear "offensive action" and a "war-winning" nuclear capability; he believes the Soviet Union is driven relentlessly to expand, and distinguished himself in March 1981 by getting quoted (as an NSC officer) saying war with the USSR was inevitable if it did not change its system. All three emerged as close advisors to the new president, with Van Cleave directing the transition at the Pentagon.[77]

Reagan's "kitchen cabinet" consists of old friends of his from southern California who had a major role in the selection of cabinet-level appointees. These include Henry Salvatori, a Los Angeles oil man; Justin Dart of Dart Industries; William Wilson, a land developer; Theodore Cummings, who built the Food Giant chain; Holmes Tuttle, an auto dealer; Jack Wrather, oil and entertainment; Earle Jorgenson of Jorgenson Steel; Alfred Bloomingdale, former board chairman of Diner's Club; and several others. All told, some sixteen millionaires are part of the group. Bloomingdale argues that "running the government is like running General Motors" (not the best analogy, given our auto industry).[78] Most of these fat cats fancy themselves self-made men, however, and unlike GM almost all of them run enterprises that have national rather than transnational interests. Dart is a hawkish nationalist who argued that the United States should have sent the marines to Afghanistan last year; the group as a whole is ultraconservative and can be expected to give a sharp nationalist cast to Reagan's thinking. Leonard Silk refers to them as "right wing populists," hostile to big business.[79] The most hawkish nationalist of the 1980 campaign was John Connally, who argued after Afghanistan: "Let's do something. Let's move. Let's use the forces of this country." His standard campaign speech included strong protectionist talk:

> I'd tell the Japanese . . . that unless they're prepared to open markets for more American products they'd better be prepared to sit on the docks of Yokohama in their Toyotas watching their SONY televisions, because they aren't going to ship any of them here.

He also remarked that Nixon was "a particularly good President in foreign policy."[80] Connally was among the first people Reagan consulted after his election, in a two-hour meeting in Los Angeles on November 15; nothing was said about the substance of their talks.

Were the CPD/team B people, the Hooverites, Connally, and the kitchen cabinet to be prominent in foreign policy, it would suggest a nationalist Reagan foreign policy that would bring sharp increases in defense spending, strong pressures on allies to share defense burdens and to favor declining American industries like steel and autos by cutting imports (fair trade rather than free trade), and an interventionist policy in the third world. There is another set of advisors, however, who represent the internationalists (such as they are) of the 1980s in the Republican party. Although pushed to the Right by the events of the 1970s, they still appear as moderates to *The New York Times* and the Eastern Establishment.

The internationalist "moderates" have one great demand, and then a host of lesser ones: that demand is to bring back Henry Kissinger, and thereby keep the "crazies" and "wild men" (Leonard Silk's terms)[81] from tampering with foreign policy. Henry the K is the bellwether figure in what *Business Week* called "the battle for the heart and mind of Ronald Reagan."[82] To the radicals, however, Kissinger symbolizes not just détente but the Rockefeller influence in Republican circles. The Right remembers the "compact of Fifth Avenue" in 1960 when, three weeks before the Republican convention, candidate Nixon met with Nelson Rockefeller and agreed on a document "tilting the Republican platform in a direction compatible with his views."[83] They remember what Roger Morris has called the *coup d'état* at the Hotel Pierre in 1968,[84] when Nixon hired

Kissinger, and then jettisoned Nixon foreign policy task force chief Richard Allen.

In 1980 Kissinger first supported John Connally and George Bush, but then drifted toward the Reagan camp. In May 1980 he had chats with Richard Allen, but journalists noted that Kissinger "seems to represent a particularly sensitive problem for the Reagan camp." In mid-July Kissinger seemed to be "edging his way" into the Reagan circle, but then was forced to withdraw from testifying before the Republican platform committee. *The New York Times* quoted a Reagan aide as saying, "he is part of a past that we don't want to see resurrected." The *Times* said "Conservatives regard Mr. Kissinger as an internationalist, soft on the Soviet Union," and blame him for SALT, détente, and the Panama Canal Treaty.[85] At the Republican convention Kissinger referred to Reagan as "the trustee of our hopes" and launched an assault on the Carter policies —somehow failing to mention his own policies of détente, SALT negotiations, and the opening to China. He called for "containing Soviet expansionism."[86]

During the convention there nearly occurred another *coup d'état* as Kissinger sought to convince Reagan to take Gerald Ford on as vice-president with greatly enhanced powers and responsibilities. Reagan aides called this "a dangerous power play," with Ford being Henry's "ticket back to power." The scheme, they thought, would reduce Reagan to a ceremonial role as Ford took responsibility for the National Security Council "and, of course, with Mr. Kissinger as Secretary of State."[87]

The *coup* in 1968 had been at the expense of Richard Allen, and just before the 1980 election it seemed another *coup* might be in the works. During the summer the muckraking magazine *Mother Jones* had revealed that, among other things, Allen had passed himself off as a Ph.D. when in fact he never got one; had "intimate ties" with fugitive financier Robert Vesco; and had been an agent for Rhodesian chrome, Grumman airplanes, Datsun cars, and Lockheed airplane sales. To the extent that the allegations were true, Allen was linked to scandals from southern Africa to Japan to the Vesco multimillion-dollar scam in Europe and the United States.[88] This article was widely ignored until a week before the election, when *The Wall Street Journal* printed a front-page story giving even more details on the allegations—surely the first time the *Journal* has taken its cues from *Mother Jones.*[89] Allen was forced to take a brief leave of absence, presumably to ease the tension by wiggling his toes in the sandbox he keeps in his office.[90] A close confidant of Carter pollster Patrick Caddell told me that the universal assumption in the White House was that Kissinger was behind the *Journal* article. On October 31 the *Times* reported the "resurgence" of Kissinger within the Reagan camp, describing it as one of Reagan's "most important assets" as the election drew near. Kissinger invited Nancy Reagan to dinner, along with George Shultz; the *Times* reported that Kissinger loved Shultz and that Shultz believed Kissinger to be "the best qualified" for secretary of state in the Reagan administration.[91] Shortly after the election, however, Richard Allen came back as national security advisor-designate.

This failure did not deter the insistent Kissinger, or his supporters. A close friend, Trilateralist David Abshire (the man who brought Kissinger to Georgetown University), became the overall coordinator of the foreign policy transition team. Abshire noted that this effort was "not designed to supplant the functions of Dick Allen." But another aide said, "right-wingers have gone to their battle stations" because they think Abshire is Kissinger's stalking horse.[92] Leonard Silk castigated the rightist "populists" and noted the comforting presence among Reagan advisors of David Rockefeller and Walter Wriston, chairman of Citicorp.[93] Soon, a chorus of liberals trumpeted the virtues of appointing Kissinger. On November 8 James Reston noted that Reagan was sounding like Kissinger, "talking more quietly now" and "selecting his aides carefully." Reston was glad to see George Shultz among the potential cabinet appointees. Three weeks later he wrote a column titled "Why Not Kissinger?" arguing for Henry for secretary of state, referring to Shultz as "a wise and experienced man," and—without even a hint of a smirk—suggesting David Rockefeller for secretary of the treasury.[94] Joseph Harsch chimed in on "the re-education of Reagan," suggesting a Kissinger cabinet appointment—which would reassure our allies—or, failing that, choosing "a person known to have Kissinger approval." He noted in passing that this would mean the second supersession of Richard Allen.[95] Allen might be excused for thinking he had a wolf pack after him.

Failing the return to power of Henry the K, the internationalists were ready to settle for Shultz; he spruced up his moderate credentials by getting named a director of the Council on Foreign Relations in the spring of 1980. John Connally was another possibility. Engineer of the NEP, supporter of the mining of Haiphong and the 1972 Christmas carpet bombing of Hanoi, his rampant nationalism frightened many internationalists then; but now the American political economy required strong medicine (not for the United States, of course, but for second world allies and third world enemies) and moderates have moved far enough Right not to include Big John among the "wild men" and the "crazies."

In the event the appointment of Alexander Haig as secretary of state fit the moderate logic. Here, indeed, is a person "known to have the Kissinger approval." As Mao promoted Wang Hung-wen, the youngest member of the gang of four, Henry promoted Haig through the ranks like a helicopter to four-star general, and then found him useful in arranging wiretaps on Henry's subordinates and, finally, in giving him domestic policy while Henry took the world during the bunker phase of the Nixon presidency in summer 1974. Haig is the perfect exemplar of the technocrat reared in the national security state; his long march was through the bureaucracy, making him arrogant in his newly found power, but insecure and dependent beneath the macho front. When the load fell on his shoulders abruptly with the assassination attempt in March 1981, the combination of power-grubbing and sweaty insecurity was caught all too clearly by the merciless television cameras.

Haig's appointment would seem to assure the dominance of the moderates in foreign policy. Indeed, in the first months of the administration the radicals under Allen at NSC were corralled and cloistered, with the NSC recalled to its original function of coordination and paper-pushing. Radicals like Pipes, Allen, and the distinctly unappealing Jeane Kirkpatrick found their every comment leaked, cropped, and placed in headlines. Haig became "vicar" of our policies, and congressmen and liberal journalists leaped forward to congratulate Reagan on his good sense. James Reston referred to "Reagan's dramatic success" with his "cautious compromise," his Rooseveltian oratory, and his "talking in gentler ways now that he has entered the White House." Those who elected Reagan were now more worried about him than those who had opposed him.[96] Leslie Gelb called on him to be a moderate but not a weak president: maybe the "imperial presidency" wasn't so bad after all. And the *Times* editorialized that the new president had chosen "the role of the moderate in a script of gradualism."[97]

Even were Haig not to survive the firestorm over his peremptory attempts at foreign policy usurpation (beginning with day one of the Reagan presidency), George Bush is now in charge of foreign policy crisis management and can be counted on to keep the ship of state on the "moderate" course. It is as if the office of the vice-president had become what Ford and Kissinger wanted it to be during the Republican convention. Furthermore, nearly all of Haig's appointments to key assistant secretary posts were Nixon/Kissinger stalwarts: Lawrence Eagleburger, John Holdridge, Walter Stoessel, Robert Hormats. (These choices were also lauded by James Reston: "Wally" and "Larry" were especially good picks.)[98] Thus it seems clear that the Republican moderates have won the foreign policy battle, although they may have to throw some bones (e.g., El Salvador) to the radicals hungry for red meat.

What is the character of this moderation? Immoderate in the third world, tempestuous with our Second World allies, it will probably move in the end back to détente. On the critical China issue, the moderates have already won: Gerald Ford journeyed to Beijing and told Deng that Reagan will move forward with the relationship. Unless the Soviets invade Poland, relations with them will move once again toward superpower accommodation. After all, American conflicts of interest *about which something can be done* are much more important vis-à-vis our old allies; West-West conflicts are the order of the day.[99] In other words, we are back to the three-world strategy of Richard Nixon. Why? Because his amoral/immoral realism accorded so well with imperial interests abroad and the vested interests at home of the national security state.

CONCLUSIONS: NIXON IS NEAR

Imagine the condition of men living in a sort of cavernous underground
chamber, with an entrance open to the light and a long passage all down
the cave. Here they have been from childhood, chained by the leg and also
by the neck. . . . At some distance higher up is the light of a fire burning
behind them; and between the prisoners and the fire is a track with a
parapet built along it, like the screen at a puppet show. . . . Now behind
this parapet imagine persons carrying along various artificial objects
. . . some of the persons will be talking, others silent. It is a strange picture,
he said. . . . Like ourselves, I replied.

Plato

Is it China or America that is inscrutable? Where do we find the boxes
within boxes? For Henry Kissinger, popular paragon of the philosopher-
king, Asia is the mystery: Japan is a Kabuki play, Chou En-lai is a genius,
Mao speaks in epigrams that only reveal their meaning upon reflection.[100]
For Richard Nixon, popular exemplar of the leader as crook, China was his
refuge. For campaign 1980, Ronald Reagan was our bull in a China shop,
stumbling back and forth because he kept tripping over "China" while
speaking of China. For Zbigniew Brzezinski, China was the talisman he
picked up in the sands of the Ogaden.

It is our politics that is mysterious, difficult to penetrate, like shadows
on the wall of a cave. A decade that begins with détente and mass resistance to war policies ends with Cold War and a whimper of dissent. Two
men who deliver us from the threat of nuclear holocaust in the first world
pursue criminality at home and in the third world; one crime is punished
and one is not; one is saved and the other lost in 1974, or so it seemed.
A new healer appears, a moral man who will always tell us the truth, yet
cannot stick to the barest of campaign promises and reneges on every
commitment. It is as if someone wants to proffer us our own morality
personified, only to take it and destroy it. Now, in 1981, we have a
president who exemplifies traditional morality; before he took office he
was whipsawed between Right and Left, barely able to form a cabinet. Is
he also offered up as a ritual sacrifice to our illusions?[101]

In foreign policy it is worse. The average American is not provided an
iota of the information necessary to comprehend foreign relations; an
election is held, a new president emerges, and at his side is the hired foreign
policy technocrat: have paradigm, will travel. Most know nothing about
him; few can pronounce his name; hardly anyone knows how he arrived
at his exalted status. The latest version comes with such scandalous bag-
gage that he was almost out before he was in; yet only the cognoscenti can
grasp the issue, and only those with their ear to the ground, paying close
attention to the telltale sounds of power struggle, have a hint of what the
conflict portends. Foreigners materialize in Washington after the election;

one question is on their minds: who has the ear of the victor? Who is up, who down? What does it all mean?

Only Vietnam lifted the veil. People were taken from the cave and thrown into the dazzling light of day; what they saw sent them reeling back into the darkness. Forget it: it's Chinatown. A few years later a film could play, *The Deerhunter,* which reversed the verdict on the war. The hero triumphed over the evil Vietcong, playing a cruel Russian roulette. The audience clapped, the film won an Academy Award. Critics retreated to a private repose.

The new president recalled in his speeches an earlier era, when America was "number one." The inaugural plugged "a new beginning," but the thick mist of nostalgia betrayed the president's intent: we will have the 1950s in the 1980s. The real meaning of Reagan's foreign policy, too, has been obscured: it is Nixonism recrudescent.

Dean Rusk liked to play dominos, Kissinger played chess, and the conflicts between column A and column B meant that Carter played pick-up sticks. Nixon's game is poker. He helped finance his law education, such as it was, through poker winnings. A good poker player, Nixon tells us, likes to keep something in the hole. Nixon's current hole card is really rather stunning: his new book, *The Real War,* might as well be the bible of the Reagan foreign policy. Written before the heat of the 1980 campaign, it etched out the program, and even provided the phrases, for many of the victorious candidate's speeches. Such an assertion will astonish those who, as in the past, have relegated Nixon to the dustbin of history; so will Nixon's outrageous language in the book.

But consider a couple of facts. Writing in *The New York Times Book Review* on November 30, 1980, William Simon recommended that *The Real War* should be "essential reading for a new President in coming to an accurate understanding of the broad spectrum of defense and foreign policy issues that will confront him in office." Turn also to the last page in the book: here Nixon acknowledges the help of William Van Cleave, head of the Reagan transition staff at the Pentagon.[102] If that is not enough, consider the following: central themes in the Reagan campaign rhetoric on foreign policy may be found throughout the Nixon book: the idea that we need a margin of safety, if not superiority, over the Russians (p. 153); that we need "the MX on land, the Trident on the sea, and the B-1 in the air" (p. 169); that Carter "greased the skids" for the Shah and Somoza through his human rights campaign (p. 239); that America is "a sleeping giant," a term Reagan used often (p. 244); that "linkage" is central to our relations with the Soviets, the first foreign policy comment Reagan made after his election (p. 267);[103] that the "Carter doctrine" in the Persian Gulf is "an empty cannon" unless we have credible forces to back it up (p. 94); and any number of specific recommendations from unleashing the CIA to restoring Radio Free Europe to increasing defense spending far over Carter's 5 percent. Nixon's central argument, moreover, was the key to the coming together of elites in the new Cold War consensus: from 1975 on, "the walls of containment have been ruptured" (p. 297); there can be no détente without containment. Nixon even uses the "rollback" language so dear to the 1950s outlook of the Reaganites (and the old Nixon): "A more fundamental step we should take is to knock down the 'no trespassing' signs that surround the Soviet empire" (p. 299). The book, in short, was the bible of the Reagan foreign policy. After the election, a photo in *Time* showed the president-elect sitting at a clean desk, *The Real War* on top.

Now here is something worth reflecting upon. Nixon does not simply presume to chart our course in the 1980s; he even gives us a lecture on leadership. Leadership is the quality that

> in one crisis after another raises the sights of the American people from the mundane to the transcendent, from the immediate to the enduring. If we determine to win . . . then the spirit gives edge to the sword, the sword preserves the spirit, and freedom will prevail. (p. 315)

Richard Nixon is going to lift us from the mundane to the transcendent. The former president, and the new one, seem to have a cyclical theory of history. Like old China, America can wax and wane, recapture the past, and retrieve leaders from history's ashcan. Mao had the better vision: history is dialectical, not cyclical, and re-creating the 1950s past in the 1980s present will spell disaster.

NOTES

1. Nixon's quotes are drawn from the Watergate tapes; Roger Morris quotes Nixon in reference to the "impossible fags," and Kissinger on his "crazy" boss, in *Uncertain Greatness: Henry Kissinger and American Foreign Policy* (New York: Harper & Row, 1977), pp. 156, 123.
2. Franz Schurmann is, to my knowledge, the first to count Nixon the architect and Kissinger the engineer. Unpublished paper presented at the Colloquium on American Foreign Policy, University of Washington, May 1979.
3. Morris, op. cit., p. 203.
4. Henry Kissinger, *White House Years* (Boston: Little, Brown, 1979), pp. 691, 695, 704, 1087, 1144, 1153, 1259. Hereafter, *WHY*.
5. Morris quotes Richard Helms's notes on Chile, after a briefing by Nixon, p. 230.
6. Ibid., pp. 210, 244.
7. Kissinger, *WHY*, p. 955.
8. See Mary Kaldor, *The Disintegrating West* (New York: Hill & Wang, 1978), p. 201; also Charles P. Kindleberger, *The World in Depression 1929–1939* (Berkeley: University of California Press, 1973), chap. 14.
9. Kaldor, op. cit., p. 85.
10. Richard Nixon, *The Real War* (New York: Warner Books, 1980), pp. 27, 82, 89.
11. Ibid., pp. 2–3, 86.

12. Ibid., p. 114.
13. Quoted in Morris, op. cit., p. 241.
14. See my "The Political Economy of Chinese Foreign Policy," *Modern China*, 5, 4 (October 1979), 450–453.
15. A particularly good example of this line of thinking is the testimony by Admiral Stansfield Turner, director of the CIA, in *Allocation of Resources in the Soviet Union and China–1977*, Joint Economic Committee, U.S. Congress (Washington, D.C.: U.S. Government Printing Office, 1977), pp. 1–15.
16. Trilateral Commission, *The Crisis of International Cooperation* (New York, 1973), p. 13; and Trilateral Commission, *The Reform of International Institutions* (New York, 1976), p. 10.
17. Zbigniew Brzezinski, "America in a Hostile World," *Foreign Policy*, 23 (summer 1976), pp. 65–96; another representative view is Tom Farer, "The U.S. and the Third World: A Basis for Accommodation," *Foreign Affairs*, October 1975; on "making the world safe for interdependence" and America as custodian, see Trilateral Commission, *The Reform*, p. 10.
18. Thomas Ferguson and Joel Rogers, "Another Trilateral Election?" *The Nation*, June 28, 1980, p. 785.
19. Laurence H. Shoup, *The Carter Presidency and Beyond* (Palo Alto: Ramparts Press, 1980), p. 43.
20. Ibid., p. 105; see also information on Trilateral appointees inserted in *The Congressional Record* by Senator Barry Goldwater, June 3, 1980, pp. S6202–6208.
21. See Carl Gershman, "The Rise and Fall of the New Foreign-Policy Establishment," *Commentary*, July 1980, pp. 13–16; also John Judis, "The Carter Doctrine," *The Progressive*, March 1980, p. 36.
22. Franz Schurmann, *The Logic of World Power* (New York: Pantheon, 1974), part I.
23. Quoted in Tad Szulc, *The Illusion of Peace* (New York: Viking, 1978), p. 14.
24. Richard Falk, "Brzezinski: Looking Out for Number One," *The Nation*, September 27, 1980, p. 265.
25. Sally Quinn, "The Politics of the Power Grab: Nine Rules of Notoriety," *Washington Post*, December 1979.
26. Thomas Ferguson and Joel Rogers, "The Empire Strikes Back," *The Nation*, November 1, 1980, pp. 436–440.
27. *The New York Times*, July 21, 1980. Hereafter, *NYT*.
28. *NYT*, January 9, 1980.
29. Jack Anderson, *Seattle Post-Intelligencer*, October 15, 1980; R. Burt, *NYT*, January 25 and February 2, 1980.
30. *NYT* editorial, August 21, 1980.
31. According to Richard Burt, National Security Decision Memorandum no. 242, prepared during the Ford administration, called for a counterforce nuclear strategy; on Nixon-Ford planning for counterforce, see also I.F. Stone, *Village Voice*, August 19, 1980.
32. Burt, *NYT*, March 30 and August 13, 1980; Anthony Lewis column, *NYT*, August 20, 1980.
33. Burt, *NYT*, January 25, 1980; obituary of the Shah, *NYT*, July 28, 1980.
34. Michael Klare, "Have RDF Will Travel," *The Nation*, March 8, 1980, p. 266 (emphasis added).
35. Burt, *NYT*, August 23, 1980.
36. Marcus Raskin, "The National Security State (Carter-Style)," *Inquiry*, April 3, 1978, p. 14.
37. *NYT*, July 21, 1980, quoting Marshal Shulman and other State Department

officials; see also Leslie Gelb's essay in *NYT Magazine,* July 20, 1980, p. 39.
38. *NYT,* November 30, 1980.
39. Banning Garrett, *The China Card* (Berkeley: University of California Press, 1981).
40. *NYT,* June 9, 1980.
41. Justin Galen (pseud.), "US' Toughest Message to the USSR," *Armed Forces Journal International,* February 1979, pp. 30–36.
42. See various articles on the Brown visit by Fox Butterfield, *NYT,* January 1980.
43. *NYT,* January 25, 1980.
44. *NYT,* January 30, 1980.
45. *Pacific News Service,* January 18, 1980.
46. *NYT,* December 8, 1980.
47. Burt, *NYT,* April 28, 1980; May 10, 1980.
48. *NYT,* August 10, October 6, November 23, 1980.
49. *NYT* Op-Ed, November 23, 1980.
50. *NYT,* May 13, 1980.
51. Arthur Macy Cox, "The CIA's Tragic Error," *New York Review of Books,* November 6, 1980.
52. Galen, op. cit., p. 32.
53. "Soviet Geopolitical Momentum: Myth or Menace?" *The Defense Monitor,* 9, 1 (1980).
54. Burt, *NYT,* January 25, 1980.
55. *NYT,* March 30, 1980.
56. *NYT,* July 10, 1980.
57. Emma Rothschild, "Boom and Bust," *New York Review of Books,* April 3, 1980.
58. Paul H. Nitze, "Strategy in the Decade of the 1980s," *Foreign Affairs* (fall 1980), pp. 81–101.
59. *NYT,* Op-Ed, February 25, 1981.
60. Fred M. Kaplan, "Our Cold-War Policy circa '50," *NYT Magazine,* May 18, 1980.
61. Papers of Dean Acheson, Memoranda of Conversation, box no. 65 (Harry S. Truman Library). See also the Papers of Matthew J. Connelly, Cabinet Meeting notes, May 5, 1950, quoting Acheson as saying, "Russia in 1954 will become very dangerous and may become very aggressive" (Truman Library).
62. In 1974 Schurmann presciently suggested that a new Soviet threat could heal divisions among the American foreign policy elite (*Logic of World Power,* p. xxvii).
63. *NYT* Op-Ed, November 8, 1980.
64. Gershman, op. cit., p. 24. Walter Lacqueur, "Containment for the '80s," *Commentary,* October 1980, pp. 33–42.
65. Lewis, *NYT* Op-Ed, March 24, 1980.
66. *NYT,* November 30, 1980.
67. David Rockefeller, "In Pursuit of a Consistent Foreign Policy," *Vital Speeches,* June 15, 1980, pp. 517–520.
68. *NYT,* September 22, 1980.
69. *NYT,* November 11, 1980.
70. Rockefeller, op. cit.
71. *NYT,* August 19 and August 21, 1980.
72. *NYT,* January 10, March 22, July 13, September 24, 1980; *NYT Magazine,* November 16, 1980.
73. *NYT,* November 30, 1980.
74. *Christian Science Monitor,* April 2, 1980; *San Francisco Chronicle,* November 7, 1980; R. Milliken, *Pacific News Service,* July 1, 1980.
75. *Seattle Post-Intelligencer,* December 7, 1980.

76. Ibid.; also *Washington Post,* November 19, 1980.
77. *NYT,* April 21, May 25, 1980; Robert Sherrill, "Gene Rostow's Propaganda Club," *The Nation,* August 11–18, 1979; see a complete listing of CPD members in Shoup, op. cit., pp. 299–301.
78. *Washington Post,* November 18, 1980; *San Francisco Chronicle,* November 29, 1980; *NYT,* May 31, 1980.
79. *NYT,* November 7, 1980.
80. *NYT,* January 15, 1980; *NYT Magazine,* November 18, 1980.
81. *NYT,* November 9, 1980.
82. Ferguson and Rogers, "Trilateral Election."
83. Kissinger, *WHY,* p. 6.
84. Morris, op. cit., chap. 2.
85. *NYT,* May 25, July 6, 1980.
86. *NYT,* July 7, July 12, July 16, 1980.
87. *NYT,* July 22, 1980.
88. "Reagan's All-in-One Erlichman, Mitchell and Kissinger," *Mother Jones,* September–October 1980, pp. 42–43.
89. *The Wall Street Journal,* October 28, 1980.
90. *NYT,* October 31, 1980.
91. Ibid.
92. Burt, *NYT,* November 12, 1980.
93. *NYT,* November 9, 1980.
94. *NYT* Op-Ed, November 9, November 30, 1980.
95. *Christian Science Monitor,* November 15, 1980.
96. *NYT* Op-Ed, January 21, 1981
97. Gelb, *NYT Magazine,* January 18, 1981; *NYT* editorial, January 21, 1981.
98. *NYT* Op-Ed, January 18, 1981.
99. On this point see Immanuel Wallerstein, "Friends as Foes," *Foreign Policy,* 40 (fall 1980), 119–131.
100. On Kissinger's genuflecting before the mysterious East, see *WHY,* pp. 699, 710, 1061.
101. See Sheldon Wolin, "Reagan Country," *New York Review of Books,* December 18, 1980.
102. Van Cleave said this of Nixonian foreign policy in *NYT,* October 12, 1980: "One might compare the situation today with 1973, when the United States was a power to be respected and a powerful force for containing the conflict [in Iran] and settling it. Today, the United States is almost irrelevant. The Soviet Union is showing the world that questions of peace and war in the Middle East and probably questions over the flow of oil rest with the Soviet Union rather than the United States."
103. Richard Nixon announced his own commitment to "linkage" at a press conference seven days after assuming office in 1969. Richard Barnet, *The Giants: Russia and America* (New York, Simon & Schuster, 1977), p. 30.

STATE AND MARKET:
ECONOMIC REGULATION
AND THE GREAT
PRODUCTIVITY DEBATE

Alan Stone

I

American political discourse has for long been characterized by the use of words or phrases rich in ambiguity and hyperbole. Prior election campaigns have centered around such phrases as "anti-communism," "states rights," a "fair deal," the "New Freedom," and so on. The phrases sometimes originate during the election campaign, but frequently do not. And campaigns sometimes include not one such word or phrase but several, although campaigners do restrict their number to avoid befuddling or taxing the attention of the electorate. It is a mistake, however, to conclude that they are as devoid of meaning as a Madison Avenue slogan intended to sell a new brand of cosmetics. While such phrases when beamed at the mass public would appear to have precious little content, they more often than not reflect important policy changes which are contemplated or which have subtly taken place. Further, the use of these slogans is deliberately ambiguous so that the particulars of policymaking disputes are resolved by elites and not by the public. Any such phrase, then, may cover up sharp divisions as well as their resolutions among important elites and groups. And while an American election provides a vehicle to help resolve differences among groups or to declare victors among candidates, it is certainly not used to consider issues seriously.

"Deregulation" as well as "overregulation" were certainly slogans in this sense in the 1980 election, just as the theme of consumer protection was important in the 1968, 1972, and 1976 elections. The central question, then, is why the terms "deregulation" and "overregulation," unknown in political discourse until just a few years ago, played a significant role in the 1980 election. President Carter, for example, in signing the Railroad Deregulation Act (the Staggers Rail Act of 1980) on October 14, 1980, during the heart of the campaign, remarked: "We deregulated the airlines, we deregulated the trucking industry, we deregulated financial institutions, we decontrolled oil and natural gas prices and we negotiated lower

I would like to thank Gordon P. MacDougall, Esq., one of the most perceptive observers of the Washington regulatory scene, for his very helpful insights.

trade barriers throughout the world for our exports. . . . We've carried out the most fundamental restructuring of our economy, the relationship between government and the private enterprise system, since Franklin D. Roosevelt's time and the initiation of the New Deal. It will be a major boost for the revitalization of the American economy, a revitalization that I intend will restore America's competitive edge and make possible full employment, and, at the same time, stable prices."[1] The remarks, made by a president often charged with doing very little of substantive impact during his term, were intended for both ceremonial and electoral purposes. In addition, they provide an important clue to the symbolic and practical purposes of deregulation. The remarks help us to understand why deregulation was placed on the electoral agenda in 1980, replacing—indeed reversing—such themes as consumer protection and "strong regulation in the public interest" of years past.

President Carter's harking back to the New Deal period and seeking to link his performance and the needs of the political economy with the New Deal are more than campaign rhetoric. For in both the current period and during the Great Depression, the economy's performance was in considerable trouble. The problems, of course, are quite different in 1980 than they were in 1930. Yet in both periods policymakers, businessmen, and others have recognized that they are not short-term, but chronic—unless something is done. Among the most important undertakings in such situations is a close reexamination of business-government relations and a refashioning of those relationships in such a way as to escape from the morass. During the early New Deal, for example, a number of regulatory statutes were intended to refashion and revitalize the banking and securities industries and, with them, the economy as a whole.[2] Similarly, the terms "deregulation" and "overregulation" and the policies that underlie them must be placed in the context of the chronic problems Carter mentioned: inflation, unemployment, the declining competitiveness of American industry including, of course, automobiles and steel. The critical question is to see how new regulatory policies are intended, together with such other policy instruments as taxation, loan guarantees, and outright subsidies, to contribute to what Carter called "the revitalization of the American economy." And in this inquiry it is important to remember that a word like "deregulation" can embrace a number of different, sometimes conflicting, sometimes overlapping, and sometimes complementary policy prescriptions, the battle over which will be fought out not before the electorate, but more quietly among important elites and groups. The electorate is, however, prepared for changes by slogans.

One must therefore be attentive to the fact that President Reagan's use of the code words might be different from President Carter's, and that their policy prescriptions in the area of regulation might (and did) differ considerably. Certainly, the people from whom Reagan derived his regulatory policy proposals differ considerably from the combination of Naderite reformers, academic economists, politicians, and businessmen who constituted the Carter group. For as *The New York Times* reported on November 17, 1980, many of Reagan's programs, including those dealing with regulation, were fashioned by a number of big business and conservative foundation-supported nonprofit institutions, including the Hoover Institution, the Institute for Contemporary Studies (ICS), the Heritage Foundation, and the American Enterprise Institute for Public Policy Research (AEI).[3]

These institutions, especially AEI, have for many years commissioned a large number of sympathetic university academics and resident fellows to prepare papers on a wide variety of regulatory (and other) topics, including environmental controls, transportation, antitrust, health, and safety. In addition, a number of educational institutions, such as UCLA and the University of Chicago, contain heavy concentrations of like-minded scholars. Not surprisingly, then, the various transition task forces President Reagan appointed were heavily laced with academics associated with these conservative think tanks and universities. It should also be noted that the transition groups included businessmen, former Ford administration officials, politicians, and state administrators. The Transportation Task Force, for example, included the co-director of AEI, a Ford administration deputy assistant secretary of transportation and senior vice-president of the holding company that controls the Chessie railroad system, a former Nebraska governor, and the commissioner of the Texas Department of Highways and Public Transit.[4]

This diversity of background provides an important clue to the need for the relative degree of ambiguity with which terms like deregulation must be—and were—used during the campaign. For a major task of each party candidate was to hold together and submerge a number of diverse and potentially conflicting ideological views and economic interests. In some respects an American political campaign resembles a war of national liberation in the Third World. As Algeria demonstrated, a set of vague slogans—in that case directed against French imperialism—aided immeasurably in holding a coalition together during the rebellion phase. But the coalition fell apart almost as soon as Algeria obtained its independence. In our system, once the task of policymaking begins, significant differences begin to surface. But instead of jailing losers, the American political dynamic consists of trying to achieve compromises and tradeoffs that will not drive significant interests from the coalition, and pretending that the end result pleases everyone.

Even during the campaign President Reagan promised to take another look at trucking deregulation, a favorite of the AEI intellectuals, but bitterly opposed by the Teamsters who endorsed him. Similarly, Reagan backtracked on the question of the Chrysler subsidy, which is also anathema to the conservative academics, but which clearly establishes an important principle for many businessmen struggling against the superior competitiveness of Asian and European firms. Ideologues may place principle first, but businessmen will always consider the probable effects on their firms of policies far more important than consistent principle or an ideology that free markets will more readily lead to economic efficiency. For this reason, businessmen will not infrequently favor government regulation while preaching the gospel of free enterprise.[5] The petroleum industry vigorously supported the Texas Railroad Commission's restrictions on the amount of oil that may be taken from the ground when that suited it, but it now favors decontrol of crude oil prices, since that currently suits it. For businessmen, profits, not the way in which principles fit into a theoretical system, are what count.

President Carter, too, faced the same problems that confront President Reagan. Let us turn again to the Staggers Rail Act of 1980. He stated: "The importance of this act is clearly reflected in the outstanding and diverse group of people who are assembled here today for this ceremony—representatives from railroad management, from labor, from such shippers as automobiles and steel and coal, retail stores, farm organizations, and also from environmental organizations. . . . This was a really good example of how the legislative process is supposed to work, attempting to harmonize all the divergent interests. . . ."[6] But one of the major problems of the Carter administration was that such "harmonization" was not very common. Too often it was difficult, if not impossible, to see even the general outlines of policy direction. Important components of the Carter constituency were almost continuously at war, and the president was more often than not unable to resolve the differences. Thus, *Fortune* reported that the Naderites, who occupied many important second-level posts in the Carter administration, were frequently at odds with the more conventional representatives of business and labor interests. Transportation Secretary Brock Adams and National Highway Traffic Safety Administrator Joan Claybrook (a former Naderite), for example, bitterly disputed air-bag recommendations because he felt that her proposals were way out of line with the automobile industry's technological and production capabilities.[7]

Only after President Carter decisively trounced Senator Ted Kennedy in the Democratic primary campaign did he begin to exercise some degree of leadership, to accommodate divergent interests within the framework of reasonably formed goals. Only after the demonstration of the glaring weakness of Kennedy's constituencies, including the Naderites and public interest groups, did Carter decide that too many concessions to obtain their support would hurt his election chances more than help them. Only then did he decide he would have to place regulatory questions within the framework of broad policy goals and not continue to stand above the fray and issue platitudes that would please no one. Only then did he move to review and then loosen the regulations that the steel and automobile industries were complaining hindered their competitiveness. Only then did he move firmly to the right instead of having his feet firmly planted in midair. But by then it was too late to overcome the widespread belief that he had no clear conception of the connections between regulatory and other micro policy areas on the one hand, and our major economic problems on the other. Clearly he had some inkling of these relationships, but he approached them in fits and starts. Clearly he had some triumphs in the regulatory area, but they were not comprehensive enough, nor sufficient to overcome the nagging feeling expressed by Robert O. Hatfield, chairman of the Continental Group, in October: "I really don't know where Mr. Carter stands. . . . The burdens on industry have increased enormously under President Carter. There is no question that Mr. Reagan is for lifting many regulatory burdens."[8]

One can almost see the shift in business support as the disparity between Carter's conflicting record and Reagan's apparent—or at least articulated—grasp of the connections between the regulation question and the larger economic issues grew during the campaign. During August, before Reagan's standing within the business community began to rise, the *Journal of Commerce* reported that some of the major steel companies had contributed about evenly—but unenthusiastically—to the Democratic and Republican contenders. The relative evenhandedness was due in part to Carter's firm stand against the liberal wing of his party's effort to introduce a $12 billion jobs program, coupled with skepticism that Reagan's proposed tax cut and higher defense spending were compatible with a less inflationary budget. Additionally, *The New York Times* reported in August that many businessmen felt that President Carter—notwithstanding his mistakes—had learned something about governance and policy in his first term. Still, August can be characterized as a month in which few spokespeople for business expressed much enthusiasm for either candidate—or for Congressman Anderson.[9]

By October, things had changed significantly. Business support for Carter had dropped. Even though business political action committees were contributing more to Democratic than to Republican Senate and House candidates, according to the October 13 *Wall Street Journal,* a marked shift to Reagan was discernible. The critical perception that caused the increase in support for Reagan the candidate, if not for Reagan the man, was his continuing association with and reliance on advisors associated with positions in which businessmen placed considerable confidence. The chairman and chief executive of Caterpillar, Inc., captured this view, stating: "It is not all that clear that Reagan would do that much better. But I have a lot of confidence and enthusiasm for people like George Shultz, Alan Greenspan and Charls E. Walker," who held positions as Reagan economic advisors. A *Wall Street Journal*/Gallup survey reported on October 30 that an overwhelming majority of company chief executives believed Reagan would do the best job of handling the economy, and that the percentage of companies who so believed had been continuously increasing.[10] Immediately after the election, executives of industries as diverse as savings and loan associations and energy could barely contain their glee at the results.[11] The key, then, to big business acceptance and then enthusiasm for Reagan stemmed not so much from a perception of the candidate's qualities, but from a perception of the qualities of the persons who would be making economic policy, including regulatory policy, in the new regime. Indeed, Reagan's limited knowledge about national economic policy was almost viewed as a blessing in disguise, since he would have to rely more on advisors and experts than a better-informed president. Mr. Carter, in contrast, was perceived to have failed in economic policymaking and, notwithstanding his recent moves to the right, to be unreliable. Naderites, trade unionists, and others comprising part of the Democratic coalition might move him to support additional "burdensome" regulation or to adopt a neutral stance on particular issues.

Reagan and Carter, then, shared many of the same regulatory goals we will examine. But the composition of Carter's constituencies, in contrast to Reagan's, made him less of a safe bet to much of the business community, especially in view of his first-term performance. Before looking at the underlying meanings of "deregulation" and "overregulation" in the 1980 election campaign, we will first have to look more closely at the idea of regulation.

I I

"Regulation" is a relatively easy word to define, but "deregulation" and "overregulation" are more difficult. A *regulation* may be defined simply as a limitation on the discretion of persons or firms that is supported by sanction. Prior to the passage of the law requiring the installation of safety belts in new cars, automobile manufacturers could exercise discretion by installing these devices, not doing so, or offering purchasers an option. After the enactment of the law, automobile manufacturers had to install such devices or face the threat of sanction—in that case, a fine. The definition, of course, does not necessarily imply that any particular sanction is effective in deterring undesirable conduct. For example, if the sanction is simply adverse publicity, a firm might be willing to violate the law because in its judgment the net benefit from violation outweighs the net benefit from compliance.

Regulation may be imposed for a variety of reasons. Restrictions on reading sex-oriented literature or on having sexual relations with water fowl are premised on moral grounds. Regulation may also be premised on grounds of preserving public order. Much of the criminal law, including the rules pertaining to such acts as robbery and murder, are premised upon that ground. Regulation may be imposed in order to carry out other functions. Examples of such procedural regulation include requirements that we file full and accurate income tax returns or that fur dealers maintain their business records in certain ways. In these cases, regulations are imposed not for some immediate substantive purpose, but to serve other substantive ends.

It is the final two categories, social and economic regulation, that most of us consider when we use the word, and that have generated most of the recent debate over the topic. The former concerns consumer health and safety as well as the quality of products and services offered for sale. Food and Drug Administration regulation of food and drug safety and efficacy, Environmental Protection Administration regulation of air and water pollution, and state laws prohibiting unlicensed persons from practicing medicine are examples of social regulation. Economic regulation pertains to price and entry controls as well as aspects of resource use on such traditional economic grounds as cost, price, and industrial structure. For example, the ICC may forbid a motor carrier to transport goods between two points. But its primary purpose will be to protect the profit position of carriers already serving those markets. In contrast, the EPA may forbid transport in an area. It will do so not on economic grounds, but to reduce the quantity of emissions inhaled by the public, an object related to health. While this distinction between social and economic regulation has a superficial appeal, we will see later that it is rejected by many in the Reagan camp and embraced as revealed truth by many in the Carter camp, particularly Naderites and public interest groups. But the distinction gives rise to more than an academic dispute and has important policy implications that may provide a sharp contrast between the two administrations. Social regulation has its counterpart in overregulation, as we will see later.

While the overregulation charge is largely confined to the areas of environmental, safety, health, and consumer affairs, deregulation is usually confined to economic problems, especially in connection with transportation, communications, and infrastructural services such as banking. Given the apparent success of airline deregulation and the widespread popular support the program enjoys, there is a clear political advantage in having a new program described in these terms.[12] Deregulation may not yet be elevated to the status of motherhood, but it now carries so many positive connotations that the three major candidates and several minor ones embraced it. Unfortunately, deregulation's ideological value far exceeds its analytical value, for the term may have three distinctly different meanings. First, it may mean complete restoration of market mechanisms and a withdrawal of government intervention. The airline industry is expected to become deregulated in that sense in the near future with respect to rates, routes, and entry, but not safety considerations. Thus, even the airline industry will not achieve the status of having all its activities determined by market mechanisms. And yet it is the industry that will move most dramatically in this direction as CAB domestic route authority expires at the end of 1981, fare authority at the end of 1983, and the agency itself on January 1, 1985. It is important to appreciate that even in the airline industry, deregulation does *not,* as a practical matter, mean the end of all government intervention and complete reliance on the market.

Airline deregulation provides a good example of deregulation's second meaning—a reduction in the extent of regulation. Translated into the language that began this section, this means that the number of activities over which firms and persons in the subject industries may exercise discretion, without fear of government-imposed sanction, increases. But in other instances it becomes difficult, if not impossible, to distinguish this second meaning of deregulation from the third one, which is merely changing the regulatory rules. The Staggers Rail Act of 1980 provides a good example, and leads to the question underlying deregulation. Why have the rules been changed in some cases, but not in others? Under the Staggers Act, railroads can avoid ICC review of a rate increase as long as the new rate is less than 160 percent of out-of-pocket (or variable) costs, a figure that will rise to approximately 175 percent in 1984. Another clause protects an existing rate if it is not successfully challenged before the ICC by shippers within six months of the act's signing. Thus railroads, unlike bubble gum prices, are still subject to a limitation on discretion in the future if they exceed the designated percentages. Similarly, the challenges that occur within six months of the law's enactment—and there will be many—can determine the range of rate discretion for the foreseeable future.

But the real kicker concerns the change in antitrust coverage that will begin in 1984. Under the old law, railroads were largely exempt from the antitrust laws enforced by the Justice Department's Antitrust Division, although the ICC had to consider antitrust impact among other factors in rendering its decisions. Under the new law, railroads are far more closely covered by the labyrinth of antitrust laws and the enormous volume of judicially imposed restrictions that have been decided under them. In this instance, it is difficult, if not impossible, to decide whether deregulation is more aptly characterized as a decline in the level of regulation or simply a change in the basic rules. Similarly, under the 1980 banking deregulation statute, it is true that Regulation Q, which sets deposit interest rate ceilings, will be phased out within six years. But it is equally true that the Federal Reserve Board was granted the right to impose reserve requirements on a large number of depository institutions over which it previously did not have jurisdiction. The Regulation Q phaseout is a clear move toward free market conditions; but the new authority over banks not previously covered is a layer of regulation in addition to that imposed by state banking authorities or a substitution for state authority. Other provisions in the statute simply changed the regulatory rules. For example, one limited mutual savings banks' commercial lending authority to 5 percent of an institution's assets, but restricted this power to the mutual's home state or to within 75 miles of its principal office.

It is a myth, then, to conceive of deregulation as a synonym for the free market, although most of the new and proposed deregulation statutes do enlarge the markets in which regulated firms may compete. But many restrictions remain. The complexity and detail of the new deregulation statutes and the older statutes that are subject to pressure for change compel us to look beyond simplistic explanations. The code words "deregulation" and "overregulation" (which we will look at later) require separate explanation. In addition, each instance of deregulation—natural gas, airlines, trucking, railroads, banking, communications—requires a separate explanation of the contending forces and compromises that led to the deregulation statute. Neither the process nor the impetus for deregulation is reflected in sharp party divisions, nor even along ideological lines. The impetus began during the Ford administration, continued during Carter's, and will probably go on during Reagan's. This does not imply, of course, that the specific deregulation statutes would be identical under all three; they probably would not be, since the enactment of each statute involved delicate compromises among contending economic interests and presidential support derived from different configurations. Nevertheless, it is instructive to note that airline deregulation drew its most fervent support from an odd coalition of consumer organizations and free market advocates. Both Ralph Nader and AEI economists strongly favored a bill uniting Senator Kennedy and future Reagan advisors.

Although deregulation embraces a collection of individually highly complex and different political and legislative histories, it is safe to assert the generalization that changing economic conditions and opportunities, particularly high and accelerating rates of inflation, triggered the impetus toward deregulation. The movement may almost be seen as the converse of the early New Deal, when policies were designed to raise prices under such statutes as the National Industrial Recovery Act. Then, artificial price enhancement was perceived by policymakers as one of the cures for depression. The NRA, fair trade laws, the Robinson-Patman Anti-Price Discrimination Act, agricultural price supports, and a host of other laws that substituted cartelization for competition may be seen as part of a consistent overall set of micro policies that would have the macro effect of enhancing prices in the economy as a whole—or at least preventing their further decline. Today, one of the most important macroeconomic problems is how to prevent rapid price increases. The cost of infrastructural services, particularly transportation, communications, credit, and energy, are reflected in the prices paid by consumers and every industrial and service sector of the economy. But inflation is not the only large-scale problem affecting recent American economic performance. In the next section, we will look in more detail at these other macro problems; but for the moment, it suffices to list supply problems, especially in energy, and the general deterioration in economic performance in certain industries, including rail and air transportation. Finally, another layer must be added —changed conditions in many regulated industries leading to pressures from those affected, including the regulated, for changes in the rules. These might include new technologies, as in the case of communications, or new profit-making opportunities, as in the case of financial institutions. This labyrinth of considerations, configured differently in each regulated industry, has led to a wide variety of new policy proposals lumped together under the label of deregulation, a label calculated to entice a large degree of public sympathy.

The most important deregulatory move during the Carter administration illustrates the complex mix of motives and forces that produce the final shape of such a statute. In order to understand the Financial Institutions Deregulation and Monetary Control Act of 1980 (hereafter the Banking Deregulation Act), the most recent of the important banking regulation statutes, one must take a long historical perspective. Specifically, why should the 1980 statute have moved in the direction of freer competition, while such earlier major statutes as the 1914 Federal Reserve Act and the 1933 Emergency Banking Act moved in the direction of more restriction? Why should bankers have accepted each of these statutes? Like the members of virtually every other business field, bankers have a contradictory stance toward regulation. As I have argued elsewhere, enterprises want to use competition to increase sales and profits at the expense of their rivals, but on the other hand they want to prevent inroads on their profit and sales positions by their rivals and thus assure stability. Regulation that forbids or reduces some areas of competition, such as interest rate or entry regulation, obviously serves the latter prong of this contradiction, while numerous activities—from advertising to giving away merchandise to customers who open a savings account—serve the former prong.[13]

Sometimes, of course, one bank opts strongly for regulation while another vigorously campaigns for freer competition, and at other times the positions are reversed. But unless one understands that banks and credit-providing institutions generally are like chameleons, changing colors as it suits their perceived interests, and sometimes expressing both motifs at once, an important aspect of the politics and public policy in this area is not understood. Of course, once a regulatory apparatus has been put in place, firms within the credit-extending field seek to use it to their best advantage against their rivals. Thus, based upon particular interests, a bank may at one time favor some form of regulation imposed on its rivals from which it is exempt, but at another time adopt the contradictory principle.

Not only must we take into account the justifications for banking regulation and the contradictory stance that credit extenders adopt toward such regulation if we are to understand the politics and policies of banking, but we must consider other factors as well. Among the most important of these are the sharp divisions within the credit-extending field. Of course, manufacturers of glass and aluminum containers engage in both intra-industry and interindustry competition. Cross elasticity of demand is high in many economic endeavors, but in competition for deposits and loans it is a peculiarly acute problem. Bankers must be concerned not only with rivalry among themselves for deposits and consumer choice between investment and consumption generally, but because of the peculiarly fluid and transportable qualities of investable funds, they must be keenly alert to every other possible use of such funds. Thus, on the liability side of their business, commercial banks must take into account in their decision-making such diverse competing instruments as commercial stocks, bonds, foreign currencies, mutual funds, and government securities. They must therefore make their moves in full contemplation of such diverse institutions as distant banks, stockbrokers, investment bankers, savings and loan associations, mutual savings banks, currency dealers, and so on. On the asset side of their business, commercial banks must consider the activities, for example, of finance companies and credit unions in consumer loans and the possibility of internal financing in the case of business loans.

The responses of commercial banks and public policy to the acute cross-elasticity problem inherent in banking provides another important overriding theme to understanding the politics and policies of banking. On the one hand, institutions seek to use public policy legally to restrict the permissible moves of their rivals. But on the other hand, institutions seek to move into the activities of their rivals—especially when opportunities for attracting deposits and making loans are great. For example, in a Texas suit with national implications, the Texas Bankers Association, representing about 1,300 commercial banks, sought to enjoin credit unions from issuing instruments called "share drafts," which are virtually identical to checks conventionally issued by commercial banks.[14] Historically, the persistent battle over the ability of banks to branch within states and across state lines that is now controlled by the 1927 McFadden Act and its amendments is little more than a reflection of the rivalries between small and large banks and between money market and local banks.[15] But while banks are constrained by the branching rules, they have also sought to circumvent them through the bank holding company device, credit cards, distant electronic funds transfer terminals, and other means. In a word, then, banking's peculiarly acute cross-elasticity problem has led to restrictive regulations, attempts to weaken or terminate such restrictions, and the development of instruments to circumvent such restrictions within a given regulatory environment. It is not rare for the same institution to adopt any of these stances, either sequentially or simultaneously, with respect to different regulatory issues.

From these observations, another important point is implied. While there are issues that unite all credit-extending institutions, it is a serious mistake to conceive of them as a permanent or stable coalition. They tend to divide on particular issues. Nevertheless, there are somewhat stable coalitions in the form of national trade associations that represent different credit-extending groups—although it is not unusual for bitter divisions to materialize within each association. Thus, commercial bankers are represented by the American Bankers Association and the smaller Independent Bankers Association, mutual savings banks by the National Association of Mutual Savings Banks, and savings and loan associations by the U.S. League of Savings Associations and the National Savings and Loan League. To some extent affiliation is determined by choice, but to a larger extent it is determined by the specific purposes for which an institution has been chartered; one should always remember that one cannot simply enter banking or many near-banking activities. Rather, one must obtain a charter that presumably limits purposes, investment opportunities, and the services that may be offered. In order to examine the nature of banking politics and policy, it is necessary to sketch the major differences among institutional types and how these differences lead to different general policy preferences.

Commercial banks are the most important type of financial institution, but are sharply divided, first, between large and small banks. Branching powers and permissible activities are among the most important issues over which they divide. In addition, money center banks often have different interests from those of other large banks. But in a general sense, although commercial banks have been interested in consumer banking, they have traditionally been associated with the financial needs of the commercial and industrial sectors. In contrast, savings and loan associations (S & Ls) and mutual savings banks (mutuals) were, prior to the 1980 statute, largely limited in their loan activities to the home mortgage business and were forbidden to offer checking accounts and other services available at commercial banks. To compensate for these disadvantages, S & Ls and mutuals were permitted to offer higher rates of interest on time deposits than commercial banks. Credit unions, still another type of regulated institution, were largely limited to consumer loans, but were also forbidden to offer checking accounts. A labyrinth of regulatory agencies at the federal and state levels supervise these institutions.

Still other types of institutions compete with these, but escape the labyrinth of banking regulation, although they may be within the jurisdiction of other agencies. Insurance companies and finance companies, for example, make consumer loans. Industrial and commercial corporations often bypass banks for short-term funds by selling commercial paper directly or obtaining long-term funds through the sale of bonds. Two institutional types have made major inroads on the traditional financial intermediaries in recent years: money market mutual funds, in attracting investment funds away from banks, and S & Ls and mutuals and finance companies, such as General Electric Credit Company, in making both consumer and business loans. Generally, then, a large number of business interests have the potential to compete with one another. In recent years that potential, we will see, has been realized as ways have been found for institutional types to invade new markets and leap over the regulatory walls that were so carefully constructed during the New Deal. The cast of players includes not only the different types of credit institutions, but other interests as well. For example, while S & Ls have sought to diversify their loans away from the volatile residential housing industry into other areas, home builders, contractors, and the construction unions prefer that the funds of S & Ls should be solely committed to them rather than having to bid competitively for funds.

Why, then, did the regulatory arrangements so carefully constructed during the New Deal fall apart, leading to the Banking Deregulation Act? Two factors stand out above all others in answering these questions: high inflation rates and strong credit demand. The increased opportunities for both loans and investments inexorably increased incentives to attract funds. When the ability of conventional liabilities such as time and savings deposits and demand deposits were insufficient to attract the funds required for loan and investment opportunities, new means were found. This led banks and their competitors, faced with some of the same problems, to invade one another's presumably walled-off areas as sources of funds. Because of regulatory restraints, banks and other institutions had to conceal these invasions and adopt techniques that circumvented restrictions. Thus, the adoption of negotiable order of withdrawal (NOW) accounts and payment orders by mutuals and S & Ls and share accounts by credit unions—from the consumer's perspective interchangeable with checking accounts—intensified competition between rival institutions and institutional types. At the same time, each institutional type, as well as various categories within each type, sought to employ the regulatory framework and the courts to rein in rivals or to extract a competitive advantage. The inevitable result was an expanding volume of litigation.

The ability to attract funds as well as the ability to lend funds depends, of course, not only on the extent of these markets, but on interest rates paid on deposits and loan rates. Both of these rates, in turn, are closely connected with the rate of inflation. The greater the rate of inflation, the more depositors—including household depositors—are attentive to interest rate differentials and market yields. Comparisons of three types are made in considering alternatives: (1) differentials between yields from alternative instruments, such as stocks or money market mutual funds, and deposit rates; (2) spreads between interest paid by commercial banks and other financial intermediaries, most importantly mutual savings banks and savings and loan associations; and (3) spreads between different types of deposit instruments offered by the same institutional type.[16] When funds flow from bank deposits to other investment opportunities because of the latter's superior yields, the process is known as disintermediation. This process has been particularly harmful to the housing sector of the economy when, on a number of occasions, funds fled rapidly from S & Ls and mutuals—the principal supplier of loans to that sector.

On the one hand, it is evident that all financial institutions would like to pay as little interest as possible and consequently would prefer not to compete for liabilities. To this extent they approve of the regulatory rules setting deposit interest rate ceilings. But because of the difficulty of attracting deposits sufficient to meet their perceived needs and their fears of disintermediation and cross-intermediation to rival types of financial intermediaries, they also resist interest rate regulation and have found ways to attract funds that, at least temporarily, are not subject to ceilings. Thus, the introduction of large negotiable certificates of deposit in 1961 by First National City Bank as an instrument outside the scope of the then legally enforceable ceilings was one of the earliest attempts to evade such regulations by offering a new instrument.[17] From that point forward, the floodgates were opened as more and more financial institutions issued instruments designed to circumvent deposit rate ceilings, and the regulatory agencies devised a complex of specific ceilings, sometimes suspending specific ones, sometimes reinstituting them, depending upon the threat of disintermediation.[18]

The dynamic of strong loan demand coupled with high rates of inflation, then, eroded traditional boundaries among institutional types, while the traditional regulatory apparatus designed during the New Deal to assure stability contributed to instability beginning in the 1960s. Institutions began ingeniously to devise new ways of circumventing regulatory boundaries, of which the development of the NOW account by mutuals is one example. At the same time, as competition intensified, operating expenses rose, squeezing profit rates, as institutions stayed open longer, offered additional services (pay-by-telephone accounts) and other inducements (gifts for opening accounts) and utilized new technology (electronic funds transfer). The ensuing litigation on the questions raised by these developments in the courts and at the level of administrative agencies made a shambles of the old regulatory apparatus, leading the District of Columbia U.S. Court of Appeals in an important 1978 decision to call for Congress to clear up the confusion and enact a new statute.[19]

But it is much easier to talk about new legislation to fit these important developments than to spell out the details of a statute. Clearly, the clock could not be turned back to 1933. But the difficulty of constructing statutory language that would attain effective compromises and not place one or another interest at a serious disadvantage was enormous. The Banking Deregulation Act—enacted almost two years after the Court of Appeals decision—was, in the words of a *Journal of Commerce* editorial, "A delicate balance . . . a broad ranging bill, with provisions that should please all types of financial intermediaries." And even though provisions that please one type of institution will displease others, "The consensus appears to be that financial institutions 'can live with it.' "[20] Mutuals and S & Ls received the right to offer NOW accounts, while credit unions were authorized to issue share drafts. Regulation Q, which limits deposit interest rates, will be phased out by 1986, a move favored by consumer groups and by commercial banks because of the differential between what commercial banks may pay and what S & Ls and mutuals may pay. S & Ls were authorized to invest up to 20 percent of their assets in consumer loans and corporate debt securities—a compromise between them and the housing interests that sought to restrict S & L loans for housing.

Space precludes examining the many other provisions of the hodgepodge that constitutes the Banking Deregulation Act. But the statute illustrates the complex dynamics involving changes at the macroeconomic level and the structure of competition as well as the impact of interest group activity. The basic impetus for both airline and trucking deregulation stemmed from the general notion that more freedom to compete would reduce the prices and costs of these infrastructural services, as well as the perception that some practices under regulation involved grossly inefficient resource use (such as rules that prevented regulated truckers from carrying return trip or full loads).[21] Moreover, in the case of trucking, a labor-intensive industry, the substantial pay hikes granted to the Teamsters in many contract negotiations have been viewed as a major cause of the increasing cost of goods. While the impact of these costs vary from shipper to shipper and industry to industry, the conclusion drawn by many in both political parties is that the antitrust immunity granted to carriers before the Trucking Deregulation Act provided no incentive to engage in hard bargaining over wages.

But although the general principles were widely accepted—except by those with a vested interest that moved them to favor continued regulation—the particulars of a deregulation statute are determined by the political infighting among the various interest groups. The regulated sector of the trucking industry, as well as the Teamsters, who regarded trucking deregulation as a threat to jobs, strongly opposed deregulation. On the other hand, the Independent Truckers Association, representing independent owner-operators, supported it strongly. The National Association of Manufacturers and consumer groups—strange bedfellows—as well as important retailers, such as Sears-Roebuck, also advocated enactment of a deregulation statute. And one survey disclosed that 91 percent of the big shippers and 89 percent of the small ones favored deregulation. Opposition within shipping circles stemmed from heavy industries that valued a stable delivered pricing system, in which all transport rates are known, more than they valued lower rates. The end result of the political infighting, which cut across party lines, was compromise legislation that made it far easier for prospective truckers to get new routes and eliminated much of the industry's antitrust immunity. But the trucking deregulation law fell far short of the original proposal sponsored by Senators Kennedy and Packwood that would have gone much further in removing controls over trucking.[22] And while support for trucking deregulation, as well as resistance to it, cut across party lines, it is highly unlikely that deregulation will proceed any further in this area under a Reagan administration. During the campaign Mr. Reagan, enthusiastically endorsed by the Teamsters, gave every indication that he would proceed warily—if at all—on this issue.[23]

Yet because of the different political configurations, Mr. Reagan will proceed more rapidly than Mr. Carter would have in the area of energy deregulation. In other areas we may be confident that Mr. Reagan will not move in the direction of *reregulation*. But again, whether the new administration will move at all or in new directions depends upon the particular facts and forces involved. Certainly, the rapidly changing technology in the communications field and the closer integration of information processing with telecommunications would lead us to expect that new rules will be devised in that area. Similarly, technology and the continuing volatile nature of competition in the area of credit provision may lead to additional pressures for changes there. But the stagnating nature of the railroad industry and the shakeout in the airline industry would not lead us to expect much pressure for change in the regulation and deregulation of those sectors. Rather, pressures will probably be exerted for special subsidies, rather than for changes in competitive rules.

Although this brief survey indicates the complexity of motives and policies that underlie the word "deregulation," they pale when one probes the underlying meaning of "overregulation," the examination of which must be preceded by a closer look at the nature of our macroeconomic problems.

III

The macroeconomic problems that beset America cannot easily be dissociated from one another. Just as the economy's functioning must be viewed systemically, so too must the set of problems that comprise the current difficulties—or crisis. Inflation, productivity, unemployment, the massive public deficit are all inextricably linked. Nevertheless, it is analytically important to separate them in order to see how regulation and deregulation fit into plans for the economy. All three major candidates agreed that inflation is the single most important economic problem, and while their unanimity does not necessarily make this judgment correct, it is clearly one of the important problems. The rate of inflation, as measured by the Consumer Price Index (CPI), rose from an average annual rate of 1.8 percent from 1950 to 1965 to 4.4 percent from 1965 to 1973, and then skyrocketed to 9.4 percent from 1973 to the first half of 1980. Moreover, the rate during the last period was frequently well in excess of 9.4 percent and subject to rapid shocks from food and oil prices. From 1976 on, the *annual* rate was accelerating rapidly although, of course, rates varied considerably when measured on a monthly basis.[24] Finally, no end to high annual inflation rates or their acceleration appears in sight.

Although sudden food and energy price increases have clearly played significant roles in the post-1973 inflation, we must not overstate their impacts. Japan and West Germany are even more vulnerable to OPEC price increases than the United States is, and yet they have much lower rates of inflation. Obviously, then, other factors must contribute to the American inflation rates, which are lower than those of some advanced capitalist nations, but significantly higher than those of others. The principal culprit in the American case is alleged to be productivity. Although the concept is admittedly difficult to measure, especially in the service sector and in management functions in all sectors, we must not throw up our hands and reject it. It is useful, for example, in measuring changes in output for production tasks. And when we focus on those activities in which the concept is most useful, something in America has clearly gone wrong compared to other major advanced capitalist countries. For example, the October 15, 1980, *Wall Street Journal* reported that although Japanese labor

247

costs per unit of output have barely changed in recent years, the United States has been experiencing substantial increases in this measure. Japan, West Germany, and France each registered annual output per man-hour increases in manufacturing industries in excess of 4 percent from 1973 to 1979; the United States lingered at 1.6 percent during the comparable period, a marked decline from the 2.9 percent compound rate from 1967 to 1973.[25] And although the United States is still the most productive economy in the world, the gap between it and other advanced capitalist countries is closing so rapidly that—unless something is done—West Germany, Japan, and others will outpace us in output per employed person.

Productivity, although it has been emphasized in the media, is only one of the serious problems affecting American industry. Productivity compels us to focus on unit costs, a particularly important factor in the competitiveness of relatively homogeneous goods. It tells us considerably less about the competitiveness of goods in which quality and product differentiation count for more. Although steel and automobiles are frequently lumped together as two of America's "sick industries," they, in fact, manifest these two very different problems. From 1973 to 1978 productivity in steel—a relatively fungible group of commodities—actually declined. An index of this decline is that at present only about 16 percent of American steel is continuously cast (a highly efficient steelmaking technique); in Japan, the comparable figure is approximately 70 percent. And, in general, America's industrial equipment is older and inherently less efficient than that of its principal competitors. For example, approximately 69 percent of American metal-cutting machinery is, according to a June 5, 1980, *Wall Street Journal* examination, more than ten years old, whereas the figure for Japan is 41 percent. Automobiles are different. Productivity in car manufacture actually increased 3.9 percent between 1973 and 1978.[26] As virtually every American knows, the problem of the American automobile industry has been one of quality. Our automobiles, until fairly recently, have not been as fuel-efficient as their European and Japanese counterparts. Probably equally as important in the long run, they have not been as durable and well constructed.

Automobiles and a number of other American industries, then, have been suffering not a productivity problem, but a quality problem stemming from objective or perceived competitive disadvantage. The effect, regardless of the cause, is the same: a declining American share of both the American and world markets. According to the June 30, 1980, *Business Week* special study, "The Reindustrialization of America," the American share of both markets has declined significantly in virtually every important industrial sector. The American share of domestic auto market sales declined from 95.9 percent in 1960 to 79.9 percent in 1979; American steel's share declined from 95.8 percent to 86 percent.[27] In general, according to an August 18, 1980, *New York Times* report, America's share of the industrial world's manufactured exports fell from 22 percent in 1962 to 14.8 percent in 1977.[28] The decline in sales and competitiveness leads, especially in the case of capital-intensive industries utilizing smaller percentages of capacity, to a tendency toward sluggish capital investment in new facilities and a decline in spending on research and development. Thus, real industrial research and development outlays as a percentage of GNP slipped from 2.1 percent in 1964 to under 1.6 percent in 1978. Capital spending fell from 11 percent in the first quarter of 1974 to about 10 percent in the first quarter of 1979. But the picture is far worse than these figures indicate, for investment in the energy sector rose from 8 percent of the total in 1973 to more than 12 percent in 1979 and promises to rise even higher in the future, starving out other important sectors. Moreover, business investment as a percentage of corporate cash flow dropped from 99 percent in the first quarter of 1970 to 81 percent in 1979.[29]

One could go on, but the cycle is clear. Productivity problems, declining research and development expenditures, domestic and international noncompetitiveness, shrinking capital utilization, quality problems exacerbate one another and the problem of inflation. The fear of those elites who reflect on such problems is that things could get even worse. American industry could fall far behind those of our major competitors, particularly Japan and West Germany. The tarnished example of Britain—once the world's industrial leader—is there for all to see. On the other hand, as Japan and West Germany show, there are ways of meeting economic difficulties that might reverse the course. This does not mean blindly imitating such policies as Japanese indicative planning, but rather closely examining the shape of American public policy, modifying some of it and replacing some of it. Phrases like "industrial policy," "supply-side economics," and "reindustrialization" were, and are, intended to embrace this process. And although there were significant differences among the three major candidates on how to undertake this process—notably in the area of taxation—there was also a surprising degree of consensus. Regulatory reform was one of the areas in which consensus on the basic thrust of policy was particularly striking.

I V

Rarely has a week elapsed during the last two years without an important business executive or the business press lambasting "overregulation" or "excessive regulation." A typical example is provided by an article written for the September 22, 1980, *Business Week* by Ruben F. Mettler, Chairman of TRW, Inc. In the article, adapted from a speech delivered at the California Institute of Technology, Mettler urged:

> Instead of formulating policies that enhance the American industrial system, we have tried to milk it to produce short-term benefits. . . . Meanwhile the American political system has launched what has seemed at

times a vendetta against American industry. In the good name of protecting the environment, consumers and workers, and of other valid concerns,
it unleashed the disastrous regulatory excesses of the 1970's.[30]

The reader should note the important distinction implicit in Mr. Mettler's
statement that provides a central theme in the current offensive against
regulation. The attack is not on social regulation itself, but on its "excesses." A strategy of outright attack on environmental, safety, and health
regulation would elicit little popular support, for distrust of American
business conduct is so widespread that virtually everyone supports *in
principle* regulatory programs aimed at raising levels above what would
probably prevail in free market conditions. Therefore, the appeal is based
upon "reasonableness" and against "excess." Who could possibly approve
of unreasonableness and excess?

Supporting the view that regulation has grown unreasonable and excessive are a number of theoretical studies conducted under the auspices
of the American Enterprise Institute and the Center for the Study of
American Business at Washington University, St. Louis. The work on this
problem done by economist Murray Weidenbaum on the cost of regulation
has been especially influential. A little flavor of this literature is in order.
According to Weidenbaum, the budgets of fifty-six federal regulatory
agencies rose from over $1 billion in 1970 to over $6 billion in 1980, while
the number of pages covered in the Federal Register by regulatory rules
climbed from approximately 60,000 in 1975 to almost 85,000 by 1980.
But the direct costs, according to Weidenbaum, are only a small part of the
total costs. The costs business firms must sustain to comply with (or
contest) these regulations—much of which is passed on to consumers—far
exceed the direct governmental costs. The annual costs of meeting federal
regulations for consumer product safety, job safety, environmental protection, and other requirements were estimated to be $102.7 billion in 1979
—or about 4 percent of GNP.[31] General Motors alone calculated that from
1974, when it first began keeping track of the costs, through the first half
of 1980, it had expended $8.1 billion, excluding the $8 billion required to
meet fuel economy standards which it charged to "competitive expenses
mandated by the marketplace." To place this staggering total in perspective, General Motors reported that in 1979 its regulatory expenses were
$3.1 billion, while its sales were $66.3 billion.[32]

Thus, the first part of the argument that now constitutes the prevailing
view is that regulation is expensive. In Milton Friedman's phrase, "There's
no such thing as a free lunch." This perception has become so much a part
of the conventional wisdom that it is difficult to remember the prevailing
legislative ideology of only a few years ago, which is still the way a
segment of the Democratic party's liberal wing conceives regulation. According to that view, the costs imposed on business are worthwhile public
benefits. Nor was there much consideration of the link between regulatory
costs and higher prices for goods and services. But the heightened and

accelerating rate of inflation, coupled with well-publicized research of the type conducted by Weidenbaum and the AEI, certainly drew that link to the attention of most of the public. Nevertheless, President Carter, because of the need to retain the support of liberals, was compelled to pay obeisance to their ideology. Thus, the Democratic platform called for: (1) vigorous enforcement of auto pollution and toxic substance regulations; (2) elimination of acid rain pollution; (3) sharp controls on noise pollution; (4) opposition to any attempt to weaken OSHA regulation; (5) opposition to authority for the federal government to override other federal or state environmental, safety, or health regulations; and (6) the enactment of additional statutes and regulations in such areas as automobile safety, food and drug safety, and clothing flammability.

Certainly President Carter's record during his last two years in office belies his devotion to the liberal ideology. But he was saddled with it, and Reagan, sensing Carter's vulnerability in this respect, frequently emphasized the purported link between "overregulation" and economic costs. In his important October 25, 1980, television address on the economy, Reagan asserted:

> Another vital part of this strategy concerns government regulations which work against rather than for the interests of the people. No one argues with the intent of regulations dealing with health, safety and clean air and water. But we must clearly re-examine our regulatory structure to assess to what degree regulations have cost jobs and economic growth. There should and will be a thorough and systematic review of the thousands of federal regulations that affect the economy.[33]

In his September 12 press release on the Endangered Species Act—a particularly vulnerable statute because of the snail darter incident—Reagan, after affirming his commitment to preserving animal life, stated: "At the same time, however, we should recognize that blind enforcement of this policy can—and often has—unnecessarily impeded economic growth and energy production. . . . In exploring all the alternatives in each instances, we must seek to strike a delicate balance in preserving endangered species and in permitting necessary construction."[34]

One could go on illustrating from speech after speech, statement after statement, Reagan's overriding regulatory theme. "Excessive" regulation is bad primarily because it enhances the prices of goods and services beyond what they would otherwise be. The November 26, 1980, *Wall Street Journal* reported that Reagan's anti-inflation effort will "include attempts to trim federal regulation. . . . Such changes could eliminate billions of dollars of cost increases on business over five years, Reagan regulatory experts say."[35]

The second major objection to "overregulation" concerns the opportunity cost problem. Corporate funds that must be invested in plant and equipment required to comply with government regulations, such as environmental control devices, cannot be used for capital investment purposes that aid economic growth. Similarly, resources employed in research and development needed to meet government requirements cannot be employed in research and development that will modernize or make more efficient use of labor or raw materials. Research funds that must be devoted to determining how to comply with regulations cannot be used to develop new or improved products. In the words of the October 28, 1980 *Wall Street Journal:* "People who prepare government required reports or develop and monitor plans to comply with regulations . . . are paid by the companies, but essentially they work for government. Instead of producing tires, hamburgers or revenue generating services, they advance the government's social goals. As their ranks increase, therefore, they tend to reduce the productivity of company work forces."[36] In brief, then, the opportunity cost argument contends that, in a world of scarce resources, overregulation shifts their use from activities that would better help achieve productivity, innovation, competitiveness, capital investment, and price stability into activities that hinder their attainment.

But what, according to Reagan and his regulatory advisors, constitutes overregulation? How does one distinguish it from the proper amount of regulation? We must remember that in his speeches and television appearances, President Reagan went to great lengths to indicate the great social benefits—including pollution control—that were produced during his tenure as governor of California. We should also remember that neither the academics nor the businessmen surrounding Reagan during the campaign rejected outright such goals as job safety or safe drugs. Rather, they carefully used such words as "balance." From the great volume of material issued, we can construct a set of questions, which must be asked in sequence, that can help us predict their *theoretical* approach to specific regulatory problems. Of course, it must be borne in mind that the theoretical approach can always be modified by the practical concerns of constituencies to whom Reagan is beholden. For example, the influence of the Teamsters on trucking deregulation might override the persuasiveness of an AEI economist lauding it and calling for its extension.

In any situation, the Reagan people start with a predisposition in favor of free markets. They accept the long line of argument beginning with Adam Smith and running through Milton Friedman that the free market is *usually* the most efficient allocator of resources and best maximizer of welfare. For this reason, they oppose both the Chrysler loan guarantee and the vast synfuels subsidy program; such interferences in the market misallocate resources that on their own businessmen will more efficiently employ elsewhere. In his September 8 press release on the Energy Mobilization Board proposal, Reagan objected to giving "federal bureaucrats the power to arbitrarily pick and choose their favorite energy projects."[37] Let the market decide whether the most promising investment for future energy resources is in shale oil, coal conversion, solar energy, and so on. At the same time, the free market advocates do not object to government

sponsoring or furthering basic research, since this activity does not inter-
fere with market mechanisms; it simply supplies additional information
upon which market decisions will be based. And, to repeat a persistent
theme, as Reagan's changing views on the Chrysler subsidy illustrate, he
is an eminently practical man willing to compromise high economic principle for political benefit. The weaker members of the American automobile
industry, Michigan voters, and other industries that might have to ask for
loan guarantees or subsidies, are all important Reagan constituencies. The
best workable hypothesis concerning Reaganism in this area is that there
is a strong presumption in favor of unconstrained market arrangements,
but that it may be overcome by political pressures.

In accordance with welfare economics, the Reaganites do, however,
recognize that there are instances of market failure which might require
government intervention as a remedy. For example, the problems of air and
water pollution are subsumed under the economic concept of externalities,
in which the market does not operate according to theoretical plan because
costs are externalized—imposed on those outside a firm's transaction decisions—rather than incorporated within cost-price decisions. But even
when market failure exists, it does not follow that the free market advocates would then agree to regulatory solutions. For they then ask whether
the market can be corrected by extending such traditional common law
notions as tort, contract, and property rights. For example, it is likely that
under the Reagan administration, EPA will extend the idea begun on an
experimental basis during the Carter years of pollution rights that are
transferable and divisible in much the same way that property rights are.
In their view, such notions will yield better efficiency results than regulation.

But even when such traditional common law notions cannot readily
be used, it still does not follow, under the Reaganite view, that regulation
is appropriate. In this respect the views of Reagan's regulatory advisors are
a sharp break from traditional liberal Democratic practice, in which regulatory solutions are inevitably proposed to cure market failures, and other
problems as well. Instead, we may expect Reagan's economic advisors to
ask first whether there is a reasonable justification for intervention in the
marketplace. These would include such theories as externalities and natural monopoly. But even if a justification is found, they will not necessarily
propose using regulation, for they will then look at its probable costs and
benefits, compare those to the probable costs and benefits under free
market conditions, and ask which will lead to better results. In the case of
extant statutes and rules, they will ask much the same questions. When
they find that nonintervention will probably lead to better performance,
they will seek to have the agency rescind the rule or Congress repeal the
statute. But even if regulation is found to yield better performance, a
further question will be asked. Is there a cheaper and/or more effective
technique that will attain the same goals? In general, we may reasonably
assume that the Reagan administration will opt for tax incentives and

other "carrot" techniques rather than use the regulatory stick when both alternatives seem to be available.

From the above scheme we may readily conclude that regulation will not be a favored technique of the Reagan administration, and that in the names of "deregulation" and "curbing excessive regulation" it will seek to cut back the federal regulatory apparatus. But even if the answers to the questions above lead inexorably to the conclusion that regulation is warranted, the theory guiding the particular regulation to adopt or the bill to promote is quite different from that which guides liberal Democrats. It is here that phrases like "overregulation" and "balance," so common in Reagan's regulatory vocabulary, can be placed in context. The underlying theory is easy to state, but the application is far more difficult. The principal tool used is cost-benefit analysis. But what costs and what benefits? Here one must draw the distinction between *aggregate* cost-benefit analysis and *marginal* cost-benefit analysis. Under the former—and fallacious—type of analysis, one looks at the annual total cost of a problem and concludes that there is a net benefit if annual total expenditures are less. For example, if the national cost of air pollution is $10 billion a year and public expenditures are $1 billion, it does not follow that we could (or should) be spending much more to curb air pollution.

The fallacy in this sort of balance sheet reasoning lies in the assumption that there is a linear relationship between costs and benefits within the whole range of costs and benefits—that is, for every dollar expended, there is a dollar's worth of benefit. The assumption is unwarranted both theoretically and practically. It is far more common in the real world of such problems as pollution, safety, and health for the marginal benefits to decline relative to marginal expenditures as one moves toward a 100 percent solution of a problem. For this reason, the appropriate way to conceptualize so-called social regulation is in terms of marginal costs and marginal benefits. The critical question under the marginalist concept is how much *extra* benefit will be obtained with the application of *additional* cost at each point along the expenditure range. If, for example, at the $2 billion expenditure point $1 of expenditure will yield $2 of benefit, the expenditure is warranted. But if at the $9 billion point $1 of expenditure will yield only 50 cents of benefit, the expenditure is not warranted. In areas where regulation is justified, the goal must be to attain the level at which marginal costs just equal marginal benefits. Points above which marginal costs exceed marginal benefits are what Reagan and his regulatory advisers would call "excessive" or "overregulation."

V

Several comments must be made about the Reaganite conception and its impact on the campaign. First, it sounds eminently sensible. Virtually everyone knows of some government program that does not work or that works badly. Television news reporters are more than delighted to tell us about some silly governmental program or one that involves paternalism or oppression. Many people are aware of regulatory programs that work at cross purposes or conflict with important goals. Most Americans are aware that while EPA seeks to reduce the use of pesticides, the Department of Agriculture promotes them; that the EPA pushes for stringent air pollution standards while the Department of Energy promotes the use of coal, the dirtiest energy source; and that the Department of Energy supports low coal rates to aid utility fuel conversion, while the Department of Transportation favors high rates to aid the railroads. Yet although these and many other examples illustrate the dangers of "overregulation" and inconsistency and the need for "reasonableness," a moment's reflection will also indicate the difficulty of applying marginal cost–marginal benefit analysis. Perhaps you and I, for example, can agree that a certain additional expenditure is unwarranted, but many others may disagree. There are simply so many subjective considerations that it is difficult, if not impossible, to quantify benefits. I may place a very low benefit value on maintaining trees that will be ruined by noxious emissions, but another person may place a much higher value on preserving such amenities.

Moreover, we must remember that marginalist analysis calls for location of the *precise* point at which marginal cost just begins to exceed marginal benefit. Thus, even if you and I agree that the cost of removing 95 percent of a particular pollutant from the air is excessive relative to the marginal benefit, we still have the difficult problem of determining the location of the precise threshold point. I might opt for 84 percent, you might opt for 73 percent, and a third person might light upon 91 percent. Surely, President Reagan is not planning a national referendum on each and every problem involving social cost and social benefit. Even if he decided on this unlikely course, few people are inclined to think in this manner. The absurdity of the notion compels us to ask how such judgments will be made. The probable answer has been supplied by the practice of the last few months of the Carter administration, especially after Carter's decisive defeat of Senator Kennedy in the Democratic primary campaign. After he saw the extraordinary weakness of Governor Brown and his radical-chic contingent, and the weakness of Senator Kennedy, Carter could move rightward—being careful, however, not to so alienate the Democratic Left that it would jump into the Anderson camp or sit out the election.

The post-primary Carter strategy, likely to be continued during the Reagan administration, consists of bargaining and negotiation between government and industry, with an eye to the interests of other groups, to determine the extent of the retreat in social regulation. Notwithstanding the facade of its being based on economic theory, especially marginalism and cost-benefit analysis, it will be no more scientific than the liberal operating standard, which employs the moralistic language of concern for the disadvantaged as a substitute for failing to incorporate cost analysis in policy proposals. The principal difference between what Carter would have done and what Reagan will do lies not in the direction taken, but where to draw the overregulation line, for Reagan does not have a liberal constituency to worry about. Speaking in Steubenville, Ohio, a working-class city, on October 7, Reagan spelled out the difference. Referring to Carter's plan to assist the steel industry, Reagan stated: "However in perhaps the most important area—overregulation—Mr. Carter's plan is but a pale imitation of my proposal. I have spoken out consistently against overregulation, and in my steel program focused on stretching out the compliance times for all steel companies. In contrast, Mr. Carter is merely proposing to amend the law to allow the E.P.A. to grant an extension if the E.P.A. decides that certain conditions are met."[38]

Nevertheless, the policy of bargaining and negotiating that Reagan will follow was begun during the Carter administration. And a look at Carter's policies is instructive to see the new direction in social policy. First, we can expect a continuation and expansion of the Carter policy adopted in 1979 at the behest of his Council on Wage and Price Stability of requiring economic impact statements from regulatory agencies. Second, we can anticipate a substantial slowdown in the number of new regulations. Third, we can readily expect, where possible, the substitution of performance standards for design standards. Under the former, firms are given a performance goal they are free to meet in any way they choose; under the latter, government regulators specify the means by which goals are to be met. But the most important regulatory direction is indicated by Carter's moves in connection with the steel and automobile industries. The process begins when the industry complains about some examples of "overregulation," showing, in the process, the adverse impact on costs (and price) and competitiveness in relation to foreign rivals. Government is reminded of the number of persons employed in the industry who might become unemployed unless something is done. The process of business-government negotiation then begins in earnest, concluding when government yields to some industry demands by reducing the extent of regulation. Perhaps the process might be called "de-overregulation."

President Carter's moves toward the automobile industry illustrate the results of this dynamic. In August, the head of EPA's program for controlling mobile-source air pollution notified the industry that a rule requiring "tamper-proof" idlers for 1982 and later models was being eliminated. According to a Ford official, "The government asked us to give them five priorities for regulatory relief. This was one of them. So we feel very pleased by the action."[39] In September EPA announced the postponement from the 1983 to the 1984 model year of several auto emission standards, although it denied others requested by the industry.[40] In October President Carter, as part of a wider aid plan for the steel industry, offered to request congressional authorization allowing EPA to permit case-by-case delays of up to three years for meeting air quality standards.[41] Given these initial successes, we can confidently expect the substantial expansion of "de-overregulation" within these and other industries during the Reagan years.

The moral of the story is not that Left-liberals should engage in plaintive hand-wringing during the Reagan-Bush years, wondering why the people elected "hopeless reactionaries" instead of them. They might do better to consider that moralistic platitudes are no substitute for devising alternative regulatory programs concerned with such problems as efficiency and productivity. They might consider that social programs do cost great sums, and that trying to measure costs and benefits in a reasonable manner should not be an exercise reserved exclusively for conservatives. Combining the economic concern for efficiency with the traditional Left concern for equity—something conservatives tend to ignore—can lead to a resurgence of Left-liberal thought not only in the realm of regulation, but in policymaking generally. Whether we can expect such a resurgence remains to be seen.

NOTES

1. Jimmy Carter, "Remarks on Signing S.1946 (Staggers Rail Act of 1980) into Law," *Weekly Presidential Documents,* October 14, 1980, p. 2226.
2. See, especially, the essays in Gary M. Walton (ed.), *Regulatory Change in an Atmosphere of Crisis* (New York: Academic Press, 1979), pp. 79–129.
3. B. Drummond Ayres, Jr., "Conservative Researchers Expect New Prominence," *The New York Times,* November 17, 1980, p. D12. See also Mary Battiata, "Think Tank Tribute," *Washington Post,* December 13, 1980, p. D2.
4. "Former Ford Officials Named to Transport Transition Team," *Journal of Commerce,* November 12, 1980, p. 2.
5. This proposition was most forcefully developed in Gabriel Kolko, *The Triumph of Conservatism* (New York: Free Press, 1963).
6. Carter, pp. 2226, 2227.
7. Juan Cameron, "Nader's Invaders Are Inside the Gates," *Fortune,* October 1977, pp. 252–262.
8. Thomas C. Hayes, "Executives Favoring Reagan," *The New York Times,* October 27, 1980, p. D8.
9. "Steel's Support for Carter Seen Hinged to Aid," *Journal of Commerce,* August 19, 1980, p. 3; and Thomas C. Hayes, "Business Supporters of President Carter," *The New York Times,* August 13, 1980, pp. D1, 14. See also Alena Wels and George Telfer, "Business Backs Carter's Battle against Inflation," *Journal of Commerce,* August 15, 1980, pp. 1, 17.
10. Jerry Landauer, "Hedging Political Bets, Firms Give to Liberals in Positions of Power," *The Wall Street Journal,* October 13, 1980, pp. 1, 11; Hayes, op. cit., p. D8; and Frank Allen, "Carter Rating from Business Drops Further," *The Wall Street Journal,* October 30, 1980, p. 27.
11. "Nuclear Industry Hails Reagan's Victory," *Houston Chronicle,* November 6, 1980, sec. 3, p. 11; Bill Paul, "Energy Executives Are Elated, Expecting Unfettered Growth under GOP Regime," *The Wall Street Journal,* November 6, 1980, p. 5; and G. Christian Hill, "S & L Industry Buoyed by Reagan's Win, Pins Hopes on Spur to Capital Formation," *The Wall Street Journal,* November 11, 1980, p. 18.

12. For a summary of airline deregulation's success, see Comptroller General of the United States, *The Changing Airline Industry: A Status Report Through 1979* (Washington, D.C.: Government Printing Office, 1980), 23 pp.
13. For a discussion of the contradictory impulses toward regulation that business firms exhibit, see Alan Stone, *Economic Regulation and the Public Interest* (Ithaca: Cornell University Press, 1977), Chap. 1.
14. Fred Bonavita, "Share Draft Suit to Explore Complex Banking Questions," *Houston Post,* September 9, 1979.
15. On branching politics, see Charles W. Collins, *The Branch Banking Question* (New York: Macmillan, 1926); and Gerald C. Fischer, *American Banking Structure* (New York: Columbia University Press, 1968), chap. 2.
16. U.S., Senate, 94th Cong., 1st Sess., Committee on Banking, Housing and Urban Affairs, *Financial Institutions Act of 1975, Hearings,* pp. 134–144.
17. See Edward M. McKelvey, "Interest Rate Ceilings and Disintermediation," *Staff Economic Studies No. 99* (Washington, D.C.: Federal Reserve Board, 1978), p. 9.
18. See *Golembe Reports,* No. 3 (1979), pp. 3, 4.
19. The decision and order are reprinted in U.S., Senate, 96th Cong., 1st Sess., Committee on Banking, Housing and Urban Affairs, *Depository Institutions Deregulation Act of 1979, Hearings, Part 1,* pp. 108–112.
20. "A Delicate Balance," *Journal of Commerce,* March 14, 1980, p. 4. See also Karen Pennar, "Bankers Expected to Support Bill," *Journal of Commerce,* March 14, 1980, pp. 1, 19.
21. Excellent summaries are provided in Paul H. Weaver, "Unlocking the Gilded Cage of Regulation," *Fortune,* February 1977, pp. 179–188, and David Welborn, "Taking Stock of Regulatory Reform," paper presented at the American Political Science Association Annual Meeting, Washington, D.C., September 1, 1977.
22. Charles G. Burck, "Truckers Roll toward Deregulation," *Fortune,* December 18, 1978, pp. 75–80, 85; "Trucking Deregulation Is Moving Fast," *Business Week,* November 27, 1978, pp. 63–72; "A Truck Law That Only Nibbles," *The New York Times,* June 25, 1980, p. A26; "An Open Road toward Trucking Deregulation," *Business Week,* June 9, 1980, p. 28; Ernest Holsendolph, "Kennedy Broadens Truck Bill," *The New York Times,* May 2, 1979, pp. D1, 4.
23. "Reagan Trucking Stance Clouded," *Journal of Commerce,* October 28, 1980, p. 2; and "Carter, Reagan Assess Transport Issues," ibid., p. 4.
24. Data from Harry Brandt, "Inflation: Still Our Number One Problem," *Federal Reserve Bank of Atlanta Economic Review,* September–October 1980, pp. 16, 17.
25. Alfred L. Malabre, Jr., "Factory Labor Costs Soar in U.S., But Hardly Budge in Japan," *The Wall Street Journal,* October 15, 1980, p. 48.
26. See Alfred L. Malabre, Jr., "As Usual in Slump, Factories Cut Capacity Use, But Degree, Timing of Decline Are Exceptional," *The Wall Street Journal,* June 5, 1980, p. 48; and "The Reindustrialization of America," *Business Week,* June 30, 1980, p. 65.
27. Malabre, "Reindustrialization," op. cit., p. 60.
28. Clyde H. Farnsworth, "U.S. Industry Seeking to Restore Competitive Vitality to Products," *The New York Times,* August 18, 1980, pp. 1, D8.
29. "What Is Blunting the Recovery," *Business Week,* November 3, 1980, pp. 34, 35.
30. Ruben F. Mettler, "The Cargo Cult Mentality in America," *Business Week,* September 22, 1980, p. 22.
31. See Murray L. Weidenbaum, *The Future of Business Regulation* (New York: Amacom, 1979), pp. 11–24. Weidenbaum, "How Much Regulation Is Too Much?" *The New York Times,* December 17, 1978, p. F16.
32. "Costly Regulations," *Journal of Commerce,* June 12, 1980, p. 4.

33. Reported in *The New York Times,* October 25, 1980.
34. Ronald Reagan, "Endangered Species Act," Reagan-Bush Committee *News Release,* September 12, 1980, p. 1.
35. Kenneth H. Bacon, "Reagan Economic Blitz to Get High Priority Despite Stiff Obstacles," *The Wall Street Journal,* November 26, 1980, p. 22.
36. Ralph E. Winter, "Many Businesses Blame Government Policies for Productivity Lag," *The Wall Street Journal,* October 28, 1980, p. 1.
37. Ronald Reagan, "Energy Mobilization Board," Reagan-Bush Committee *News Release,* September 8, 1980, p. 1.
38. Ronald Reagan, "Excerpts from Remarks—Steubenville, Ohio," Reagan-Bush Committee *News Release,* October 7, 1980, p. 2.
39. Quoted in Reginald Stuart, "Auto Makers Benefit as E.P.A. Cancels Rule," *The New York Times,* August 27, 1980, p. D6.
40. Ernest Holsendolph, "Pollution Limits Deferred to Help Auto Industry," *The New York Times,* September 18, 1980, pp. D1, D6.
41. Edward Cowan, "White House Seeks Delay in Pollution Rules," *The New York Times,* October 1, 1980, pp. D1, D5.

BY FORCE OF REASON: THE POLITICS OF SCIENCE AND TECHNOLOGY POLICY

David Dickson and David Noble

I

Shortly before Ronald Reagan's inauguration as president, *Business Week* published an article on his administration's likely attitude toward science and technology. In striking contrast to other areas of government policy, no major changes were expected from the new administration. The article noted that key advisers in the president-elect's transition team had played prominent roles in the previous administration's effort to improve the climate for technological innovation, and predicted that many of President Carter's policy recommendations were likely to remain intact. "The science and technology field is not one in which there are radically different views on different issues," a former presidential science advisor explained, while an advisor to the Reagan transition team reaffirmed the incoming president's commitment to "upgrade science, technology and productivity."[1]

Despite later rumors about a possible restructuring of the science advisory apparatus within the White House and some proposed budget cuts in "marginal" areas such as education and space exploration, such words were reassuring to the science-based business and research community. Many remembered the anti-intellectualism of the Nixon era, when research budgets declined for the first time since World War II, and the Republican president sacked the whole of his science advisory team after some of its members publicly opposed his views on antiballistic missiles and the environmental acceptability of supersonic transport aircraft.[2] Mr. Reagan's approach—including his apparent intention to retain the Office of Science and Technology Policy, also abolished by Nixon—seemed to reflect his agreement about the centrality of science and technology to the political economy of the United States.

Indeed, few issues in American politics are more important than the use of state power to regulate technological development. That this issue seldom intrudes in traditional campaign rhetoric makes it no less vital. At home, rapid technological innovation has become critical to the health of the domestic economy, where such "high tech" science-based industrial sectors as computers, semiconductors, telecommunications, aerospace, and biotechnology now play the leading role once assigned textiles, steel, or automobiles. Abroad, resource wars and the accelerated pace of international economic competition have underscored the importance of technological expertise in preserving international market shares. A recent report from the Organization for Economic Cooperation and Development (OECD) voiced international business community consensus in declaring that "intellectual capital—scientific resources and the aptitude for technological innovation—constitutes the major asset of industrialized nations in the new modes of international competition and interdependence."[3] Figures from the National Science Foundation bear out the observation for the American case. Between 1967 and 1977, the U.S. balance of trade surplus in R&D intensive manufacturing goods more than tripled, from $8.8 billion to $27.6 billion. Particularly significant—and crucial to understanding debates over our economic relationships with the Third World—is the large proportion of this surplus accounted for by exports to developing countries. The exchange of computers, machine tools, and military equipment for petroleum and mineral resources from predominantly developing countries during the period was a trade acting in favor of the United States, with a surplus that grew from $3.7 billion to $16 billion. By contrast, the American trade deficit with Japan deepened from $115 million to $3.5 billion.[4]

Given the striking economic importance of science and technology, the assurances of continuity in goals (if not means) from the Reagan team were particularly welcome. But the promise of continuity masked a fundamental shift in the content and political function of science and technology policy that had taken place during the Carter years. This shift has implications extending well beyond such conventional issues as government selection of research topics and levels of budgetary support. Put briefly, the dominant themes of science and technology policy were previously those which focused on the allocation of resources to meet national needs. The new theme is a desire to reshape the political and administrative apparatus of the state in the interests of its private corporations. Such a goal is not new to American politics. What is new is the way it is now pursued and justified through science and technology policy.

Established in the early 1950s, the office of science advisor to the president and the members of the President's Science Advisory Committee (PSAC) concentrated for the first decade or so on supporting defense and space research. As late as 1962, defense research was absorbing 70 percent of all federal funds for R&D (down from 80 percent in 1960). Three years later, 34 percent was going to space research, while the civilian share of federal R&D funding stood at a modest 16 percent. But in the late 1960s and early 1970s, the main focus of federally supported research shifted, in line with general social priorities, toward the role of science and technology in meeting social needs more directly. This was particularly evident in the fields of health, energy, and the environment, federal expenditures on which more than doubled the civilian share of federal R&D funding to 40 percent by 1978.[5]

All these fields have remained high on the agenda of the science advisor, and to most of the outside world technology policy still implies the selection of technological goals and priorities by the federal government. But over the past three years a significantly new policy initiative has also emerged. Its formal substance has been efforts, boosted by the Carter administration and continued under President Reagan, to accelerate technological innovation and productivity improvement in the private sector. Its explicit agenda has included the need to reduce the burden of "unnecessary" government obstacles to industrial innovation, in particular by promising changes in regulatory legislation, which is claimed to impede the introduction of new products and processes into the factory and market. Its goal, justified by appeals to rationality and efficiency, has been to create an environment in which the private sector can manage its affairs with a minimum of interference from government authority. Its effect has been to mount a counter-offensive against pressures for increased public control of research and the pace and direction of technological change, returning responsibility for these to the private sector in the name of progress and reason.

Responsibility for this policy shift does not lie solely with the Carter administration. The decisions announced by President Carter and his science advisor, Dr. Frank Press, continued a process of policy realignment initiated under the administration of Gerald Ford. Reacting to pressure from both the scientific community and industrial leaders, Ford had resurrected the science advisory apparatus Nixon had dismantled, taken steps to reverse the decline in the federal R&D budget, and pointed his science advisors toward the private sector productivity problem. In 1975, as part of the planning for a new Office of Science and Technology Policy (OSTP), Ford established an advisory group on technology and economic strength. The group was asked to examine "issues and opportunities involving the improved utilization of technology in fostering economic strength and in assuring that economic goals are achieved along with environmental goals." It was chaired by Dr. Simon Ramo, co-founder and vice-chairman of TRW, Inc., and science advisor to Reagan during the 1980 campaign. At the same time, by the mid-1970s many private corporations were claiming links between their declining economic performance and the need to meet the growing demands of federal regulation, and arguing that growth and productivity could be guaranteed only if the regulatory burden was lightened.

But if Ford sowed the seeds for the change in science and technology policy, it was the Carter administration that brought it into bloom. Early in Carter's term, science advisor Press urged consideration of industry demands for an improvement in the environment for innovation. What was needed from the federal government, Press and business leaders argued, was not greater financial support for industrially oriented research and development (the previously offered panacea), but a revision of tax, patent, antitrust, and other regulatory policy. The proposed shift in science policy emphasis soon became formal administration policy. By the middle of his administration, Carter was putting the need to stimulate innovation in industry at the top of his list of priorities for federal R&D policy. In his March 1979 message to Congress on science and technology policy, industrial innovation ranked higher than the traditional goals of meeting energy, natural resource, food, and health needs.

This shift in the *content* of science policy toward industrial innovation and regulatory reform had two important implications for its *form*.

The first was a change in the dominant conception of science and technology as these are integrated into the political process. Previously technology, and the science that supported it, was conceived primarily as a way of achieving specified social objectives. A report prepared by the National Academy of Sciences in 1974, for example, stated explicitly that "the view of science and technology which the presidency requires is that of means by which opportunities can be identified and problems can be met or obviated."[6] Two years later, when Vice-President Nelson Rockefeller was describing President Ford's reasons for reinstating the Office of Science and Technology to a congressional subcommittee, he described the role of science advisor primarily as one of using science and technology to meet national goals and address national problems.[7] And in his State of the Union message in January 1978, Jimmy Carter singled out the need to support science and technology for essentially the same reasons.

The private sector, in contrast, has never seen technology primarily in terms of its social function, but as a source of profit. What the Carter administration's new concern with industrial innovation illustrates is the degree to which this alternative way of looking at technology—which might be described as emphasizing its *exchange value* rather than its *use value*—is spreading from the private into the public sector. No longer does the president or his science advisor see the president's function as prescribing bold strategic goals for the nation's scientific and technological efforts (an omission that has frequently been criticized by Congress, which specifically called on the president to perform such a function in the National Science and Technology Policies Act of 1976 reinstating OSTP and the science advisor post).[8] Today the main interest in technology policy is neatly summed up by Carter chief inflation fighter Alfred Kahn's definition of an airplane: "a marginal cost with wings."

The second fundamental change relates to the political function of the science policy apparatus. Increasingly science policy has become a vehicle for attempts to change the structure of government bureaucracy. The prime mechanism for this has been the close relationship established between the Office of Science and Technology Policy and the Office of Management and Budget (OMB). Although their relationship is commonly described as a mechanism for generating support for the adequate funding of research and development throughout federal agencies—and hence as a way of providing OSTP with some political clout—the two agencies have, less publicly, worked closely together on a score of policy initiatives whose scope extends well beyond budgetary administration.

Prime examples are the domestic policy review on industrial innovation, efforts to streamline the activities of the government's regulatory agencies (including the OMB's move to establish a regulatory budget, and its attempt to remove health effects research from the Environmental Protection Agency), and measures to reduce the impact of federal accounting rules on government research.

OSTP's role here is frequently described, by Press and others, as one of bringing some order into the frequently conflicting and even contradictory mandates imposed by Congress on federal agencies. Speaking at a meeting organized by the American Association for the Advancement of Science (AAAS) in 1979, Press complained: "We have a regulatory structure which is highly segmented, wide-ranging in its impact, economically important, highly politicized, very aggressive, relatively independent, and almost totally uncoordinated."[9] The key word in justifying OSTP's broader role has been the need to "rationalize" government.[10] At the same AAAS meeting, OMB Executive Director Bowman Cutter, Press's close associate in many of his management initiatives, used the word "rational" three times in quick succession when he declared that the purpose of decontrolling oil prices was to create a more rational price regime, so that society would be able to hold rational expectations and make rational decisions on energy investment matters in the future. William Carey, executive director of the AAAS, later congratulated Dr. Press for helping to "rationalize" regulatory hysteria in the interests of productivity.[11] Dr. Lewis Branscomb, chief scientist at IBM and chairman of the National Science Board, warned of dire consequences should rationality in government action not be achieved. At a congressional hearing in 1979, Branscomb emphasized that "the development of more rational decision processes related to public strategies for generating, introducing and managing technology are vital to the survival of democracy itself."[12]

Three points may be made about the way this desire for rationality should be interpreted. The first is that the need for greater rationality is frequently used to justify a more hierarchical and authoritarian way of running the government, with agencies responding less to the details of their congressional mandates and more to the directives coming out of the White House. Frank Press has described the role of the Regulatory Council, in which the various regulatory agencies in the environmental and health fields come together to exchange details about future programs, as a mechanism for bringing some "coordination and consistency" into the regulatory system. Addressing a meeting at the American Enterprise Institute, Alfred Kahn may have provided greater insight into current political realities when he described the council as "an attempt to introduce into the regulatory process integration and rationality, both economic and scientific, which means the setting of priorities, and the knocking of heads together to see that the regulatory agencies, pressed by the council on one side, and by RARG (Regulatory Analysis Review Group) on the other, follow the lead of the president."[13]

The second aspect of this push for rationality is that the principal matrix for rational decisions is neither enlightenment philosophy nor overt political ideology, but the "free" operation of the market. The market, it is argued, should be the principal framework within which decisions are made and assessed. Left to the freedom of individual choice, consumers can be trusted to make rational decisions on whether to consume energy or conserve it, whether to shield themselves from potential carcinogens or rationally expose themselves to risk. Industrial managers can decide rationally whether to pay insurance premiums for their work force or install protective equipment. From this point of view, the rationality of federal policy is not measured by the yardstick of democratically determined social objectives, but by the extent to which it permits the unrestricted operation of market forces. The "reasonable goal" of government regulation becomes, in the words of Bowman Cutter of OMB, the achievement of an open market structure with sufficient predictability that expectations can remain constant over time, and investment decisions "can be made rationally."[14]

The third point to be made about appeals for rational government is that such appeals are frequently used to counteract pressure for increased public participation in decisions about the allocation of technical and scientific resources. In the late 1960s and early 1970s a series of political and social events, from the horrors of the Vietnam war to a growing awareness of the environmental side effects of indiscriminate industrialization, led to increasing demands, if not for social control of technological choices, at least for public discussion of their respective costs and benefits.

Ironically, as much of this move to evaluate the social consequences of science and technology was initiated by "insider" scientists as by any popular movement. The Environmental Protection Act of 1969, for example, was precipitated partly by groups like the President's Science Advisory Committee, which had carried out a major study of the environmental impact of pesticide abuse as early as 1966 and concluded that the long-standing claims of such environmentalist critics as Rachel Carson, Barry Commoner, and Ralph Nader had a basis in fact. Despite claims that the new environmental legislation of that period was a product of popular demand, it might be noted that Earth Day in 1970 came a year after Senate action on a host of environmental issues, including the mandate for a White House Council on Environmental Quality. Similarly, President Nixon's final abolition of PSAC stemmed directly from that group's attack on the SST, expressed in a mixture of economic and environmental arguments.

Whatever its origins, concern over the regulation of science and technology was quickly linked to broader challenges to the political system. "Technical choices" regarding the environment, worker safety, energy, and national health were politicized and made the object of mass mobilization. To the extent that they reflected and determined the degree of popular control over science and technology, related policy fields like tax, industrial policy, foreign relations, manpower planning, and international trade and development were also subjected to new scrutiny. Science policy thus became social policy, and popular mobilization around what former PSAC member James Coleman has described as a vast "expansion of the class of *science-laden* policies"[15] (emphasis added) constituted a fundamental challenge to conventional state-industry relations. This challenge took a variety of forms, including the search for alternative solutions to scientific and technological problems, the intellectual critique of objectivity and the claimed neutrality of science, wider citizen participation in activities formerly the preserve of experts, popular resistance to highways, the SST, nuclear power, and recombinant DNA research, and the institutionalization of issue-oriented political action through regulatory legislation and the establishment of EPA, OSHA, CPSC, and TSCA. All these challenges called into question the staples of capitalist apologetics—faith in the unidimensional benefits of industrialization, the rationality of the market, the authority of experts, and the idea of progress itself—while they affirmed with renewed vigor the principles of democracy and social welfare.

In its third new meaning, "rationality" is set in opposition to such popular participation. Widespread democratic challenge to traditional science policy is lumped directly with what are claimed to be antiscience and antitechnology movements. Popular criticism of a particular type of rationality—that which underlies production for profit and for military purposes—is purposefully confused with a critique of reason in general. Any dissident can thus be dismissed as, by definition, irrational and unreasonable.

Seen in this light, the redefinition of "reason" is but the most visible aspect of a broader political struggle including but not limited to the issue of popular control over science and technology. From its inception, the social legislation of the 1960s and early 1970s and the popular challenge to corporate domination of the political system which it reflected engendered broad resistance in the American business community. In retrospect, the actual strength of the popular challenge during the period is less important than the decisiveness and scope of the response it triggered. By the mid-1970s, working through a variety of trade associations, domestic and international think tanks, universities, policy institutes, planning agencies, foundations, and select offices within the Executive branch,*

*The number and variety of these institutions preclude their full discussion here, but we note the following important ones: the Trilateral Commission, Organization for Economic Cooperation and Development, German Marshall Fund, Committee for Economic Development, Conference Board, Business Roundtable, Industrial Research Institute, Chemical Manufacturers Association, and the American Petroleum Institute. The critical White House offices include the Council on Wage and Price Stability, Council of Economic Advisors, Regulatory Analysis and Review Group, Office of Management and Budget, and the Office of Science and Technology Policy. In the "tertiary" sector are the National Academy of Sciences, Council on Foreign Relations, major foundations (Ford, Rockefeller, Mellon, and Sloan), *ad hoc* commissions established to legitimate specific policy directives, and, of course, the universities.

highly mobilized business elites had forged a counterattack. This counter-attack disparaged what was called the "antiscience" movement and pro-claimed a new age of reason while remystifying reality. It entailed four interrelated campaigns:

1. The rediscovery of the self-regulating market, the wonders of free enterprise, and the classical liberal attack on government regulation of the economy, all in the name of liberty.
2. The reinvention of the idea of progress, now cast in terms of "innova-tion" and "reindustrialization," and the limitation of expectations and social welfare in the quest for productivity.
3. The attack on democracy, in the name of "efficiency," "manageabil-ity," "governability," "rationality," and "competence."
4. The remystification of science through the promotion of formalized decision methodologies, the restoration of the authority of expertise, and the renewed use of science as legitimation for social policy through deepening industry ties to universities and other "free" insti-tutions of policy analysis and recommendation.

That science and technology policy should be an arena for such mas-sive elite mobilization again underscores the critical economic roles of science and technology, while indicating as well their current political function. On the one hand, science-based high-technology industries now comprise the most competitive sectors of the economy. In a time of ac-celerated global economic integration and domestic stagflation, they carry the greatest hopes for domestic revival and continued American interna-tional economic dominance. On the other, the Enlightenment ideals of applied reason and shared inquiry such industries claim to embody provide needed legitimation for the modern, executive-centered, interventionist state. Not accountable to democratic or juridical norms, state action when cloaked in the mantle of science may still be justified as "rational," while consensus on the value-neutral character of scientific enterprise effectively sanitizes the policy formation process, justifying its removal from the control of mass democratic institutions. What is at stake in the current struggle over science and technology policy is not merely the technocratic redefinition of reason, but the redefinition of democracy itself. What has been altered by elite counterattack is not merely the pattern of choice within a limited area of government policy, but the entire shape of Ameri-can politics.

II

If nothing else, the burgeoning regulation of the 1960s and early 1970s challenged once-dominant conceptions of the market as the socially optimal allocator of goods and values. Not surprisingly, the first and most visible part of the business counterattack was a rediscovery of the wonders of the self-regulating market. A broad-based attack on government regulation began to take shape along several fronts, in the mass media, Washington, and the courts, proclaiming the virtues of the market and the tyranny of big government.

In the forefront of the media campaign were the petrochemical firms, the focus of much regulatory legislation and, in the public eye, primary perpetrators of a toxic environment. Mobil spent millions buying a regular columnist spot in the nation's leading newspapers. Dow preached "Common sense—uncommon chemistry." Du Pont offered the reassurance: "You and Du Pont—there's a lot of good chemistry between us." Monsanto gave the nation a science lesson: "Without chemicals, life itself would be impossible." Union Carbide reminded an already anxious population that "we don't live in a risk free world," and organized an "issues management team" to help people put the risks of modern life "in perspective." The Chemical Manufacturers Association hired the J. Walter Thompson advertising agency to put together a $5 million media blitz with the message that risk was part of life itself. The naturalness of chemical pollution was also a major theme at Dow, whose ads included the message that "the chemicals we make are no different from the ones God makes . . . There is an essential unity between chemicals created by God and chemicals created by humans . . . Birds, for example, are extraordinarily beautiful products produced by God."

Not long ago America's young science-based corporations shared a vision of a better world. Posing as bearers of enlightenment, they declared that progress was their most important product, and promised better living through chemistry. In the mid-1970s, with that vision having darkened, they peddled a more scientifically "neutral" message, calling for a neonaturalistic accommodation to the grim realities of life in industrial society. Science and Nature, once opposed, were joined by corporate capital to discipline a still idealistic humanity.[16]

Elsewhere, the lawyers of monopoly headed for Washington to hold the line for liberty. Here, as in the media, science and nature were coupled for a defense of the rights of science-based industry in an Edenic marketplace. The nineteenth century was revisited and computerized. "Grassroots" lobbyists dispatched by the Business Roundtable, Business Council, and United States Chamber of Commerce railed against government interference in the God-ordained and science-sanctified free enterprise system.

The major theme, however, was not theological or political, but economic. Against a backdrop of soaring inflation, corporate representatives deluged Washington with seemingly scientific studies of the disastrous economic consequences of regulation prepared by the Chemical Manufacturers Association, the American Petroleum Institute, the Business Roundtable, and the American Enterprise Institute's Center for the Study of American Business. They soon succeeded in altering the framework of regulatory analysis and decision-making to include close assessment of compliance costs. In 1976, President Ford issued an Executive Order calling for "inflation impact statements" (later, "economic impact statements") for all regulatory decisions. The Ford move was later seconded by Jimmy Carter in his general order for systematic regulatory review.[17]

According to science advisor Press, Carter at first viewed regulatory reform as a way of eliminating paperwork for business, but soon after taking office began to realize the "enormous impact of regulation, an idea brought home to him by outside industrial leaders" and Charles Schultze of the Council of Economic Advisors, an authority on the "economic alternatives to regulation."[18] Just before joining the Carter administration, Schultze warned an audience at Harvard that government "is imposing command and control solutions over an ever-widening sphere of social and economic activity."[19] Once settled with the Carter team, Schultze initiated a general review of regulatory activities, working through the Council on Wage and Price Stability (headed by Barry Bosworth), the newly formed Regulatory Analysis and Review Group (headed by William Nordhaus), and the OSTP (headed by Press, who was also a member of RARG and whose office did work for COWPS on regulatory analysis). These White House groups worked, as Michael Baram has observed, "in a setting of free-wheeling *ex parte* contacts between presidential aides and the agencies," pressuring the regulators, with the weight of the White House, into the "tradeoffs" and compromises before executive power described by Kahn. COWPS analyses, though sanctioned by the OSTP, were never articulated for the public, Congress, or the courts. Both "significant" and "unaccountable," they go far to explain the dulling of regulations on photochemical oxidants, acrylonitrile and toxic substances in general, airbags, noise pollution, and coal emissions, to name but a few.[20]

The backroom activities of the White House groups did not go unnoticed or uncriticized. Nicholas Ashford, for example, chairman of OSHA's science advisory board, declared them "antidemocratic." And Senator Edmund Muskie called for hearings before the Senate Subcommittee on Environmental Pollution "to assess the merit, legality, and political ramifications of the economic-oriented White House groups' role in environmental regulation." But business interests were generally delighted with the development. Jeffrey Joseph, director of government and regulatory affairs of the U.S. Chamber of Commerce, voiced the dominant business view when he told a *Newsweek* reporter, "It's very helpful to have the Administration's economists whacking away at all this."[21]

The courts were another arena for the corporate counterattack, as trade associations such as the American Petroleum Institute and Chemical Manufacturers Association kept EPA and OSHA swamped in litigation. Here too the primary focus has been on the costs of regulation, with plaintiffs demanding compliance with Executive Orders, cost-benefit analyses of protections before implementation, and a standard of proof for claiming adverse effects of products and processes that defies the present capacities of science. The legal campaign has recently scored impressive victories with the Supreme Court decisions on benzene and cotton dust standards, which push OSHA to do more quantitative cost-benefit analysis and risk assessment. As *Newsweek* reported, "Carter's anti-inflationists contend that the benzene case is a classic example of the kind of cost-benefit analysis that must now be done if the burden of regulation is to be cut." Thus the legal battles, which delay and neutralize regulations, are intimately tied in with the industry-sponsored promotion of new and seemingly scientific methodologies for risk assessment. These have the double effect of depoliticizing debates over environmental safety and reestablishing an antidemocratic regime of technical expertise.[22]

Meanwhile, the courts are being prepared for the continued legal attack on regulation. At the University of Miami's Center for Law and Economics, funded by Exxon, Mobil, General Electric, IBM, Alcoa, and other firms, federal judges are receiving training in "economics" designed to give them "a significantly new perspective on the world." This "new perspective" is one which sees government as inefficiency incarnate, and regulation as an assault on freedom itself. The center is directed by Henry Manne, a corporate lawyer who has undertaken to demolish what he calls the "myth of corporate responsibility." "Every time businessmen acknowledge a public interest in what they do," Manne warns, "they invite political control of their activities." At Manne's center in Miami, interested judges learn how to write decisions against such outside political control couched in the new (old) norms of market efficiency.[23]

Whether in the media, in Washington, or in the courts, however, the campaign against government regulation, even in its most sweepingly ideological free market form, remained an essentially negative campaign, and almost transparently self-serving for corporate interests. To be credible, business needed to link the attack on regulation to a more positive program of general benefit capable of commanding widespread support and sacrifice. The second prong of the corporate counterattack provided this positive program in the form of a reinvention of the idea of progress, and its specific linkage to issues of industrial innovation and productivity.

The issue of industrial innovation had of course been around for some time, both in academic circles and the government. In the 1960s Herbert Hollomon raised the issue while assistant secretary of commerce, and the Charpie Report on innovation appeared in 1967. By the mid-1970s, a vast literature on the subject had emerged. People in the field tended to agree on at least three things. First, innovation appeared to be linked to small entrepreneurial firms. Second, large firms tended to retard innovation. Third, government regulation of the economy could be a boon to innovation in forcing changes in product and process design, such as in automobile design. There was also some agreement that innovation and economic growth were related and that it would therefore be good to have more innovation, although there was little agreement about how to stimulate it.

As the deregulation campaign gathered momentum in 1976 and 1977, innovation surfaced as a major issue in industry circles, but in this renewed discussion there was little mention of the stimulating effects of regulation or the retarding effects of monopoly or excessive scale. On the contrary, the call for innovation had become a new twist in the campaign *against* regulation. Thus Chemical Manufacturers Association president Robert Roland lamented that, because of regulation, "innovation has been stifled, productivity curtailed, inflation fueled, our ability to compete in foreign markets hampered and our domestic markets opened to cheaper foreign competition." John Connor of Allied Chemical likewise warned that if regulation were to continue "business will become increasingly reluctant to develop products." Eugene Berman of Du Pont observed that the 1975 TSCA regulations would have a "stifling effect on new chemicals development," and W. R. Corey of Monsanto predicted a "substantial drop-off in the commercialization of new chemicals" due to excessive government interference. More generally still, Procter & Gamble's Thomas Mooney warned that "we seem to be on the road to freezing science." Inevitably the link to economic growth was made. Hewlett Packard chairman David Packard concluded that "the mushrooming of government regulations is a major cause of the productivity decline in our economy over the last five or ten years . . . I think we have to recognize that what has taken place is a major change in our priorities—one which has slowed up growth by unduly emphasizing the environmental quality of life over our traditional goals of economic growth."[24] In short, regulations were cast as obstacles to innovation, science, productivity, growth, and progress.

The general theme was echoed in the major trade associations and industry think tanks. Already the industry-dominated National Academy of Engineering, at a 1976 meeting on technology, trade, and the U.S. economy, had concluded that "a general inquiry should be organized into all possible ways and means to foster technological innovation in the United States. This inquiry should range broadly over tax policy and incentives, regulatory policy, anti-trust practices and other federal laws and policies affecting innovation." The Industrial Research Institute was also discussing the problem. Established by research executives of science-based electrical and chemical firms back in 1938, the IRI has always been dominated by such corporate giants as Du Pont, Exxon, GE, Westinghouse, Procter & Gamble, American Cyanamid, Monsanto, Bell Labs (AT&T), ARCO, Merck, Pfizer, and the like. In September of 1979, IRI held a symposium on innovation in U.S. research. Most of the speakers echoed the new theme of innovation through deregulation. Hollomon was almost alone in voicing the things industry did not want to hear, when he pointed out that innovation "requires an economy not dominated by giant monopolies which cannot be entered by other firms who threaten the monopoly" and acknowledged the "excesses which industry is guilty of in the face of free goods, free air, free water, free places to dump refuse— instances where industry, because of the system we have, did not act in the social welfare." More typical of the speakers at the IRI meeting was Thomas Vanderslice of GTE, chairman of a Committee on Economic Development subcommittee on technology which had conducted a major new study on the stimulation of innovation and technological progress. Vanderslice outlined the study and reported its major recommendations. The report differed strikingly from Hollomon's position.[25]

The CED report argued first and foremost that there was a perceived decline in innovation and that this was a major cause of the decline in the rate of productivity. Neither the innovation lag nor the connection with productivity was substantiated (and indeed the phrase "perceived lag" later became widespread, presumably to avoid having to prove the innovation decline).[26] Nonetheless, the lag was attributed to excessive regulation, which created uncertainty and undue expense, tax policies that prevented the capital formation required for investment, and patent policies that were not uniform and failed adequately to reward innovators for risk-taking. To correct the situation and stimulate innovation, the CED recommended patent policy reform to allow *inter alia* contractor patents on government-funded research, a more liberal tax policy, and a significant reduction in regulatory uncertainty and expense. It also encouraged greater industry-university cooperation. The report warned against too much direct government involvement in stimulating innovation. It called for government support of basic research but urged caution, to "avoid interference with private sector research and development," and concentrated instead on possible "incentives" to innovation (tax and patent policy), and the removal of "disincentives" (regulations). "We see selectively enlarged direct federal support of research and development," Vanderslice concluded; "however, we believe that the other tax, regulations, and patent policy recommendations . . . are even more important" in stimulating innovation.[27]

The CED report on stimulating innovation was soon almost directly translated into official government policy in the area. How that translation came about is an interesting story. Frank Press, as we have seen, had already become deeply involved in the deregulation campaign as a member of RARG and as informal scientific aide to the COWPS, particularly in the latter's attack on EPA air pollution standards. He had also begun to work closely with OMB, particularly with Bowman Cutter (a former assistant to the president of North-West Industries, parent of Velsicol, a pesticide producer recently found guilty of withholding information from the EPA, and former assistant to the president of the *Washington Post*, whose chairman, Katherine Graham, was a director of Allied Chemical). In the summer of 1977, Press became aware of the industry innovation campaign then in the making. At an MIT seminar two years later he explained in detail how the Carter administration's position on innovation was developed.

"When I took the job at OSTP," said Press, "I went out of my way to meet with leaders of industry. I asked them what their concerns were, as opportunities for me to address important national problems. There was unanimous agreement that there was a perceived lag in innovation." "They couldn't prove it," Press continued, but industry leaders were sure that government was to blame for this lag, and they cited tax, regulatory, and patent policy as the prime offenders. Undaunted by the lack of evidence either of a lag in innovation or the relationship between previous government policy and this supposed decline, Press was moved by the industrial leaders' insistence. He concluded that "the time for innovation, as a policy issue, is here."

"From my point of view," Press explained to a Senate Commerce Committee subcommittee hearing in March 1979, "any improvement on innovation, whether we are behind or whether we are not behind, any improvement is bound to help this country, to improve its productivity growth, help in the fight against inflation, to help our balance of payments, to help in the creation of new jobs and services. And for this reason alone we should be concerned with enhancing innovation." At the MIT seminar, under challenge about the alleged lag in innovation, Press conceded again that the decline was unproved, but here too insisted that "whether or not there is a lag in innovation, spurring innovation is a good thing."

Accordingly, the president's science advisor picked up the industry banner and launched a major Domestic Policy Review study on innovation, only now he publicly assumed that there was indeed a serious decline in innovation and set about to identify the reasons for it and propose solutions. To direct the study, Press turned to Jordan Baruch in the Commerce Department. In private life Baruch is a member of the MIT Sloan School of Management faculty, and a director of the Cambridge-based engineering firm of Bolt, Baranek & Newman. He had long been involved in the industry discussions of the alleged innovation problem.[28] Meanwhile Press and OMB's Bowman Cutter went to work before Congress promoting the industry innovation campaign. Their statements before the House Committee on Science and Technology sound like transcripts of the Vanderslice report. "During the period . . . when we were formulating this policy," Press told the members of Congress, "we saw together a number of leaders in industry and we asked them their views. . . . They were not looking for large R&D expenditures; they were concerned about other Federal policies which affect their ability to innovate (patent, tax, and regulatory policies)." Press then offered his own views on the matter: "I think we have to examine this question from many points of view, not simply R&D support . . . we should examine all Federal policies that affect the ability of industry to innovate." Moreover, he went on, "we must rely on our competitive system to provide signals to the industrial sector" rather than government directives. Bowman Cutter also stressed the importance of market mechanisms rather than government interference, and proposed the creation of incentives and the removal of disincentives: "You won't see substantial investment in an area like this until you see a more predictable and better performing economy." "We must join together in providing an environment of stability," Press insisted. Chiming in was

Exxon's Edward David, who warned against "capricious government actions in various areas."[29]

As if the industry orientation were not clear enough, Press made it additionally plain. "Our approach is consistent with that of industrial leaders who ask the Federal Government for a climate that fosters innovation, rather than for direct support of R&D with near-term commercial pay-off." The Baruch innovation study itself, he continued, "reflects very extensive collaboration between the Administration and industry." The Domestic Policy Review was intended to provide the president "with guidance as to possible modifications of policy that would improve the climate for innovation." Addressing the IRI a while later, Press again left no room for doubt: "The focus of our work is . . . on the various ways that the decisions-makers in the country's industrial firms can be provided with better incentives and opportunities to stimulate innovation. . . . Just as important as providing various incentives for industrial innovation is reducing the disincentives to the innovation process. . . . [T]he Administration is attuned to industry's views on this, and regulatory reform has been one of its major efforts."

Frank Press, science advisor to the president, had become an industry lobbyist in the White House. The Domestic Policy Review on innovation that Baruch developed in Commerce, reviewed by the OMB and CEA and passed on to the president by the OSTP, was no more than the industry campaign against regulation, now sanctioned by science and presidential authority. Finally appearing in October 1979 (three months after publication of the CED report), the review echoed the CED's call for less regulation, extensive patent reform, and increased government-funded industry-university cooperation in research.[30] Business leaders praised this near-total White House capitulation to industry demands on the innovation issue as a breakthrough in creative policymaking. Even after the Carter defeat, IRI spokesman Jules Blake published a letter in *Science* magazine defending the record of the OSTP. "During the last four years," Blake wrote, "there has been important interaction established by the OSTP with the industrial research community. Furthermore, this interaction was carried out without an adversarial relationship which sometimes obtains between industrial and Federal agencies. The interactions were frequent and led to the involvement of many industrial researchers in activities such as the Domestic Policy Review on Technological Innovation. We in the research and development community feel that our voice has been heard and that we have made a contribution."[31] Indeed they had.

The innovation campaign, an affirmative transformation of the corporate attack on regulation and government-generated "uncertainty," set the stage for the more sweeping "reindustrialization" crusade. At the core of this bipartisan movement were the same concerns about regulation, tax policy, and the assault on free enterprise, only now they were integrated into a broader canvas depicting general American decline. The causes for the decline, according to industry leaders, included regulation and the famous lag in innovation, but also high wages and, perhaps most critically, popular expectations that had "outpaced" reality. Although the origins of the reindustrialization campaign have been traced variously to Congressman Jack Kemp and resident White House sociologist Amitai Etzioni, it was really developed first in the business community, and then raised to political maturity within the White House by Carter aides William Drayton and Stuart Eisenstat.[32]

As early as 1972 the National Planning Association, a liberal management organization first established in the 1930s, issued a special committee report called "Changes in National Priorities during the 1960's: Implications for 1980." Committee members included representatives from Hoffman LaRoche, GE, ITT, Exxon, Western Electric, Babcock & Wilcox, and Northeast Utilities (many of whom had been recent targets of antinuclear demonstrations). They noted with alarm the "shift in priorities" that had taken place in the 1960s as a result of an expanding economy, political ferment, and the extension of democratic processes. All these developments pointed to continuously rising aspirations and expectations among the working population: "Americans are demanding many more services from government in education, health, law enforcement, pollution control, recreation, social welfare, and other areas," the report observed, all of which require "the transfer of more of the economy's resources from the private to the public sector." If continued, the NPA committee warned, the trend could lead to inflation, expectations outstripping resources, deepening balance of payments deficits, and a weakening of the American competitive position in world markets.[33]

Two years later, at a series of meetings sponsored by the Conference Board, leaders of America's largest corporations addressed themselves to similar problems and generally anticipated the deregulation, innovation, and reindustrialization campaigns. Attending the meetings were Leonard Silk and David Vogel, who later reported that "the central tension of American capitalism, according to the common business view, is between people's rising aspirations and the inability of the American economic system to satisfy them without weakening its long-term viability." The executives themselves phrased the challenge in less academic terms: "Desires are becoming necessities." "More and more goods and services are being classified as necessities rather than luxuries." "The public is demanding more and more goods. If they can't get them through the marketplace, they will get them through government." Some of the executives blamed themselves for the problem: "We have been hoist by our own petard. We have raised expectations that we can't deliver on." "We have promised too much." "We have created our own Frankenstein monster." Others blamed rabble rousers: "We must deflate false expectations planted by demagogues." But all agreed on the common threat to industry: "We may be engulfed by a rising tide of entitlement."[34]

Thus by the mid-1970s corporate leaders had come to the conclusion that they had to deflate expectations and discipline a population reared upon corporate promises of the past.[35] Voicing the new consensus of the business community, Du Pont's Irving Shapiro, chairman of the Business Roundtable, declared: "There has to be a return to a period of more self-restraint. . . . People have to disavow some of the things they have come to expect. The public sector is taking too much of the wealth that is being created." Initiated by the business community, relayed by the media, authorized by the White House, and legitimated by the apparent imperatives of science and technology, the industry campaigns against regulation, and for innovation and reindustrialization, were all opening moves in the massive project of turning back public expectations of industry and government. But they only treated symptoms of what was considered a deeper and more persistent problem, the "disease" apparent in a political system still sufficiently open that it permitted such expectations to gain articulation and public authority. Now business resolved to treat the disease. "While critics of business worry about the atrophy of American democracy," Silk and Vogel observed, "the concern in the nation's boardrooms is precisely the opposite. For an executive, democracy in America is working all too well—that is the problem."[36]

Thus business developed the third prong of its counterattack: the direct assault on democracy itself. Industrial leaders resolved to get more involved in direct political action, and simultaneously to transform the political system, rendering it more compatible with modern realities. Always the assault on democracy was cast in terms of a need for a more efficient, competent, streamlined government to match the technologically sophisticated requirements of a changed political economy. Science and technology, not counterrevolution, demanded the abandonment of democratic norms. In the new formulation, democracy had become not the hallmark of Enlightenment, but of popular reaction, not the highest expression of progress, but its major obstacle.[37]

At meetings sponsored by the Conference Board in 1975, business executives delared that "we can no longer muddle through." "We don't have a democratic system designed for coping with the modern world." The American system was decried as "inefficient and unpredictable." "Our government is simply not organized to make cost-benefit analysis." Koppers chairman Fletcher Byrom, vice-chairman of the CED, declared that "under conditions of today's technology" democracy has become an anachronism. He later called for a constitutional convention to begin restructuring the American political system in the name of modern technology. For the executives present, such a restructuring was both welcome and necessary, and need not even entail the abandonment of democratic forms. Democracy would remain, but drained of political content. As one participant pointed out, "the market is more democratic than the government" anyway, since in the market "every person gets a vote every day."[38]

The industrialists at the Conference Board meetings were not the only business leaders preoccupied with the new problem of democracy. The Trilateral Commission's study, *The Crisis of Democracy,* was also published in

1975. The authors of the report were authorities on Western Europe, the United States, and Japan. They had been commissioned to grapple with the question "Is political democracy, as it exists today, a viable form of government for the industrial countries of Europe, North America, and Asia?" Samuel P. Huntington, professor of government at Harvard, undertook to answer the question for the United States.

Huntington addressed the issue from the perspective of one who had spent much of his career among the elite circles of government, consulting for the State Department, the Pentagon, and the White House. For him, the previous decade had been marked by a "democratic distemper," an "excess of democracy" that posed a serious threat to established government. His description of the 1960s and early 1970s characterized the period as marked by "privatistic youth," "oppositional adversary intellectuals" who had not been sobered by the experience of governing, an iconoclastic liberal media, a "reassertion of Congress" and the related weakening of the institution of the presidency, an excess of bureaucratic interference in the economy, rising expectations and increasing popular demands on a government whose legitimate authority had been seriously diminished, a decline in the strength of the traditional political parties, the related inclusion of heretofore "marginal groups" in the political process, and a general instability and "overloading" of the institutions of government. In short, Huntington concluded, there had been a dangerous "democratic surge" during the previous decade, and a barely tolerable widespread "democratic challenge to authority."

"Truman had been able to govern the country with the cooperation of a relatively small number of Wall Street lawyers and bankers," Huntington observed, but by the mid-1960s "the course of power in society had diversified tremendously and this was no longer possible." The result had been a "decline in the governability of democracy at home," and an ensuing "decline in the influence of democracy abroad." To restore order, he recommended "a greater degree of moderation in democracy"—that is, less democracy. In particular, he called for the strengthening of the presidency, the restoration of confidence in the political process coupled with the exercise of tighter party discipline over that process, and a restriction of democratic claims in the name of rationality, efficiency, and competence. Again, the attack on democratic forms and processes is promoted in the name of science and expertise: "The arenas where democratic procedures are appropriate are, in short, limited. . . . In many situations, the claims of expertise, seniority, experience and special talents may override the claim of democracy as a way of constituting authority."[39]

For business leaders, the restoration of public confidence in government and in the virtues of working within the system that Huntington called for had to go hand in hand with a restoration of corporate control over the political system. Otherwise the "crisis of democracy" would only worsen. This was the theme of a 1976 CED conference on major challenges likely to face our economy in the future. The session was chaired by MIT faculty member and former presidential economic advisor Carl Kaysen, who also serves as a German Marshall Fund trustee, member of the CED advisory board, and a director of Polaroid.

Like his counterparts at the Conference Board and Trilateral Commission, Kaysen described what he called the "increasing and accelerating democratization of the polity," a process characterized by the decline of political parties and the valorization of "issue group" politics at the expense of "interest group" politics. "The biggest change is that the equity issues have come increasingly to the fore," together with an "adversary stance . . . enhanced by recent changes in the political process, by the emphasis on wide public participation, on openness, on the avoidance of or control over conflicts of interest." Kaysen noted that the educational level of the population was on the rise, and reminded the audience that "it is known that political activism rises with the level of education. Thus the nation is producing a population that will be more interested in political activity, more ready to listen to the kinds of political entrepreneurs who create issue politics, whether they are called the Friends of the Earth or Defenders of the Consumer or the Preachers of Energy Doom or the Savers of the Rare Species."[40] "In some respects," he continued, "this change is a good thing. If we Americans believe our own professions of the democratic faith we can only welcome a process that brings a larger share of the population into active political life and engagement in the political process. On the other hand . . . it must be recognized that interest groups (e.g. corporate interest groups) tend to have a long political life and a high degree of persistence while issue groups tend to be more volatile." In order to foster stability within the system, Kaysen recommended the restrengthening of interest groups, and a reassertion of their control over the political system. He argued finally that "realistic solutions to the problems . . . may increasingly require a negotiating process of accommodation in detail, a tolerance of asymmetry and discrimination and differentiation impossible to achieve in a legalistic, public, adversary process." In other words, a more controlled political process with state-sanctioned power hierarchies and the erosion of democratic and juridical norms.[41]

A final example of the new business consensus on democracy is offered by the November 1980 issue of Du Pont's house magazine *Context*. There, in an article entitled "Five Directions for Government Reform," Brookings Institution scholar James Sundquist both crystallizes corporate thinking on democracy over the past five years and reflects renewed industrial confidence in treating the disease. Echoing the sentiments of business leaders, Huntington's Trilateral report, Kaysen, and others, Sundquist calls for a strengthening of traditional political parties, a restoration of presidential leadership to correct the "Congressional excesses of the last decade," a rationalization of the process of selecting presidents (to overcome the "extreme hazard that can lie in leaving the nominating process almost wholly to millions of rank and file voters," a situation resulting from the shift to direct primaries in both parties after 1968), and the creation of a "corps of professional government managers" grounded in scientific management techniques and evaluated by merit rather than political affiliation.[42] "To move in these directions will not be easy," Sundquist acknowledged; "Many of the necessary changes go against the trends of many decades, against settled patterns of political behavior, against popular attitudes and conceptions." Yet he confidently predicted that "we can begin to make progress in improving the competence of government only when we recognize that our problems are not in our leaders . . . but in the *system* that produces the leaders and which, after their election, obstructs and hampers them" (emphasis in original).[43] Democracy, in short, must give way to managerial competence.

The effects of the corporate campaign against the "democratic distemper" are already evident in renewed calls to strengthen the authority of the president, civil service reforms geared to the creation of an elite corps of government executives accountable and loyal only to the White House, bipartisan efforts to reform the presidential nominating process, a tightening of party discipline within Congress, the restriction of government support for mass education (together with a major shift toward industry support in the elite schools), an increasingly successful counterattack on equal opportunity, affirmative action, and antidiscrimination legislation, the rationalization of the regulatory process to curb citizen participation in the name of efficiency, and legislation requiring cost-benefit and risk assessment analysis by appointed experts for all regulatory decisions prior to enactment and implementation.

The rationale for many of these measures has been "science," which has now taken on an extended and distorted meaning that includes dominant conceptions of efficiency, competence, predictability, uniformity, stability, and control. Science thus appears as "management," where management in turn means increasingly authoritarian command over the myriad exigencies of a high-technology-based, corporate-dominated political economy. In the view of industrial planners, democracy is too slow, too unwieldy, and too uncertain to respond to private imperatives in a competitive international system. Thus democracy must be reduced to techniques of management, but these in turn require a legitimacy no longer provided in an atrophied democratic process. As a source of values and consensus which are claimed to lie beyond the commands of politics and power, science appears finally as legitimation. The fourth prong of the corporate counterattack—the remystification of expertise and the revival and extension of industry links to academic establishments—makes this legitimating function explicit.

The role of science as legitimator for undemocratic government action is most obvious in the ongoing "rationalization" of policy evaluation. Seemingly scientific methodologies which have evolved from business cost accounting, such as cost-benefit analysis and, more recently, quantitative risk assessment, are urged by industry and the new breed of professional policy analyst as guidelines for government action. "Whether government understands, accepts and applies risk benefit analysis to regulation," Monsanto's John Hanley has observed, "will be the most consequential question facing the chemical industry in the 1980's." Indeed, despite the often cited and widely acknowledged technical, logical, epistemological, political, and moral shortcomings of such evaluation techniques (MIT Professor James Fay, a jaded expert in the various methods, crystallizes all the criticism in calling them "scientific pornography"), they are fast becoming the dominant, hegemonic paradigm for policy analysis and decision-making.

There is little cause for wonder here, since the use of such techniques offers the user many distinct advantages. Perhaps most important, they provide a seeming monopoly on rationality itself, relegating all qualitative and subjective reflection on policy matters to the realm of irrationality and naked emotion, eliminating at a stroke people's reliance upon experience and intuition (analysts are most proud of their counter-intuitive results) as a guide to judgment. Democratic responsibilities are surrendered to adroit experts who are more than willing to place popular concerns "in perspective." All but the technically initiated are excluded from the debate from the outset, forced to become spectators rather than participants in the central political struggles of the day. Once restricted to the depoliticized realm of "objective analysis," policy evaluation neutralizes passions and abandons principle. In the alchemy of the experts, horrible "bads" are magically transformed into relative "goods," "wrongs" into "rights." "So It's a Carcinogen," *The New York Times* conceded after the Supreme Court decision on benzene, "But How Bad?"

Anything goes in this new utilitarianism. Everything is subject to "tradeoff," including human lives. The scientistic techniques obscure the political questions of equity, justice, power, and social welfare behind a technocratic haze of numbers, substituting statistics for issues and the calculations of a few for the judgment of many. For the growing army of professional analysts, the techniques afford an opportunity to display hard-won technical competence and to achieve some scientific respectability, even to do good, without requiring any untidy or risky confrontation with power. For already harassed and intimidated regulators, the new techniques forced upon them by the White House and the courts keep them busy, though not with regulation. OSHA officials, for example, estimate that the new economic impact assessments required by the White House have extended from three to six years the time required to put a new regulation into effect. In short, the methods of what *Science* magazine has called a "new religion" have added to the corporate arsenal in its campaign against regulation and democracy, rigorously and routinely ratifying the status quo in the name of science.[44]

Industry cost-benefit and risk analysis studies now abound, proffered in support of corporate-sponsored legislation by the Chemical Manufacturers Association, the Chemical Industry Institute of Toxicology, the American Petroleum Institute, the Business Roundtable, and a host of consulting firms. But business leaders well understand that industry studies lack in credibility whatever they have in the way of support resources. In their search for scientific legitimation, industry has again discovered that academic and professional associations can provide both at a cost-effective price.

Industry spokesmen like Hanley of Monsanto have long considered the National Academy of Sciences the prime candidate for an "impartial science court," and not without reason. Since its revival by George Ellery Hale during the World War I preparedness campaign, the academy has functioned as a clearinghouse for corporate science. Under the recent guidance of president Philip Handler (who doubles as a director at Squibb–Beech-Nut), the academy has been prepared for a major new role in the corporate campaign. In his last presidential address, outgoing president Handler (who has been succeeded by Frank Press of OSTP) exhorted his colleagues to condemn the "charlatans" and "nay-sayers" in their midst, those who impetuously sound the alarm on environmental and health hazards and harp on questions of academy conflict of interest. In the same talk, Handler hinted at the group's future functions.

"Substantial external pressures seek to enlarge our role in educating the public to understand relative risks," he explained, "among tnem a consortium of chemically-oriented companies that would like to encourage legislation that would call upon the Academy to study and render judgments on risks of all types associated with chemicals utilized in industry. . . . Another group of companies has requested us to sponsor a meeting on the role of science in guiding public policy in regulating carcinogens." In response to these and other requests, the academy has created a committee on risk and decision-making. Chaired by Harvard Business School and Kennedy School of Government professor Howard Raiffa, the committee will serve as a mechanism for the "scientific" oversight and review of the regulatory process.[45]

The National Academy of Sciences, of course, is only the tip of the iceberg. As the composition of its own newly formed risk committee indicates, consulting authorities and the respectability they bring to corporate social policy are ultimately to be found in the secular churches of academia. It is the universities that serve as the industrial research centers, the stables for mobile experts, and the suppliers of a whole new generation of risk accountants. More important, the universities offer droves of professional academics willing to purify, resurrect, and sermonize about the new (old) gospels of market economics and progress, while at the same time lending an aura of science to the hackwork of cruder corporate "analysts."

For the third time in this century, the universities are undergoing a major transformation, both in response to a fundamental shift in the political and economic climate and in preparation for a new, enlarged role in corporate policymaking. During the first decades of the century, the elite liberal arts colleges were expanded and rapidly transformed into research and training centers for the then emergent science-based electrical and chemical industries. In the 1940s the universities' primary ties were transferred from private industry to the federal government (although the ties with industry were never severed) as they became centers of contract research for the military and other branches of government. This phase reached its full flowering in the think tank multiversity of the 1960s. Now the universities are shifting their primary allegiance back to the private sector, in response to a new corporate-initiated courtship and grave financial problems and out of resistance to government red tape and scrutiny. In this new phase, the universities are being geared to provide research and training in new industrial areas—notably semiconductors, automation, and biotechnology—and to bestow scientific legitimacy and ideological sanction upon the corporate campaigns for deregulation, innovation, and reindustrialization, and against democracy.

Industry's drive for closer collaboration with academia nicely complements the needs of the universities. The universities themselves, of course, had experienced firsthand the "democratic distemper" of SDS, the antiwar movement, civil rights, equal opportunity legislation, and the critical challenge to the corporate service center, military think tank conception of higher education. Thus they are well attuned to the corporate campaign against the "excesses" of the last decade and a half. Moreover, having restored order on the campus and recaptured the administration building, university leaders find themselves confronting falling enrollments, fiscal austerity, and mounting demands from the government for accountability and affirmative action. Not surprisingly, they see corporations as their knights in shining armor. What Exxon's Ed David calls the "industrial connection" offers a promising new source of funds and welcome respite from government scrutiny. According to the annual survey of the *Chronicle of Higher Education,* universities have, in the last three years, received the largest increase in industrial financial support since 1920, when the *Chronicle* began its survey.

Emboldened by this infusion of private support, the universities have begun to denounce government "interference" as passionately as they not so long ago welcomed it. Thus Charles Overberger, vice-president for research at the University of Michigan, complains about recent limitations on the peer-review system, which in the past gave the universities control over government funding (and enabled private colleges to become state-supported without surrendering the prerogatives of private control), challenges to indirect costing practices, restrictions on faculty salaries, and the growing emphasis on accountability in government research contracts. MIT's Jerome Wiesner, former science advisor to Presidents Kennedy and Johnson, rails against "arbitrary political pressure on research" as he witnesses the erosion of the once cozy arrangements worked out by Vannevar Bush (MIT), James Conant (Harvard), Frank Jewett (AT&T), and others for a state-supported, professionally controlled, private research establishment.[46]

In the controversy over the OMB Circular A21, which called for greater fiscal accountability from universities, academia's own campaign against regulation moved into high gear. Echoing the corporate innovation theme, Wiesner, for example, protested vigorously that alleged attempts to "shackle (the universities) to a detailed and rigid set of nationally administered rules and regulations . . . swap progress for administrative convenience." He bemoaned the "erosion of mutual confidence, the spirit of collaborative partnership with the government," and decried what he labeled "despotic regulation." "What we need and what the country now needs," said Wiesner, "is regulation of regulation." Happily enough for the universities, the A21 crisis was resolved through a softening of OMB demands that followed the intervention of Bowman Cutter. But widespread academic resistance to government "interference" remains on the rise, reflected most clearly in the orientation of the Sloan Commission on Government and Higher Education's 1980 report, of which Carl Kaysen was research director. From all the colleges and universities surveyed, Sloan Foundation president Nils Wessell reported, "we have been hearing expressions varying from concern to frustration to disbelief regarding the enlarging influence of government on their affairs. The mutually beneficial relationship between government and higher education characteristic of the years immediately following World War II has given way to an atmosphere of friction and confrontation. Growing involvement of the government with higher education is producing growing tensions." Thus the universities' own concerns about government interference dovetail perfectly with industry's concern. The universities are sensitive to the challenges confronting corporate America, and primed to aid business in confronting them.[47]

In addition to the business schools, which serve industry directly, there are centers, schools, and institutes that provide legitimation for the political corporate campaign and an educational fast track for entry into the higher levels of management and government service. The Woodrow Wilson School of Public and International Affairs at Princeton is one, and the new School of Management and Public Policy at Yale (headed by German Marshall Fund treasurer William H. Donaldson) is another. But the center of such academic action in support of corporate policymaking is the Kennedy School of Government at Harvard, including its Institute of Politics. It is not hard to explain the corporate, liberal orientation of this institution, with an outside advisory committee consisting of high-ranking executives from such firms as IBM, ARCO, Hewlett-Packard, Raytheon, TRW-Fujitsu, Texas Instruments, Xerox, Du Pont, Tosco (formerly Monsanto's oil business), Exxon, Chase, Salomon Brothers, Goldman Sachs, First Security Trust, U.S. Trust, Time, CBS, and NBC. Such industry integration into the school's institutional structure is reciprocated by school faculty integration into industry and select business associations. Graham Allison, dean of the Kennedy School, is one of a handful of academics invited to join the Trilateral Commission, for example.

The Kennedy School, which is now undergoing a significant expansion of facilities, is engaged in the whole range of industry policy concerns. Just established is the new Executive Sessions Center, devoted to fostering closer business-government relations through the medium of high-level intimate brainstorming sessions among corporate and government leaders. "Universities can help provide the knowledge and understanding from which a new working partnership between business and government can be constructed," Dean Allison explains. "An excessively litigious society paralyzed by conflicting goals and a rapidly changing set of problems needs to explore new ways to develop informal consensus and mutual accommodation." School faculty are well on their way to accommodation. At a recent conference between Kennedy School advisory committee members and the staff of the school's Energy and Environmental Policy Center— held in the school's avant garde ARCO forum—the faculty voted unanimously against government controls on oil prices, to the delight of the corporate executives. In addition to a wide range of energy-related studies, the center conducts research on risk assessment (funded by the utilities industry Electric Power Research Institute and the General Electric Foundation), with an emphasis on chemical carcinogens and regulation. Faculty there are currently exploring economic alternatives to such "command and control" regulatory legislation as the Clean Air Act.

Elsewhere at the Kennedy School, the Faculty Project on Regulation, headed by Christopher DeMuth, is also at work on economic alternatives to existing regulatory policy, and is currently promoting the idea of a "regulatory budget" that would place a ceiling on government regulatory expenditures while providing for White House oversight through a proposed OMB office of regulatory budget. The project does additional work on risk assessment and cost-benefit analysis in the regulatory context, and conducts a regular seminar series on regulation. Prominent business leaders are commonly invited to address this seminar, thus assuring faculty and students steady exposure to industry concerns. On a recent visit, David Rockefeller endorsed the Business Roundtable's recent legislative recommendations on regulation, which call for cost-benefit analysis for all regulatory actions, a mandatory "economic review" before implementation, and "executive oversight of regulatory bodies." "In order to achieve the acceptable goals of regulation in a constantly changing world," Rockefeller declared, "the U.S. must enlist the cooperation of the world's most qualified experts in change: the nation's businesses." Bolstered by their intimate connection with "experts in change," institutions like the Kennedy School lend corporate power a veneer of academic respectability while servicing business with a stream of risk accountants and other properly habituated students well on their way to corporate, foundation, academic, and government posts.[48]

Because of their traditional respectability and aura of objectivity, their relative immunity from public scrutiny and challenges of conflict of interest, and their identification with "pure science," universities provide the perfect vehicle for current corporate campaigns. Moreover, the elitism endemic to the most powerful schools ideally complements and reinforces the corporate campaign against democracy and "the masses." Industry is well aware of all this. In a recent address to academics at MIT, Du Pont's Edward Kane, for example, argued that "none of us is well-served by inefficient and uneconomic regulations. You in the universities are in a good position to present the argument and point the policy-makers to sensible decisions." And in *The Regulation Game,* a recently published how-to book for managers, authors Bruce Owen and Ronald Brautigan explicitly advised businessmen on how to use university personnel to their best advantage. "Regulatory policy is increasingly made with participation of experts," they commented, "especially academics. A regulated firm or industry should be prepared whenever possible to co-opt these experts. This is most effectively done by identifying the leading experts in each relevant field and hiring them as consultants or advisors, or giving them research grants and the like. This activity requires a modicum of finesse; it must not be too blatant, for the experts themselves must not recognize that they have lost their objectivity and freedom of action."[49] But corporations have also moved beyond the crude tactics of individual cooptation to a strategy of institutional cooptation on a grand scale. In their search for legitimacy, they are buying into basic laboratory science, toxicology, epidemiology, and other areas of public health, as well as policy-oriented disciplines such as economics, political science, and management, and creating from scratch new "policy institutes" on campuses throughout the country. In all these fields, the leased school will provide the reams of data, the scientific publications, the cost-benefit and risk assessment analyses, the policy recommendations, and the new generation of students lured by ample fellowships, new programs, and large research grants. Industry will provide some cash.

Exactly how such extensive industry tie-ins to universities are orchestrated is illustrated by the recent experiences of three elite universities: Harvard, MIT, and Stanford. Beginning roughly in the spring of 1978, during the height of the corporate deregulation advertising campaign, both Stanford and MIT received requests from industry to begin discussion on the problems of risk and regulation.[50] In November of that year, the provosts of the two schools sent memoranda to selected faculty members soliciting comment. At MIT, it was suggested that a faculty group be formed to explore "the problem of assessing and coping with risks resulting from scientific and technological innovation." This faculty workshop, it was hoped, would ultimately launch "a serious long-term investigation, for which outside funding would be sought." This early initiative by then–MIT provost (and Kaiser Industries director) Walter Rosenblith culminated in a new MIT-Harvard Joint Program on the Impact of Chemicals on Human Health and the Environment.

The central thrust of the program was indicated in the report of a

Harvard committee formed to consider that university's participation: "While strenuous efforts are being made and will continue to be made to prevent the further introduction of deleterious substances into the environment and, if possible, to eliminate those already present, one cannot believe that such efforts will ever be completely successful. Accordingly, there is now and will continue to be a need to deal in an ablative sense with the effects of exposure to one or another of these man-made environmental contaminants." In October 1979 the program was formally unveiled by MIT president (and Celanese director) Jerome Wiesner, bringing together under one umbrella health sciences, environmental sciences and engineering, regulatory policy analysis, and the resources of the schools of law, government, management, medicine, public health, and arts and sciences.[51] The new program's dominant theme faithfully reflected broad industry concerns.

Christopher DeMuth, a Harvard participant and director of the Kennedy School Project on Regulation, observed: "There is growing agreement among scholars that the process of adversarial regulation suffers from inherent shortcomings." These include what DeMuth characterized as a "disregard of fundamental economic aspects of regulation and a well nigh universal suppression of innovation and competition, and protracted and unnecessary disputes between business and government over information disclosures, plant inspections, etc." Accordingly, he and his colleague suggested that economic alternatives to traditional regulatory policy must be explored. Funding for the joint program has already been forthcoming from the Chemical Manufacturers Association, Dow, Monsanto, Exxon, and Du Pont, and Wiesner noted in his formal opening announcement that the search was underway for further funding "at a level that will make such an ambitious program possible." Meanwhile, Provost Rosenblith and his academic and corporate colleagues look forward to the establishment of a "new institution whose competence, objectivity, and integrity would be unquestioned."[52]

At Stanford, three thousand miles away, early expressions of industry interest brought a call from the provost's office for a conference on risk assessment and regulation centered on a similar notion of an "objective, unbiased examination of risk." As a university statement phrased it, "the current drive to reduce risk through government regulation is having and can have a severe negative impact on business, the economy and society, far out of proportion to the benefits society can expect to gain. . . . Over-regulation, based upon emotion rather than sound science and logic, can soon become socially unacceptable. . . . There is now a strong need for an objective examination of these issues." Here too the challenge is to depoliticize debates over risk and regulation by conjuring up an "objective" basis for decision-making, and in the process to defuse the political energies that gave rise to the protective legislation in the first place. After toying with the symposium idea for a while, the Stanford administration and faculty decided that rather than merely talking about these problems, they would prefer to pursue some long-term projects with industry. Recently, preliminary negotiations with B. F. Goodrich and other firms began to yield plans for a collaborative approach to the regulation problem.[53]

The corporate invasion of academia is not restricted to the scientific and policy-oriented disciplines. Beyond the need for scientific credibility, industry must gain broader sanction for its political campaign. In recent years it has turned as well to the social sciences and humanities. Throughout the United States, interdisciplinary programs bringing together philosophers, historians, sociologists, and political scientists, as well as representatives from the "harder" technical fields, have been established to explore the social and political implications of technological choice. Funded heavily by the Sloan (General Motors), Mellon (Gulf), and Exxon foundations, they are known generally as "science, technology and society" programs. Among the first was a program at Cornell, founded and directed by Franklin A. Long (a trustee of the Sloan Foundation and a director at Exxon). Cornell researchers are closely connected with such institutions as the OECD and German Marshall Fund, and have been distinguished by their extensive studies on citizen participation in technological decision-making. Probably the most ambitious program was the one set up at MIT in 1977, at the initiative of Wiesner, Rosenblith, and others. First directed by Donald Blackmer (formerly director of the Center for International Studies, where he was replaced by Eugene Skolnikoff, chairman of the German Marshall Fund), the MIT program includes Wiesner and Rosenblith among its membership. It is currently directed by Polaroid director Carl Kaysen (research director of the Sloan Commission on Government and Higher Education, advisor to the CED, and trustee of the German Marshall Fund). Current activities include symposia on risk, innovation, and reindustrialization.[54]

At Duke, Dartmouth, Cornell, Pace, Colorado, Northern Michigan, and other universities, the corporate connection with academia has also taken the form of "executives in residence" programs. Former Schaefer Corporation chairman Robert Lear, who is doing his residence at Columbia University, explains that his "major effort is to get more business executives more interested and more concerned as to what is being taught and researched at the school. . . . I'm a teacher . . . yet even in school I am still in business, still a part of the corporate scene." "The executives," Dean H. Jerome Zoffer of the University of Pittsburgh observes, "have an opportunity to plumb the contemporary student mind, and to participate in the training of their successors. And the students have an opportunity to see that executives are people like everyone else." The executives thus become "role models for the student body."

The hiring of executives as professors is one way of bringing the corporate scene directly into the academy. At the same time, corporations are finding ways of bringing academics directly into the corporate scene. Larger firms have long sponsored conferences for academics as a form of public relations. Having cut down on this sort of activity during the last decade and a half—when academic ties to corporations came under challenge—corporations are now beefing up their university affairs departments and trying new approaches. Du Pont is among the most ambitious. A full-time ambassador spends most of his time flying around the country, identifying established and up-and-coming academics. He then invites them to give lectures at Du Pont headquarters, attend seminars, write articles for Du Pont publications and otherwise become a part of the expanding corporate world.[55]

A particularly fertile area for industry-university cooperation has been the reindustrialization issue. Here the universities have performed a dual function, lending academic sanction to industry slogans, as at the spring 1980 Harvard conference on productivity,[56] and serving as an institutional conduit for taxpayer subsidies for industrial research and training.

At Cal Tech, the National Commission on Research, established in 1978, specifically endorsed the industrial research connection with universities. And little wonder. Members of the commission included Exxon's Edward David, Monsanto's Monte Thordahl, and Raymond Orbach (a UCLA physicist and consultant to the Aerospace Corporation, of which David is a director, along with William Carey). Officially charged "to study the relationship between the government and the research universities," the commission complemented the work of the Sloan Commission on Government and Higher Education, focusing upon accountability, peer review, alternative funding mechanisms, the development or research personnel, and industry-university-government relations. Funded primarily by the Exxon, Carnegie, Mellon, and Hewlett foundations (but also by the Air Force, Navy, DOE, and NSF), the commission issued its report, "Industry and the Universities: Developing Cooperative Research Relationships in the National Interest," in August 1980. Appropriately enough, the report begins with a quote from the industry-initiated Carter Domestic Policy Review, citing the famous alleged lag in innovation. It recommends that "the Federal Government encourage the application of research results to product development by permitting universities to retain title to inventions developed under federally-supported research," thereby assuring greater "financial rewards to universities and industry for assuming the risks of bringing highly uncertain scientific and technological programs to fruition and usefulness." "The Federal Government," the report points out, can "provide financial incentives to initiate and maintain closer industry-university ties," such as tax incentives, but recommends that government "encourage and support the relationship by becoming a facilitator rather than an ongoing participant in direction or management." Thus the proper role of government is one of simply providing seed money and then leaving the rest to the academic-industry partnership. Not surprisingly, the report concluded that "university-industry cooperative research relationships are beneficial and should be encouraged," and ends on the reassuring note that "hazards to university academic freedom from university-industry research relationships are manageable."[57]

With the blessings of the Commission on Research, not to mention the government, industry, and the universities themselves, the industry-university connection is growing apace. Although the relative decline in government support of university-based research has turned around, with a 70 percent increase in Department of Defense funding in the last three years (after a sharp dropoff during the "antiwar" decade), the overall trend is toward greater infusions of money from the private sector, stimulated by government incentives. Between 1955 and 1978, industrial support of academic research had dropped from 10 percent of overall support to less than 3 percent, while government support swelled. Now the pendulum is swinging back the other way. Universities are seeking long-term research support from corporations, free of government overhead and red tape, and corporations are seeking greater control over the direction of new scientific and technological developments and a greater proprietary interest in their commercialization.[58]

The financial infrastructure of the industrial connection includes government incentives for corporate-university cooperation in research, such as tax breaks and more direct government seed money for joint ventures (such as the National Science Foundation's and Department of Commerce's "generic technology centers" and "innovation centers"); long-term contracts in basic and applied research (such as recent Monsanto-Harvard and Exxon-MIT contracts); cooperative research agreements, involving several firms and one or more universities, which allow for joint efforts without any clear violation of antitrust laws (such as MIT's Polymer Processing Lab); reform of patent policy to foster uniformity from one contract to another and greater proprietary control over marketable research results; cross-fertilization between industry and universities, including institutionalized consultant relationships, personnel exchanges, visiting faculty appointments, more elaborate industry oversight of research and teaching (through advisory committees and the like); and more extensive contacts between students, faculty, and industrial recruiters. All these facets of the industrial connection are being promoted in the name of innovation, reindustrialization, and American industrial competitiveness.[59]

Thus far the major areas of research include industrial automation (for example, Rensselaer Polytechnic Institute's work on computer interactive graphics, with the International Business Machines Corporation, General Electric, Grumman, Lockheed, Prime Computer, and Bethlehem Steel; Carnegie-Mellon's collaboration with Westinghouse on a major NSF-funded robotics project; and Stanford's new Computer-Aided Design/Computer-Aided Manufacturing Center); integrated circuit design, especially for very large-scale integrated systems, at Cal Tech and MIT; materials structures and processing (Cornell's submicron structures lab, the University of Delaware's composite materials project, and the Polymer Processing Lab at MIT, which now involves some two hundred corporations, including such giants as ITT and GM). Elsewhere the new MIT-Exxon "combustion" project is touted as a model for long-term cooperative research. Calling for the expenditure of $8 million over ten years, the contract is one of the largest and longest in duration of any university-industry collaboration in research. MIT proposes the specific research projects from which Exxon selects the ones to be pursued, and Exxon gets an irrevocable, worldwide, nonexclusive, royalty-free license to any marketable results. MIT retains the patents. Exxon's Ed David, who negotiated the contract, sees it as an important step toward long-term industry-university partnership and predicts that before too long industry will be underwriting 10 to 15 percent of university-based research.

University-industry collaboration in automation and computer technology has been going on for decades. Much newer is the widespread cooperation in "biotechnology." This latest growth industry is likened to the electronics explosion of the 1950s and 1960s and reflects, first, major new advances in recombinant DNA technology which render heretofore arcane laboratory techniques adaptable to large-scale production and, second, the move of the petrochemical firms, by means of merger, acquisition, and research, into the agricultural products and pharmaceutical fields that will make the most use of the new production processes. As *Chemical Week* put it in a recent headline, "DNA Is on the Way to Chemicals." "The backdrop," explains Monsanto's Louis Fernandez, "is that many of our traditional businesses—plastics, fibers and organic and bulk chemicals—will be growing at a rate substantially less in the next ten years than in the previous decade or two. We see greater potential for growth in the life sciences." Accordingly, Monsanto recently named Howard Schneiderman, dean of the School of Biological Sciences at the University of California at Irvine, to be its new senior vice-president for research and development. Similar moves into the biological fields, and especially into the new microbiological world of recombinant DNA, have been made in recent years by Standard Oil of Indiana, Union Carbide, Standard Oil of California, Shell, and Occidental Petroleum.[60]

By far the most ambitious bit of collaboration in the biomedical area thus far is Monsanto's $23 million cancer research project at the Harvard Medical School. More recently, the Harvard School of Public Health established an industrial associates program—modeled on the industrial liaison program at MIT (and indeed, set up by a former administrator of the MIT program)—to keep fee-paying firms abreast of the latest developments in biotechnology and to foster individual and institutional consulting relationships and, possibly, more specific industry-sponsored research projects. In addition, Yale Medical School has established close ties with Miles Laboratory, and Stanford Medical School has stepped up plans for a new Institute of Biological and Clinical Investigation, which is essentially a biotechnology job shop. The architects of the institute "propose to develop a long-term continuous collaboration with the chemical, pharmaceutical and engineering industries." "Collaboration with industry," they go on, "will be businesslike, with contracts made by both parties involving commitment of the entire Department of Medicine faculty." Calling their program "a model of industry-university collaboration," the promoters claim to "see few liabilities, if any, in terms of academic freedom," and anticipate "no negative influence on individual initiatives."[61]

Such extensive industry-university collaboration on research projects of great commercial potential has inevitably led to a new species of university entrepreneurship. Reminiscent of the state-university "spinoffs" of the electronics revolution, a host of university-generated new genetic engineering firms have lately become the darlings of Wall Street. Like the electronics firms, the new biotechnology corporations profit from research paid for with public funds. Herbert Boyer of the University of California at San Francisco started the new wave when he founded Genentech in 1976. He has since been emulated by scientists at the University of Michigan, Harvard, and MIT, who have rushed to form new companies with names like Genex and Biogen. The stampede was stimulated by several factors, not the least of which, of course, were the advances in biotechnology itself. But other factors have included relaxed regulations on recombinant DNA work (even the controversial National Institutes of Health guidelines do not as yet apply to industry, although the hazards multiply with competitive commercial development), a flow of venture capital into this new growth sector, federal support for research in bioengineering, the support of (and acquisition by) capital-rich petrochemical companies, and the recent favorable Supreme Court decision on the patenting of living organisms.

Given such a favorable climate, universities such as Harvard and Yale have seriously contemplated and begun to organize for going into partnership with their own faculty. Neil Reimer, the chief of Stanford's office of technology licensing, is representative in his enthusiasm for the Supreme Court ruling, and looks forward to the day when Stanford's patents on bioengineering techniques could become "Stanford's Gaterade" (a reference to the commercially successful drink developed by researchers at the University of Florida).[62] Elsewhere Herbert Fusfeld, the director of NYU's Center for Science and Technology Policy (and former research director of Kennecott Copper, director of Hazeltine, member of the OECD "Expert Group," and past president of the Industrial Research Institute), editorialized in the July 1980 issue of *Science* that "strong industry participation in mission-oriented research institutes at universities and long-term projects between university research teams and single companies can provide opportunities for combining university research careers with economic growth of the private sector."[63]

But in addition to widening faculty career paths, such participation by industry in putatively pristine university-based research will also reinforce and legitimate the corporate campaigns for deregulation, innovation, and reindustrialization, while furthering the attack on democracy by encouraging continued private appropriation of the publicly supported resources of academia. As these resources are auctioned off to the highest bidder, university research will inevitably reflect less than ever the interests of less endowed and mobilized portions of the population—consumers, environmentalists, and working people generally. In addition to the dampening effect it is sure to have on university researcher criticism of corporations, the industrial connection thus additionally furthers the concentration of economic, political, and ideological power in the political system. In short, universities will effectively contribute to the already overwhelming power of large corporations while lending to that power the double sanction of academic respectability and scientific credence.[64]

The industrial connection is not merely the final prong of the corporate counterattack on the reforms of the 1960s and early 1970s, but a microcosm of all the changes in American politics the success of that attack has entailed. With little fear of exaggeration, we can see in it not merely the replacement of one research funding source by another, but a vast shift in the terms and direction of political conflict generally. The redefinition of political decisions as purely technical choices, the concomitant valorization of elite expertise at the expense of mass decision-making, and the progressive replacement of free discourse by commercial interest, democratic norms by private imperatives, legislative debate by executive action, and the demands of science by the demands of power all serve to blur or eradicate those fundamental distinctions of authority and procedure around which American political life has traditionally devolved. What is announced by the multifaceted corporate campaign, its industrial spokesmen and academic mandarins, is not merely a technically more complex political universe, but a quieter one, in which the voices of popular resistance and control are no longer heard.

III

Science and technology policy has been a central arena for domestic political struggles, but it functions equally well as a vehicle of realignment in foreign policy and affairs, where many of the same economic dynamics are at work. Indeed, with the accelerated pace of global economic integration, the drives of the domestic and international economies converge in market interdependence. Already noted is the role the export of high-technology R&D-intensive manufacturing goods to developing countries plays in generating income for the purchase of petroleum and essential minerals, and the frequency with which appeals for domestic innovation and deregulation are explicitly tied to the demands of the international economy. At the same time, many of the social and environmental effects of technological change, from potential climatic changes induced by fossil fuel combustion to the proliferation of nuclear weapons, have become international in scope. These two trends have become both a reason and an excuse for building a substantial science and technology component into U.S. foreign policy, while linking foreign and domestic policy generally. As the Atlantic

Council concluded in a recent report on nuclear proliferation, "The isolation of domestic from foreign affairs may have been tolerable in simpler times. Now policies for energy, nuclear power, non-proliferation and natural resources demand integration of foreign and domestic considerations."[65]

Awareness of the significance of the science and technology dimension of foreign policy first emerged in the early 1970s, largely in response to the traumas of the OPEC oil crisis, and flowing from a general realization that the political demands of the developing countries (for a substantial change in the terms under which technology was transferred from rich to poor nations) could no longer be safely ignored. Henry Kissinger told the United Nations in a 1974 speech that "no human activity is less national in character than the field of science. No development offers more hope than joint technical and scientific cooperation." Two years later, addressing the United Nations Conference on Trade and Development (UNCTAD) in Nairobi, Kissinger acknowledged that developing country demands for a New International Economic Order (NIEO), which included demands for a change in technology transfer rules, could not be ignored, even if they could not be accepted. Kissinger stressed the economic interdependence of rich and poor nations, and their mutual interest in economic health and technological development: "The advanced nations have an interest in the growth of markets and production in the developing world; with equal conviction we state that the developing countries have a stake in the markets, technological innovation and capital investment of the industrialized countries."

Within the State Department, the stress on interdependence, coupled with the recognition of science and technology's potential value as a source of international bargaining chips, resulted in growing pressure to build links between technology and foreign affairs. In 1976, Deputy Secretary of State Charles W. Robinson commissioned a report on the topic from consultant Dr. T. Keith Glennan. In his later introduction to the report, Robinson noted that science and technology were becoming "major factors" in the conduct of foreign affairs with an "increasingly critical" role to play.[66] Glennan's report came to the same conclusion, warning that "the relationship of technology to foreign affairs is now a vitally important part of the business of the Department of State," but that "adequate awareness of this relationship, and of the potential of American technological leadership, is generally lacking throughout the department."[67] Similar conclusions were reached by the Congressional Research Service in a major study called "Science, Technology and Diplomacy in an Age of Interdependency" released in June 1976. The study also argued for increased attention to science and technology at the State Department, and accused the United States of neglecting technological expertise as a potentially powerful instrument of policy formation. It suggested that technology and technology transfer offered "many opportunities" for the achievement of foreign policy objectives.[68]

Responding to these pressures, the State Department upgraded its science and technology activities, primarily through raising the status of, and providing additional funding for, its Bureau of Oceanic and International Environmental Affairs. The need for an additional science emphasis in foreign policy was formally recognized in the department's authorization bill for 1979, which gave the secretary of state explicit responsibility for developing the science and technology component within the department. As Carter administration Undersecretary of State for Science, Technology and International Security Lucy Wilson Benson put it: "We have come to a transition. We are leaving an era in which science and technology were thought of as independent activities throwing an occasional roman candle . . . into the foreign policy arena. We have entered an era in which the interactions between science and technology and foreign affairs are recognized increasingly as continuous and central to many of the important foreign policy problems with which we are dealing—among them energy, food, nuclear proliferation, communication, the environment, and so on."[69]

The motives behind the spate of reports and eventual State Department response were not entirely altruistic or even scientific, however. Coinciding with and largely responsible for heightened official concern with the science and technology component in foreign policy was a growing concern among multinational corporations that they secure reliable government assistance in developing markets for their goods and maintaining stable supplies of cheap labor and raw materials for their international operations. Talk by the developing countries had centered on the need for access to Western technology on terms that the developing countries would determine, and NIEO threats of a legally enforceable international code of conduct to achieve this redetermination triggered a chorus of multinational demands for government intervention. A 1971 OECD report on science policy had already warned of the growing tensions between rich and poor nations over the technology transfer issue, and warned of potential threats to "world stability."[70] A 1976 seminar of managers from several major corporations, organized by Glennan and Herbert Fusfeld (then Kennecott Copper research director) to discuss State Department initiatives in the science and technology field, reached the conclusion that the transfer issue "could have serious consequences affecting positively or negatively the ability of U.S. industry to engage in international operations," while posing "serious difficulties for both foreign policy and business opportunities if not resolved, and great opportunity to improve both if approached thoughtfully."[71] Similarly, another 1976 meeting organized by the National Academy of Engineering concluded that while the developing countries' assertions about the structural imbalance in technology transfers were "unfounded or exaggerated," and significant primarily as a reflection of their aspirations and frustrations, it was nevertheless important to discuss "ways and means by which the United

States might accommodate its policies in some measure towards relief of the frustrations and support of the aspirations."[72]

As in the domestic transformation of science and technology policy through the innovation and reindustrialization campaigns, government officials explicitly assumed that eventual policy should be guided by the imperatives of the relevant corporate actors, in this case the giant multinationals. The CRS study complained that "multinational corporations are recognized as the primary mechanism for international transfer of technology, yet the United States has no policy for enlistment and coordination of this great resource to advance the purposes of U.S. diplomacy."[73] The Glennan-Fusfeld seminar also recommended that the State Department establish better contact with the multinationals, counseling that "American industry would welcome an opportunity to consult with government officials in advance concerning major proposals which might be made in the field of international technology."[74]

Such "advice," "consultation," "contact," and dominance eventually came in a number of forms and from a variety of business quarters, but is most dramatically illustrated by the Trilateral Commission's attention to the technology issue. Established by commercial banker David Rockefeller in 1973 as a mechanism for coordinating the interests of multinationals from the United States, Western Europe, and Japan, the commission evidenced an early interest in the technology transfer issue and "interfaced" almost perfectly with the State Department in the policy formation process. Two prominent Trilateralists, Patrick Haggerty, chairman of Texas Instruments, and Dr. Marina v.N. Whitman, professor of economics at the University of Pittsburgh, were members of the sixteen-person committee established by President Ford in 1975 to study "the contribution of technology to economic strength," prior to the reestablishment of the OSTP. Another member of the same committee was C. Fred Bergsten, author of one of the commission's many task force reports and long active at the Council on Foreign Relations, who became assistant secretary of the Treasury for international affairs under the Carter administration. After leaving the State Department in 1977, Robinson, who had commissioned the Glennan study on technology and foreign affairs, joined Blyth Eastman and Dillon and the commission's executive committee. He was succeeded at the State Department by Benson, another Trilateral Commission member and past president of the League of Women Voters.

Several other Trilateralists, in addition to Secretary of State Cyrus Vance, joined the State Department and were given various indirect responsibilities for scientific affairs. Perhaps most significantly, three commission members who had played a prominent part in its discussions of the transfer problem and related science and foreign policy issues were appointed "ambassadors at large." Elliot Richardson, previously U.S. Ambassador to Britain, was put in charge of the American delegation to the UN's Law of the Sea negotiations, where the United States was keen to establish rights for its mining companies to retrieve ocean bed minerals, but reluctant to accept Third World demands for access to its mining technology. Henry Owen, a commission co-founder and previous director of foreign policy studies at the Brookings Institution, was given responsibility for "economic summit affairs," and played a leading role in forging plans for the ill-fated Institute for Scientific and Technical Cooperation, an earlier version of which had been proposed in a Brookings study. And Gerard Smith, a corporate lawyer who had been chairman of the commission's North American branch, was given responsibility for nonproliferation issues. Nonproliferation is another problem of general concern to multinationals and the commission, who wish to devise a way of permitting the growth of nuclear power without the destabilizing political effects attendant upon nuclear proliferation (an interest reflected in Carter's proposal of an International Nuclear Fuel Cycle Evaluation).

Given this extraordinary domination of the relevant State Department offices by multinational representatives, it is unsurprising that President Carter made the international aspects of science and technology a central platform in his science policy. In his science and technology message to Congress in March 1979, Carter stressed four aspects of this platform, emphasizing (1) the need to build up programs and institutions to help developing countries use science and technology; (2) the pursuit of new international initiatives to advance the United States' own research and development objectives; (3) the development and strengthening of international scientific exchanges "to bridge political, ideological and cultural divisions"; and (4) cooperation with other nations, both developed and developing, to manage technologies with global impact.[75]

Although international scientific activities are frequently described in terms of "cooperation" or "exchange," this is commonly acknowledged by government officials to be a thin veil for the pursuit of more clearly political and economic objectives. On the economic side, for example, Carter admitted that international R&D activities can be used to "foster commercial relationships,"[76] and one of the principal foreign policy successes of his administration, the full normalization of relationships with the People's Republic of China, relied heavily on the use of science and technology as commodities. The Chinese desired access to American technology to support their bid for rapid modernization. The United States, in return, was interested both in the potential markets that close links with China would open, and the access to important raw materials that the Chinese possess. While more formal diplomatic initiatives were stalled over the recognition of Taiwan, presidential science advisor Frank Press was able to negotiate a United States–China Agreement on Scientific and Technological Cooperation, building on scientific and academic contacts that had been taking place through such private channels as the National Academy of Sciences since the early 1970s. Cooperation was agreed upon in such broad research areas as space, energy, agriculture, and health, as well as in academic exchanges, and the general agreement was signed in 1979. In this case, the United States had relatively little interest in Chinese science, but saw the rewards of making science and technology available. Press later observed that "the developing scientific and technological relations with China proved to play a significant positive role in the broader effort to normalize relations between our two countries."[77]

A similar pattern was followed, albeit usually on a smaller scale, in a series of science and technology agreements signed with other countries. In general, these agreements were structured like the Chinese one. The United States offered scientific and technological assistance in return for access to some other desired asset. An agreement with Mexico, for example, was signed as part of negotiations that were to give the United States access to Mexico's abundant supply of oil and natural gas. A similar arrangement was reached with Nigeria, the United States' second largest supplier of petroleum, where an extensive series of science and technology agreements were reached and signed by Press in 1980. Others were signed during a similar visit to Latin American countries in 1979, shortly before a meeting of the Organization of American States at which the United States was keen to head off Cuban influence in Latin America. They promised scientific and technological assistance in exchange for economic and political cooperation.

Many of these countries are commonly described by policymakers as "middle-tier." In American eyes, this means that they offer a potential market for high-technology goods, while frequently (as in the case of China, Mexico, Nigeria, or Venezuela) possessing resources the United States badly needs. Economic and political ties with the "middle-tier" countries have therefore taken on special significance. "These nations are often politically important, and by helping them we help ourselves," Press explained in congressional testimony in 1979. "Since science and technology are particularly important to middle-tier countries . . . the transfer of technical knowledge and capability are a likely foundation for our relationships with these countries."[78] Linkages with middle-tier countries were to have been one of the principal goals of the proposed ISTC. Such countries, because of their relatively high per capita income, do not qualify for the technical assistance programs that come under the category of foreign aid.

In seeking such links, the Carter administration had the full support of the private sector. But corporations were less than happy with administration attempts to use technology for direct political leverage and sanction, particularly when this took the form of shutting down technology exports. Speaking to the Japan-American Society of Southern California in 1979, for example, David Rockefeller criticized two such cases. One was the decision to ban the sale of $268 million worth of turbine generators by Allis-Chalmers to Argentina, because of "human rights" violations. Another was the Defense Advisory Board's refusal to approve Dresser Industries' export of oil drilling equipment to the Soviet Union. In both cases the bans were reversed after pressure from the companies concerned.

But Rockefeller also cited the administration's successful refusal to permit export of a $6.8 million computer system to the Russian news agency Tass as an example "of how politics has frustrated doing business abroad."[79]

Despite such periodic criticisms, there are at least three ways in which the political use of science and technology in foreign affairs has been encouraged and supported by the private sector. The first has been the attempt to use the nation's scientific and technological preeminence to exercise a hegemonic role in addressing global problems, as in the proliferation of nuclear weapons, and hence achieving a resolution acceptable to the United States. Given the many conflicts that have resulted from tensions and structural changes in the global economy during the 1970s, Carter National Security Advisor (and former director of the Trilateral Commission) Zbigniew Brzezinski spoke frequently of the need for the United States to "manage the peaceful process of global change." Picking up on this theme, Charles Dennison, executive director of the Council on Science and Technology for Development, told a 1979 meeting of the American Association for the Advancement of Science that "science and technology are principal tools for the management of global change," representing resources "with which this nation is still well-endowed and that the developing nations seek most urgently."[80] Although the policy has found many supporters, its most ambitious effort, the Nuclear Non-Proliferation Act of 1978, has also been its most outstanding failure. Under the act, the United States attempted to deny developing countries access to American nuclear technology unless they agreed to open all nuclear facilities to international inspection. But this commitment to the monitoring of peaceful nuclear development was soon abandoned with the decision to export enriched nuclear fuel to India, which refused to comply with the inspection requirement. At the time, the Carter administration cited overriding "broad foreign policy considerations," namely the desire to balance the influence of the USSR on Indian Prime Minister Indira Gandhi. Although the export control policy had been contested from the outset by the nuclear industry in the United States, it had initially been supported by many multinationals as an appropriate and welcome use of technological dominance.

The second corporate-supported political use of science and technology has been their transfer under conditions designed to support and extend existing patterns of ownership and control of knowledge. Multinationals have accepted the principle that both developed and developing countries can benefit from accelerated technology transfer, but they have equally put substantial effort into making sure that such transfer occurs only under conditions that ensure their proprietary rights to technical knowledge and have contested claims by the developing countries that such knowledge should be freely available. Nat C. Robertson, for example, chairman of the international subcommittee of the Industrial Research Committee, told Congress in 1979 that demands from developing countries "would dilute the proprietary rights of private sector firms" and would "surely be counterproductive at a time when our firms should be encouraged to provide useful technologies to the poorer countries." Robertson expressed approval of the United States paper submitted to the United Nations Conference on Science and Technology for Development (UNCSTD), which had argued that technology transfer should be an effort "in which private industries or organizations enjoy due protection, and due return on their investment and inventiveness."[81] In a similar vein, Elliot Richardson has expressed his frustration with Third World demands for access to American sea-bed mining technology, declaring that the U.S. government actually has "no deep-sea-bed mining at all," since the technology involved is entirely owned by private companies, and even the U.S. government cannot simply demand access to it. Richardson has also ridiculed the idea that technology developed by multinationals in the developed countries should be considered "the common heritage of mankind."[82] In line with these sentiments, U.S. foreign policy has consistently reflected the belief that, where technology and technical knowhow are being transferred, priority should be given to the retention of private property rights.

The dispute over the rights to ownership and control of proprietary technology are part of a larger struggle over the control of scientific and technical resources in general. One of the central demands of the New International Economic Order has been for a major shift in technical resources from the developed to developing countries. At present, developed nations account for over 95 percent of the world's research and development, and are inevitably its major beneficiaries. In an attempt to redress this imbalance and gain greater control over technology transferred to them by multinationals, developing nations have attempted coordinated prohibition of "package" sales in which they are forbidden to take apart the technology they buy, as well as denials of patent protection. Such moves have generally outraged the multinationals. Reflecting their concern, Richardson has declared that "in the eyes of the Group of 77, the position of technological and scientific capability and the assets thereby derived are in themselves the manifestation of the newest form of economic imperialism. The consequence of this, in turn, is that the Group of 77 is probably more unitedly organized today in an assault on the citadels of technology than on any other single effort."[83]

The third corporate-supported political function of science and technology policy grows directly out of this challenge of concerted developing nation action on technology transfer, and takes the form of an attempt to head off and contain such challenges to the orderly expansion and operation of the multinationals. One goal has been to seek a voluntary code of conduct on technology transfers, rather than submit to any legally binding commitment which corporations feel could reduce their effectiveness. Another has been congressional efforts to confine American technical assistance to those countries that support United States foreign policy. The latter have brought American lawmakers into conflict with the World Bank, which refuses to accept restrictions on the money it is provided for loans.

A third related trend is the general move away from supporting the science and technology activities of the multilateral aid agencies operating out of the UN, since the one nation–one vote decision procedure of the governing body has resulted in a major shift in control of these agencies' resources to Third World countries. In contrast, additional support has flowed to bilateral aid projects whose terms can be more closely monitored to ensure that they do not conflict with multinational interests.

Each of these three elements of the corporate-supported role of science and technology in foreign policy—as a tool for exercising American hegemony in international problems, as a way of injecting marketplace relationships into the development process, and as a mechanism for containing Third World demands for greater effective control over the allocation of global resources—can be seen in the behavior of the United States delegation to the 1979 UNCSTD meetings in Vienna. The delegation faced a delicate task. On the one hand, aware of the potential damage caused by the apparent failure of other North-South negotiations, it was keen to establish "dialogue" and not be identified as entirely hostile to developing nation demands. On the other, it did not want to give away anything significant on the general technology transfer issue.

Many American scientists complained at the time about the lack of explicit consideration given at the conference to the particular needs of the developing countries in science and technology. But the United States delegation was in little doubt about the real agenda of the meeting. As Lucy Benson candidly described it to a Senate committee, "UNCSTD was a political conference, since the principal issues were the concerns in developing countries about inequality and dependence. Those are really the catalytic forces that gave cause to this conference. It's the desire of the developing countries to overcome this technological dependence and overcome this inequality."[84]

Little such open admission of the political nature of the conference was forthcoming from Notre Dame president Father Theodore Hesburgh, however, the head of the United States delegation. Hesburgh, who serves as a director both of the Council on Foreign Relations and the Chase Manhattan Bank, gave a speech to the plenary session at UNCSTD that closely reflected the multinational consensus on technology transfer issues. It complained that "the patterns of worldwide technology generation, diffusion and utilization lack the cohesion that would incorporate and benefit the majority of people," spoke of the "anomaly" that 95 percent of world R&D is conducted by the developed world, argued strongly for "cooperation not confrontation," recommended the creation of "a more equitable relationship between the developing countries and international private enterprise, so that in the global transfer of technology the interest of both is enhanced," pointed out that it was impossible to ignore the private sector as "a major source of innovation, a major factor in the diffusion of technology," and finally rounded off with an appeal to "usher in a new age" that would produce both "a new realm of reason" and a "new realm of reality."[85]

Father Hesburgh's corporate sermon reflected many of the comments that the State Department had solicited from private corporations in preparation for the UNCSTD. This process of official preparation had begun in 1976, when Henry Kissinger organized a meeting of business representatives to assess the transfer issue. At the 1979 meeting, two slightly different forms of business response were evident, similar in message but distinguishable in tone. A report to the meeting prepared by the Council of the Americas and the Fund for Multinational Management Education had taken a hard line in the protection of American interests. Council of the Americas managing director Harvey W. Wallender III recognized the potential importance of the conference for future trade relations, but warned that "if a frank and constructive platform does not emerge from Vienna, the United States and especially its international business and labor interests will be faced with increasing conflict and serious disruptions."[86] Others, however, suggested a more accommodating approach. One of the most influential documents was a report called "The Contribution of Transnational Enterprises to Future World Development," prepared at the suggestion of conference secretary-general Frank João de Costa by an *ad hoc* advisory group consisting of senior managers from twenty-six American and European multinationals. This group stressed the need for flexibility in negotiations—which meant that in debates between multinationals and host governments, both sides were encouraged to respect the objectives of the other. As the chairman of the *ad hoc* group, James D. Grant of CPC International put it, "both parties must be satisfied with the arrangement if a successful investment is to be made. Transnationals must receive a return for their investment and proprietary knowledge, and certainly the host country's political, social and economic objectives must be met as well."[87]

It was this somewhat ambiguous second report that set the tone for the United States delegation to UNCSTD. The developing countries, negotiating through the Group of 77, came to Vienna with a demand for a new fund that would total $4 billion by the end of the 1980s, and be used to double the research and development capabilities of the developing countries. The developed countries agreed with the objective and its rationale —that the poor countries would only be able to develop economically through building up an adequate scientific and technological infrastructure —but few were willing to increase their commitment to providing financial and technical assistance. Most developed nations also opposed Third World demands for increased control over the science and technology apparatus within the UN and the major changes in the terms and conditions of technology transfer suggested by the NIEO and similar programs.

In the end, little was achieved in Vienna, although the appearance of outright failure was avoided by agreement on an "interim fund" for science and technology, to be run by the United Nations Development Program with an initial voluntary contributions target of $250 million over a two-year period. The figure was modest compared to the original $4 billion demand, yet even the smaller money pool seems unlikely to materialize. The United States has yet to provide any money for the fund, although the State Department had previously indicated that the United States would be prepared to contribute "its fair share"—thought to be between $50 and $60 million—and, using this as a cornerstone, had persuaded other developed countries to accept the idea.[88] By the time the contribution had appeared in President Carter's budget request to Congress for 1981, however, the figure had been reduced by the Office of Management and Budget to $15 million, and subsequently to $10 million. Congress, sensing a lack of commitment on OMB's part, finally deleted the whole contribution from the foreign aid budget.

The future of the interim fund, virtually the only concrete result of the Vienna meeting, now seems dim. When Carter science advisor Frank Press wrote a retrospective article in *Science* magazine listing the Carter administration's achievement in science policy, no mention was made of the UN-CSTD conference.[89] Many observers felt that, faced with Third World demands for greater access to and control over American scientific and technological resources, the $2 million the United States had spent on preparing for the conference and its provisional commitment to support the interim fund had merely been ways of buying peace. Certainly the American tactics won few friends at the conference. Other developed countries felt they were being pressured to accept an arrangement they did not in principle approve, since they were unwilling to provide extra funds for technical aid, while developing countries were additionally frustrated at achieving none of their objectives. As the *Chronicle of Higher Education* headlined shortly after the conference closed, "To Many, the United States Was the Biggest Culprit at the UN's Conference on Science and Technology."[90]

The Reagan administration's attitude toward the use of science and technology in foreign policy remains unclear. Certainly there is likely to be even less support for foreign aid, either through multilateral or bilateral channels. The U.S. delegation to the United Nations Educational, Scientific and Cultural Organization (UNESCO) was cut in half at the end of 1980, and similar reductions are expected in support for other specialized agencies. Nor is there likely to be much enthusiasm for denying private technology transfers on "human rights" grounds.

Yet despite likely changes in these two directions, the three basic trends that have recently dominated the foreign policy application of science and technology are almost certain to remain. First, the United States will continue attempts to use its supremacy in science and technology to impose its preferred solutions on global problems, although mounting challenges to this supremacy from other advanced industrial states like Japan and West Germany will make such unilateral imposition difficult. Second, with the continued integration of the world economy, the internationalization of labor markets and production sites, and the growth of Third World economies, the United States will continue to seek "market solutions" (meaning private appropriation and incentive structures) to the allocation of scientific and technological products and expertise. Third, in approaching the technology transfer issue, the United States will continue to stress the need for international "stability" at the expense of satisfaction of Third World demands for access and control.

As in the domestic arena, these trends will be justified by appeals to "reason" and "rationality," obscuring the political choices they portend. Father Hesburgh's plea for a "new realm of reason" is nicely complemented by the U.S. Chamber of Commerce's demand for a "new rule of reason" in technology transfer agreements.[91] The "new rule" would be one stressing voluntary rather than legal codes of conduct for the multinationals, and is informed by an understanding of technical knowledge as private property. In the long term, the principal goal of multinationals operating in the Third World is the achievement of a stable and attractive investment climate. This was stressed in the multinationals' report to the UNCSTD meeting in Vienna, which emphasized the need for "the promise of stability of policies, attitudes and relationships" on the part of host country governments, and recommended as features of a stable international economic regime "a pragmatic approach to regulation, the acceptance of international arbitration in disputes, and freedom to repatriate a reasonable level of funds."[92] Thus in international relations, as in domestic affairs, the "reasonable" use of science and technology is defined as use conforming to the imperatives of private capital.

I V

From this survey of the domestic and international use and transformation of science and technology policy, several conclusions emerge. First, science and technology have assumed a new centrality in the modern political economy. The economic dimension is evidenced in the growing dominance of science-based industries. The political dimension appears in the growing technological component of traditional social policy. Second, and precisely because of this centrality, science and technology policy formation enjoys considerable insulation from the institutions of mass democracy and electoral politics, exhibiting a recent continuity in policy formation that has withstood changes in political administration from Republican to Democrat and back to Republican again. Third, the content of science and technology policy has shifted in the past several years from the structuring of scientific resource delivery to national problem areas to encouragement of the decision procedures and allocative mechanisms of private enterprise and the market. Fourth, this shift in content is traceable to elite mobilization against the popular demands for participation and equity characteristic of the late 1960s and early 1970s. Fifth, in the process of this elite mobilization and the transformation in government structures it entailed, science and technology have played an increasingly important role as legitimizing executive-centered state power and corporate domination of the political system.

Linking all these observations on science and technology policy is a consideration of the forms of governance appropriate to an industrially advanced, technologically based society. This most basic of concerns was raised recently by Dr. John Kemeny, chairman of the presidential commission established to investigate the 1979 accident at the Three Mile Island nuclear power plant, when he described to an audience at the Massachusetts Institute of Technology what he saw as a growing tension between Jeffersonian democracy and the demands placed on political institutions by advanced technology. Referring in particular to the tangle of misjudgments that had led to the TMI accident, Kemeny commented: "I've heard many times that although democracy is an imperfect system, we somehow always muddle through. The message I want to give you, after long and hard reflection, is that I'm very much afraid it is no longer possible to muddle through. The issues we deal with do not lend themselves to that kind of treatment."[93] Speaking in a broader context, Dr. Lewis Branscomb, chief scientist at IBM and chairman of the National Science Board, also noted the tensions between democracy and technology. "Each time the Congress and the executive are unable to achieve a public consensus on a technologically complex issue," said Branscomb, "we witness another failure in the consensus process of our democracy. If this continues to happen with increasing frequency, the pressures to alter the political foundation of our society inevitably grow."[94]

The dilemma is a real one. If we cannot learn to develop institutions capable of controlling technology in an acceptable and desirable way, then its undesirable consequences will be experienced by default. Yet precisely because of the importance of science and technology, efforts to submit them to popular control encounter deep and abiding resistance. In a corporate-dominated political system such as that of the United States, demands that the direction and utilization of science and technology should be determined within the institutions of mass democratic politics represent a direct challenge to the power of private corporations. In return, the representatives of corporate power suggest not that the development of technology should be molded to social demands as expressed through these institutions, but that the institutions themselves be sacrificed to the "demands" of technological development. Ed David, vice-president for research at Exxon, has noted that "the adversary relationship between government and industry in the U.S. . . . has its roots in the populist attitudes that have long pervaded our culture. But this style may have become seriously counterproductive."[95] Fellow Reagan science advisor Simon Ramo of TRW has a similar message: "We see in the United States today a severe mismatch between the high potential of technological advance and the low potential of the country's social-political progress. The problem is not technology per se. We are simply not organized to use science and technology to the fullest."[96]

For corporate leaders, the full utilization of scientific and technological knowledge therefore requires the retreat from democratic norms and procedures in the interest of "rationality" and science. Thus William O. Baker, president of Bell Laboratories and a past PSAC member, speaks of the "bizarre conflicts between the presumptive laws and regulations of pervasive government in a low risk, welfare society, and the present realities of technical and scientific advance, which, more than ever, demand the freedom to experiment and innovate boldly."[97] And Frank Press tells the American Association for the Advancement of Science that "science is essentially rational and as scientists we generally support more analysis and fact-gathering, to bring reason to bear on our regulatory decisions."[98]

Former MIT president and presidential science advisor Jerome Wiesner has made the political significance of this push for rationality explicit in a recent interview with *U.S. News and World Report* entitled "After Affluence, Americans Are Not Prepared to Go Back." There Wiesner echoes and seconds the antidemocratic sentiments of corporate executives. "In the past two decades," he comments, "the U.S. has moved a long distance in the direction of becoming a more open and democratic society, and we are still trying. While this is an admirable goal, in the process of trying to do this we have created a society that is unmanageable because we no longer have established ground-rules for decision-making, to say nothing about significant knowledge or material goods. Our problem at the present time is not that the world has become much more complex but that we have become a society in which we have let a lot more people have a voice without at the same time figuring out a way to keep the system operating. A multitude of people are now able to participate in the decision-making process—without adequate knowledge—and all have either something to gain or something to lose. This leads to a paralysis of decision-making. What is needed," Wiesner concludes, "is the reestablishment of a governmental mechanism to end the paralysis." In short, what is needed is government by the experts, a stronger, more technocratic executive, and perhaps a new American constitution.[99]

Thus for the representatives of corporate interest, the conflict between science-technology-"rationality" and democracy is easily resolved. Democracy must be abandoned in the name of a cynical notion of "progress," where "progress" refers to the continued development of science and technology within a structure of private direction and gain. Such a sacrifice of democracy is "easy" for those who already command vast private resources of money and power, because their interests do not rely on democratic norms and procedures for their expression.

But for the rest of the population, the abandonment of democracy is neither "easy" nor affordable. For them, democracy is not the anomalous luxury of a previous age, but the only possible present guarantee of political power in a system that otherwise rigorously reinforces harsh inequalities in the distribution of income, wealth, and political clout. It is not something that can be sacrificed in the name of corporate progress, but the only means of achieving social welfare and equality, health and environmental integrity. For the working population, abandoning democracy is not an option, and the "easy" corporate solution to the problems of democracy and technology is therefore no solution at all.

But the corporate conclusion is not the only one. Implicit in all of the foregoing analysis is an alternative view of the problems of democracy and technology that sees those problems as rooted in a lack of democracy rather than an excess. Under this alternative view, what is currently needed in American politics is not the closure of democratic institutions but their revival and extension, which implies as well a need for more social regulation of private enterprise, and the subordination of science and technology to democratic choice, socially determined need, and human and ecological survival. In sum, what is needed is the articulation of a more hopeful notion of progress and the future development of American political institutions in which the apparent contradiction between the principle of democracy and the possibilities of science and technology can be reconciled or resolved in the interests of humanity instead of power and profit. Such an alternative view can only be suggested here. Its full exploration awaits resumption of those popular deliberations on equity and participation begun in the 1960s and early 1970s, whose achievements are now being erased. The political struggles of that period were prematurely closed. But the questions they raised about the future direction of American politics remain unanswered, and are now more urgent than ever. Thomas Jefferson once wrote that "whenever the people are well informed, they can be trusted with their own government." At present, the people are neither well informed nor in control.

NOTES

1. "Steady Gains in R&D Spending," *Business Week,* January 12, 1981, pp. 86f.
2. For a description of some of these tensions, see Richard L. Garwin, "Presidential Science Advising," in William T. Golden, ed., *Science Advice to the President* (New York: Pergamon Press, 1980).
3. *Technological Change and Economic Policy* (Paris: OECD, 1980), p. 20.
4. *Science Indicators 1978* (Washington, D.C.: National Science Board, 1979), p. 34. Source: Department of Commerce, Domestic and International Business Administration, Overseas Business Reports, August 1967, April 1972, April 1977, June 1978.
5. Ibid., p. 182.
6. *Science and Technology in Presidential Policy-Making: A Proposal* (Washington, D.C.: National Academy of Sciences, 1974), p. 3.
7. Testimony to House of Representatives Science and Technology Committee, June 10, 1975.

8. For a criticism of the failure to meet this congressionally mandated goal, and some of the reasons, see: "The Office of Science and Technology Policy: Adaptation to a President's Operating Style May Conflict with Congressionally Mandated Assignments," General Accounting Office Report, PAD-80-79, Washington, D.C., September 3, 1980.

9. Don I. Phillips, Gail J. Breslow, and Patricia S. Curlin, eds., *Colloquium on R & D Policy*, American Association for the Advancement of Science, Report no. 79-R-14, October 1979, p. 18.

10. Referring to various steps introduced by President Carter to stimulate innovation and reduce the burden of regulation, Press told the meeting that "a major goal of these actions is improved care and rationalism, in both substance and process." Phillips et al., eds., op. cit, p. 19.

11. William D. Carey, "Science Policy: New Directions?" *Science* 210, 4472 (November 21, 1980).

12. Lewis M. Branscomb, "Science Policy Issues in the 1980s," evidence presented to the Committee on Science and Technology of the U.S. House of Representatives, reprinted in *National Science and Technology Policy Issues 1979: Part 1* (Washington, D.C.: Government Printing Office, 1979), p. 122.

13. *A Conversation with Alfred B. Kahn*, report of a meeting held at the American Enterprise Institute, April 3, 1980, p. 18.

14. Quoted in Phillips et al., eds., op. cit., p. 32.

15. James Coleman, "The Life, Death and Potential Future of PSAC," in Golden, ed., op. cit., p. 135.

16. *Rural Advance Newsletter* (Rural Advancement Fund/National Sharecropper's Fund), summer 1979; Monsanto, *Chemicals and Life* (also advertisement in *Seven Days*, June 5, 1979, p. 25); Hugh Menzies, "Union Carbide Raises Its Voice," *Fortune*, September 25, 1978. See also David F. Noble, "The Chemistry of Risk," *Seven Days*, July 1978; David F. Noble, "Cost-Benefit Analysis," *Health PAC Bulletin*, July–August 1980; "New Aura, Old Karma," *Mother Jones*, February–March 1980; "Cleansing the Chemical Image," *Business Week*, October 8, 1979, p. 73.

17. Jackson Browing, "Cancer, Chemicals, and the Environment," talk given before the Florida Audubon Society, October 27, 1978.

18. Frank Press, seminar at the Center for International Studies, MIT, November 1979. See also David Dickson, "U.S. Seeks to 'Rationalize' Health and Safety Regulation in the Interest of Profits," *Nature*, June 28, 1979, p. 746.

19. Charles Schultze, quoted in George and Joan Melloan, *The Carter Economy* (New York: Wiley, 1978), p. 75.

20. Michael Baram, "Regulation of Health, Safety, and Environmental Quality and the Use of Cost-Benefit Analysis," Final Report to the Administrative Conference of the United States, March 1, 1979.

21. Nicholas Ashford, "A Plea for a New Kind of Realism," *The New York Times*, December 17, 1978, p. 16B; Jeffrey Joseph, quoted in Merrill Shiels, "What Price Regulation?" *Newsweek*, March 19, 1979.

22. Shiels, op. cit.

23. Walter Guzzardi, Jr., "Judges Discover the World of Economics," *Fortune*, May 21, 1979; Henry Manne, "The Myth of Corporate Responsibility, or, Will the Real Ralph Nader Please Stand Up," *Business Lawyer*, November 1970, p. 539.

24. Roland, quoted in Luther Carter, "An Industry Study of TSCA; How to Achieve Credibility," *Science*, February 1974; Connor, quoted in Marvin Zim, "Allied Chemical's $20 Million Ordeal with Kepone," *Fortune*, September 11, 1978, p. 91; Corey and Mooney, quoted in "Chemical Industry and EPA

Square Off on TSCA Rules," *Chemical Week,* January 31, 1979, p. 27. See also "Are Health Rules Unhealthy to Innovation?" *Chemical Week,* January 24, 1979.

25. W. N. Smith and Charles F. Larson (eds.), *Innovation and U.S. Research,* ACS Symposium Series, No. 129, 1980.
26. Not everyone agreed that there was a lag in innovation. *Fortune* magazine, for example, noted on December 17, 1979, that "the state of innovation in the U.S. has been the subject of much anxious commentary of late: many fear that the spirit of invention is dying. But most of the discussion is impressionistic, and a detailed inquiry shows that the true situation varies enormously by industry and fields of endeavor. In some instances, the pace of American innovation is more breathtaking than ever." Dr. Bruce Hannay, research director of the Bell Labs, concurred with *Fortune's* judgment, describing a *Time* headline about "vanishing innovation" as "utter nonsense."
27. CED, *Stimulating Technological Progress.* See also Thomas Vanderslice's contribution to *Innovation and U.S. Research.*
28. Press, CIS Seminar. See also Will Lepkowski, "Jordan Baruch Makes His Mark on Innovation," *Chemical and Engineering News,* January 1, 1979; and Lepkowski, "White House Awaits Huge Innovation Report," *Chemical and Engineering News,* February 12, 1979.
29. Press, *Hearings Before the Committee on Science and Technology, U.S. House of Representatives,* 96th Cong., 1st Sess., April 3–5, 1979. Cutter, David, ibid.
30. *Hearings; Domestic Policy Review Innovation Initiatives,* released October 31, 1979.
31. Jules Blake, "OSTP: The Last 4 Years," *Science,* December 12, 1980.
32. See William Tabb, "Playing Productivity Politics," *The Nation,* January 5, 1980; Sidney Lens, "Reindustrialization: Panacea or Threat?" *The Progressive,* November 1980; David Moberg et al., "Reviving Industry on Whose Terms?" *Working Papers,* December 1980; and *Business Week's* Special Issue "The Reindustrialization of America," June 30, 1980. See also: "Six Myths in Steel," United Steel Workers *Local 65 News,* reprinted in *Labour Notes,* September 25, 1980, p. 4.
33. National Planning Association, *National Priorities during the 1960's: Implications for 1980.*
34. All quotes from Leonard Silk and David Vogel, *Ethics and Profits* (New York: Simon and Schuster, 1976).
35. Before its more sophisticated expression, the attack on "false" expectations of corporate performance and democratic procedures took the form of directly stifling consumerist protest. An example is the 1971 Conference Board Report on "Handling Protests at Annual Meetings." The report documents confrontations at the annual stockholder meetings of AT&T, ARCO, Boeing, CBS, Dow, GE, Gulf, Honeywell, IBM, Olin, RCA, Exxon, Texas Instruments, Union Carbide, and United Aircraft, where protesters had challenged corporate involvement in the war in Vietnam, environmental destruction, hiring discrimination, and the manufacture of unsafe products. In response, corporate leaders had undertaken to "review and refine admission procedures" to annual meetings, and made physical arrangements which would facilitate management control at the meetings, "such as the design, operation, and protection of the public address system" and the tightening of security (including the tripling of security guards, close coordination with local police, surveillance, and intelligence work). The Conference Board recommended "rearrangement of the order of business," if necessary, "prompt and firm action in removing unruly persons," and "restriction of discussion" in order to "stick to the agenda." Managers were now "resolved that future meetings would be planned on the assumption that irrational and destructive actions were entirely possible."

36. Shapiro, "Interview," *Context;* Silk and Vogel, op. cit.
37. Ibid.
38. Ibid.
39. Michael Crozier et al., *The Crisis of Democracy* (New York: New York University Press, 1975).
40. Which is one of the reasons why the Sloan Commission on Government and Higher Education, of which Kaysen is vice-chairman and research director, recently recommended a cutback in government scholarship support for needy students. The commission supported preferential allocation of resources to the elite colleges in order to offset what Sloan Commission President Nils Wessell referred to as the government-engendered "pall of uniformity," "homogeneity," and "levelling" which has settled over higher education during the last decade. The main thrust of the commission's work has been to legitimize a restriction of the role of government in university affairs, in the form both of financial support and, more important, government oversight and regulation of admission, appointments, curriculum, and research. The commission justified these measures in the name of academic "autonomy," "diversity," and "independent critical thought." See generally *Alfred P. Sloan Foundation Report,* 1977, "President's Statement," and "Sloan Commission on Government and Higher Education."
41. Kaysen in CED, "Improving the Long-Range Performance of the U.S. Economy," 1977.
42. Carter's civil service reforms of 1978, with the creation of an elite mobile "senior executives service," constitutes an important step in this direction. Loyalty to the president is assured both by the mobility and by the performance bonuses determined by the White House.
43. James Sundquist, "Five Directions for Government Reform," Du Pont *Context,* No. 2, 1980.
44. James Fay, talk given at MIT Technology and Policy Program Symposium on liquified natural gas policy, January 1979; *The New York Times,* July 9, 1980. See generally Noble, "Cost Benefit Analysis."
45. Handler, "Presidential Address"; Howard Raiffa, form letter about the Committee on Risk and Decision Making, March 26, 1980.
46. "Business Gifts to Universities Rise 23.3 Percent," *The Chronicle of Higher Education,* June 8, 1971, p. 1. See also "Corporate Aid to Higher Education," *The Wall Street Journal,* October 5, 1978; Robert Rheinold, "Pentagon Renews Ties with Colleges," *The New York Times,* May 13, 1980; Charles Overberger, "Universities and the Federal Government: A Marriage That Has Survived," *Chemical and Engineering News,* December 4, 1978; Jerome Wiesner, "Universities and the Federal Government: A Troubled Relationship," *Chemical and Engineering News,* December 11, 1978; David Kevles, "The National Science Foundation and the Debate over Postwar Research Policy," *ISIS,* 68, 1977.
47. Wiesner, "A Troubled Relationship"; *Sloan Foundation Report,* 1977.
48. John F. Kennedy School of Government, *Bulletin,* fall–winter, 1980–81. See also William Zeckhauser et al., "Incentive Arguments for Environmental Protection," typescript.
49. Bruce Owen and Ronald Brautigañ, *The Regulation Game* (Cambridge, Mass.: Ballinger 1978).
50. Donald L. M. Blackmer, "Possible Study Group on Risk Assessment, Regulation and the Individual," Memorandum, Program in Science, Technology and Society November 20, 1978 (MIT).
51. "Report of the Committee to Consider Harvard's Possible Participation in a Joint Program on the Impact of Chemicals on Human Health and the Environment" (Harvard); Jerome Wiesner, "Report of the President, 1978–79" (MIT).

52. DeMuth in "Harvard's Policy Analysis Component," Joint MIT–Harvard Program on the Impact of Chemicals on Human Health and the Environment," typescript, April 30, 1979 (John F. Kennedy School of Government, Harvard University); Blackmer, "Possible Study Group"; Walter Rosenblith, form letter on meeting, April 5, 1979 (Provost's Office, MIT); Raiffa, "The Committee on Risk and Decision Making," National Academy of Sciences, March 26, 1980.

53. William F. Miller, Provost's Office Memorandum, "Proposed Conference on Risk Assessment and Regulation," Stanford University, November 24, 1978.

54. *MIT Report on Activities,* 1980. Not all these centers are formally tied to the universities or even on campus. An important example of an independent institute is the National Humanities Center. See David F. Noble, "Corporatist Culture Ministry," *The Nation,* March 21, 1981.

55. Leonard Sloane, "Business on Campus," *The New York Times,* February 20, 1980, p. D1; Gene Maeroff, "Education and Industry Narrowing the Gap," *The New York Times,* January 7, 1979; Du Pont *Context.*

56. Co-sponsored by Harvard, the New York Stock Exchange, and the U.S. Senate Subcommittee on International Trade, the conference brought together academics, congressmen, and leaders from the corporate and banking communities (but no representatives from regulatory agencies, consumer or environmental groups, or labor). The most tangible product of the conference was a full-page advertisement in *The Wall Street Journal* (July 23) proclaiming that the United States "must strengthen its competitiveness" by, among other things, reducing the burdens of regulation and fostering innovation through government tax and other incentives. "The American people," the ad read, "are aware of a fundamental crisis in our economy and are ready to support extraordinary measures to reverse it."

57. National Commission on Research, *Industry and the Universities.* This was not the consensus among faculty at Harvard in the fall of 1980 when the Harvard administration proposed that Harvard go into the biotechnology industry, in partnership with resident researchers. President Derek Bok and his associates in the effort encountered stiff resistance to the plan on the grounds of violation of academic integrity and freedom. They were compelled to drop —or, more likely, postpone—the commercial venture. See David F. Noble and Nancy E. Pfund, "Business Goes Back to College," *The Nation,* September 20, 1980.

58. MIT Symposium on Innovation, *Proceedings;* R. E. Lyon, "A Bridge Reconnecting Academia and Industry through Basic Research," spring 1980 (typescript); see also "MIT, ER&E Enter Research Agreement," MIT *Tech Talk,* April 30, 1980. Also Jerome Wiesner, "Has the U.S. Lost Its Initiative in Technological Innovation?" *Technology Review,* July 1976.

59. Edward David, "Science Futures: The Industrial Connection," *Science,* March 2, 1979. See also Denis Praeger and Gil Omenn, "Research, Innovation, and University-Industry Linkages," *Science,* January 25, 1980.

60. Fernandez and Schneiderman in "For Monsanto, A New Direction: Health Care," *Business Week,* July 9, 1979; Praeger and Omenn, op. cit.; "Department of Medicine Proposal to Stanford University to Establish an Institute of Biological and Clinical Investigation" (typescript), Stanford University.

61. Lyon, op. cit.

62. Philip J. Hilts, "Ivy Covered Capitalism," *Washington Post,* November 10, 1980; Paul J. Bass, "Yale Ponders Setting Up Own Research Company," *New Haven Register,* October 29, 1980; "Discussion Memo: Technology Transfer at Harvard," *Harvard Gazette,* October 9, 1980; "Harvard Considers Commercial Role in DNA Research," *The New York Times,* October 27, 1980; Richard Lewontin, "A Grave Threat," *Harvard Crimson,* October 16, 1980. See also Joel

Gurin and Nancy Pfund, "Bonanza in the Lab," *The Nation*, November 22, 1980. Riemer in Diana Dutton, et al., "Entrepreneurial Biology" (typescript), Division of Health Services Research, Stanford University.

63. Herbert Fusfeld, "The Bridge between Universities and Industry," *Science*, July 11, 1980.

64. Barring, of course, the success of the California Rural Legal Association suit against the University of California. This unprecedented suit, which charges the university with misuse of public funds because, in developing harvesting machinery, it served agribusiness at the expense of small growers and farm-workers, could have far-reaching consequences for the future conduct of university-based research. See Bernard Taper, "The Bittersweet Harvest," *Science 80*, November 1980.

65. *Nuclear Power and Nuclear Weapons Proliferation*, Report of the Atlantic Council's Nuclear Fuels Policy Working Group, The Atlantic Council, 1978.

66. U.S. Department of State, *Technology and Foreign Affairs*, December 1976, p. iii.

67. Ibid., Appendix A, p. 2.

68. *Science, Technology and Diplomacy in the Age of Interdependence, Report Prepared for the Subcommittee on International Security and Scientific Affairs of the Committee on International Relations of the U.S. House of Representatives*, Congressional Research Service of the Library of Congress, June 1976.

69. Evidence given to the U.S. Senate Commerce Committee's Subcommittee on Science, Technology and Space, July 17, 1979. Report 96–43, p. 9.

70. *Science, Growth and Society* (Paris: OECD 1971), p. 53.

71. *Technology and Foreign Affairs*, Appendix E, p. 2.

72. *Technology, Trade and the US Economy, Report of a Workshop Held at Woods Hole, Massachusetts, August 22–31, 1976*. National Academy of Sciences, Washington, D.C.: 1978, p. 9.

73. *Science, Technology and Diplomacy*, Vol. 1, p. 5.

74. *Technology and Foreign Affairs*, Appendix E, p. 6.

75. For a description, see Frank Press, "Science and Technology in the White House, 1977 to 1980: Part 2," *Science*, 211, January 16, 1981.

76. *The Science and Technology Message of the President*. Message to the Congress, March 27, 1981, p. 13.

77. Press, op. cit.

78. *National Science and Technology Policy Issues: Part 1*, Committee on Science and Technology of the U.S. House of Representatives, 36–106, 1979, p. 14.

79. "A Lack of Clear-cut Policies." Interview with David Rockefeller, *Business Week*, March 12, 1979, p. 74.

80. Don I. Phillips et al. (eds.), *Colloquium on R & D Policy*, AAAS Report No. 79-R-14, October 1979, p. 137.

81. Evidence presented to U.S. Senate Commerce Committee Subcommittee on Science, Technology and Space, on U.S. policies and initiatives for the UN Conference on Science and Technology for Development, July 17, 1979, p. 89. Report 96-43.

82. Phillips et al., eds., op. cit., p. 132.

83. Ibid., p. 131.

84. See Senate Report 96-43, pp. 32–33.

85. Father Theodore Hesburgh, Address to Plenary Session, United Nations Conference on Science and Technology for Development, Vienna, August 20, 1979.

86. Senate Report 96-43, p. 67.

87. Ibid., pp. 76–77.

88. Ibid., p. 35. Letter from J. Brian Atwood, assistant secretary of state for congressional relations, to Senator Adlai Stevenson, August 17, 1979.

89. See Press, "Science and Technology in the White House," *passim*.

90. *Chronicle of Higher Education,* September 10, 1979, p. 3.
91. *Technology Transfer and the Developing Countries,* U.S. Chamber of Commerce, 1977.
92. *The Contribution of Transnational Enterprises to Future World Development,* UNCSTD Background Document, 1979, p. v.
93. John Kemeny, "Saving American Democracy: The Lessons of Three Mile Island," *Technology Review,* 83, 7 (June–July 1980).
94. Branscomb, op. cit.
95. Edward E. David, "Technology and Society: Prospects for the 80s," keynote address at the dedication of the Bechtel Engineering Center at the University of California in Berkeley, June 6, 1980, p. 15.
96. Simon Ramo, *America's Technology Slip* (New York: Wiley, 1980), p. 4.
97. William O. Baker, *National Science and Technology Policy Issues: Part I,* op. cit., p. 66.
98. Phillips et al. (eds.), op. cit., p. 22.
99. Jerome Wiesner interview, "After Affluence, Americans Are Not Prepared to Go Back," *U.S. News and World Report,* August 11, 1980. See as well the extraordinary October 10, 1980, letter to *The New York Times* signed by Wiesner and others. Written in response to a *Times* editorial on the significance of the accident at the Three Mile Island nuclear power plant and the likely implications of the not-yet released Kemeny Commission report on the accident, the authors of the letter attempted to anticipate and preempt "the possible public and governmental reaction to the Kemeny Commission report," and defend the continued use of nuclear power. Assuming that the report would condemn the nuclear industry, they urged that nuclear power "be evaluated realistically" in comparison with alternative sources of energy. "We hope (the Report) will not be misconstrued by the public, its leaders, or the press as a definitive statement on the future use of nuclear power." As it turned out, their fears were unwarranted. The Kemeny Report did not condemn the continued use of nuclear power outright, but instead called for more attention to the "human factor" in power plant operation, and the ideological scientistic "mindset" that nuclear power was "safe." Indeed, as noted above, Kemeny was soon telling an MIT audience that such technological issues defied public and governmental oversight, and noting the possible irrelevance of democracy in an advanced industrial age. However embarrassed for having jumped the gun, the authors of the letter could not have been more pleased. Epitomizing the convergence of industry and university, profit and objectivity, science and power, antidemocratic social policy and elitist science policy, they included, in addition to Wiesner: physicist David S. Saxon (University of California), physicist Marvin Goldberger (Cal Tech), physicist Harvey Brooks (Harvard, and a director at Raytheon), Irving Shapiro (chairman of Du Pont and the Business Roundtable, director at Citicorp, IBM, and the Conference Board), Thomas A. Murphy (president of General Motors and the Business Roundtable), W. H. Krome George (president of Alcoa, director at Mellon Bank and Pullman), and John D. Macomber (president of Celanese Corporation, director at Chase and R. J. Reynolds).

A RADICAL DEPARTURE: SOCIAL WELFARE AND THE ELECTION

Ira Katznelson

The 1980 presidential election was a battle about social policy fought by combatants of unequal conviction. The Reagan campaign defined the place of the contest: the crossroads of the market and the state. It convinced a majority of voters to choose the path of nineteenth-century liberalism. The market should specify matters of production and consumption, and governmental policies should be restricted to the minimum necessary to protect the marketplace. This achievement was a considerable one. Most Reagan voters had a stake in the social policies of the federal government. Further, since the New Deal, Republican and Democratic administrations alike have accepted a modest consensus about social policy. This broad agreement about collective provisions, regulations, and redistributive activities of government has defined the limits of political common sense and public policy for nearly a half a century. The causes of the radical departure signified by the 1980 election are not self-evident.

I

The public record of a political campaign records, charts, and directs political change. It may be thought of as a text that invites critical readings. Such interpretations are complicated by the deliberately evocative and opaque features of much political language, which is designed to secure new supporters without forfeiting traditional constituents. Democrats are usually careful to balance their recital of past luminaries and legislative accomplishments with reassurances about fiscal prudence and support for the business economy. Pledges by Republicans to resist big government are often tempered by comforting noises of compassion and support for social policies they once opposed.[1]

Each election, nevertheless, has a revealing integrity of its own which can be discerned, and which tells us a great deal about the balance of social forces and policies more generally. If politicians tell voters what they think

I wish to thank James Johnson for his research assistance.

voters would like to hear, their rhetoric not only reflects opinion but leads it. Candidates tell voters what to think.

The major review of trends in the American electorate, *The Changing American Voter*, considered the available survey data on public attitudes about various issues from the late Truman administration through Nixon's first term. The authors found that social policy questions stood out as most important only in the Truman years. Concerns with welfare state programs took a secondary place to issues of foreign policy (Korea, communism, atomic weapons) in the Eisenhower years. Race became the dominant mass issue in the Kennedy administration; poverty and Vietnam in Johnson's; and a cluster of daily life issues—drugs, crime, delinquency, abortion, and urban disorder—in Nixon's. Nie, Verba, and Petrocik concluded a bit obviously, but importantly, that "the way in which citizens conceptualize the political realm is dependent on the political content to which they are exposed."[2]

This content is an agglomeration of fact and interpretation. Some three decades ago David Truman made the point that interest groups and politicians fashion mappings of the facts in order to create those attentive publics most likely to support their interests.[3] In 1972, for example, Nixon tried with some success to talk to blue-collar workers about noneconomic issues, and in this way to create a public these workers could join, even as he opposed most of the policy proposals made by their trade unions. His task was made easier than it might have been by George McGovern's sanctimonious and soft demeanor, and by his poorly presented economic proposals. McGovern's rejoinder to Nixon, nonetheless, was an attempt to mobilize a working-class public, concerned with social policy.

A striking feature of the 1980 campaign is that it explicitly and directly placed issues of social policy at the heart of the competition for votes. Fundamental questions about what may be called the social democratic agenda were politicized in a way they had not been since the Truman years. Apart from the nationalization of industry, a subject that has never been included in the ordinary give and take of American politics, this agenda has been concerned with the following: (1) the capacity of government to regulate, plan for, and modify the private economy; (2) the choices government makes in creating macroeconomic policies to deal with unemployment and inflation; and (3) the scope and character of welfare state programs, including social insurance, such as social security, and nonmarket transfers of money, including food stamps and welfare payments. Each of these areas of policy is concerned with the appropriate scale of state intervention in the marketplace, matters of equity and utility, and fundamental questions about capitalism, socialism, and democracy.

The 1980 election was distinguished by an antistatist rhetoric, which signaled a loss of faith in the social democratic image of society and in its promise. This change in public philosophy did not happen all at once, of course. In its electoral outcome and in the way its debates were conducted, however, the election ratified a shift in initiative to the opponents of welfare capitalism, and it signified the disarray of the keepers of the social democratic impulse.

This election was hardly the first in which American voters have heard a rhetoric of limited government. But apart from foreign policy questions about the role of America in the world, the campaign revolved around the question of whether social policy should be an adjunct to the market, and should be called on only in cases of clear market incapacity; or whether social policy should aim for a redistribution of resources based on nonmarket principles.[4] In this discussion the terms were set by the Reagan campaign, before and after his nomination, and by the clusters of conservative intellectuals in the academy and selected East and West coast think tanks who provided a rationale for the candidate's conservative impulses and stump speeches. Reagan avoided making the kind of specific proposals that got him into political trouble in 1976, when he said he had a plan to transfer responsibility for many federal programs to the states in order to save $90 billion each year. Instead, his 1980 campaign pledged itself, in more general terms, "to restore to the Federal Government the capacity to do the people's work without dominating their lives," and to "the clarity of vision to see the difference between what is essential and what is merely desirable." He did call, more precisely, for turning welfare financing back to the states (along with tax resources equivalent to current block grants), and for cuts in federal spending "of ten per cent by fiscal year 1984." As an advocate of tax reduction and a massive increase in military spending, Reagan made clear that his cuts would be made in welfare state programs. He hastened to add on many occasions that his "strategy for spending control does not require slashing necessary programs," a reassurance consistent with his distinction between the necessary and the desirable. Further, he attacked federal planners and regulators, pledging to "remove from the backs of industry in America unnecessary federal regulations." He disdained using fiscal and monetary policy to minimize unemployment, promising instead that tax cuts and deregulation would promote noninflationary growth.[5]

These themes and proposals established the larger frame of reference for the contest for the presidency. After all the candidates had declared but before the primary season opened, George Bush spoke at the American Enterprise Institute. In contrast with past campaigns, he observed, "I do not think there is a wide array of differences among the candidates. . . . There is more of a matrix, more of a center, more of an agreement among the Republican candidates this year than in the past."[6] His own proposals as the "moderate" in the campaign were virtually indistinguishable from those of Reagan—limitations in public spending, regulatory cutbacks, and supply-side tax cuts, with new tax credits for business. With the exception of his tax proposals, even John Anderson, as a Republican and later as an independent candidate, was part of this consensus. The Ford reassurances at the Republican convention of 1976—"We will make sure that this nation does not neglect citizens who are less fortunate, but provides for their needs with compassion and dignity"—were displaced by a different rhetoric of compassion in 1980. "We have forged a giant government out of compassion for the needy," Ford told the convention in August. "Now we can trim that government out of compassion for the taxpayers."[7]

By contrast to the assertive Republican assault on the social policy role of the state, the Democratic candidates were placed on the defensive. Carter's main response was a series of overdrawn attacks on Reagan as threatening to dismantle all major domestic programs, including social security, coupled with an endorsement of the Reagan goals of limited government. Carter favored restraint in the growth of federal spending, and indicated that he hoped to hold federal spending to little if any real growth in his second term. Unlike 1976, when he proposed national health insurance and an expensive overhaul of the welfare system, including the federalization of expenditures, in 1980 Carter pledged to work only for a modest start on health policy and for a very limited program to help some states pay their welfare bills. He identified inflation as the main current economic problem, rather than unemployment, which he stressed in his first campaign.[8] And he boasted of his achievements in deregulation: "We have accomplished the deregulation of airlines, trucking and financial institutions. We're working hard to get rail deregulated. We are also working on communications-system deregulation." In sum, he told *U.S. News and World Report* in a preelection interview: "There has never been an administration that's been so successful in getting the government's nose out of the free enterprise system."[9] Carter's boasts were rather like Reagan's promises.

Even Edward Kennedy, the keeper of the social democratic impulse (a role he discovered at Georgetown University only after initial primary election defeats and a waffling inability to define a coherent rationale other than personal ambition for his challenge to a sitting Democratic president), produced an exceptionally mild campaign in social democratic terms. Other than wage and price controls, a policy last implemented by President Nixon, and a $12 billion countercyclical jobs program, Kennedy's campaign was rather longer on the language of empathy than on specific proposals for an expanded government role in any of the main dimensions of social policy. Even his proposal for comprehensive national health insurance was hardly mentioned on the stump, and only in passing in his moving speech to the Democratic convention. Rather, as the most "progressive" candidate in the race, Kennedy defended existing gains and programs from Republican attack, and from the Carter retreat. "The Carter budget," he proclaimed in the primary season, "flies a Republican banner. It seeks to take food from the mouths of 2 million children in the school lunch program. It seeks to slash public housing below the rockbottom levels of the Nixon years. And the cuts may go deeper as pressure on the President mounts from the Republican candidates." He then defined his role as a defensive one: "Unless some among us are willing to make a stand, to hold our ground, the pressure for drastic cuts in the Federal spending may result in a reign of budget terror that will devastate the lives of millions of citizens and shatter the dream of America for millions more."[10] He combined his stress on unemployment and his protective posture on social programs with an enthusiastic embrace of the cause of deregulation, albeit to be accomplished more selectively than the other candidates indicated. Harvard law professor Stephen Breyer, a close Kennedy advisor, produced a detailed consideration of regulatory failure and principles for reform in 1979. It may be read as the most coherent statement of the Kennedy position. Breyer argued that regulation should be limited to the worst cases, that it should rely on inducements rather than penalties, and that the government should examine the problems of regulation through a "procompetitive lens." Energy, health, transportation, safety, and environmental regulations, he claimed, were ripe for reform.[11]

The "Left" candidate, in short, did not resist the deregulation impulse, but promoted it; did not advocate an expansion of social welfare programs, but only their defense; and differed chiefly from the other candidates of both parties in his macroeconomic proposals. Although he was the most friendly overall to the traditional social policy agenda of the Democratic party and to social goals more generally, Kennedy helped reveal the central domestic feature of the campaign: an exhaustion of ideas and political capacity on the Left, and an abdication of initiative to the Right. The changes in the preferences of politicians and voters recorded in the campaign put at issue many of the assumptions and programs of the American welfare state. Confirmed in the election was a broadly coherent world view which identifies the growth of government as the major source of economic problems, and which sees a less bridled marketplace as the solution. Moreover, this perspective, in the absence of coherent and committed articulate opposition, was presented successfully as not partisan in class terms, but as a program in the interest of all Americans. In 1972, the Republican candidate sought to mobilize blue-collar support not by talking economics and social policy, but by creating an alternative public. In 1980, Reagan talked with effect directly about these issues. Asked why blue-collar workers should vote for him, he answered in terms of deregulation and the bounty of employment his social and economic policies would create.[12] "The Republicans might be for the rich man," a New Jersey spot welder told *The New York Times*, "but when they are in there they provide jobs."[13]

I I

How is this text to be read? For a very long time, analysts of social policy have tried to explain the dramatic growth of social policy expenditures by governments throughout the West, and they have tried to assess the impact of these programs on the private marketplace. The lessons we have learned in making these accounts are not irrelevant to attempts to assess the current hard times for social democratic policies. For if the tools we developed to explain the expansion of the welfare state are in fact good ones, they should be helpful in accounting for this moment of ideological, if not yet actual, contraction. Or at least minimally, they should allow us to conceptualize how we wish to think about current events.

This is not the place for a full-fledged review or critique of various accounts of the development of social policy. Nor is it obvious, and this is a theme to which I will return, that the welfare state in fact is about to contract. Just yesterday, as I noted in a related paper,[14] the majority of observers talked about the welfare state in terms of uninterrupted growth. Objections to these trends and proposals of the kind made by the Reagan campaign to undo parts of it seemed quixotic and utopian. Measured against this inheritance of apparently irreversible and virtually automatic growth in state programs, the 1980 campaign appears to herald a very different trend. We would do well to be agnostic. It is far from clear that American social policy is in more difficulty today than, say, a quarter-century, or half-century ago. The chronological comparisons that provide justifications for considerations of the conservative resurgence have a more condensed time frame. My second reservation concerns the future. It is not possible to extrapolate long-term trends from the current situation, for obvious methodological reasons. These cautionary words having been said, the "text" of antigovernment assertiveness in 1980 deserves a reading; and the tools for this reading should be crafted as part of a more general approach to the development of social policy.

Without reviewing the positions of others, let me restate my own, in condensed form.[15] The social policy activities of Western democratic governments in capitalist societies develop in two interrelated ways. First, the ordinary operation of the capitalist political economy, in a particular time and place, requires a variety of state activities for the re-creation of the productive and social relationships essential to the economy. We do not have a precise understanding of what these requirements are; we lack such a theory. But even if its precise content is not known, it seems beyond doubt that a *minimum* of social policies is required to ensure the process of economic accumulation, and to give it broad social acceptance. The level and content of this minimum, however, cannot be the subject of calculations that hold equally well for all capitalist democracies. The minimum varies from state to state and from time to time because it represents an amalgam of what has come to be economically, politically, and culturally necessary. The minimum is in part genuinely a minimum by intention that connotes widely shared meanings and understandings about the appropriate dimensions and character of government interventions in the market. Although largely the result of past group and class struggles, the minimum at a given moment is no longer the subject of struggle. It is accepted as a given by all classes in society. The existence of a National Health Service in Great Britain and the social security system in the United States are cases in point.

An institution in being defines reality for its participants, and constitutes a definition of problems and ways to work them out. The welfare state at the level of the minimum in a given society at a given moment presents a common set of problems that appear technically and politically neutral for politicians, administrators, and client-citizens. To such problems, civil servants and contestants for the vote are compelled to respond. In constructing these responses, they may draw on elaborate and sophisticated tools from welfare economics and theories of public finance that provide a framework for the identification of an appropriate welfare state minimum. This technical literature understands state growth as the product of social overhead requirements and external costs generated by private sector development, and it seeks to find alternative guidelines to public sector expansion in the absence of price tags to link specific outlays to specific contributions by taxpayers. The definition not only of public goods but also of appropriate merit goods is the object of such analyses, linked explicitly to the externalities generated by ordinary capitalist development.

But the welfare state does not only develop in this "problem-solving" way. Under certain conditions, various political parties and social movements may succeed in utilizing the democratic process (including protests as well as elections) to push welfare state advances forward at a pace more rapid than that dictated by the emergence of manifest "problems." When such attempts succeed it makes sense to speak of a social policy *surplus,* required neither by the logic of capitalist nor of democratic relations understood in their own terms, independent of the distinctive tension between the functional requirements of capitalism and democracy and the dynamics of class and group organization and demands in specific settings.

The level of welfare state expenditures as well as their character at a given moment is the sum of the minimum about which there is broad communal consensus, and the results of current factional group and class conflicts. The dimensions of the minimum inherited from the past, and struggles about whether and to what extent a surplus will be fashioned in the present, are functions of the capacities of organized groups and classes.

I should stress that it does not follow from these considerations that policies now part of the "minimum" are necessarily more functional for market capitalism than those generated by struggles about the "surplus." In part this is because, as Cohen argues, "class insurgency is more likely to achieve its object when the object has functional value. . . . There is victory [for the working classes] when capitalism is able to sustain itself only under the modification the reform imposes on it."[16] It is also the case because, in contradictory fashion, any expansion of the nonmarket sphere, at whatever level of welfare state development, entails at least short-term costs for investment and productivity and for some privileged economic actors. Further, it should be recalled that a present minimum is yesterday's surplus, and, as such, was the occasion for struggle. For this reason it is difficult to say that the welfare state is in more trouble today than at many

other periods. Struggles about the welfare state are structurally condi-
tioned by the distinction between minimum and surplus; struggles are
endemic about where the line between minimum and surplus is to be
drawn, and about the potential surplus itself. These struggles about the
definition of minimum and surplus and about the content of the surplus
consist in a set of limits which are set in part by the functional requirements of capitalism and democracy, in part by the inheritance of past
policies and compromises, and in part by factors that affect class and group
capacity.

I think these observations are of some use in diagnosing the 1980
campaign. The logic of the welfare state that I have sketched has not
changed. The new resolve of the Right and the incapacity of the Left to
define the terms of political discourse have not altered the existing welfare
state minimum in basic ways in the United States or in any of the other
societies of Western Europe and North America. Indeed, it is rather a
commonplace to note that once social policies cease to be the targets of
group and class contests, and once they provide a set of givens that inter-
twine other social and economic policies in complicated ways, they prove
extremely difficult to undo. Thatcherite Conservatives in England do not
dismantle the British Health Service to return to fee for service medicine,
though they might try to reduce increases in health spending. Conservative
Republicans in the White House and Congress are equally unlikely to
dismantle social security, or Medicare and Medicaid, which they once
fought so hard to prevent, even though they will work to stop their
expansion. The costs to the social order of doing more simply would be
too high. In the afterglow of the Reagan victory such staunch conservatives
as Republican Congressmen Jack Kemp and David Stockman, the new
director of OMB, reassured Americans that the New Deal will not be rolled
back, and that most social policy expenditures are locked in by law. I return
to this point below.

On the record of conservative governments in the past, here and
abroad, it is reasonable to say that governments on the Right have been
compelled to address social problems in ways that actually expand the
scope of the welfare state. What has occurred in the past few years, and
was ratified in the 1980 campaign, was an intensification of the resistance
to this process of expansion of the "minimum," and, concurrently, an
erosion of the ability of various popular movements within and outside the
Democratic party to secure a welfare state surplus. It is this double trend
that demands explanation.

III

The stagflation that has persisted in the United States, and in the West
more generally, since 1973 provides the context for such an evaluation.

The combination of low, and at times negative, economic growth and high rates of inflation has altered the climate for both principal ways in which social policy initiatives have been developed in the past. Government and private economists and technocrats have begun to think out loud about the contradictory effects of social policy, and especially about the constraints the social democratic agenda places on the logic of the market and its mechanisms. The inability of the capitalist economies of the West in recent years to find a formula to provide for growth, high employment, and low inflation has also hurt the social democratic political forces. The economic crisis, together with other factors, has diminished the political capacity of the organizations and movements that wish to fight for what I have called a social democratic surplus. Instead, like the Kennedy campaign, they have been placed on the defensive. Conversely, stagflation has made the arguments of the Right seem considerably more persuasive than they are.

The two decades after World War II were years of economic prosperity. At the end of the war, 1946 and 1947 were years of negative growth, as the economy demobilized and returned to a peacetime footing, and many economists and politicians feared a return to prewar crisis conditions. These concerns proved unfounded. Between 1947 and 1967, there was real annual growth in the GNP of just under 4 percent; the average unemployment rate was about 4.5 percent; and inflation averaged only 2 percent a year. Since 1967, and especially since 1973, there has been a dramatic deterioration of the American economy in each of these aspects. Real annual growth from 1969 to 1979 dropped to under 3 percent; average unemployment moved up to 5.8 percent; and inflation jumped to an average of 6.7 percent (and to almost 9 percent since 1973, and more than 13 percent in 1979).[17]

The poor performance of the American economy (and of Western economies more generally) has produced a crisis of Keynesian economic theory. It is worth lingering on this theoretical impasse, because both the technocratic and political mechanisms of the expansion of social policy depended on Keynesian theory, which was seen to work, and to produce a surplus that was available for nonmarket programs. At the end of the period of high prosperity and growth, Robert Gordon observed, an activist view of fiscal policy based on Keynesian assumptions "appeared to have achieved an unassailable victory over its critics." In 1966, Walter Heller summarized this consensus, when he proclaimed that "we now take for granted that the government must step in to provide the essential stability at high levels of employment and growth that the market mechanism, left alone, cannot deliver."[18] The problem-solving mode of welfare state expansion dealt with the externalities of capitalist growth, which it took for granted; and the social democratic groups and movements created a marriage between Keynesian demand management and attempts to secure a welfare state surplus. That is, they made claim to the tools that could make capitalism flourish, while undermining the logic of the marketplace in a way that ultimately might transform capitalist social and economic relationships. If the expansion of social policy was thus rooted in Keynesian doctrine and in its successes, the crisis of economic theory and performance has challenged the underpinnings of each.

Perhaps the greatest macroeconomic puzzle of the past decade or so has been the very great deceleration of labor productivity (output per hour). Between 1947 and 1967, productivity grew at an annual rate of 3.2 percent; since 1967 it has grown at a rate of less than 1.5 percent, and at under 1 percent since 1973.[19] This productivity crisis has proved a severe challenge to Keynesian theory, because it appears to invalidate the axiom that adequate demand will maintain supply; that productivity is determined by demand. Peter Drucker, a critic of this view, has summarized the new skepticism:

> It was . . . not totally frivolous to assume, as Keynes did 50 years ago, that productivity would take care of itself and would continue to increase slowly but steadily, if only economic confidence prevailed for both businessmen and workingmen, and if only demand stayed high and unemployment low. In the early 1930's Keynes' was a rational—albeit optimistic—view (though even then Joseph Schumpeter and Lionel Robbins could not accept it). But surely this can no longer be maintained. And yet, within the Keynesian system there is no room for productivity, no way to stimulate or spur it, no means to make an economy more productive.[20]

The failures of post-1967, and especially post-1973, capitalism have thus been read as the failure of the Keynesian promise that markets would function as the neoclassical economists said they would if aggregate demand was maintained. A former Keynesian, Mark Willes, now a member of the extremely conservative "rational expectations" school associated with Robert Lucas of the University of Chicago, has produced a typical critique of Keynesian models, which, he tells us, "flatly failed":

> As recently as the early 1970's they uniformly predicted that the United States could push its unemployment rate down to 4 percent if it accepted an inflation rate of about 4 per cent. If it accepted a slightly higher inflation rate, according to these models, it could reduce unemployment still further, and with a 5 per cent rate of inflation, it could practically assign unemployment to the history books. Clearly, these predictions were far off the mark. Unemployment did not drop when inflation went up—unemployment went up too.[21]

These comments capture another aspect of the attack on Keynesian theory—the assault on the Phillips curve assumption of a tradeoff between inflation and unemployment that can be exploited by policymakers. In 1958 New Zealand economist A. W. Phillips published an empirical study of the relationship between wage rates and unemployment in the United Kingdom between 1862 and 1957. MIT economist Robert Solow, who along with his colleague Paul Samuelson fashioned an equivalent time series for the United States and suggested that the Phillips findings had major policy implications, recalls: "What Phillips found was really pretty astonishing. The simple bivariate relation, relating only to one real and one nominal variable, held up very well over a very long time during which the nature of British industry and labor changed drastically. Here was evidence for a strong and apparently reliable relation between the nominal world and the real world." This relationship, Samuelson and Solow wrote, demonstrated that there is a "menu of choice" between levels of unemployment and inflation.[22]

The Phillips curve became the conventional wisdom of the 1960s, but it has come under fire by conservative economists ever since Milton Friedman's celebrated attack in his presidential address to the American Economics Association in 1967. He suggested that the Phillips curve was an illusion; that in the long term unemployment settles at its "natural" rate, whatever the rate of inflation. This speech, based on the assumption that unemployment is essentially voluntary—individuals are unemployed because they mistakenly think they can get better wages by waiting or by searching for employment other than that which is available—denied the key policy prescription of Keynesian theory: that unemployment could be reduced by stimulating demand. It also argued, in a corollary way, that restrictions on monetary growth could dampen inflation without unemployment in the long run.[23]

"Economic ideas," Robert Gordon observes, "rarely lead economic events but usually follow them." There had been many dissenters from the Keynesian consensus before 1967, but only after that year did the case against it make much headway. It would be misleading to think that the departures from Keynesian orthodoxy have come entirely on the Right. In the past decade there has been a vigorous, and important, revival of Marxist economic theory (which *has* paid attention to questions of production and productivity, rather than mainly to issues of distribution and demand), and there has been a new flourishing of Left or radical Keynesianism under the label of post-Keynesian economics. Yet there is also no doubt that there has been a massive shift in the conventional wisdom of the economics profession to the Right; that with this shift key assumptions of the "problem-solving" bureaucratic, technocratic, and apolitical approach to defining a social policy minimum have been undermined; and that it has entailed a major attack on the credibility of social democratic initiatives more generally.

This move to the Right has had three main components: an emphasis on supply-side economics; monetarism; and the development of the rational expectations school. The supply-siders stress the related issues of capital formation, savings, productivity, and technological changes. Although to date supply-side economists have not produced a model that incorporates the issues of productivity and capital formation or links their microeconomic and macroeconomic concerns, they have been vigorous in an eclectic way in insisting that issues of supply dominate questions of demand; in focusing on the price extracted by government regulation; in drawing attention to the decrease in the proportion of GNP devoted to research and development; and in drawing attention to the decrease in the growth of the capital to labor ratio.[24]

Monetarism (the term was coined in 1968 by Karl Brunner) is identified principally with Milton Friedman and the University of Chicago, and is based on a simple set of ideas. The more money available in circulation, the more inflation; the less money, the less inflation. Changes in the stock of money also critically influence production and employment; the actions of government authorities in managing the supply of money are critical to the functioning of the economy.

The rational expectations school can be seen in part as an extension of the monetarist perspective, in that it proposes revisionist tenets to be appended to monetarism. Whereas Milton Friedman conceded to the Keynesians that there might be a short-term tradeoff between unemployment and inflation (while denying the longer-term relationship), the rational expectations school argues that even such short-term tradeoffs depend on the assumption that economic actors can act adaptively in nonrational ways. They rejected this assumption and, as the name of the school implies, argued that even in the very short term all actors "optimize and use information efficiently when forming their expectations."[25] In the 1970s Robert Lucas and some other economists took this assumption and created macroeconomic models based on classical principles to rival, and in their view to replace, Keynesian macroeconomic models.

Each of these main nodes of conservative economic thought agrees on an antistatist position. The supply-siders think that government and business are in competition for resources; and that tax cuts and a smaller government budget (especially with regard to such "nonproductive" programs as those of the welfare state) will make vigorous growth possible again. The policy implications of monetarism are also noninterventionist, and they have been popularized in Milton Friedman's past and present best sellers and television extravaganzas. If anything, the rational expectations folk are even more resistant to the role of government in the economy and in social policy. Since they stress that the rules of the economic game need to be well understood and stable, they give to government this single function of the specification of the rules, but leave the play of the game entirely in private hands. "Instead of activist policies we need stable policies" is their slogan.[26]

The shift to the Right in the economics profession has fundamentally altered the way in which social policy and the role of the state more generally are discussed in the "nonpolitical" policymaking community. These conservatives notice a provocative correlation between the growth of government—in particular, the growth of social welfare transfers and new health, safety, environmental, and transport regulations—and the reduced vitality of the capitalist economy. And they proceed to argue that this correlation identifies the principal causes of economic disarray. The National Bureau of Economic Research's important new volume, *The American Economy in Transition,* opens and closes with clear statements of this view. The organization's president, Martin Feldstein, notes that "the expanded role of government has undoubtedly been the most important change in the structure of the American economy in the post-war period," and he concedes that "the extent to which this change in structure has been the cause of the major decline in performance cannot be easily assessed." Nevertheless, he goes on to argue in the remainder of the essay, "there can be no doubt that government policies do deserve substantial blame for the adverse experience of the past decade." He holds that transfer payments which aim at redistribution have had the direct consequence of lowering rates of savings and investment.[27] In similar terms, Arthur Burns concludes the volume by enumerating a list of the current failures of American capitalism, and by finding cause for hope[28]

> by noting a highly constructive development in our country. We as a people now know what our problems are and we have begun to do something about them. Inflation is now accepted as our nation's number one economic problem. The zeal for government regulation is diminishing. The importance of encouraging savings and business capital investment is no longer questioned. Expenditures on research and development are again rising in real terms. . . . A conservative financial trend is developing in our country, and I think it is gathering momentum.

This new center of gravity of the economics profession has been reflected in the changes in initiative and impact of the major social policy think tanks in the United States: the Brookings Institution, the American Enterprise Institute and, to a lesser extent, the Institute for Policy Studies. That this should be so is hardly surprising, since economists have played a critical role in shaping the intellectual climate in these institutions, even as they have been concerned with more than economic policy narrowly conceived. In the 1960s, Brookings was in the ascendant, pushing and probing on the center and the left of the Keynesian consensus of the Great Society years to find new ways to achieve Walter Heller's injunction. Though small, the Institute for Policy Studies housed a vigorous research program tied explicitly to the various social movements of the period. By contrast, the American Enterprise Institute was a rather weak, fringe institution. Today, all this has changed. IPS, torn a few years ago by internal dissension, is still doing important work, but it has not succeeded in defining a clear role for itself in the absence of vigorous movements for radical change. Brookings continues to be the largest and most respected of the establishments, but as even a cursory bibliographical review of its recent publications on social policy would indicate, it has turned its attention rather more to fine-tuning existing social policy than to proposing new departures. AEI, by contrast, has grown very rapidly, and in a vigorous publication program has challenged the major social democratic programs and policies of the federal government.

In short, the terms of reference and tools policymakers have for considering the social democratic minimum have changed dramatically in the past decade. Although the problems to which social democratic solutions have been addressed in the past have stayed with us and, if anything, have grown more pressing, the interpretive lenses worn by those who process and identify this minimum are now very different. Quite obviously, the way we see reality affects the choices we think we have in managing and shaping reality. If politicians by their discourse tell voters how to think, economists and the policy community more generally have been telling politicians how to think. By the evidence of the 1980 campaigns, the politicians have been rather assiduous pupils.

I V

Nevertheless, the lessons they have been taught have significant flaws and limits. These are intellectual, budgetary, political, and structural. Each set deserves at least a brief discussion in its own right; and each should be taken into account in an assessment of the likely impact of the results of 1980 on social policy in the near and middle-range future.

The new scholarly matrix fashioned by policy intellectuals comes equipped with the imposing authority of erudite presentation, models from the simple Laffer curve to the learned mathematics of Robert Lucas, and the happy circumstance of not having yet been tested too often in practice.[29] Its intellectual flaws—that is, those features which are vulnerable by the ordinary canons of scholarship—however, are not inconsiderable. Here I will confine myself to noting just two.

The anti-Keynesian, anti-Phillips curve view of unemployment depends on the radical and simplistic assumption that unemployment is never involuntary. At every moment, the argument goes, there is employment to be found for all who are willing to work at the going wage. The unemployed are people who refuse, thinking that if they wait and keep looking they will find something better. In so doing, they make bad assessments of their situation. This view, as Kenneth Arrow has pointed out, "can only be defended on the extreme view of smoothly working labor markets," in "which prices clear markets at every instant," and which takes no account of "market disequilibria that persist over months or even years."[30] Such an approach elides discussions of structural unemployment, dual labor markets, and race and sex discrimination; and has nothing to say about such recent trends as the extraordinary change in the job prospects of black teenagers, the increase in white-collar unemployment relative to blue-collar unemployment, and the upward drift in definitions of the "natural rate" of unemployment.[31]

Consider the latter issue. Estimates of "full employment" were put at 3 percent in the 1950s, 4 percent in the 1960s, 5 percent in the early years of the 1970s, and over 6 percent today. Noneconomists like myself might notice that these "natural" rates creep up to come close to the existing average rate, thus avoiding difficult questions by definition. Neo-Keynesian economists like James Tobin have also noticed that this upward drift poses a problem for theorists who associate the "natural" rate "with an equilibrium in which unemployment represents voluntary choice and efficient search."[32] Tobin argues in a recent Brookings paper, convincingly I think, that only a tiny fraction of the increase "has been credibly explained in terms of the labor market itself, as voluntary leisure disguised as unemployment, or rational job search, or friction, or persistent misinformation." Similarly, such government policies as minimum wages, unemployment compensation, and welfare state transfers have had, at most, only a tiny effect on the unemployment rate. As Tobin observes, the changes in the 1970s in these programs were far smaller than alterations in unemployment rates; and perhaps more important, most of these programs were created *in response to* higher unemployment, and thus can hardly be considered its cause. It is just possible, he concludes, that there is no natural rate of unemployment, "except one that floats with history."[33]

History does not appear to be a strong suit of the new conservative orthodoxy in public policy, and neither is comparative analysis. It is an article of faith of the new social policy analysts that there is an inverse relationship between economic growth, on the one hand, and the size of government and the level of social policy expenditures on the other. It follows that the private economy would work better if only the share of national income spent on social services would decrease. Popular accounts of this view linger on in the British case, and treat it as a morality tale of the perils of social democracy. Even the current prime minister in Downing Street takes the lessons of this story as an article of faith. But what a flawed story it is, in historical and comparative terms.

The most cursory kind of research a college freshman is capable of reveals that there has been no correlation whatsoever in the postwar years between rates of growth and relative shares for the market economy and the state. The growth rates of Sweden and the Netherlands have exceeded the best achievements of the American economy in this era, yet their public sectors capture more than half of their gross national products. West Germany takes a larger share of GNP in taxes than either the United States or Britain. Britain itself hardly is to be found at the top of the "league tables" of social democracy, but in the middle; the United States, one of the poorest economic performers of all, is resolutely stuck at the bottom. How is it, we may well ask, that the society with the smallest social democratic establishment of the major capitalist democracies has had one of the most sluggish economies? The simple refrain, "cut the state to unfetter the economy," is not a little problematical in this light.

In all, the intellectual underpinnings of the assault on social policy are, conservatively speaking, composed as much of ideology as of science. Science is invoked as part of a campaign to reduce the size of government and to overturn the redistributive effect government has had. In the United States, as Benjamin Page has recently shown in a valuable summary article, such impacts have been exceedingly limited. The largest social welfare program is social security, and it has only a very limited redistributive effect.[34] Unemployment insurance helps those who usually get work at a reasonable wage rather than those at the bottom of the economic ladder, who are out of work for long periods. And cash transfers like AFDC are quite meager, accounting for only some 3 percent of the federal budget; less, Page points out, than is spent on veterans' benefits and farm price supports.[35]

The American provisions for social welfare have been relatively modest, I have argued elsewhere,[36] because the United States lacks a regular political vehicle—a social democratic party or movement—for securing a social democratic surplus. With the exception of brief periods of angry and *ad hoc* popular mobilizations, as in the 1930s and 1960s, the welfare state has expanded principally as a result of technocratic, problem-solving initiatives by policymakers. In the years from the New Deal to the present there has developed an elaborate and sophisticated set of analytical tools to identify a social democratic minimum for the United States. "We may infer," I have written, "that the role of the state may be understood as being very close to the structural minimum necessary for system reproduction. A surplus social democracy does not exist because those who would be served by it lack the capacity—that is, both the disposition and the ability—to bring it into being."[37] As the tools used to identify the minimum have come under challenge, however, the minimum of the past is now identified by an increasing number of analysts as not really required, but as part of a surplus that can be rolled back.

Such a rollback will be very difficult to achieve, however, for a number of reasons. The first is budgetary. Most of the social democratic minimum —the prevailing agreement which is the product of past conflicts—has been enacted into legislation that produces "entitlements" to benefits linked to the cost of living quite outside the annual appropriation process. George Shultz, who directed the Office of Management and Budget for President Nixon, and Kenneth Dam, his assistant, have written in frustration about the "myth of budget tuning." Using data for fiscal 1977, they observe that the main constraint on budget policy is the uncontrollable character of 73 percent of the budget; if we leave defense spending aside, only about 10 percent of the budget is part of the normal consideration of the budget in Congress.[38]

There are several reasons why expenditures may be legally uncontrollable. Much spending in any given year is the fulfillment of obligations undertaken much earlier. Interest payments are another factor. But most important are the use of trust funds, as in social security, or legal entitlements which trigger payments to people when they enter certain categories like the unemployed. Shultz and Dam explain this process in political terms: advocates of specific programs want to shelter them from annual budgetary reviews. Legislative committees protect their programs from appropriations committees; and executive departments protect theirs from OMB. Correct as this assessment may be, it misses the point that this sheltering process signifies the existence of a deeply rooted social democratic minimum that would prove extremely difficult to undo. The political costs are likely to be very high. No one expects the Reagan administration to create a social democratic surplus, but an attempt to roll back the existing minimum would probably generate a severe electoral reaction: people typically are in favor of budgetary restraint except where their own programs are concerned. A genuine rollback would also create a national social crisis; the poor may not pay the costs of fiscal prudence quietly.

The aspirations of the conservative policymakers and intellectuals are also limited by what might be called structural constraints. As many economists of varying ideological persuasions have noted, capitalism simply could not exist in its current form without a significant array of social programs, including many that are sensitive to cyclical trends in the economy. David Stockman has bemoaned the fact that unemployment drives up federal income support expenditures, but precisely this kind of sensitivity has helped stabilize the economy by keeping shifts in demand relatively small. Even when revenues fall on hard times, spending stays up. The result, Robert Gordon notes, echoing a quite broad agreement among economists, is that "government has introduced an inertia into the quarter to quarter changes in spending that may have made a greater contribution to stability" than many of its other activities.[39] For this reason, and others, a rollback in state programs, including the social democratic ones, would impose major costs not only on the working class and the poor, but on capital as well. Recent evidence from Britain hardly contradicts this claim.

For all these scholarly, budgetary, political, and structural reasons, the conservative policy intellectuals are unlikely to command the exclusive right to define the social democratic minimum. An intellectual reaction has already begun. It can be found in the newly assertive Keynesianism represented in Tobin's paper on stabilization policy, in the institutional and historical orientations of the post-Keynesians, and in the stubborn insistence by many economists and policy analysts that questions of ethics, justice, and equality cannot be wished away in the name of unbridled personal liberty.[40]

But these rejoinders to the initiatives of the Right will not reimpose the Keynesian consensus of the middle 1960s. Rather, I suspect, discussions at the technical level about social democratic minimums will be concerned increasingly with fundamental issues in the relationship of state and economy; and these discussions will be compelled to address what in the Marxist lexicon might be called "the contradictions of the welfare state," and which in non-Marxist discourse have been associated with Joseph Schumpeter, who asked if capitalism could survive.[41]

The Reagan politicization of these questions will produce a more general discussion of the basic issues the Keynesian–social democratic marriage obscured. This discussion will be helpful to the Left, which hardly wishes to be in the position of allocating equal shares of poverty. Thus, while the Right mistakenly implies that advanced capitalism without the welfare state is a formula for a workable society, and while it is implausible that the welfare state in fact could be rolled back even if that were desirable on efficiency criteria, the conservative issues of disincentives to investment and work cannot be dismissed out of hand. Nor can the issues recently raised by Tibor Scitovsky, in the 1979 Richard Ely lecture, who argues that welfare capitalism has made the price system more rigid than it was, thus rendering capitalism increasingly inflexible and unadaptive to new situations; and that the growing role of the state in the economy has fragmented the economy into relatively self-contained parts. The result is a much less uniform economic environment than was the case a generation ago. As a result, governmental macroeconomic interventions have a very uneven impact in a situation where "insufficient demand in one part of the economy creates unemployment, and excess demand in the other part creates inflationary pressures."[42] This new, inflexible, and heterogeneous situation presents a challenge not only to the Right, but to any social democratic program. In the absence of coherent economic theory and policy proposals, the Left is unlikely to compete successfully with the Right to define the society's social democratic minimum.

V

The combination of stagflation and the crisis in Keynesian theory, together with the new assertiveness of the policy community on the Right, has left the adherents of social democracy in a weakened condition, even where they have traditionally been much stronger than in the United States. Whatever the precise merits of the conservative argument may be, there is no question but that stagflation has raised the perceived costs of welfare state expenditures for investment and productivity. The economic crisis of the 1970s has made it much easier for the Right to argue that the economic system would work better if only the share of national income spent on social services were to decrease. In much of Western Europe, moreover, social democratic parties were in power for significant periods in the early and middle 1970s, and they could hardly escape electoral recriminations. The Swedish SAP and the Labour party in England were especially vulnerable to the charge that their management of the welfare state contributed to growing economic difficulties. The inability of Keynesian nostrums to deal with the stagflation of the 1970s left social democratic parties, including the Euro-Communists, without a coherent economic program with which to confront the pro-market advocacy of the Right.

The result for the parties of the Left was a series of unappealing choices. They could either, as the British Labour party did in 1976, announce that they were prepared to contract the welfare state and claim that they could do a better job of restricting government than political parties to the Right, or they could push ahead with the advocacy of new social policies to create a social democratic surplus in the absence of a coherent strategy to manage the existing capitalist economy. Such programs to expand the sphere of nonmarket rationality (including further measures of nationalization of industry, land, and credit) have made their appearance. But these options are very difficult to convince voters to bet on because they invite investment rebellions by capitalists who wish to avoid allocations that are suboptimal with respect to profits. Proposals that might deepen the current crisis in the name of socialist or social democratic theory, or future prosperity and equality, hardly constitute a realistic basis for achieving electoral majorities.

These features of the current political scene in Europe, which have weakened the advocates of social democracy, have had an even more intense impact in the United States. To understand why this is so, we should remember that the Democratic party is at best only partially analogous to the European parties of the Left; and that in the absence of socialist, social democratic, or laborist political parties, the American welfare state has been pushed beyond the "minimum" only at those moments when the pressures of extraparty social movements were very strong and threatening. Such was the case in the 1930s and 1960s. But in the 1970s, both the labor and the black movements, which have been in the forefront of struggles for a social democratic surplus in the past, became considerably weaker. As a result, with the exception of *ad hoc* interest groups that pay attention to particular programs, there were no vigorous political forces outside the social service bureaucracies capable of posing a social democratic vision and program to oppose the antistatist program of the Right.

Over three decades ago, C. Wright Mills observed that the only mass, multiracial, progressive organizations in the United States were trade unions; and that the future of social policy depended heavily on the zeal of their members and on the choices of their leaders. Mills was pessimistic because of the cautious and defensive stance the unions were taking in the Truman years, and because they were limiting their attention mainly to workplace issues, and to social insurance policies that affected their membership directly.[43] Today, there are even more reasons for concern. Apart from the gains in organizing public employees, and what have proved to be relatively ephemeral efforts at constructing rank and file insurgent movements in older CIO unions, the story of trade unions in the past three decades is mainly a tale of a bad time for labor. The proportion of private sector workers who are unionized has fallen gradually since the middle 1950s. In 1956, 34 percent of nonagricultural private sector workers belonged to unions; by 1974, only 26 percent did. Since that year, unions have lost a half-million members, while the economy has gained 6 million jobs. In 1950, unions won three in four NLRB elections to secure representation; by 1976 the rate was under 50 percent, and it is continuing to decline. Gallup poll data, which in the 1950s found that almost eight in ten Americans approved of labor unions, today finds about half in favor. Industries like construction and printing, which only ten years ago were said to be dominated by unions, are today bastions of employer resistance. Less than half the buildings under construction today use unionized workers. Computerization has destroyed the skilled printing craft.[44] Not surprisingly, in the face of these trends and challenges organized labor has become, if anything, more defensive, and more concerned with the health of specific industries. Despite the falling rate of growth in the dues-paying membership of unions, labor has achieved some victories in recent years: pension plan regulation, the creation of OSHA, and an expansion of the obligation employers have to bargain with unions under the National Labor Relations Act. But overall, organized labor has become increasingly disinclined to engage in larger political battles.

The hard times of American labor have a number of causes. Labor ceased to be a movement, equipped with organizing zeal and an ideological vision. Labor also remained aloof, and at times was in opposition to, the three great mass movements of the 1960s: civil rights, sexual equality, and the antiwar protest. Helped in part by changes in the law which unions opposed (Taft-Hartley, and a number of NLRB and Supreme Court decisions enhancing management's "free speech" rights in opposition to unionism), capital has been increasingly aggressive in resisting collective bargaining. "Nowadays," Richard Freeman notes, "managements contest elections, making extensive efforts to convince workers to vote against unions, and often employing specialized labor-management consultants to advise or run their campaigns."[45] This opposition has had an effect. Where unionization is unopposed, workers select unions some 97 percent of the time; but where opposition is intense, the figure declines to between 30 and 40 percent. Moreover, there is good evidence to indicate that employers are resorting to illegal means to resist trade unions. All this activity is of compelling importance in the South and West, which are gaining in population and jobs but which traditionally have had very low rates of unionization. It is hard at this moment to resist A. H. Raskin's judgment that "without an enthusiastic membership and a persuasive appeal to the three quarters of the nonfarm workforce now totally outside its ranks [labor] will keep going nowhere economically, socially, or politically."[46]

It has long been a commonplace to observe that it is easier to maintain collective organizations at work than off work, since the plant and industry situation itself provides a system of incentives to organization. The decline of the black movement, described accurately in my view by Lerone Bennett as "the most serious crisis for blacks since the Civil War,"[47] is a case in point. In the 1960s, a remarkable combination of mass insurgency, growth in membership and visibility of national civil rights organizations, the flowering of new locally based groups, often focused on single issues, and the development of appealing if opaque ideologies of black power and nationalism fashioned a movement that had to be reckoned with from the city block to the White House. Today this movement is in disarray. What happened?

A politics of disorder is notoriously hard to sustain. In city after city a mix of repression and institutional reforms heightened the risks of street action and turned a local leadership to participation in government programs. In New York City, for example, school decentralization absorbed the energies of many activists on behalf of community control; and Mayor Lindsay's programs of neighborhood government enticed local groups into political dead ends by providing resources too meager to make a difference but sufficiently large to make them nearly impossible to spurn. In this way, leaders, thought to be providing only for themselves, lost followers, and their groups disintegrated.[48]

At the national level the nationalist impulse, frustrated by the erosion of its base, fragmented and weakened. By 1971, Pan-Africanism had replaced black power for most nationalists, who reacted "to the cooption of key phrases, concepts, and even personalities by the dominant media and culture." This rubric was sufficiently general to be an umbrella for the great majority of black activists and intellectuals, but it also masked highly divergent tendencies: an increasingly Marxist "left-nationalism," a cultural nationalism, and electoral strategies. These tendencies were brought together in March 1972, in the founding convention of the National Black Political Assembly, attended by about 12,000 people in Gary, Indiana. Convened by Mayor Hatcher, Congressman Diggs, and Imamu Baraka, the meeting agreed on a progressive Black Agenda, written in nationalist language. But shortly after the black elite's unity shattered, and the tacit divisions became apparent. Black elected officials needing white votes broke with the more radical nationalists. By 1974 the elected politicians stayed away from nationalist gatherings. These meetings of militant students, community organizers, intellectuals, and some workers divided between the cultural nationalists and the black Left. By mid-decade, there was much polemic and little organization; and those blacks "in the system" were increasingly cut off from the mobilized support of those outside it. The nationalists who aspired to lead a mass movement found themselves without funds, and without a national grassroots presence of any dimension. At the same time, the traditional national civil rights organizations —the NAACP and the Urban League being the two most important ones —were themselves faced with a decline in membership and a hard time in defining a coherent program for black America.[49]

There were, nevertheless, two new sources of organizational strength for the black community in the 1970s. The first was the dramatic growth in the number of black elected officials, who increased from 103 in 1964 to 1,469 in 1970 to 4,311 in 1977. From the black caucus in the Congress to local sheriffs, this group constituted a more progressive category of politicians than any other in the country. And yet its capacity was limited by its diversity of location and authority, by the very small fraction its members composed in different representative and executive bodies, and by the need to enter electoral and governing coalitions with those who had increasingly lost faith in the social democratic agenda.

The second main organizational development had very different implications. Black professionals and businesspeople, capitalizing on new opportunities created by the end of formal discrimination, affirmative action, and government programs to foster black capitalism, and growing access to college and postgraduate education, created a host of new organizations. The National Association of Black Manufacturers, the National Association of Black Accountants, the National Association of Black School Educators, and literally dozens of others, have been the only interest groups growing in size and number in the black community. They tend to be moderate to conservative in their politics, mainstream in their tactics, and indifferent if not opposed to the social democratic agenda.

Their very existence points to the central change in black America in the past two decades: the growing schism between the black middle class and underclass. As William J. Wilson has argued in the most influential treatment of race relations of the last ten years, this division is deeply rooted in the sectoral and geographical divisions of the American economy, and is thus not simply or exclusively a question of race.[50] The class divisions fostered by the impact of the larger political economy on the black political economy not only raise questions about whether all blacks share a single interest in racial change, but have also left the best off the best organized; the weakest and poorest are without leadership, without a coherent voice, and in despair.

To be sure, there is a plethora of progressive black and white groups operating in many communities in the United States; one recent survey discovered scores of direct action groups and alternative institutions.[51] But they tend to be disconnected, obsessed with single issues, not tied to the trade union movement, and without a national presence. Put side by side with the organizational network of the Right, they appear puny indeed.

VI

The Reagan campaign, in brief, ratified the intellectual and political trends of the 1970s, both of which were hostile to social democratic policy initiatives and goals. In much of Western Europe, political parties of the Left are in waiting to form governments when the shallowness of the antistatist Right is exposed. But in the United States, with no such party, intellectual and political alternatives will have to be developed nearly from scratch. If they are not, the winter of social policy may prove very long and very hard.

The large task defined by the assault on social policy is not, however, impossible or quixotic. The flawed analysis underpinning the Reagan policies is untested. Various social policies have their articulate defenders and the conviction of precedent. The organizational structure of unions, black groups, and community-based organizations, though weakened and in disarray, nevertheless exists, providing the basis for future institutional efforts. Conversations about how to resist the Reagan attack on social policy, and about how to build an appealing progressive politics more generally, have already been stimulated by the shock of the election, by the seizure by the Right of the ability to command the terms of discussion, and by the obvious gap between the current organizational capacity of an assertive Right and a fragmented and relatively incoherent Left. These stimuli help define the magnitude of the task of political reconstruction. Here, I wish only to make a partial and tentative contribution to the conversations that have already begun, less by the way of proposing a blueprint or specific program than by making a number of broad substantive and strategic suggestions.

It is worth remembering that just a very short time ago many of us would have keenly anticipated the development of a national debate focusing on the failures of the capitalist economy, and on the baleful and biased features of government interventions. The post-1973 crisis, still very much with us, and likely to be for some time to come, has in fact provided the occasion for such a debate, but it found the Left rather unprepared and vulnerable. We would do well to ask why, and to understand why the Right has succeeded, at least temporarily, in defining the economic crisis as a crisis of Keynesian theory rather than that of capitalism; and why it has been able to identify a key cause of the economy's troubles as being redistributive social policy.

A key reason, in my view, has been one of intellectual abdication. The response on the Left to the economic crisis has been a differentiated one. Some have argued, often in abstract ways, that the crisis provides evidence for the failures of capitalism *tout court,* and that only with a socialist transformation will the crisis be overcome. Others have continued in a more reformist vein to focus on questions of allocation and redistribution in isolation from matters of growth and supply. And yet others have continued to look to traditional Keynesian nostrums to manage the economic crisis.

None of these foci has provided the intellectual tools the Left must have in the current situation. The goal of the transformation of capitalism to socialism can guide short- as well as longer-term activity, but divorced from a coherent movement and program for the present, it is more romantic than meaningful. The issue before us is not one of the relative merits of democratic capitalism or democratic socialism abstractly considered. Rather, it is how to think and act in a situation in which, for the foreseeable future, the economy is likely to be organized by capitalist principles. The focus on distribution disconnected from considerations of production in a capitalist economy renders the Left intellectually vulnerable and politically marginal, since voters are hardly likely to wager on a program that promises to distribute poverty. All the major parties of the European Left have understood this fact of life, even as it has been a source of considerable tension between their immediate and long-term aspirations. Keynesian theory, which the social democratic (and Euro-Communist) parties, as well as the American Democratic party, have embraced once provided for a link between the aim of making the short-term economy work in the interests of longer-term changes in the balance between market and nonmarket economic forces. But a continuing commitment to traditional Keynesianism seems dubious at best, indeed for many of the reasons the Right cites. It seems incapable of delivering growth, employment, and acceptably low inflation.

The Left's postdepression commitment to Keynesian theory, in both Western Europe and the United States, moreover, gave away more than it had to to the current organization of production. By not focusing on matters of productivity and supply directly, Keynesian theory relies on mechanisms that place "primary responsibility for economic disturbances upon the failure of public policies," and proposes solutions that "deal only with aggregates, leaving the basic structure of the industrial system unchallenged and largely unnoticed."[52] But short of a socialist transformation, the Left needs a strategy for economic supply, productivity, and growth that does not simply take current arrangements for savings and investment for granted. With such a strategy, radical policies of allocation may be convincingly proposed. Without one, little is politically possible.

Reagan economics, which underpin the attack on social policy, must be addressed, in short, on the terrain of supply, and not just on that of demand. Alternative strategies for how to create pools of investment capital (some of which could be under state control, and some of which could be constrained by regional planning policies) should be developed and proposed; and debates about them could proceed. Such an effort, conspicuously lacking in recent years on the Left, would counterpose to views that stress how the state, through taxation policy and deregulation, should encourage market-governed investment decisions an alternative strategy of marrying productive economic investments to a coherent set of social goals. Whatever the precise focus of such alternatives, whether based on models drawn from our own New Deal or savings and equity plans under discussion in Scandinavia, or other possibilities, we can no longer afford to avoid these questions or assume that attention to the management of demand by itself will provide a coherent economic program.

With such a program, the traditional elements of the social democratic agenda of planning, employment policy, and social welfare expenditures can prove a principled alternative to the idea that the market will automatically solve social problems. This possibility is likely to become more compelling with the passage of time, since Reaganite economics and social policy are likely at best to produce extremely uneven and inegalitarian economic growth, with many losers and a heightened possibility of social crisis. In that circumstance, even some of the winners might pause to rethink.

In the immediate future the central problem for the Left is less likely to be the expansion of social policy, but rather the protection of past gains. Present and future attempts to cut back on the social democratic minimum provide a chance to define a coherent set of principles with which to think about the federal budget. It would be ironic indeed if those of us who have argued in the past that many federal programs which fall under the rubric of social policy have a regressive impact now mobilized to save present programs in an indiscriminate way. Instead, we need to be selective in our mobilization, and to be willing to emphasize not only the total size of expenditures, but their redistributive quality. Medicaid, for example, aimed at the poor, is currently saddled with high overheads and doctors' fees. By one estimate, only 68 cents on a dollar reaches the patient.[53] American public housing, for another, is a pitifully small program, and a good case could be made for expansion. But the present organization of public housing has rarely done more than create slums and help the construction industry. In these two cases and in many others, fiscal prudence and progressive politics may go hand in hand.

In the face of the coherent, well-organized, principled, and capably led politics of the Right, an *ad hoc,* issue-specific politics of protest and demonstration led by interest groups most affected by budget cuts is likely to be terribly ineffectual. Because the assault on social policy is so total, the various *ad hoc* groups may form situational coalitions. But even such coalitions, joining civil rights groups, church organizations, day care and education lobbyists, and issue-oriented groups like the Children's Defense Fund or the National Association for Retarded Citizens, are unlikely by themselves to be able to do more than seem a loosely coupled grouping of special pleaders who defend all current social spending without regard to overarching principles, analyses, or goals.

The fact that most Americans who pay attention to politics do so only at election time compels the Left not to eschew or withdraw from electoral politics. This does not mean an uncritical plunge into mainstream Democratic party affairs, nor does it imply a commitment to third-party and third-candidate strategies. As the radical Right has discovered, the choices between mainstream and more fringe electoral politics are not exclusive ones. Rather, elections provide opportunities to define basic choices, to occupy the public space, and to persuade.

What organizational vehicles can be crafted to build a coherent opposition, to affect electoral politics, and to propose economic and social policy alternatives? Two complementary possibilities suggest themselves. The first is based on the model of the Progressive Alliance founded in 1978. Less than a political party but more than an interest group, the Progressive Alliance joined together more than 150 labor, community, and pressure groups on the Left under the banner of common aspirations. Given funding and leadership by the United Automobile Workers, the Alliance had a number of significant features. It was multiracial. It bridged the gap in American political life between the labor movement and labor politics, on the one side, and community organizations and territorial politics on the other.[54] It tried to connect academics on the Left with political activists. It aspired to influence debates in Congress and party platforms, yet it was independent of any specific political party, whether in the mainstream or on the fringe. It was concerned with the political process—in particular, how to mobilize nonvoters, who compose a potential constituency for social democratic, if not socialist, politics—and with public policy. And its leadership understood, if possibly only in a loose way, that social policy is intimately connected to broader economic strategies.

The Progressive Alliance, though still existing in form, is now largely defunct. The Kennedy campaign deflected the energies of its leaders. The large investment of the UAW proved a weakness as well as a strength, because its commitment was secondary to other organizational goals, and because its dominance gave other organizations a more token role. But the example of the Progressive Alliance remains, in my view, the most compelling one we have capable of building connections between the various mass organizations of the Left, and for incorporating the trade union movement within a broader politics of social change. The revival of the Alliance in the light of recent experience, or the creation of a new organization in its image, would allow for effective mobilization both within and outside the electoral arena.

The second possibility is the creation of an organization on the model of The Liberal Project of 1960, which brought together academics willing to think about fundamental policy issues in seminars with progressive political officials and bureaucrats in Washington. This project became the basis for the Democratic Study Group in the House of Representatives. In today's climate, where universities provide the only major autonomous centers of scholarship, this kind of initiative might provide the foundation for an American equivalent of the Fabian Society, which could utilize the resources of groups like the Institute for Policy Studies, and which could draw from a national pool of social scientists. It has become a commonplace to say that progressive politicians are looking for fresh ideas. And if the recent election has taught us nothing else, it is that ideas still count.

NOTES

1. Benjamin I. Page, *Choices and Echoes in Presidential Elections: Rational Man and Electoral Democracy* (Chicago: University of Chicago Press, 1978).
2. Norman H. Nie, Sidney Verba, and John R. Petrocik, *The Changing American Voter* (Cambridge, Mass.: Harvard University Press, 1976), p. 121.
3. David B. Truman, *The Governmental Process: Political Interests and Public Opinion* (New York: Knopf, 1951), pp. 216ff.

4. For a discussion, see Richard M. Titmuss, *Social Policy: An Introduction* (London: Allen and Unwin, 1974), esp. chap. 2.
5. *The New York Times,* July 18, 1980, p. A8, and October 25, 1980, p. 8; *U.S. News and World Report,* October 6, 1980, pp. 59–62; *Christian Science Monitor,* April 4, 1980, p. 12; *The Wall Street Journal,* May 6, 1980, p. 12.
6. *A Conversation with George Bush* (Washington, D.C.: The American Enterprise Institute, 1980), pp. 19–20.
7. *The New York Times,* August 20, 1976, p. 1; July 15, 1980, p. B7.
8. *The New York Times,* June 26, 1980, p. B9; August 12, 1980, p. 8; August 15, 1980, p. B2; September 2, 1980, p. 7; *Business Week,* November 3, 1980, pp. 74ff.
9. *U.S. News and World Report,* October 6, 1980, p. 64.
10. "The Basic Speech: Edward M. Kennedy," *The New York Times,* p. A11.
11. Stephen Breyer, "Analyzing Regulatory Failure: Mismatches, Less Restrictive Alternatives, and Reform," *Harvard Law Review,* 92 (January 1979).
12. *U.S. News,* op. cit., October 6, 1980, pp. 59–62.
13. *The New York Times,* July 22, 1980, p. B4.
14. Ira Katznelson, "Accounts of the Welfare State and the New Mood," *American Economic Review,* 70 (May 1980).
15. I draw in the following paragraphs from the paper cited in note 14, and from my "Considerations on Social Democracy in the United States," *Comparative Politics,* 11 (October 1978).
16. G. A. Cohen, *Karl Marx's Theory of History: A Defence* (Princeton, N.J.: Princeton University Press, 1978), pp. 295–296.
17. Martin Feldstein, "The American Economy in Transition: Introduction," in Feldstein, ed., *The American Economy in Transition* (Chicago: University of Chicago Press, 1980), pp. 1–2.
18. Cited in Robert J. Gordon, "Postwar Macroeconomics: The Evolution of Events and Ideas," in Feldstein, op. cit., p. 133.
19. Ibid., pp. 104–105.
20. Peter Drucker, "Toward the Next Economics," *The Public Interest,* special edition 1980, pp. 10–11.
21. Mark Willes, " 'Rational Expectations' as a Counterrevolution," *The Public Interest,* special edition 1980, p. 84.
22. Cited in Daniel Bell, "Models and Reality in Economic Discourse," *The Public Interest,* special edition 1980, pp. 66–67.
23. See James W. Dean, "The Dissolution of the Keynesian Consensus," *The Public Interest,* special edition 1980, pp. 26ff.
24. See Drucker, op. cit.; and Irving Kristol, "Lessons in Political Economy," *The Wall Street Journal,* December 21, 1980, p. 12.
25. Willes, op. cit., p. 90.
26. Ibid., p. 95.
27. Feldstein, op. cit., p. 3.
28. Arthur Burns, "Concluding Comments," in Feldstein, op. cit., p. 676.
29. Where they have been, as in Thatcher's England or Barre's France, they have hardly solved the problems they claim to be able to address.
30. Kenneth Arrow, "Real and Nominal Values in Economics," *The Public Interest,* special edition 1980, p. 150.
31. Richard B. Freeman, "The Evolution of the American Labor Market, 1948–80," in Feldstein, op. cit., p. 388.
32. James Tobin, "Stabilization Policy Ten Years After," *Brookings Papers on Economic Activity,* 1 (1980), p. 58.
33. Ibid., pp. 57ff.
34. "Nearly half of the beneficiaries are not poor at all. Most of the others are poor only in the sense that they have retired after having worked and earned

substantial lifetime incomes." Benjamin I. Page, "Why Doesn't the Government Promote Equality?" in Robert A. Solo and Charles W. Anderson, *Value Judgment and Income Distribution* (New York: Praeger, 1981).

35. The Page paper provides an excellent summary discussion.
36. Katznelson, "Considerations," op. cit.
37. Ibid., p. 93.
38. George Schultz and Kenneth Dam, *Economic Policy beyond the Headlines* (New York: Norton, 1977), pp. 28–29.
39. Gordon, op. cit., p. 108.
40. For a discussion, see Dean, op. cit., p. 32.
41. Claus Offe, "Some Contradictions of the Modern Welfare State," Paper presented to the Facolta de Scienze Politiche, University of Perugia, Italy, February 12, 1980; Joseph Schumpeter, *Capitalism, Socialism, and Democracy* (New York: Harper & Row, 1944).
42. Tibor Scitovsky, "Can Capitalism Survive?—An Old Question in a New Setting," *The American Economic Review*, 70 (May 1980), 7.
43. C. Wright Mills, *The New Men of Power* (New York: Harcourt, Brace, and World, 1948).
44. Freeman, op. cit., pp. 367–372; Nicholas von Hoffman, "The Last Days of the Labor Movement," *Harper's*, December 1978, pp. 22–28; A. H. Raskin, "The Big Squeeze on Labor Unions," *The Atlantic Monthly*, October 1978, pp. 41–48.
45. Freeman, op. cit., p. 369. He notes that "in Canada, where the same unions and management often deal with one another but where the method of recognizing unions does not allow for management campaigns against organization, trade union organization of the workforce has grown."
46. A. H. Raskin, "Management's Hard Line: 'Class War' or Labor's Chance to Reform?" *Monthly Labor Review*, 102 (February 1979), 36.
47. Cited in Larry Reidman, "The Condition of Civil Rights Advocacy," *Civil Rights Digest*, 2 (spring 1979), 35.
48. I discuss these themes in my *City Trenches: Urban Politics and the Patterning of Class in the United States* (New York: Pantheon, 1981).
49. The best available treatment of these matters is Manning Marable, "Black Nationalism in the 1970's: Through the Prism of Race and Class," *Socialist Review*, 50–51 (1980), passim.
50. William J. Wilson, *The Declining Significance of Race* (Chicago: University of Chicago Press, 1978).
51. Janice Perlman, "Grassroots Groups in 1970's USA," paper prepared for presentation at the International Sociological Association Conference on the Sociology of Regional and Urban Development, Messina/Reggio Calabria, Italy, April 1976.
52. Ronald King, "Hegemonic Considerations in U.S. Taxation Policy," Ph.D. dissertation in progress, Department of Political Science, University of Chicago.
53. Page, "Why Doesn't the Government," op. cit.
54. This long-standing division in American political life has proved a key barrier in the past to the development of a broadly based progressive politics. Attempts to create such a politics now need to be self-conscious about this inheritance and willing to work to overcome it.

NOTES ON CONTRIBUTORS

Walter Dean Burnham is professor of political science at the Massachusetts Institute of Technology. He is the author of numerous books and articles on the evolution of American party politics and electoral behavior, including *Critical Elections and the Mainsprings of American Politics,* and the editor, with William Chambers, of *The American Party Systems.*

Alexander Cockburn is a journalist with the *Village Voice,* where he writes a weekly column on the press and, with James Ridgeway, a column on national politics. He is a regular contributor to *Harpers, The Wall Street Journal* and *The New York Review of Books,* the author of *Idle Passion: Chess and the Dance of Death* and, with James Ridgeway, *Smoke: Another Jimmy Carter Adventure,* and the editor, with James Ridgeway, of *Political Ecology: An Activist's Reader.*

Bruce Cumings is assistant professor of political science at the University of Washington. A former editor of the *Bulletin of Concerned Asian Scholars,* he is the author of a two-volume study of the origins of the Korean war, of which the first volume, *The Origins of the Korean War: Liberation and the Emergence of Separate Regimes,* has recently appeared.

David Dickson is the Washington news editor for the British weekly science journal *Nature.* A graduate in mathematics from Cambridge University, he worked for two years with the British Society for Social Responsibility in Science before becoming a science journalist. He is a member of the editorial collective of *Radical Science Journal* and the author of *The Politics of Alternative Technology.*

Gerald Epstein is assistant professor of economics at Williams College. He recently completed a dissertation on the Federal Reserve system and United States monetary policy.

Thomas Ferguson is assistant professor of political science at the Massachusetts Institute of Technology. He is the author of the forthcoming *Critical Realignment: The Fall of the House of Morgan and the Origins of the New Deal.* A member of the editorial boards of the Sage Series in Political Economy and *democracy*, with Joel Rogers he writes a regular column, "The Political Economy," in *The Nation*.

Ira Katznelson is professor of political science at the University of Chicago. The founding editor of *Politics and Society* and currently a member of the editorial board, he is the author of numerous books and articles on urban politics, social welfare issues, and political theory, including *Black Men, White Cities: Race, Politics and Migration in the United States, 1900–1930, and Britain, 1948–1968* and *City Trenches: Urban Politics and the Patterning of Class in the United States.*

David Noble is an assistant professor in the Science Technology and Society Program at the Massachusetts Institute of Technology. He is the author of numerous books and articles on the development and control of science and technology in the United States, including *America by Design: Science, Technology and the Rise of Corporate Capitalism,* and the forthcoming *Forces of Production.*

James Ridgeway is a journalist with the *Village Voice*, where he writes a weekly column on national politics with Alexander Cockburn. He is the author of numerous books and articles on American politics, including *The Closed Corporation, The Politics of Ecology, The Last Play, Who Owns the Earth,* and, with Alexander Cockburn, *Smoke: Another Jimmy Carter Adventure* and the editor, with Alexander Cockburn, of *Political Ecology: An Activist's Reader.*

Joel Rogers is assistant professor of political science at University College/-Newark, a division of Rutgers University. He is currently completing a dissertation on American labor policy since the New Deal. A member of the editorial board of *democracy*, with Thomas Ferguson he writes a regular column, "The Political Economy," in *The Nation*.

Alan Stone is associate professor of political science at the University of Houston. He is the author of numerous books and articles on law, economic regulation, and the American power structure, including *Economic Regulation and the Public Interest, Regulation and Its Alternatives,* and, with Kenneth Prewitt, *The Ruling Elites,* and the editor, with Theodore Lowi, of *Nationalizing Government.* He is currently completing a study of the relationship between capitalist economic development and the changing structure of law.